Systematics Critical and Constructive 1

Systematics Critical and Constructive 1

Biblical—Interpretive—Theological—Interdisciplinary

Ronald R. Ray

☙PICKWICK *Publications* · Eugene, Oregon

SYSTEMATICS CRITICAL AND CONSTRUCTIVE 1
Biblical—Interpretive—Theological—Interdisciplinary

Copyright © 2018 Ronald R. Ray. All rights reserved. Except for brief quotations in critical publications or reviews, no part of this book may be reproduced in any manner without prior written permission from the publisher. Write: Permissions, Wipf and Stock Publishers, 199 W. 8th Ave., Suite 3, Eugene, OR 97401.

Pickwick Publications
An Imprint of Wipf and Stock Publishers
199 W. 8th Ave., Suite 3
Eugene, OR 97401

www.wipfandstock.com

PAPERBACK ISBN: 978-1-5326-0016-6
HARDCOVER ISBN: 978-1-5326-0018-0
EBOOK ISBN: 978-1-5326-0017-3

Cataloguing-in-Publication data:

Names: Ray, Ronald R., author.

Title: Systematics critical and constructive 1 : biblical—interpretive—theological—interdisciplnary / Ronald R. Ray.

Description: Eugene, OR: Pickwick Publications, 2018. | Includes bibliographical references and index.

Identifiers: ISBN 978-1-5326-0016-6 (paperback). | ISBN 978-1-5326-0018-0 (hardcover). | ISBN 978-1-5326-0017-3 (ebook).

Subjects: LCSH: Theology, Doctrinal. | Bible—Theology. | Theology—Study and teaching. | Hermeneutics.

Classification: BT75.2 R15 2018 (print). | BT75.2 (ebook).

Manufactured in the U.S.A.   08/15/18

To the intellectual giants from whom I have sought to learn, and to my loving, wise, and radiant Diane, who daily enlightens and enlivens our discipleship adventure, and from whom I have even more sought to learn.

Condensed Contents

Understanding the Discipline | 1

    Preface and Introduction | 3

1. Systematic Theology's Nature, Purposes, Tasks and Methods | 7
2. Jesus Christ as God's Past and Present Revealing Word | 19
3. Bible as Witness to Jesus Christ, God's Past and Present Revealing Word | 32

Developments toward the Testaments, Authority of Each | 39

4. Developments toward Old Testament Canon | 41
5. Authority of Old Testament for New Testament Christians and Christians Today | 50
6. Developments toward New Testament Canon, Their Theological Implications—General Canonical Conclusions | 95

Canon and Interpretation | 127

7. Canonical Interpretation Plus Its Perils and Promise | 129
8. Dynamic Traditioning Process in Scripture and beyond | 158

More Interaction with Related Disciplines | 165

9. Utilizing Christian Religious Experience, Reason/Apologetics, Historical and Biblical Theology in Systematics | 167
10. Question of General Revelation or Natural Theology | 193
11. Evaluating Arguments That Attempt to Prove God's Existence | 207
12. Relationship of Philosophy to Systematic Theology | 218
13. Dialogues, Meeting Points Involving Natural Science, Philosophy, Christian Theology | 232

    Appendix Highly Relative Summary concerning Relativity, Quantum Theories | 252

Service to Other Related Disciplines | 255

    14. Proclamation and Teaching | 257

    15. Congregational Preaching and Biblical Interpretation | 264

General Interpretation and Additional Biblical Interpretation | 273

    16. General Hermeneutics, Its Relationship to Biblical Hermeneutics | 275

    17. Biblical Hermeneutics | 288

Thematic Exposition Begins | 303

    18. Relationship of Christian Faith to Historical Revelation | 305

    19. Christian Knowing, Believing, Sharing in Faith | 324

    Conclusion | 333

        Glossary with References | 335

        Bibliography | 343

        Index | 353

Expanded Contents

Understanding the Discipline | 1
   Preface and Introduction | 3
      Preface | 3
      Introduction | 5
1 *Systematic Theology's Nature, Purposes, Tasks and Methods* | 7
     1. Names for the Discipline | 7
     2. Its Nature | 7
     3. Is It Necessary? | 9
     4. Its Purposes | 10
     5. Dialectical Method and Christocentric Focus | 12
     6. Relationships between Revelation, Scripture, Systematics and Preaching | 12
     7. Separating Word from Words, Kernel from Husk | 13
     8. Spirit's Leading, Sense of Wonder and Astonishment | 13
     9. Learning Ever Afresh | 14
     10. Thorough Theology Inherently Hellenic | 15
     11. Utilizing Abstract Thought in Systematics | 15
     12. Systematizing Method Encourages Consistency, Has Capacity to Disconfirm Truth Claims | 16
     13. Is Systematic Theology a Science? | 17
2 *Jesus Christ as God's Past and Present Revealing Word* | 19
     1. Christ's Risen Presence as Operating Premise | 19
     2. Primary Object of Christian Faith is God, not Our Experience | 19
     3. Transcending Mere Subject-Object Knowing | 20
     4. God in Her Word | 21
     5. Revelation as God's Self-Disclosing Communicating | 23
     6. Use of Analogical Language | 26
3 *Bible as Witness to Jesus Christ, God's Past and Present Revealing Word* | 32
     1. Scripture as Witness to Jesus Christ | 32
     2. Instrumental Understanding of Scripture | 33
     3. Exposition between Remembrance, Expectation | 36
     4. Need for Critical Discernment | 37

DEVELOPMENTS TOWARD THE TESTAMENTS, AUTHORITY OF EACH | 39

4 *Developments toward Old Testament Canon* | 41
    1. Development of Jewish Understandings of Written Sources of Authority | 41
    2. Judaism's Evolving Pre-Old Testament Scriptures | 42
    3. Jewish Factors for Accepting Books as Authoritative Scripture | 44
    4. Evidence for Christians' Use, Canonizing of Septuagint and Utilizing of Greek Language Testimony Books | 45
    5. Post New Testament Church Opinions concerning Apocrypha | 47

5 *Authority of Old Testament for New Testament Christians and Christians Today* | 50
    Part A | 50
        1. Introduction to Non-Historical, Non-Literary Ways Early Christian Writers Interpreted Old Covenant Texts | 50
        2. Pre-New Testament Christian Message Determined What Would Be Creatively Utilized from Available Pre-Old Testament Traditions | 53
        3. Jesus's Use of Old Covenant Traditions | 54
        4. Old Testament Prophetic Hopes That Build toward New Testament Fulfillments and beyond | 55
        5. Old Testament Prediction, Its New Testament Use, New Testament Prediction | 58
        6. New Testament Midrashic Interpretation | 64
        7. New Testament Pesher "Translations" of Old Testament Texts as Sub-type of Midrashic Method | 68
        8. Direct Allegorizing | 69
        9. Typology | 69
        10. Typology Illustrated: God's Servant Humiliated and Exalted (Isaiah 52:13–15; 53:1–12) | 71
    Part B | 77
        11. Ethical Similarities between Testaments | 77
        12. New Testament's Setting Aside or Abandoning Many Old Testament Traditions | 80
        13. Additional Examples of Specific Conflicts between Old and New Testament Convictions | 83
        14. Marcion in Context of Second Century Christianity, His Rejection of Textually Disconnected Readings of Old Testament, His Christocentric/Soteriological Focus | 90
        15. Proposals for Christian Use of Old Testament | 92

6 *Developments toward New Testament Canon, Their Theological Implications, General Canonical Conclusions* | 95

1. Christian Faith in Earliest Period Primarily Communicated Orally, Pauline Exception, Pre-New Testament Book Dating and Composition | 95
2. Pre-New Testament Writings Crucial to Early Christians Though Many Illiterate in Greek | 97
3. Paul's Epistles Understood to Carry More Authority Than Mere Letters | 98
4. Pauline Epistles, Pauline Corpus | 99
5. Oral, Written Gospel Traditions | 101
6. By Early Second Century the Following Were Used More Than Emerging Old Testament: Paul's Epistles Plus Ephesians and Colossians, Then Individual Synoptic Gospels, Later the Fourth Gospel | 105
7. Catholic or General Epistles, Acts, Hebrews, Revelation | 105
8. Marcion's New Testament Collecting, Editing in Context | 107
9. Little Direct Canon-Determining Influence from Reactions against Montanist and Gnostic Direct Revelations and Their Proliferation of Writings | 108
10. Influence of the Codex Book-Making Technique on Development of the New Testament Canon | 110
11. Canon-Encouraging Indirect Effect of Diocletian Edict | 111
12. Eusebius's Canonical Listing of Undisputed and Disputed New Testament Books | 112
13. Constantinian Push toward New Testament Canonical Uniformity | 112
14. Solidifying of Western Opinion by Athanasius, Augustine | 114
15. Scripture-Canon Distinction, Textual Versions and Variations, Necessity of Written Attestation, Then of Canonization | 115
16. Criteria Used in Determining Composition of New Testament Canon | 119
17. Conclusions concerning Canonizing Process, Historical Circumstances | 125

CANON AND INTERPRETATION | 127

7 *Canonical Interpretation Plus Its Perils and Promise* | 129
1. Primarily Concerning Long Existing Differences among Churches Regarding Precise Content of New Testament Canon | 129
2. Canon's Scope in Principle Open to Revision | 131
3. New Testament as Interpretation | 131
4. Evaluation of Brevard Childs's Canonical Approach | 134
5. New Testament as Whole not Source of Church Unity | 136
6. Use of Intracanonical New Testament Norms—Canons within the Canon | 138
7. Essential or Normative Beliefs | 140
8. Inerrancy's Errors Including Absence of Christian Freedom | 148

8   *Dynamic Traditioning Process in Scripture and Beyond* | 158
    1. A Preliminary Illustration: Biblical Reinterpretations to Take Account of Eschaton's Delay | 158
    2. Scripture and Traditioning Process | 160
    3 Dialectical Traditioning Process | 160
    4. Critical Dialogue of Revisable Science with Revisable Theology | 161
    5. Need for Theological Restatements in Transmission of Biblical Tradition | 163

MORE INTERACTION WITH RELATED DISCIPLINES | 165

9   *Utilizing Christian Religious Experience, Reason/Apologetics, Historical and Biblical Theology in Systematics* | 167
    1. Brief Discussion of Sources and Their Relationship | 167
    2. Christian Religious Experience and Wilhelm Herrmann's Understanding of Its Relation to Faith, Knowledge, Science | 169
    3. Interaction of Reason and Experiential Faith within Systematics | 171
    4. Christian Faith above Natural Reason but Interrelates with Rational and Empirical Truth | 172
    5. Sin's Corruption of Various Academic Disciplines' Use of Reason | 176
    6. Apologetics | 177
    7. Some Aspects of Kierkegaard's Apologetics | 181
    8. Christian Interpretation of Natural Experience | 185
    9. Differences, Relationships between Systematic Theology and Various Forms of Historical Theology | 186
    10. More on Biblical Theology, Its Differences from, Relationships with Systematic Theology | 187
    11. Systematics's Social Context: Creative and Critical Dialogues with Yesterday's and Today's World Church, Possible to Extent of Its Obedience to the Living Christ | 189
    12. Critique of Biblicism's Illusions, Dialectical Attitude toward Early Post-Biblical Orthodoxy, Seventeenth Century and Modern Protestant Varieties | 190

10 *Question of General Revelation or Natural Theology* | 193
    1. The Contemporary Context of This Discussion | 193
    2. Mainly on Need to Here Discuss "Image of God" Teaching | 194
    3. Old Testament Meanings of Human Creation in God's Image | 195
    4. Theological Expansion of Old Testament Image of God Understandings | 197
    5. Brief Reference to New Testament Image of God Usage | 198
    6. Other Alleged Biblical Bases for General Revelation or Natural Theology | 199
    7. Calvin's Contradictory Views: Original Gift of Natural Awareness of God as Currently Implying Only Guilt and Accountability, Versus Idolatry and Impiety as Evidence of Sense of God's Presence | 202

8. Awareness of Our Own Deathward-ness not Implying Natural Theology or General Revelation | 203
9. Willingness to Learn from All Quarters not Natural Theology | 204
10. Risen Christ's Word Spoken through Nature and amid Human Words and Events. This also not Natural Theology | 205

11 *Evaluating Arguments That Attempt to Prove God's Existence* | 207
1. Preliminary Conclusion: Existing Realities Convincingly Known and Experienced, but Providing no Argumentative Proof | 208
2. Ontological Argument | 210
3. Cosmological Argument | 211
4. Design or Teleological Argument | 213
5. Moral Argument | 216
6. Religious Experience as Basis of Conviction | 216

12 *Relationship of Philosophy to Systematic Theology* | 218
1. Natural Reason and Christian Faith | 218
2. Christian Theology's Unique Philosophical Contribution | 219
3. Rejection of Monism | 220
4. Existence as Relational | 221
5. Exposition, Evaluation of Buber's "I-Thou" Personalism | 221
6. Kierkegaard's Existentialist Philosophy in Criticism of Hegel's System | 222
7. Kierkegaard's Category: Individual as Responsible to God | 224
8. Systematics's Dialectical Use of Philosophy: Evaluative, Selective, Eclectic | 224
9. Theological Method in Light of Kantian Philosophy | 226
10. A Little "Hegeling" | 226
11. Use of Critical Realism and Critical Idealism by Those Open to God's Transcending Word | 227
12. Whitehead Further on Realism-Objectivism | 229

13 *Dialogues, Meeting Points Involving Natural Science, Philosophy, Christian Theology* | 232
1. Preliminary Indications of Relationships | 232
2. Commonalities, Differences between Science and Philosophy | 233
3. History of Science | 234
4. Induction and "Laws of Nature" | 238
5. Newtonian Physics, Its Modifications | 240
6. New Scientific Theories Needed to Interpret Direct or Indirect Evidence | 241
7. Understanding Problem Solving, Scientific Discovery | 243
8. Polanyi's Philosophical/Gestalt Psychological Understanding of Understanding | 248
9. Non-Scientific Values Required by Science | 250

Appendix: Highly Relative Summary concerning Relativity, Quantum Theories | 252
  1. Theory of Relativity | 252
  2. Quantum Theory: Functioning of Atomic Components as Particles or Waves | 253

SERVICE TO OTHER RELATED DISCIPLINES | 255

14 *Proclamation and Teaching* | 257
  1. Proclamation According to New Testament | 257
  2. Convincing Power Belongs to God | 258
  3. Divine Authorizing and Sustaining of Proclamatory Ministers | 258
  4. Evaluation of Proclamatory Witness | 260
  5. Meaning, Purpose, Method of Christian Learning and thus of Christian Teaching | 261

15 *Congregational Preaching and Biblical Interpretation* | 264
  1. Some Possible Theological Patterns in Early Congregational Preaching | 264
  2. Homily as a Form of Congregational Preaching | 267
  3. Christ—Not Congregation—Source of Authority | 267
  4. Congregational Preaching Method | 269
  5. Interpreting Related to Congregational Preaching | 270

GENERAL INTERPRETATION AND ADDITIONAL BIBLICAL INTERPRETATION | 273

16 *General Hermeneutics, Its Relationship to Biblical Hermeneutics* | 275
  1. Need for Hermeneutics | 275
  2. Role of Philosophical and Theological Presuppositions | 276
  3. Hermeneutical Circle. | 277
  4. Cultural Context for Hermeneutical Endeavour | 278
  5. Understanding Truth amid Ambiguity of Spoken, Written Communication | 282

17 *Biblical Hermeneutics* | 288
  1. Jesus's Parables as Hermeneutically Challenging | 288
  2. Facets of Christian Hermeneutical Activity with Reference to Scripture | 290
  3. A Culture Critical Warning | 298

THEMATIC EXPOSITION BEGINS | 303

18 *Relationship of Christian Faith to Historical Revelation* | 305
  1. Essential Problem not Temporal Distance, but Gap Caused by Sin | 305
  2. Need for Inward Appropriation of Biblical Tradition | 306
  3. Resurrection-Enabled Experience of Justifying Faith Contemporizes Past Revelation in Christ | 307
  4. Hiddenness of Revelation in Jesus Christ | 308
  5. Eternal in Finite: Lack of Direct Knowability | 309

6. Conflicts with Judaism, Islam, Rationalism, Mysticism, Kantian Moralism, Lessing about Normative Historical Revelation in Christ | 310
7. General History is not Revelation, but Revelation Occurs There: Evaluating Two Philosophies of History | 312
8. A Dialectical Perspective Concerning Historical-Critical Biblical Scholarship | 314
9. Use of Historical Criticism in Biblical Analysis Theologically Motivated | 317
10. Accuracy of Bible's Historical Details Requires Historical Evidence | 318
11. Work of Historian | 318
12. Interim Reflection | 322
13. Could Christian Faith Be Historically Disproven? | 322

19 *Christian Knowing, Believing, Sharing in Faith* | *324*

Part A. Jesus, Paul, and Johannine Tradition | *324*
1. Faith/Belief in Dawning of Kingdom in Jesus's Ministry, but . . . | 324
2. Faith/Belief according to Paul | 324
3. Faith/Belief according to Johannine Tradition | 325

Part B. Biblically Responsive Theological Reflection | *327*
4. Faith and Divine Transcendence | 327
5. Christian Faith as Gift | 327
6. Faith as Evoking Affection for God Leading to Relationship with God and Trust in Her | 328
7. Christ-Centered Faith Implies Cognition | 329
8. Christian Faith Involving Whole Personality as against Cognitive, Voluntaristic, Emotional Distortions | 330

Conclusion | *333*
Glossary with References | *335*
Bibliography | *343*
Index | *353*

# Understanding the Discipline

Preface and Introduction

Preface

IN BOTH THE PASTORAL ministry in the U. S. and a considerably longer ministry of ecumenical seminary teaching in Africa, I combined *an affirmative theological emphasis with enthusiasm for facing critical issues* wherever and whenever they arose—being unwilling to sweep evidence under the carpet.[1] This systematics similarly integrates critical reflection into constructive theological reformulations without being overwhelmed by the critical reflection.

Every systematic theology is to a degree a synthesis, but the breadth of interdisciplinary interaction distinguishes some from others. Such widespread involvement does not establish these as superior. But in a discipline that is to a considerable extent concerned to interrelate knowledge, those manifesting extensive dialogue have that advantage—but only if their breadth is accompanied by considerable depth.

I am not writing a specialist tract on the latest in systematics or concerning the related fields with which I interact. *This is the beginning of the summation of a lifetime of reflection about the nature of Christian Faith.*

In its critical and constructive effort this work is much indebted to the writings of a wide range of systematic[2] and biblical[3] theologians, Christian ethicists, general philosophers, hermeneutical ones, and other specialists. Having learned from *widely disparate scholars and disciplines*, I have sought to perceive how unlikely conversation partners can enrich our thinking and living. I offer interpretations, evaluations, contractions or expansions—and attempt to pull these into a unified whole and to reach well-founded conclusions. Sometimes in the background and often in the foreground is *biblical analysis and interpretation.*

It is hoped that the reflections in these pages will provoke and stimulate careful thinking about the Christian Faith and about the living of the Christian life. More importantly, that they will contribute to an upbuilding of Christian Faith and more

---

1. Two of my previous books in Christian theology and ethics were privately printed in Nigeria and two quietly published in Kenya.

2. See the systematic theology definition in chap. 1, sec. 1 and in the glossary.

3. Biblical, Old Testament (OT) and New Testament (NT), theologies limit their subject matter to these sources.

faithful living. It is also hoped that those with ministerial responsibilities will discover theological insights to help with preaching and teaching on particular biblical themes.

When one does theologically what H. Richard Niebuhr encouraged—learning as much or more from those who are not of one's own denomination—theological insiders from one's tribe may become suspicious. Even so, systematics should not be understood as a denominational activity, but as a search for understanding of God's disclosure in Christ, with interpretive help from whatever quarters. Barth and Brunner do not attract me because they came from a Reformed background, any more than Kierkegaard (SK) intrigues me because he was a Lutheran (with strong Anabaptist/Mennonite tendencies); nor does Ellul fascinate me because he was a Huguenot with Anabaptist leanings. Brunner was particularly interdenominational, most influenced by Kierkegaard, with Luther as a close second. Neither Brunner nor Barth was uncritical of Calvin, but, as should all denominations, the Reformed is always to be in the process of being reformed on the basis of a clearer understanding of God's disclosure in Christ. The theologians who have most influenced me, including Hendrikus Berkhof, were ecumenical Christians first, and denominationally aligned second.

I am no praise singer concerning particular theologians. This writing *never just expounds* particular theologians, but utilizes them where helpful for articulating Christian Faith.

As for other kinds of scholars who are especially influential: James Barr, a biblical theologian specializing in biblical interpretation, who has been highly critical of Barth; Alfred North Whitehead and Michael Polanyi, who were both scientists and philosophers. Whitehead would be regarded by many as the polar opposite of Barth, and in some respects he is. Concerning science and philosophy much is to be learned from him. As for Polanyi, his understanding of the nature of scientific discovery and his gestalt psychology[4] as applied to interpretation are invaluable. See the index for other diverse scholars to whom this writing is also particularly indebted.

Here needs to be explained various ways in which I attempt to be gender inclusive in the language used. The NRSV is quoted and cited where it seems in this respect to improve upon the RSV translation.[5] Concerning extra-biblical quotations—many of which are from modern authors who wrote (and in some cases were translated) before the linguistic aspect of the women's rights movement came to prominence—I make no alteration. To minimize gender emphases in non-quoted, gender undetermined contexts referring to individuals, I usually use either feminine or masculine pronouns and possessives, though I sometimes utilize plurals.

The greater gender inclusive problem concerns pronouns or possessives referring to God. Since God is an Active Subject and no "It," and since I am averse to using such words as "Godself," or "S/He," my choice was between She or He, Her or

---

4 This psychology regards perception as having to do with the intuitive interrelating of parts, thereby enabling the understanding of the whole. See chap. 13, sec. 10.

5. I also use the NRSV for material from the Apocrypha/deuterocanonical books.

Him, Hers or His. All of these are used and without regard to stereotyped images. The reader should regard such usage as merely English language ways of referring to *God* as a Personal Agent. As for pronouns and possessives referring to Jesus, I use He, Him, and His, doing so because Jesus was male.

Jesus spoke of God as "Abba," Father, and so do I, but the meaning of "Abba" as "Daddy" has considerable kinship with the term "Mother" or "Mommy." This is an additional reason for freely referring to God as Mother, but not for the sake of eliminating the Father term. When signifying the presence of the Risen Lord, masculine pronouns are used for an obvious reason. To avoid implying a tritheistic understanding of Divine Triunity, plural pronouns are avoided with reference to God.

Introduction

Numerous chapters are highly dependent on the descriptive findings of Old Testament and New Testament theologies. Though many chapters have philosophical components, chapters 11–13 and 16 have much philosophical input. Similarly, though many chapters deal with aspects influenced by historians, chapters 4, 6 and 18 entail high levels of interaction with historical disciplines.

Much in this volume attempts to comprehend the Bible's authority. Chapter 3 offers a constructive statement concerning the Bible as witness to Jesus Christ, which is the primary understanding of how Scripture[6] should continue to speak to Christians. Chapters 4 and 6 are devoted to the history of the development of the writings eventually included in the canon[7] and to the historical movement toward canonizing. Chapter 5 deals with the problem of the authority of the OT for NT Christians and for Christians today. That chapter's analysis of the areas of agreement and disagreement between the Testaments may help one to render interpretive judgments as to where Christ-centered NT faith concurs with or challenges the OT. Though no Marcionite rejecter of the OT, my attitude toward it is more critical than is common in Reformed theology, including the ecumenical type of Barth and Brunner.[8]

One of the first topics a theological student should study is precisely how the Bible came to be, and its authority in the light of that history. In the absence of such consideration, students are likely to have unrealistic attitudes concerning Scripture. But such a field of study has not been a common part of theological curriculums, and I am not aware of another effort to integrate such material into systematic theology. In regard to my use of scholarship from the above technical area, this study is indebted to

---

6. As a synonym for "Bible" the term "Scripture" is used and (unlike some of my sources) is capitalized, since "Bible" is usually capitalized. However, when referring to Christian texts yet to be included in a closed canon, the term "scripture" is not capitalized.

7. A closed collection of authoritative writings.

8. My agreement is with the Reformed OT scholar Th. C. Vriezen, that the NT took a selective, critical and yet appreciative stance toward the OT (*OT Theology*). Having learned much from the NT, Christians should attempt to distinguish in the OT between what is normative and what is not.

a host of specialists, who, like many specialists, are much accustomed to communicating almost exclusively with one another.

The topic of interpretation (hermeneutics)[9] connects with the interpretive aspects of the biblical chapters previously mentioned. In particular, the chapter 5 assessment of the OT's authority for early and contemporary Christians involves an examination of the methods utilized by writers of books that came to be included in the NT, who found meaning in some of the books that came to comprise the OT. In the more explicitly hermeneutical chapters we will further assess whether such pre-NT writers' interpretive methods are still legitimate. Chapter 7 considers how understanding particular biblical books and verses in a canonical context may be valid in some respects, but invalid in others. The chapter 8 analysis of the traditioning process in Scripture should be of hermeneutical use in helping to regard Scripture more dynamically and developmentally—and may assist in rethinking how we conceive the Bible's authority. Chapter 13, section 10 discusses Polanyi's Gestalt understanding of understanding. Of the three specifically hermeneutical chapters, 15 relates biblical interpretation to preaching, 16 considers hermeneutical philosophy in general, and 17 deals with further aspects of Christian hermeneutical activity with reference to the Bible.

This critical and constructive writing is primarily for students studying theology in universities or seminaries, for their teachers, for congregational preachers and teachers, and interested lay people. Especially for the sake of the latter, but perhaps also for others, technical terms are kept to a minimum. Where these are needed synonyms or definitions are offered in close proximity to their first usage, and a glossary provided so that those who do not read chapters in sequence can find earlier terminological guidance.

First volumes usually assume that the following volume or volumes will be in the same style. Because of the time constraints for a person who is not exactly beginning his career, I cannot presume that in the future I will be able to be as comprehensive as here. But neither will I offer breezy treatments of beliefs.

This volume considers many complex theological themes, and is thus not merely procedural. It already steps into the subject matter, and so does not consist of "things to be said beforehand, but of things to be said first."[10] That is, what is said here will not comprise topics discussed before we get to the heart of the matter. But will concern essential themes regarding how we come to God, and offer first indications concerning the God who is hereby known. Such a preliminary work is necessary because without understanding how knowledge of God is possible, further elucidation of doctrines would be neither well-founded nor clear.[11]

---

9. Seeking to understand how we understand or interpret, and various theories concerning how we do so.

10. Karl Barth as quoted in Busch, *Karl Barth*, 213.

11. One procedural matter should be mentioned: Needing a term to refer to an immediate preceding new reference within the same explanatory note, "same source" is used. "Ibid.," to the contrary, refers to an immediate preceding single source note.

Chapter 1

Systematic Theology's Nature, Purposes, Tasks, and Methods

1. Names for the Discipline

SEVERAL NAMES HAVE BEEN attached to the thematic study of the beliefs of the Christian Faith. Though I exhibit terminological variety in referring to this discipline, all titles I use are intended to refer to studying the *normative* meaning of the Christian Faith topic by topic.

As for some of the specific names that have been attached to this discipline, each has something to be said against it. "Systematic theology" or "systematics" seems to summarize the enterprise in question, but some mistakenly think such titles imply direct linkage to philosophy. "Dogmatics" has also been used to refer to this activity. I employ this term, but neither I nor many others wish to be dogmatic, nor regard this discipline as involving the articulation of official dogmas. I even use the free-standing word "theology" for this enterprise. However there are many other types of theology, such as that which regards the Bible as its sole subject matter or that studies later historical understandings of Christian Faith. Systematics is informed by biblical and historical theology and much else, but having learned from these sources proposes *norms* or *standards* concerning Christian Faith.

2. Its Nature

Systematics is undertaken by those who listen for the Word of Christ spoken primarily amid the scriptural witness and reflect concerning what ought to be the content of the church's teaching and preaching.[1] Though pure doctrine can never be perfectly achieved, it can be approximated insofar as theological thought and language become faithful witnesses to God's manifestation in Christ.[2]

---

1. Barth, *CD*, 1/1:1–3; 1/2:743–58.
2. Barth, *CD*, 1/2:758–82.

Understanding the Discipline

To clarify the nature of systematics I will briefly refer to the relationship between the systematician and the congregational preacher, remembering that such preachers are also teachers. Neither theologian nor preacher is above the other, but stand side by side representing two inseparable activities—theological reflection and proclamation of the Christian message. The theologian and preacher are so bound together that neither can work properly without recourse to the other. The concerns of both activities are needed in the life of each Christian and congregation.[3] This does not mean that all Christians need to be highly cogent theologically, nor that such knowledge is as important as Christian love.

Both dogmatics and preaching seek to amplify the meaning of Christian Faith. An essential difference between these pertains to the way this is done. Dogmatics takes a more systematic and biblically comparative approach, whereas preaching focuses on the theme of a text or several texts as related to a pastoral situation. The preacher seeks to voice the Christ-centered Faith within the concrete situation of a particular congregation; the systematician reflects upon Christ-centered faith in order to test its elements and improve their consistency, while entering into constructive and critical dialogue with other knowledge.

Each particular sermon should be sustained by the dogmatic consideration of the wholeness, truth and intelligible coherence of the Christian message. The sermon ought to be like the smaller part of an iceberg visible above the water, whereas the totality of the message committed to the church should float beneath the surface.[4] Systematic activity can help the congregational witness to be faithful to the total Christian message in part by helping to move historical/critical scriptural understanding (exegesis) and biblical theology toward congregational application.

Systematics urges preachers to "be more intelligible, . . . more self-critical, less trivial, and less intimidated by dominant cultural assumptions."[5] Systematics seeks to acknowledge and systematically articulate the unity and wholeness of the Divine Reality to which individual sermons give a concrete but more one-sided witness. In this way it helps preachers to become more faithful to Christ-centered, biblically grounded content.

Theology takes its rise from the intrinsic unrest that is an inescapable part of the existence of the church within history. This restlessness arises from her deep concern that human words pertaining to God and lives attesting Her shall become faithful witnesses.[6] As the church honors the interpretive aspect of such concerns she will engage in careful theological reflection and strive to avoid using ambiguous language about God.

Systematicians cannot assume that currently articulated doctrines are adequately formulated, but must test those in openness to the Living God speaking amid the

---

3. Johnson, *Authority/Protestant*, 167, 166–67, interpreting Barth, *CD*, 1/1:84–85; 1/2:800–801, 853–54.
4. Ott, *Theology/Preaching*, 55, 26–27.
5. Migliore, *Faith Seeking*, 206–7.
6. Ott, *Theology/Preaching*, 166, 168.

scriptural witness. Though there can be considerable givenness to the theological insights that a theologian has perceived, such knowledge is not sacrosanct, but is subject to continuing scrutiny and correction, more directly from God's leading or as God confirms aspects of the criticisms of others.

3. Is It Necessary?

In the exact form it takes today this discipline did not exist in the NT period. However, Paul and Pauline writers, First Peter, the Fourth Gospel and First John exhibit well-developed systematizing abilities, thereby inspiring further systematizing labor. When the church came to have an entire canon of Scripture the systematizing task became even more important, for the canon exhibits much diversity, which needs to be sorted out, lest confusion reign. Even just prior to the canonizing of the NT, the analyzing and synthesizing of separable themes—systematics proper—began to occur, and is well-exhibited in the writings of Augustine.

Emil Brunner argues that because systematic theology did not exist during the NT period it is not essential to Christian Faith, for the essence of the church "consists only in that without which she could not possibly exist. But the church existed for two hundred years without dogmatics."[7] In terms of current understandings of when the canonizing occurred that greatly increased the need for systematics, one can extend Brunner's time line. The church seems to have existed for over three centuries without *formal* dogmatics. However, "*informal* dogmatics"—evidencing concern for clarity and consistency pertaining to what is believed, spoken, and written—is well reflected in the earliest NT writings (those of Paul). Thus one can reverse Brunner's reasoning and recognize strong continuity between the activity that was theologically vital to the early church and what was essential later. If, as Brunner argues, formal dogmatics is only necessary under some circumstances, systematizing reflection common to both informal and formal dogmatics has always been vital.

Brunner regards the post-NT church's need for systematic theology in the formal sense as due in part to a degree of contradicting multiplicity within the NT witness. Because the truth of revelation must be sought in and behind the diversity of the different testimonies to Christian truth, a systematic and evaluative discipline became indispensable.

Because of scriptural contradictions systematics cannot merely reproduce biblical teachings, but must provide biblically informed reasons for the choices it makes. As this work will continually imply, every theology that claims to only repeat biblical doctrines is accomplished by an unacknowledged and possibly unconscious process of selection and harmonization.[8]

---

7. Brunner, *God*, 9.

8. Ibid., 12. For example see chap. 7, sec. 5. If one includes the OT even more contradictions are apparent, as seen in much of chap. 5.

Understanding the Discipline

4. Its Purposes

In most dogmatics the various purposes are intertwined, though the amount of emphasis varies. Consistent with the Christ-centered nature of Christian Faith,[9] *the first and primary reason for studying systematic theology is to gain a clearer and deeper understanding of Christian Faith for ourselves and for sharing with others.* By clarifying what should be the content of Christian preaching, teaching, and catechetical instruction[10] theology hopes to encourage greater Christian faithfulness.

Because Christian Faith is founded upon historical revelation in Jesus Christ, the church's preaching and teaching needs to communicate the doctrinal content of that. Because the meaning of God's manifestation in Christ is far from self-evident, study and interpretation are required. In proceeding, dogmatic statements must not only not contradict revelation nor themselves, but must be formulated so as to not deny or distort other facts and ideas that we have good reason for regarding as true.

Though theologians strive for doctrinal clarity, neither they nor other Christians should confuse correct doctrine with faith. Though doctrine is needed to clarify the content of faith, such affirmations cannot by themselves establish or guarantee relationship with God. Because faith is distinguished from doctrine, Protestant doctrinal standards (including the two most ancient creeds) are in the Reformed tradition and some others regarded as instructional "confessions," not "dogmas" that *must* be accepted.[11] With reference to existing doctrinal confessions, the theologian stands on the threshold that separates the existing confession of faith from future, improved ones, and serves that transition.[12]

Secondly, are the interrelated communicative and apologetic purposes for engaging in systematics, though here we will primarily consider the former.[13] Traditional biblical and theological language is unfamiliar to many inside and outside the church. Thus some amount of alternative terminology needs to be employed and encouraged. Because word meanings continue to develop and change over the centuries, the church sometimes needs to use different terminology even when agreeing at particular points with traditional understandings.

---

9. Systematics's nature (sec. 2) implies a good deal concerning its purposes.

10. Though the polemical element was strongest in the post NT church, several prominent dogmatics books were intended for catechetical instruction and for doctrinal clarification, as, for example, some writings of Gregory of Nyssa and Augustine's *Enchiridion*. Similarly, in the Middle Ages systematics was often studied to elucidate and unify scriptural exposition and help one to understand the church Fathers. In the medieval period Melanchthon's dogmatics aimed to assist the Bible reader in comprehending its message. Calvin's *Institutes* arose originally as a doctrinal handbook on Luther's Catechism. However the purpose of the final *Institutes* was to help the reader comprehend the Bible. Barth's teachings and writings sought to clarify what should be the normative content of congregational preaching, that it would in turn aid Christians toward fathoming the faith.

11. Unfortunately these confessions have sometimes been interpreted less flexibly.

12. Brunner, *God*, 58.

13. For a fuller discussion of apologetics/polemics, see chap. 9, secs. 6–7.

To be effective systematicians need to become knowledgeable of the mentality and cultural situation of the people to whom the Christian Faith is to be communicated. In modern times (and yet also as early as Aquinas) such acquaintance has involved becoming deeply familiar with the secular assumptions influencing many, but can also entail learning of non-Christian religions or other commitments. Study of cultural presuppositions should not, however, be for the sake of adapting to those,[14] but that we may help people from various backgrounds perceive the meaning of Christian Faith.

Closely related to its communicative-apologetic purpose, systematics has *thirdly, helped combat false teachings that corrupt Christian Faith from within*. Controversy and polemics have played an important role in the dogmatic labors of the church. Those arguments with heresy that are today often dismissed as mere theological quarrels, in earlier times had a most stimulating effect. Then the line between polemics against heresy within the church and apologetics as conflict with non-Christian faiths outside the church was not sharply draw, because non-Christian views, Gnosticism and Traditional Religion in particular, had penetrated the church itself. Today's Church also faces non-Christian penetration.

Theological controversies are "no better or worse, and no more superfluous, than controversies in other areas of life."[15] Though the Reformation was greatly concerned about exegesis and edification, the polemical element was prominent. Luther's most important writings concerned controversies with the Catholic Church (of which he had been a priest), but he was also critical of Protestant humanistic and fanatical understandings of Christian Faith.[16]

Related to the other purposes of systematics, the *fourth is to serve the missionary outreach of the church*. Christian Faith needs to be articulated, not only that Christians may gain a clearer understanding of their faith, but that they may communicate and defend it in the face of conflicting views (even false teachings within the church), that through their witness people may realize what is entailed in decision for Christ.

---

14. Aquinas wrote *Summa Theologica* as an attempt to refute rising Averroistic Aristotelianism, but in doing so expressed Christian faith in terms of Aristotle's "modern" categories. Unfortunately, in the process he misinterpreted Christian content to a considerable extent. Similarly, in the nineteenth century Schleiermacher sought to refute the secular assumptions of the cultural despisers of Christianity, but proceeded by accepting many of their presuppositions. In recent times Paul Tillich used the language and thought forms of existential philosophy and, like Aquinas and Schleiermacher, to an extent misconstrued Christian faith for the sake of communicating it. Recently some African theologians (such as Balaji Idowu) have been so intent on relating Christian faith to African traditional religion (Animism) that they have distorted Christian faith in the process. It is not unfair to conclude that theologians who have highly emphasized apologetics have often compromised Christian content for the sake of "effective" communication.

15. Barth, *1961–1968 Letters*, 143.

16. Brunner, *God*, 93–94, 94.

5. Dialectical Method and Christocentric Focus

Dialectics concerning the thinking and communicating process involves the polar, multi-sided, tension filled, or paradoxical (only seemingly contradictory) aspects of complex ideas, or of ideas in relation to other ideas. Dialectical ideas also provoke questions—and thereby energize and open the mind. Consider the dialectical thought process involved in affirming the following examples.[17] If we are to speak of the glory of God in creation, we must emphasize God's concealment within creation (as in Romans 8:18–39). Even God's glory is a complex notion, since it was disclosed when God humbled Himself in Christ. Another example: In pondering death and the transitory quality of this life we should remember the majesty of the God who meets us in death and recall God's creational desire to share His life with human beings. Again, in considering human existence in God's image we must recall that we are sinners, and yet in considering sin we should emphasize divine forgiveness and empowerment.[18]

Christocentrism helps us to keep in mind our understandings of God's manifestation in Christ even as we reflect anew concerning the meaning of divine disclosure. Barth described his Christocentricity as rethinking previous ideas from the standpoint of God's grace in Jesus Christ. He found that such concentration enabled him to take a critical, though still sympathetic approach to church tradition, the Reformers, and Calvin in particular. He found that in this way he could express himself more clearly and confessionally, freely and comprehensively than before.[19]

6. Relationships between Revelation, Scripture, Systematics, and Preaching

Revelation is historically and normatively prior to Scripture, and Scripture is historically and normatively prior to systematics and today's proclamation. Systematics can become normatively prior to current proclamation insofar as it comprehensively clarifies the meaning of biblically attested divine manifestation. But preaching/teaching is more common as a means of grace, and systematics should also learn from this source.

Systematic theology helps to equip Christians for proclamation and teaching not by providing formulations to be directly repeated in those contexts, but by offering

---

17. See chap. 9, sec. 4 for a more extensive discussion of Christian paradoxes.

18. Barth, *Word of God/Man*, 208, 207.

19. Barth, *Changed Mind*, 43–44. Barth's christologically grounded theology first came to expression in *CD* 2/1 in relation to the question of God's being. In this regard he advanced the thesis that "God is who He is in the act of revelation" (257). Two of the many other consequences of centering all theological thinking in Christ were that there can be no doctrine of creation and providence without reference to God's covenantal purposes, and none of human nature without reflection upon the restored humanity disclosed in Christ (McCormack, *Barth's Dialectical Theology*, 454).

articulations to be pondered in preparation for such activities.[20] Even at its best, dogmatics cannot be equated with the Word of God/Revelation, but neither can proclamation nor Scripture.[21] Like these others, systematics can bear faithful witness to Jesus Christ, thereby becoming an instrument for God's disclosure.

Because systematics as watchdog and guardian is much concerned that the church's doctrinal message be faithful to God's self-communication in Jesus Christ, there is likely to be a degree of tension between systematic theologians and the church's preachers and teachers. In a parallel way some tension is expected between congregational preachers—charged with proclaiming the whole Gospel—and local congregations, who may want an easier and less holistically biblical and ecumenical faith. If systematicians and Christian preachers-teachers are truly faithful to Christ they must often challenge popular assumptions.

7. Separating Word from Words, Kernel from Husk

Because not everything found within the Bible agrees with God's disclosure in Jesus Christ, systematic theology's effort to point toward the Christ-centered Word of God in Scripture must distinguish what it thinks is of binding authority from what it regards as theologically incompatible with Christ or merely time-bound and thereby relative. The "kernel" of Christian Faith must be separated from the "husk" of the Bible's culture and world view. Though we learn of Jesus Christ through the biblical witness,[22] "Scripture is the conditional norm; Jesus Christ the unconditional norm."[23]

8. Spirit's Leading, Sense of Wonder, and Astonishment

As with all Christians, theologians can become God's interpreters and witnesses only as they receive the gift of God's forgiveness and guidance; otherwise such sinners should not have the audacity to undertake such a high and holy task. Only by God's gracious leading are Christians authorized to add human words of interpretation to the witness of Scripture—that its message concerning Jesus Christ may be better understood.[24] The Holy Spirit can empower us to accomplish that of which we are incapable (2 Cor 12:9–10).[25] Though human words of themselves denote only what is creaturely, by the free leading of the Spirit, God can enable us in our writing and speaking to share in

---

20. Barth, *CD*, 1/1:322.
21. Barth, *Göttingen Dogmatics*, 287.
22. See chap. 3.
23. Brunner, *God*, 81.
24. Barth, *Word of God/Man*, 183, 191–92.
25. Barth, *CD*, 1/2:751, 753, 756, 743.

His truth—and thereby can raise our words from death.[26] "Unless the Lord builds the house, those who build it labor in vain" (Ps 127:1a).[27]

"*Astonishment* stands at the beginning of every theological perception, inquiry, and thought" and if it is lacking, the whole enterprise degenerates. Furthermore, "no one can become and remain a theologian unless he is compelled again and again to be astonished *at himself*," becoming for himself "an enigma and a mystery."[28] Because God must overcome our inability, the person who is God's instrument is humbled by a sense of incapacity, as was Moses.[29] "Moses said to the Lord, 'O my Lord, I have never been eloquent, neither in the past nor even now that you have spoken to your servant; but I am slow of speech and slow of tongue.' Then the Lord said to him, 'Who gives speech to people? Who makes them mute or deaf, seeing or blind? Is it not I, the Lord? Now go, and I will be with your mouth and teach you what you are to speak'" (Exod 4:10–12 NRSV).[30]

9. Learning Ever Afresh

Granted our sinfulness and fallibility and God's holiness and transcendence, we must learn ever afresh. "Yesterday's memories can be comforting and encouraging for such work only if they link to the recollection that even yesterday's work had to begin at the beginning."[31] By doing this, theological activity can set an example for all intellectual activity.

Such dynamism of renewal does not mean that we benefit from no memory of the meaning of the concepts and doctrines we affirmed yesterday, as though every new day erases our entire theological understanding. It does mean that theological study should occur with openness to God's judgment and correction. We must not lock into interpretations, but be ever ready to critically reexamine and reformulate.

Since our entire lives are to be lived in God's presence and subject to His kingship, so also our theological lives. For Christians there can be no separate and autonomous kingdoms where we no longer need to be faithful to Christ, as, for example, where

---

26. Barth, *CD*, 2/1:23. Though we are obligated to try to witness faithfully, God can also speak in and through unfaithful witness—though he does so by overruling the interpretation offered.

27. Barth, *Theology/Church*, 302.

28. Barth, *Evangelical Theology*, 64, 71.

29. Barth, *CD*, 2/1:221. See below, chap. 14, sec. 3 concerning the divine authorization or calling of proclamatory ministers.

30. God's overcoming of the sense of human inadequacy was also attested when the author of Isaiah 6 wrote, "'Woe is me! I am lost, for I am a man of unclean lips, and I live among a people of unclean lips; yet my eyes have seen the King, the Lord of hosts!' Then one of the seraphs flew to me, holding a live coal that had been taken from the altar with a pair of tongs. The seraph touched my mouth with it and said: 'Now that this has touched your lips, your guilt has departed and your sin is blotted out'" (5–7 NRSV). See also Jer 1:6–9; Ezek 3:27a; Deut 18:18; Isa 50:4; Dan 10:15–19 (ibid., 221).

31. Barth, *Evangelical Theology*, 165.

mere scholarship holds. Theological endeavor must involve an offering in which everything is placed before the Living God, praying "Not as I will, but as you will."[32]

Without minimizing what has been said, we need to more thoroughly consider the intellectual dimension of theological work. But before we attend more directly to that we must be cognizant of the intellectual background influencing the work of systematic theologians.

10. Thorough Theology Inherently Hellenic

Insofar as Christian communication goes beyond the less systematic channels of preaching, congregational teaching, and informal Christian writing—it presupposes not only Greco-Roman respect for reason, but utilizes a generally Hellenistic approach. Hellenism refers not only to the ideas and culture of ancient Greece, but to the spread of such influence to non-Greek speaking areas conquered by Alexander the Great and the Roman Empire. Christians need not agree with the explicit ideas of any philosopher. Nevertheless, the systematic and thorough approach that the Greco-Roman philosophers pioneered is still essential for everyone who wishes to approach any subject thoroughly and with exactitude.

Systematic theology could not exist as a discipline without the kind of intellectual curiosity of which Greece is the source. It is not that other ancient peoples, including the Israelites, did not ask concerning the whys and wherefores of the world. It is rather that in ancient Greece the practice became a matter of principle. The Greeks asked persistently and systematically, and their questioning led to the development of the very idea of disciplines—areas of knowledge defined by principles and investigated by appropriate methods of inquiry.

Systematic theologians take the systematic search for reasons for granted, but this is something learned from the Greeks. An essential part of the Hellenic influence on Christian theology is the valuing of coherence, the asking why and how things are, the organizing of diverse material according to principles, the seeking of a basis for every claim made, and the effort to interrelate knowledge of one type with that of another. Though Christian theology requires much more than the relentlessly curious Hellenistic spirit, it also requires this spirit and these procedures.[33]

11. Utilizing Abstract Thought in Systematics

The philosophical traditions originally emanating from Greece employ abstract thought and encourage the same. To think abstractly is to perceive connections between disparate ideas, texts or objects. This activity is utilized in scientific classifications and

---

32. Ibid., 166, 167, as influenced by the Lutheran theologian David Hollaz.
33. Allen, *Philosophy/Theology*, 4–5, 28, 5.

in systematic theology's drawing together of relevant biblical and post-biblical texts that shed light on the meaning of each doctrine. But this aspect of systematics's process is even more complicated, since it first requires the perception of doctrines from the abundance of biblical texts. The abstracting capacity also lays the groundwork for recognizing compatible and incompatible texts and ideas. In somewhat overlapping ways, creativity, imagination, and even humor also have much to do with thinking abstractly—discerning patterns or connections even where none are obvious—even if only to twist them humorously.

12. Systematizing Method Encourages Consistency, Has Capacity to Disconfirm Truth Claims[34]

The need for a systematic expression of the Christian Faith is not only rooted in belief in God's oneness, indivisibility of attributes, and congruence of Her actions with themselves and with Her self-consistent nature, but is also grounded in the systematic quality of much human thought and expression. *The systematic form of writing encourages consistency, and "genuine consistency is one of the hardest tasks in theology (as it probably is in every cognitive approach to reality), and no one fully succeeds. But in making a new statement, the necessity of surveying previous ones in order to see whether or not they are mutually compatible drastically reduces inconsistencies."*[35]

The present systematizing work is in the *loci* tradition exemplified by Calvin and Barth:[36] Though everything must be tested by one's understanding of Jesus Christ, exposition does not try to encompass everything under one central doctrine concerning Christ's person or work, as, for example, the Son's self-emptying or kingship, or His justifying or sanctifying activity. Rather, with consideration of their exegetical bases, a whole series of biblically-grounded beliefs are discussed one after another, and one continually struggles to be congruous across all of these diverse but interrelated topics. *With this method the systematizing task becomes more difficult, but has more likelihood of being faithful to the biblical content.*[37]

The implicit assumptions behind the effort to take close account of the relationships between doctrinal themes is that *because Christian Faith is concerned about*

---

34. For a related discussion comparing contradiction with paradoxicality see chap. 9, sec. 4.

35. Tillich, *ST*, 3:3, my emphasis. "It often happens that those who attack the systematic form are very impatient when they discover an inconsistency in someone else's thought," but it is precisely the systematic form that helps to reduce self-contradiction (Tillich, *ST*, 1:58).

36. Karl Barth was highly systematic in sensing interrelatedness, and thorough in the extreme, but because even major topics were re-discussed many places, his fascinating and inspiring writings became extraordinarily repetitive. Unlike Barth, I try to place major discussions of particular beliefs in individual places, thereby seeking to avoid verbosity.

37. Out of attachment to a pre-established dogmatic position and for the sake of logical coherence, *on occasion* Calvin did violence to biblical texts and adapted them to the requirements of his doctrines, as in his biblical defense of infant baptism (*Institutes*, 2:1324–59; Wendel, *Calvin*, 359).

truth, various doctrines need to be understood in such ways that what one says concerning each is self-consistent and in harmony with what one says of the others and with what one otherwise regards as true. Systematics assumes that a self-contradictory belief cancels itself out, that beliefs that conflict with other beliefs cancel each other, and that beliefs that conflict with other well recognized truths cancel those beliefs.[38] *Truths must be unifiable.* Though revelation is the constructive basis for Christian truth, the *coherence test* can disconfirm what one thought to be true. Thus "in the process of theological reflection and reconstruction the truth content of the tradition itself is, in fact, at stake."[39]

Since the systematic form enables one to make comparisons and to discover relationships between the various doctrines or beliefs that otherwise would not be readily apparent,[40] it also enables the perception of incompatibilities that otherwise might not be apparent.

Where systematicians uncover genuine and unresolvable conflicts, they must insist on the need for choices and should indicate their own decisions and reasons for so choosing. For example, if because of strong biblical evidence one believes that the God of considerable power loves all people, it may be inconsistent to argue that He will eternally damn most. A willingness on God's part to damn most would seem to provide strong evidence against the premise that a considerably powerful God loves everyone. Systematicians must insist that those who affirm both beliefs are inconsistent unless they can indicate how God's damning of most people can be consistently understood as expressing His love. Mere assertions to that effect (as with Calvin) will not do!

13. Is Systematic Theology a Science?

Whether or not one classifies systematic theology as a science depends on one's understanding of the defining characteristics of science.[41] Systematics seems to agree with aspects of what many people commonly regard as essential features of science, but disagrees with other facets. As for systematics's agreement: Scientific activity presupposes that some existing reality is to be investigated and elucidated by the use of analytical and synthesizing concepts that demonstrate its comprehensive orderliness and cohesiveness, as when considering nature.[42] Systematics not only uses such pro-

---

38. Of course general learning must be critically scrutinized before becoming a cause for theological reformulation of related Christian convictions.

39. Pannenberg, *ST*, 1:23. Though striving to avoid genuine incompatibilities, seeming incompatibilities can sometimes be understood as paradoxes (involving only logical tension). See sec. 5; also see chap. 9, sec. 4.

40. Tillich, *ST*, 3:3.

41. See chap. 13, secs. 1–2, 9–11.

42. Berkhof, *Christian Faith*, 35. Dogmatics is more self-conscious and strict in seeking systematic coherence through analytical and synthesizing methods than is congregational preaching/teaching or informal forms of Christian writing. It is also more scientific in being able to pursue knowledge

cedures, but (like science) openly gives account of its methods,[43] though some differ considerably from those of natural and social science.

Recent philosophies of science emphasize that science is much dependent on tradition and history and requires particular moral commitments. In this respect it is similar to theology and to other fields of knowledge.[44]

Systematic theology certainly works in ways that drastically differ from what is *commonly regarded* as scientific. Many wrongly think that science assumes convictions and uses methods of verification that in principle are everywhere assumed. To the contrary, natural science can be practiced only by those who, among other things, believe the outward world is real, which millions of Hindus and Buddhists do not.[45] Scientists of all types must also have confidence concerning scientific method, and many people do not, but in addition must have worked to master the procedures used in their particular scientific disciplines.[46]

Certainly systematics's central convictions—for example, concerning God, Christ, and human sinfulness—are not accepted by non-Christians. Whether or not non-Christians regard systematics as "scientific" does not make much difference concerning this discipline's convictions and methods. But it may be correct that systematic theology should insist that in its own way it is scientific and that universities need its presence to help to prevent an empiricist narrowing concerning what constitutes scientific method.[47]

In systematics's concern to be regarded as scientific it must be careful not to forget its older heritage concerning its identity and purpose. It has long been regarded as a form of wisdom—that can and should translate into more faithful living.

---

comprehensively. These scientific advantages, however, do not mean that regular dogmatics is superior to the irregular types just mentioned.

43. Weber, *Dogmatics*, 1:49–50.

44. See chap. 16, sec. 4, especially n18 for a discussion related to issues mentioned in this and the preceding paragraph.

45. See chap. 13, n1.

46. See chap. 13, sec. 9. For non-scientific values required for scientific activity also see chap. 13, sec. 9.

47. Berkhof, *Christian Faith*, 35–36.

Chapter 2

Jesus Christ as God's Past and Present Revealing Word

1. Christ's Risen Presence as Operating Premise

CHRISTIAN SYSTEMATIC THEOLOGY AND proclamation can testify on behalf of God because as risen from the dead Jesus Christ here and now speaks, and also does this amid faithful Christian interpretation on His behalf. Without validating all that is said, He authenticates the truth that is reflected amid such witness. The One to whom Christian proclamation and teaching point is more extra-ordinarily present than as one merely remembered, or known only through the activating of a timeless ever-present spiritual possibility implanted in human nature via creation. The Risen Christ as Spirit freely manifests His reality by "interrupting the continuities of our lives and calling us into community with the Living God."[1]

2. Primary Object of Christian Faith is God, not Our Experience

Reasoning from God's disclosure in the past and seeking faithfully to respond to the present leading of the Risen Christ as Spirit, systematic theology *seeks to attest the activity of God, and thereby Her nature, and thus Her reality.* As personal encounter with people leads to knowledge of them, not mere relationship, so it is with God. Though we come to know God only amid communion with Her, we thereby come to know *Her*, and do not merely gain comprehension of our fellowship with Her (Schleiermacher, often), let alone mere self-understanding (Bultmann, sometimes). That the primary object of systematic theology is God, not our experience, means that Christian theology should interpret Christian discourse as "referentially transparent" and "reality depicting."[2] Though "we see in a mirror dimly" (1 Cor 13:12a) and never gain a perfect grasp of God—we can and should obtain genuine awareness of Her.

---

1. Dalferth, "Barth's Eschatological Realism," 22.
2. Ibid., 23–24, 17.

God's manifestation in Jesus Christ in the past and the Holy Spirit's present enlightening revelation are the working premises from which systematic theology begins—with trust in Jesus Christ based on experience of the Spirit. Granted that God in these ways discloses Herself, systematics inquiries concerning these processes and seeks to deepen knowledge of the revealed God.

3. Transcending Mere Subject-Object Knowing[3]

In Christian Faith and elsewhere subject-object modes of knowing can be transcended. Particular ways in which supposed subject-object knowing differs from how we know God are these: First, though in much western understanding knowing is seen as implying human control over what is known, and manipulation of it, such a conception oversimplifies how we gain any kind of knowledge.[4] As for learning of God, though we should study the Bible carefully, truly to know God we must place ourselves at His disposal. Secondly, if we try to know something only in a subject-object manner we do not know it deeply and it does not affect our hearts and lives. In contrast, knowledge of God received in response to His Living Word affects the whole person. Thirdly, mere subject-object understandings do not cause us to be less lonely, whereas God through Christ rescues us from solitariness by setting us in relationship with Himself, with fellow Christians, others, and the world.[5]

Because God as Holy Spirit freely reveals Herself, knowledge of God occurs amid a *subject-subject* context, with the divine subject taking the primary initiative. By disclosing Herself in Jesus Christ, God has in a sense also placed Herself within the *subject-object* context of human knowing. But only in a sense, for God's past revelation is hidden within the Bible amid the fallible words of human witnesses, and requires contemporary interpretation, also by other fallible witnesses. These things being so, God's presence as Holy Spirit—Subject—is required for properly understanding Her disclosure amid hiddenness. Furthermore, ongoing dynamic relationship with God as Holy Spirit must overcome sinful resistance and is required for sustaining and growing in such relationally based cognition.

God as subject hides Himself primarily in Christ and secondarily in the biblical witness to Christ and amid preaching and teaching and other testimony, that He as Holy Spirit may *freely* disclose the meaning of His primary revelation. Because our sinful resistance is real, the divine knowledge we think we derive cannot be assumed to be valid without ongoing scrutiny.

---

3. See chap. 10, sec. 6; chap. 12, sec. 5; and chap. 18, sec. 7.
4. See chap. 13, sec. 8; chap. 19, secs. 1, 3.
5. Brunner, *Truth As Encounter*, 116.

4. God in Her Word

Whether spoken or with sign language, words are important for communicating, for understanding communication, and for maintaining personal relationship. Word of God terminology is, however, generally metaphorical—for God can speak directly to our inner selves.[6] Thus we should not confuse a theology of the Word of God with one of divine chatter.

Word of God terminology is often used as an equivalent for *revelation* as divine self-disclosure. More specifically the Word can denote God's communicating as dynamic and concrete, as for example when God's Word *came* to the prophets and caused them to speak and act in particular ways.[7] In this regard the Word can be so strongly spiritual and personal and may come so unexpectedly and vehemently that Amos compared it to the roaring of a lion (3:8). In all regards the distance between us and God is indicated by the Word as required to bridge the gap.[8]

With reference to God's activity, the Old and New Testaments draw no essential distinction between "words," articulated statements, and "deeds," historical acts.[9] "God acts by His Word and speaks by His action."[10] In Christ the Word, the fundamental unity of word and action was realized. After Christ's resurrection, Word of God is the active presence and power of the Risen Lord as Spirit (2 Cor 3:17a).

Paul Tillich admitted that the Word appearing *as a person* is the fulfillment of biblical personalism: God being so personal that He is most clearly seen in one focused presence. Tillich also conceded that such biblical personalism is incompatible with the classical ontology to which he was committed (a philosophy based on an analysis of the concept of "being"). He further conceded that such an understanding of God, which focuses on His being in and beyond everything, seems to depersonalize knowledge of God.[11] Yet Tillich chose ontology against biblical personalism and proceeded to reinterpret Christian concepts to make them compatible with his analysis of "being." Methodologically paralleling many forms of Liberal Theology, he, for example, regarded Jesus as illustrating the timeless ontological possibility of new creation knowable and realizable apart from Jesus.

In opposition to Tillich's epistemology (theory of how we are able to know) Barth moved from the particularity of God's personal communication in Christ and through the Holy Spirit to an understanding of God:

---

6. Tillich, *Biblical Religion*, 78, 79.

7. Jer 1:4–12; Ezek 2:1–7; Hos 1:1–5.

8. Vriezen, *OT Theology*, 94, 253.

9. Ramseyer, "Word," 460. See sec. 5 for a biblically and theologically more thorough discussion of this point, though under the heading of "revelation."

10. Ibid., 460. Of course humans also communicate in ways that transcend words, as through gestures, facial expressions, and deeds.

11. Tillich, *Biblical Religion*, 38, 39.

(a) The experience of God's Word *does not confirm and reinforce the naive confidence that humans have the natural capacity to experience and know God*. To the contrary, such an experience severely shakes such assurance, else we would not be dealing with *God's* Word. God says something dramatically new.[12]

(b) According to biblical understanding, *"Word of God" refers to the miracle of God's free activity and speech in which She shares Her very self*, not mere information about Herself.[13] As freely acting and speaking here and now, God in Her Word cannot be mastered or domesticated.[14] We cannot speak God's Word to ourselves, but must always remain hearers or receivers. We know of God's Word insofar as God has spoken to us, the reality of God's Word preceding and grounding our possibility of knowing Her. Knowledge of God involves acknowledgment and thinking after.[15]

Because God is truly known through Her action and communication, the OT ascribes to the Word of God what belongs to God Herself (Isa 40:8; 55:10–11). The Word is God once more, God in self-disclosure, God speaking to people. The Transcendent God claims us here below. That the One God can and does exist not only in Herself but in Jesus Christ and through the Holy Spirit indicates God's capacity for Triunity: God distinguishing Herself from Herself and yet remaining one.

(c) Since God is truly known through His doing and speaking, *His Word involves intelligent communication*.[16] By the power of the Holy Spirit God enables us to understand something of the meaning of His manifestation in Christ. Thus we must not (with Rudolf Otto) anti-intellectually put irrational shaking in place of knowledge of God. Because God's Word is the bearer of truth, the prophetic and apostolic witness takes the form of words, and this is why we are called to speak about God, not to babble or mime or offer *only* instrumental music.[17] So much can our Spirit-enlightened reason participate in God's Word that human language can ever anew be qualified to become a bearer of revelation.

(d) God's Word as God's free speech is *mysterious*. "We cannot produce conditions, on the fulfillment of which hearing the Word is assured. There is no method of converting revelation into revelation really apprehended,"[18] no method of scriptural exegesis that of itself brings the Spirit, above all, no method of proclamation, that really impinges upon the hearers in an ultimate sense. There is nothing of that sort because the Word of God really touches people only through the Holy Spirit from God's side.

---

12. Barth, *Way of Theology*, 39.

13. Though "Word of God" conveys a similar meaning to "revelation" (see the next section), the former term is more commonly used in the Bible.

14. Jer 23:16–18; 1 Cor 2:3–5; 2 Cor 2:17; 4:2; 1 Thess 2:4.

15. McCormack, *Barth's Dialectical Theology*, 425, quoting Karl Barth, *Die christliche Dogmatik im Entwurf*, 136.

16. See the next sec. and chap. 19, sec. 7.

17. Barth, *Göttingen Dogmatics*, 62–63.

18. Barth, *CD*, 1/1:209.

(e) *God's Living Word is God's purposeful action whereby He implements His rule in our lives.* Not surprisingly, the Greek word for "obey" builds from the same root as the word to "hear." Amid scriptural proclamation, teaching, readings attesting God's historical revelation, and in other ways God directs His Living Word purposely toward us—claiming our lives.[19]

(f) *God's Living Word is powerful—able to accomplish much.* "For as the rain and snow come down from heaven, and do not return there until they have watered the earth, making it bring forth and sprout, giving seed to the sower and bread to the eater, so shall my word be that goes out from my mouth; it shall not return to me empty, but it shall accomplish that which I purpose, and succeed in the thing for which I sent it" (Isa 55:10–11).

5. Revelation as God's Self-Disclosing Communicating[20]

Biblical. "Word" and "revelation" terminology jointly help us understand God's communicating, each biblical term paralleling and overlapping with the other. Because we can know God only because She speaks Her Word or reveals Herself to us, OT revelation language presupposes that God is the Hidden One (Isa 45:15) whose acquaintance becomes possible through self-manifestation. In disclosing Herself God concedes to our powers of comprehension—but remains the initiator and master of Her self-disclosing action.[21]

The NT commonly uses the term "revelation" to indicate God's future death-triumphing fulfillment[22] or that of Christ,[23] who brings final judgment and salvation.[24] The NT recognizes that such future fulfillments have already begun in Christ.[25] The idea of present revelation/salvation through Christ is carried to the extreme in John, who regarded the final judgment as already completed with the coming of Jesus.[26] Though Paul believed that the last judgment will occur beyond death, according to him Christ's death and resurrection signified present salvation, God's way of setting us

---

19. Ibid., 209, 170.
20. See chap. 18.
21. The OT occasionally claims that God reveals Herself amid nature (Ps 18:7–15; 19:1–4; 29:3), but 1 Kgs 19:11–13a conflicts with this. God is also said to sometimes disclose Herself in visions accompanied with words (Exod 33:22–23; Num 24:4; Isa 6:1–8) and in dreams (Gen 28:11–17; 1 Sam 28:6). God is more commonly said to directly speak her revealing Word (Isa 5:9; Jer 23:18, 22) or to disclose herself by granting insight into the meaning of her activity in the events of individuals (Ps 3; 118:13–14) or of the nation Israel (Exod 15:1–13; Ps 98:2–3; Jer 33:16). The OT looks forward to the final revelation in the day of the Lord (Hos 2:19–23; Jer 31:31–34).
22. 1 Cor 13:12; 1 John 3:2.
23. Luke 17:30; 1 Cor 1:7; Rev 1:7.
24. Rom 8:18–25; 1 Cor 3:13; 1 Pet 1:5.
25. Heb 9:26b; 1 Pet 1:20.
26. John 3:17–19; 9:39; 12:31, 47–48.

in right relation.²⁷ Consequently, the *gospel as preached* continues the saving action of God, and can also be described as revelation,²⁸ faith's arrival²⁹ and love's disclosure.³⁰

According to the NT God is the Revealer as an object of remembrance, through personal relationship in the present and with universal disclosure in the future. Present manifestation is veiled because though eternal life was revealed with the Son's coming (1 John 1:1–2) the final revelation, consummation, or Son's return is yet to happen.³¹

Theological. Though Christians can and should gain knowledge concerning God from revelation, such knowledge involves "first of all and in every instance an actual event,"³² past, present or future. Whether NT revelation denotes the removal of a veil, the disclosure of what had been concealed, the declaration of what had been unknown, or the communication of what was otherwise unavailable, all refer to what God supernaturally supplies—not to the mere possibility of finding God³³ or to a natural capacity that God implanted within creation.³⁴ Scripture emphasizes the event character of revelation by regarding it as an act of God. "As actual event, revelation has a thoroughly temporal nature: it is not happening all the time, but at a specific time; and it is not a constantly open possibility, rather its possibility can only be recognized in that it actually happens."³⁵ Because revelation exists only in action, humankind is not continually open to God, but becomes so when God as Holy Spirit opens blinded eyes and closed minds.³⁶

The triune God is the source and agent of revelation.³⁷ The Spirit reveals the Son, who discloses the Father. God is not content to have once-and-for-all been manifested, but is ceaselessly disclosing Himself,³⁸ that people may understand and love Him (Matt 11:27; 1 Cor 2:10–14; 12:3).³⁹

Since our thoughts are not God's thoughts and our ways are not His ways (Isa 55:8–9), revelation confronts us with "what no eye has seen nor ear heard, nor the human heart conceived" (1 Cor 2:9 NRSV). God's self-manifestation in Christ is a source of offense to those who think they already know who God is and how He ought to act.

---

27. Rom 1:16–17; 3:21; 5:1; 2 Cor 4:10–11.
28. Rom 1:16–17; 2 Cor 2:14–17; Col 1:24–29.
29. Gal 3:23.
30. 1 John 4:9–10.
31. 1 John 2:28; 1 Pet 1:13. Bultmann, "Revelation/NT," 45.
32. Weber, *Dogmatics*, 1:173.
33. Ibid., 173.
34. As with Arminian/Wesleyan prevenient grace teaching.
35. Weber, *Dogmatics*, 1:173.
36. Barth, *Göttingen Dogmatics*, 58.
37. Matt 11:27; 1 Cor 2:9–16.
38. Matt 16:17; 1 Thess 2:13.
39. Biber, "NT Revelation," 173.

Thus in the first century the message of the Crucified Christ seemed to the Gentiles folly and to the Jews a stumbling block (1 Cor 1:23).

Like God's Word, Christian Faith focuses upon God's revelation in Christ, which by its very nature includes knowledge. Preaching, teaching and systematic theology teaching seek to make such knowledge explicit—thereby contributing to the upbuilding of Christian Faith. Theological inquiry as moving from knowledge of divine disclosure to clearer understanding of that is a feasible activity. Yet this is not mere knowledge—for God's grace involves an act of aggression that contradicts our self-will by calling us to repentance and costly discipleship. Thus we are able to differentiate our experience of God from our own subjectivities.[40]

God distinguishes Herself from fate by the fact that She is not inherently in history or consciousness or nature, but comes to us through these.[41] Though God and the creaturely medium come together, no synthesis occurs.[42] Divinity never passes into humanity, and humanity is not divinized. In the language of traditional Reformed dogmatics, "the finite is not capable of the Infinite," though the Infinite is capable of revealing Herself in the finite.

From time to time in manifesting Herself God grants wisdom concerning the meaning of present events. Such disclosures do not merely draw attention to their inherent content, but shed light upon our lives. These manifestations can help to make other events intelligible. Revelation in this aspect is like a luminous sentence we come across in a difficult book, from which we gain some comprehension of the whole.[43]

We now need to sharpen our discussion by considering *understandings of revelation in history* that overemphasized historical acts of God in contrast with disclosure through God's communicative Word.[44] Some within the "revelation in history" school of OT theology, and G. Ernest Wright in particular, gave such priority to outer events as to conceive of "*divine* speech" as but the *human* interpretation of events, rather than as God's communication that can condition what will occur,[45] as well as itself interpreting events. James Barr was adept at criticizing this distortion of biblical understanding: With various nuances he repeatedly insisted that as biblically understood, divine speech is often a precondition for events—not their mere interpretation—and

40. Torrance, *Barth's Early Theology*, 183, 25.

41. Barth, *Way of Theology*, 40. See chap. 10, sec. 10; chap. 12, sec. 5; chap. 18, sec. 7.

42. McCormack, *Barth's Dialectical Theology*, 269.

43. Niebuhr, *Meaning/Revelation*, 93.

44. For a broader discussion of revelation in history, see chap. 18. In particular see sec. 11 for a discussion of the work of biblical and other historians.

45. Other than Wright, James Barr in this regard mentions only Barth, but this latter reference is wildly inaccurate (*Concept/Biblical Theology*, 351, 678 for note). Barth has continually emphasized the togetherness of revelation through divine deed and Word. Because Rad stressed Israel's rehearsal of the events of her sacred history, Barr could have mentioned him. But, unlike Wright, Rad did not sharply pair off God's acts against His communicative Word, and emphasized Israel's ongoing reinterpretations of her historical traditions. In NT studies Oscar Cullmann was considerably guilty of splitting God's action from His speaking (see chap. 18, sec. 7), but the debate occurred largely in OT studies.

is essential to the story's progress. Seen in this way, Wright's emphasis on divine events plus merely human interpretation is a secularized interpreting away of divine speech.[46]

The Bible includes substantial amounts of material that do not purport to comment on specific events, for example, the OT's wisdom literature, many Psalms, and most of the teachings in the gospels and epistles. Even such favorite historical texts as the story of the exodus do not depict that occurrence as the basis for knowledge of God, but describes God as communicating before, during, and after. "Only God's previous communication with Moses made the exodus event intelligible or even possible." "Far from the incident at the burning bush being an 'interpretation' of the divine acts, it is a direct communication from God to Moses of his purposes and intentions."[47] If God had not informed Moses concerning what He would do, Moses would not have told the Israelites that God would help them to escape from Egypt, and that therefore they should leave.

As for another insight of Barr's, that "story" or "narrative" might better describe much of the framework of the OT, rather than "history," I do not object. Yet other categories, such as "myth," as describing early portions of Genesis, should be included. And many of the theological and moral teachings of each Testament either link only to such general narratives as God's disclosure in Israel's history or in Christ or do not directly connect even with those.

Having encouraged future narrative theologians to regard large portions of the Old Testament narrative as story, rather than history, Barr insisted that even these aspects interlace with history. "This narrative spirals back and forward across what we would call history, sometimes coming closer to it and sometimes going far away from it." For this and many other reasons we should not be indifferent concerning historical issues.

Primarily pertaining to the Old Testament, story/narrative is cumulative in that each stage provides material essential for what follows. Narrative sequences are not evolutionary in the sense of rising to ever higher forms. But new elements are made meaningful through what has gone before, while tensions introduced into the existing tradition lead to the formation of new traditions. "Each stage of tradition has an influence on the religion of the following stage, and it is through the religion that the older tradition is mediated to later stages."[48]

6. Use of Analogical Language[49]

Colin E. Gunton has written persuasively concerning the use of analogies and metaphors in general and in theological communication. He says that metaphors transfer words from one context to another and in the process give words fresh and unusual

---

46. Ibid., 351.
47. Ibid., 351, 346.
48. Barr, "Revelation in History," 748.
49. See chap. 5, sec. 3; chap. 17, sec. 1 for related discussions concerning Jesus's use of parables.

meanings. Metaphors "'teach old words new tricks,' and are 'affairs between predicates with pasts and objects that yield while protesting.'"[50] Even science is now recognizing the essential roles metaphors play in discovery.

Classical physics developed with the metaphorical description of the universe as a machine. Advances beyond classical physics took place with the help of another metaphor, that of a field. New language and discovery occur together, with metaphor as a vehicle of discovery. We understand facets of the world as we find new words or redeploy old ones in our search for comprehension. Metaphor is not a preliminary tool to be discarded when a non-metaphorical way of saying things is found—but one of the many devices for understanding the world.[51]

When Christian theology uses a variety of analogies to describe the meaning of Christ's atoning life, death, and resurrection, its use of language is not as different from science as has often been supposed. It was once widely believed that genuine knowledge must be expressed in literal terms, with metaphors having been appropriately "translated." Such thinking presupposes that privileged words correspond to things, while others do not. To the contrary, no words as sounds in the air or marks on a page are identical with what they signify. All words only indirectly connect to their referents, doing so because people agree that particular words point toward specific things or meanings. Analogies differ from regular words in reflecting an additional layer of indirectness, as can be seen by comparing the more direct statement, "You are fat" with the analogical one "You are *Thick as a Brick*."

Since all words stand for other things and are symbolic or representational, analogies in their additional ways attest the true nature of language. The world is largely known indirectly, through the medium of language, and therefore metaphor, being doubly indirect, adds a further creative dimension to language.[52]

Though there is no revealed language, we can speak of God only by using words we otherwise employ to describe the realities of this world. Of course theology does sometimes use technical terms, but these have parallel extra-theological meanings, as, for example, with the word "transcendence." Though the Bible and Christian theology often communicate concerning God by using analogies—language that compares Her with familiar realities—the biblical contexts and employments of such words indicate the differences between everyday word meanings and their theological redeployments.

Because the God of love chose to enter into personal relationship with humankind, the most symbolically adequate comparisons for referring to God are those derived from personal relationships. Because of God's involvement with Israel, and more specifically with her prophets and leaders, the OT applies personal analogies to God, such as Creator, Father, Mother, King, Shepherd, Judge. Similarly, it describes God as judging and yet forgiving, merciful, loving.

50. Gunton, *Actuality/Atonement*, 29, 28, citing Nelson Goodman.
51. Ibid., 30, 31, citing Richard Boyd.
52. Ibid., 34, 37, 34, 37.

The Johannine writings (see especially John 1), Paul and most of the rest of the NT regard God's decisive *Word* of communication as a *person*. The NT also says many things about the Holy Spirit, in particular that through the Spirit the Risen Christ remains with us. Such focus on Christ and His Spirit contributed to the NT's preeminent use of *personal comparisons* to describe God.

The Bible and Christian theology use nonpersonal symbols only secondarily, to illumine particular aspects of God. We may, for example, refer to God as "Rock of Ages" to emphasize how unchangeable is Her steadfast love. In similar ways nonpersonal symbols are often used secondarily to clarify people's characteristics.[53]

In using analogical language biblical writers did not confuse God with humankind. Scripture knows that fallen humanity lacks the commonality with God to justify unequivocally generalizing from us to God. The OT indicates that humankind is not God, and not even the image of God (as Christ is called in the NT), but is created "*after*" God's likeness and "*in*" Her image (Gen 1:26a).[54] Such propositions respect the permanent differences between God and humankind. Unlike us, God, for example, is all holy and inherently immortal.

Nevertheless, the Bible encourages us to use such words as "father" and "lord," "justice" and "mercy" to refer to God because aspects of such meanings apply to Him. Revelation demonstrates that God is not less than what these terms can denote, but much more and in particular ways different. *God's revelation should be the norm and limit for the use of particular comparisons.* We, for example, can find out which of the characteristics of an ideal earthly father we may analogically ascribe to God by focusing on God's disclosure in Christ, on the meaning of Jesus's common reference to God as *Abba*, Daddy, and by considering other biblical terms and concepts that surround this one or that are otherwise used to refer to God. We should not characterize God in His manifestation with a single word, since every comparison loses its relevance and transparency when detached from what other terms express. Thus we should not only speak of God as a *loving* father, with whom we can have intimate fellowship, but also as a *caring* mother, a *patient* and *persistent* shepherd, a *fair* judge, and so on.

All analogies only go so far. By making a variety of comparisons and thereby encouraging the correcting of one analogy by another, Scripture shows the precise breaking points of particular analogies as applied to God. Thus God's self-disclosure can determine meaning, rather than being subordinated to everyday understandings of terms. Symbolic language referring to revelation can also serve a critical function more generally. In Jesus's parables God is presented as a father, the owner of a house, a farmer, an employer, etc., who reacts differently from how such people generally do.[55] That He is different does not mean, for example, that God is not really Father,

---

53. Kaufman, *ST/Historicist*, 128–9.
54. See chap. 10, sec. 1.
55. See chap. 5, sec. 3; chap. 17, sec. 1.

but that human fathers are imperfect examples.⁵⁶ Thus fatherhood and all else must be rethought having taken account of God in His manifestation (Eph 3:14, 15).

Barth and Aquinas defended the use of analogy in theology. Aquinas rightly rejected the claim that language can only inadequately and ambiguously express the things of God—which would mean that we can have no genuine knowledge of God. He also conceded that human language is not completely adequate for speaking of God. (One might add that it is not completely adequate for speaking about anything!) Insisting that God can be known—but that such knowledge is imperfect—Aquinas defended the use of analogy. Though some knowledge can be grasped in this way, a direct equation between every day and sacred meanings of terms is out of the question. Barth agreed with what Aquinas affirmed so far.

Unfortunately the theological basis of Aquinas's reasoning did not protect against confusing God with humankind, nor against moving too directly from common word usage to generalizations about God. Optimistically he seems to have based his argument for using metaphorical language to refer to God on a belief in a natural image of God continuity between humankind and God. To the contrary, since humans are sinful and finite, knowledge of God cannot convincingly be based directly on non-biblical analogies—but should be attentive to revelation's correction, transformation and redeployment of normal word usage.⁵⁷

From Barth's point of view to base the possibility of the knowledge of God on that similarity to God that is ours and the world's by virtue of createdness distorts revelation into only confirming and strengthening what is already known. With this understanding "grace" is seen as only perfecting nature. Such a perspective misunderstands revelation, which judges us and discloses what we did not previously know and cannot tell ourselves.⁵⁸

Aquinas's "analogy of being" or "being mysticism" may have lain behind his theological method. This supposes that by created nature we and everything share in "Being Itself."⁵⁹ But this presumes that we have the same "isness" as God and by nature relate to Her, which denies God's transcendence, our sinfulness and our need for revelation for knowledge of God and relationship with Her.⁶⁰

Analogy of being means that our transition to explicit faith need not be disruptive. Aquinas's arguments for God's existence assume that natural humankind can know a good deal about God apart from revelation, secular knowledge being the first story of the Christian theological house. "*Can we ever speak properly of grace and faith if at*

---

56. Berkhof, *Christian Faith*, 65–69.
57. Kaufman, *ST/Historicist*, 127–28.
58. Barth, *Way of Theology*, 39.
59. This seems to assume that humans are the image of God, rather than only created *in* God's image or *after* Her likeness (Gen 1:26).
60. For the specific issue under debate here see *Summa contra Gentiles*, book 1, sec. 29, 4–5; and *The Dogmatic Constitution of the Catholic Faith*, Vatican Council, 1870.

the very outset we have provided ourselves with a guarantee of our knowledge of God which has nothing to do with grace and faith?"[61] In splitting knowledge of God Aquinas dishonored the revelational work of God in favor of a general being of God that he assumed God has in common with all that is. How can we possibly stand on the same plane with God in Her being by the mere fact that we are? Certainly God exists and we do, She is and we are. We use identical terms because that is the language we have, but we do not exist as She does, and our being is very different from Hers. God is holy and we are sinful; God is immortal and we by nature are finite; God is all wise, we are considerably foolish.

Closely related to these differences with Aquinas, Barth considers Christian knowledge of God as Creator, Reconciler and Redeemer as against three analogical bases for learning of God's existence. As against Aquinas' cosmological argument for knowledge of God the Creator, though we know of causes within creation, these differ from the Transcendent God's creating all that is from nothing (*ex nihilo*). Yet if we recognize the qualitative difference between causes within creation and God's creation of a universe, analogically we can use creational language from the former to refer to the latter, but must not confuse the two nor suppose that such language provides a proof of God.[62]

Though scientific investigations may summarize the earliest cosmological development science can trace, they are theologically irrelevant as attempts to find God. To learn of the Creator who is beyond this world we must come under the Lordship of the Father through the Son by the Spirit.[63]

Similarly, though we are familiar with many human examples of reconciliation, to be useful as analogies for helping to communicate concerning God as Reconciler, these must be reshaped and transformed in service to biblically defined divine reconciliation. For in contrast with overcoming human conflicts and disagreements, divine reconciliation cannot be humanly achieved, not through clever problem solving, subtle dialectics, the most astute social analysis, profound politics or other human efforts. These cannot bring the peace that passes understanding. Though we have a general idea about the work of reconciliation as a human activity and though we can use the same term to refer to God's work, God in His disclosing activity must indicate what divine reconciliation entails. We know of God as Reconciler and of His reconciling work because in and through Christ, God has reconciled us to Himself.

As for God as Redeemer, though we know something of goals and efforts to attain those and of the future as the time still before us, the nature and being of God in His redeeming capacity is not accessible through such conceptual analogies, though

---

61. Barth, *CD*, 2/1:85; my emphasis. See chap. 10 below on "General Revelation or Natural Theology."

62. Ibid., 76–78. See below chap. 11, sec. 3 for a more thorough discussion of Aquinas's cosmological argument.

63. See chap. 11, sec. 4.

terminological overlap is inevitable. Nor does redemption mean that the world will evolve in a particular direction, but that Jesus Christ will bring the world to fulfillment.

Contrary to Aquinas, Barth defended the theological use of metaphor from the Incarnation-inspired insight (shared with Calvin) that God in Christ accommodated His revelation to our capacities for learning. Yet because of our sinfulness and God's transcendence, revelational correction of everyday terms is required. Rejecting Aquinas's anthropologically optimistic understanding of the "analogy of being," Barth defended a revelation based "analogy of grace" or "analogy of faith" correction,[64] though he could still employ Aquinas' terminology. "If there is a real analogy between God and man—an analogy which is a true analogy of being on both sides, an analogy in and with which the knowledge of God will in fact be given—what other analogy can it be than the analogy of being which is posited and created by the work and action of God Himself [in revelation], the analogy which has its actuality from God and from God alone, and therefore in faith and in faith alone?"[65]

The linguistic comparisons appropriate for theological use must be reformulated in the light of God's manifestation, not uncritically based on the relationship of two static substances (God as Being and humans as existent). Only God's gracious association with humankind justifies the use of analogical language to refer to Him.[66]

---

64. Barth, *CD*, 2/1:78, 74–85.

65. Ibid., 83.

66. Barth recognized that modern Roman Catholic thought also knows something of the analogy of grace/faith (ibid., 81–83). Aquinas sometimes seemed to recognize that God is not in a class or kind with creation, differing only in degree (*Summa Theologica*, 1, 3, 5; Barth, *CD*, 2/1:310). But how is such a recognition consistent with the "being mysticism" that Aquinas utilized in his understanding of the analogy of being? Though Aquinas was targeted, Barth's argument may have been more directly against the Neoplatonism of Augustine and the analogy of being viewpoint affirmed by Vatican I (Barth, *CD*, 2/1:310), which has not been overturned.

Chapter 3

Bible as Witness to Jesus Christ, God's Past and Present Revealing Word

1. Scripture as Witness to Jesus Christ

THE NT NOT ONLY attests God's revelation in Jesus Christ, but the Risen Christ as Holy Spirit can and does use the biblical witness to disclose Herself and to address people today. The Bible is not self-communicating or self-interpreting; for understanding we most of all must listen to the Living God as She speaks through this medium. "The Word of God is a *happening*, not a thing. Therefore the Bible must *become* the Word of God, and it does this through the work of the Spirit." "Word is a *living* reality, not something abstract. It exists in God's action toward us. We must hear and become obedient."[1] In our understanding of Scripture we should honor what the Scripture says about Revelation/Word of God as God in action.

Apparently in response to Jewish attitudes concerning their developing scriptures, the Fourth Gospel articulated a *Christ-centered instrumental understanding* of those and of the emerging Christian ones: "'*You search the scriptures, because you think that in them you have eternal life; it is they that bear witness to me . . .* '" (John 5:39, my emphasis). Though this statement was written before Christians had a closed collection of officially sanctioned, authoritative Scripture (canon),[2] it attested that some pre-scriptural writings could draw people closer to Christ—that God could thereby claim their lives.

Because the writings now contained in the Bible were written before their inclusion in the canon, there *is not* and *could not be* a statement concerning the *Bible's* authority within the Bible. Jesus and Paul apparently had no formal doctrine about the then available scriptures of the old covenant known to them, nor Paul of a scriptural use of his writings. One finds a different perspective in Second Timothy—a late writing not written by Paul, but influenced by him[3]—concerning the then available, pre-

---

1. Barth, *Table Talk*, 26, 42.
2. See chap. 6, sec. 15 for a more extensive examination of the meaning of canon.
3. See chap. 6, n49 and chap. 7, sec. 3 for issues bearing upon the authorship of the Pastorals (1

canonical scriptures known to the author. But this is no officially recognized statement of the delimited status of a group of writings. "All scripture is inspired by God and useful for teaching, for reproof, for correction, and for training in righteousness, so that everyone who belongs to God may be proficient, equipped for every good work" (3:16–17 NRSV).[4] A textual difficulty leaves us uncertain whether these verses refer to the usefulness of all scriptures known to the author, or mean that all scriptures that are inspired will be profitable. Even if the reference were to all scriptures known to the author, it could not have included all of the books later incorporated into either the OT or NT. Many such books were yet to be written and the forming of the NT canon occurred centuries later. Since Paul's ten-book corpus was available at the time of the writing of the Pastorals, the author might have had that in mind, and possibly those writings from the old covenant then available. The Second Timothy text is remarkably low key, and says nothing of infallibility/inerrancy (no errors of any kind).[5] It speaks instead of the usefulness of scripture for accomplishing God's purposes.

2. Instrumental Understanding of Scripture

As did the Fourth Gospel, Luther considered the Bible in terms of *its capacity to witness to Christ*. His conception of scriptural authority is located in its center, Jesus Christ. This being so, Luther could be very critical of certain books, such as James or Revelation. Yet he could regard later confessions as nearly canonical, as long as they witnessed to Christ in the right way.[6] Luther's central belief in justification by God's grace received through faith in Christ and his comparative and critical reading of Scripture caused him to recognize some parts as more authoritative than others. This prevented him from affirming the Bible's authority in general terms, as though all writings are of equal value. He believed that whatever does not teach Christ is not

---

and 2 Tim and Titus).

4. Second Timothy 3:16 is biblically exceptional not only for its use of the Greek word *theopneustos*, "inspired by God," but also for its attribution of inspiration to the resultant text rather than to its in-breathing impact upon the author (Goldingay, "Inspiration," 314). This verse contrasts with another passage about inspiration and inspired-ness: Second Peter 1:20–21, also from a late writing, speaks of the in-breathing impact of God upon the prophets who in turn prophesy. "No prophecy ever came by the impulse of people, but people moved by the Holy Spirit spoke from God" (v. 21). Because such prophets were inspired by God, their oral or written communications were not to be regarded as matters of their own interpretations (v. 20). Neither, however, was everything they said and wrote to be considered God's Word. As far as scriptural *writings* are concerned, this text implies only the secondary influence of God upon the writings of some prophetic portions of the emerging OT and perhaps of some prophetically influenced portions of what is now contained within the NT.

Matthew insists that prophets' sincerity must be assessed by considering their fruits (7:15–16), and Paul in describing spiritual gifts insists that those must be tested within the church (1 Cor 12:7–11), and by the standard of love (13:1–3;14:1–5). Neither perspective entirely agrees with Second Peter 1:20–21 nor Second Timothy 3:16.

5. Concerning the concept of biblical inerrancy, see chap. 7, sec. 8.
6. Lohse, *History/Doctrine*, 219.

apostolic, even if taught by Peter or Paul. The Bible is thus a witness to the Word of God—but the Word of God is not identical with the words of Scripture.

Granted Luther's instrumental understanding of Scripture we can understand why he was able to assign varying degrees of authority to different biblical books and even argue that particular books should be excluded from the canon. He made evaluative remarks about the writings that comprise the Testaments, their historical origins, and the conditions under which they were written, many of which have been confirmed by later biblical scholarship. Luther represented a biblical faith that could combine with biblical criticism, and therefore differed from the authoritarian view of the Bible that eventually culminated in the belief in scriptural inerrancy.[7]

Barth agreed with the Fourth Gospel's and Luther's conviction that the Bible should be understood as *witnessing* to Christ. The Bible does not call attention to itself, but points to Him. Barth, however, makes an additional point with which Luther would have agreed: That the content (Jesus Christ) cannot be separated from the form (Scripture), but directly or indirectly comes to us in and through the (fallible) form. Barth recognized *considerable unity, but not identity of content between Jesus Christ and Scripture.*[8] Because we live long after the time of God's Incarnation, the Bible is necessary for knowledge concerning Jesus Christ, and is the normative written witness to Him. But "God is not an attribute of something else, even if this something else is the Bible."[9] God is the Subject, the Lord, who speaks especially amid the biblical witness and other testimonies to Christ.

We experience the Bible as the essential written witness to Jesus Christ because through this means we have come to know the Father through the Son by the power of the Spirit. We could not have received this answer had we not listened to the voice of the church and respected its biblical exposition as far as possible. But we cannot receive this answer unless (as we are able) we also accept responsibility for the Bible's correct exposition.[10]

Brunner also understood Scripture as the essential witness to the Word, Jesus Christ, not as God's Word directly. As with Luther and Barth, Brunner thought the

---

7. Brunner, *God*, 109–10, 110–11. The first generation Reformers, Luther and Zwingli, were not favorable to the belief that God inspired all of the words of Scripture, whereas Melanchthon, Calvin, and Bullinger agreed with that. Calvin fondly spoke of the oracles of God and was happy with the concept of divine dictation. Such critical pronouncements as Luther made about the Testaments are unthinkable in Calvin. (Emil Brunner, *Offenbarung und Vernunft, die Lehre von der Christligher Glaubenserkenntnis*, 126, mentioned in Baillie, *Revelation/Recent Thought*, 32.) The earlier Reformation generation's recognition of the togetherness of biblical word and interpretive guidance by the Spirit in the eighteenth century split apart: Orthodoxy became preoccupied with the Bible and interpreted it rationalistically, whereas Pietism became obsessed with religious experience and simplistically interpreted Scripture (Lohse, *History/Doctrine*, 224–25).

8. Barth, *Table Talk*, 35.

9. Barth, *CD*, 1/2:513.

10. Ibid., 462. That God does not require Christians with intellectual disabilities to carry out such an obligation is no excuse for the rest of us to not try.

authority of the Bible emerges indirectly, as an implication of our having by this means more directly or more indirectly come to faith in Christ.[11] In the same act of disclosure, faith in Jesus Christ is created or renewed and a degree of confidence arises or is sustained concerning Scripture's instrumental value.

Brunner explained that the Bible as a means of grace is like a record having many scratches, yet still able to convey the master's voice.[12] It is like a window through which we can see Beyond. Though wonderfully useful in this way it is not perfectly transparent. We see through a window dimly (1 Cor 13:12a).

We do not believe that Jesus is the Christ *merely because* the NT says so, yet *without* that witness we who live many centuries after Christ could not with a degree of accuracy learn of Him. The term Brunner used to describe the relation of scriptural words to the personal Word was "pointer." Not only is even the NT's authority only that of means, but not all within it is equally binding even in this instrumental sense.[13]

Though the Bible is the essential witness to the divine Word it is a human book replete with the imperfections and defects that connect to all that is human. *Scripture is not God's Word, but the human word about God's Word, who is Jesus Christ.*[14] "God's Word of revelation is broken in the element of the world. Unfortunately the dogmatizing church has never taken seriously Paul's famous dictum, '*We know in part.*'" Scripture as an historical document written by people participates "'in the frailty of all that is human, in the relativity of all that is historical.'"[15]

Jesus Christ stands above the biblical witness to Him in part because as we read the various NT accounts about Christ and affirmations concerning His meaning, historical-critical insight helps us compare these accounts, and in that context God's Spirit encourages good judgment as to who Christ was and is.

The revelation of God/Word of God that speaks through scriptural passages is wrapped in mystery and thus cannot be read off directly from the texts—not even with the aid of the historical-critical method. Nevertheless, with help from available interpretive methods, but also under the guidance of the Spirit, we can penetrate to the inner meaning of the outward texts and thus gain degrees of understanding.

---

11. Brunner, *God*, 110.

12. Brunner, *Our Faith*, 10–11, drawing an analogy with the great Caruso.

13. Jewitt, "Brunner/Scripture," 219, 220, 223, referring to Brunner's *Offenbarung und Vernunft*, 128. See below, chap. 7, sec. 8.

14. Ibid., 230, referring to Brunner's *Dogmatik*, 1:40.

15. Ibid., 230, quoting from *Brunner's* "Christligher Glaube nach reformierter Lehre," in *Der Protestantismus der Geggenwart*, 254; my emphasis.

3. Exposition between Remembrance, Expectation[16]

Over against the supposed objectivism of the historical science of his day, Hofmann insisted that it is impossible for biblical interpreters to be neither Christian nor non-Christian, but merely interpreters. A person approaches Scripture from experiences, has a definite character, and is not a blank sheet for Scripture to inscribe upon. So-called neutrality can more appropriately be called indifference.[17] Similarly, for Barth alleged freedom from presupposition merely means that another presupposition is presumed—namely that God's revelation is not to be reckoned with, that one can adopt a neutral attitude to Him to whom Scripture points.[18] "This neutrality, this unconcern about God's revelation, and therefore this 'freedom from presuppositions' is a presupposition [as much as] any other."[19]

In contrast to seeking to be purely descriptive and presuming thereby to be neutral, the position of the Christian expositor is with "*remembrance*, and indeed a *thankful* remembrance of the Word of God already heard, and *expectation*, indeed *joyful* expectation of hearing God's Word anew."[20] The Christian assumption behind the anticipation that God will continue to speak His Living Word is that the Risen Christ as Holy Spirit is with us.

Without the work of the Spirit, Scripture is veiled (2 Cor 3:4–6, 12–18). "No one comprehends the thoughts of God except the Spirit of God. Now we have received not the spirit of the world, but the Spirit which is from God, that we might understand the gifts bestowed on us by God. And we impart this in words not taught by human wisdom but taught by the Spirit, interpreting spiritual truths to those who possess the Spirit" (1 Cor 2:11b–13). "Those who are unspiritual do not receive the gifts of God's Spirit, for they are foolishness to them, and they are unable to understand them because they are spiritually discerned" (1 Cor 2:14 NRSV).

It is advantageous that the meaning of Scriptural texts is unveiled only through the activity of the Spirit—since this means that a spiritual relationship with God is imperative for true understanding. Without the guidance of the Living God biblical words do not lead to new life, and in practical terms the open book remains closed.

The strangeness of the NT's message also indicates the need for personal encounter. It talks of God's Holy Spirit, but most people know only of human spirit. It talks about new birth, but most know of only one birth. It talks about God become human—a most peculiar way for the Holy God to reveal Herself! We can read the words of the NT, but the information is so strange we hardly know what to make of it. Some may try to convince themselves that they believe; others may just walk away.

---

16. For explicit biblical hermeneutics also, see chap. 7, secs. 3, 6; chap. 15, sec. 5; chap. 17.
17. Harrisville, *Bible/Modern Culture to Childs*, 130.
18. Karl Barth, *Credo*, 177.
19. Ibid, 178.
20. Karl Barth, *God Here/Now*, 54.

One thing is certain—*only if God Herself opens our eyes can we truly understand the NT's strange message. Only by the free revelation of God do we know ourselves as sinners in need of God's forgiveness, sinners in need of God's Spirit, sinners in need of new birth, and sinners in need of God incarnate in Jesus Christ.*

4. Need for Critical Discernment

Individual scriptural teachings must be evaluated in the light of the Christ we have come to know through the Bible's cumulative and critically compared witness. As free and responsible friends of God we can and must exercise critical discernment, as did Jesus and Paul.[21] Paul taught that reading Scripture according to "letter" is to interpret wrongly by valuing blind obedience to the law. Against this the NT conceives of open-eyed obedience as the attitude of those to whom the Father's loving heart has been revealed. Reading Scripture under the guidance of the Spirit is to become faithfully discerning through participation in the New Age inaugurated by Christ.[22]

Though we should use the New Testament to critically evaluate the Old, we should look to Christ as Savior and Lord to evaluate both. *We know of God's saving revelation in Christ by the Spirit through the biblical witness and our confirming experience. Having come to know the triune God in this way He becomes the standard by whom we are to evaluate the means through which we have come to learn of Him.* This circular reasoning must be allowed to stand, for spiritual/theological/moral authority must impress itself upon us. It is not synonymous with mere assent to ideas or documents. Each of us must respond to the Christ we have come to know through the biblical testimony—but the Bible as a means of grace is fallible—as are we.

---

21. See chap. 7, sec. 3 and chap. 8, sec. 5.
22. Käsemann, *NT Questions*, 270–71.

Developments toward the Testaments, Authority of Each

Chapter 4

Developments toward Old Testament Canon

THOUGH WE MUST DISTINGUISH between God's revelation and the book that attests that, more is required than such a distinction, else the Bible's humanity becomes a mere assertion that faith easily forgets. The complexities of the developments that led to the acceptance of particular books into the Bible need to be faced—and by systematic theology—which will help us to understand why Scripture evidences much diversity. If bibliolatry is to be avoided, theological students and Christians in general need to learn a good deal from the specialists who have spent lifetimes studying the complexities surrounding the creation of the writings that comprise the Bible and the human decisions concerning the writings to be included. Yet even canonicity specialists admit that much is unknown. Historical science is limited to studying available evidence, and "recent scholarship has been made painfully aware of the lack of solid historical evidence by which to determine large areas of [OT canonical] development."[1]

1. Development of Jewish Understandings of Written Sources of Authority

For Judaism the final authority is the God known through revelation concerning His will and ways, especially regarding His commandments. Largely for this reason written attestations of God's communicating came to be regarded as important (Exod 24:12; 32:15; 34:1; Deut 4:13). Moses is said to have recorded the commandments of the Lord (Exod 24:4a; 34:27), and the same is said of Joshua (Josh 24:26a) and Samuel (1 Sam 10:25ab).[2]

A variety of written scriptures had long been used in ancient Israel and Judah without being given canonical (delimited) status. Shortly after the 621 BC discovery of the Book of the Covenant, King Josiah read it to the assembled people, and King and people vowed to keep the commandments and statutes enunciated there (2 Kgs

---

1. Childs, *Biblical Theology OT/NT*, 56.
2. McDonald and Sanders, "Introduction," 9.

23:1–3).³ Second Kings reflects no statement of canonizing principle, no circumscribing of some writings as of greater authority than others for determining the nature of Jewish faith. Yet the divine inspiring of the content of the Book of the Covenant is more than implied by describing these words as directly spoken by God.

Within its Deuteronomic placement, where the Book of the Covenant provides only a small part, comes a warning (supposedly directly from God) not to change the text of the whole of Deuteronomy. These Dueteronomistic words, perhaps put into God's mouth, are not likely intended to delimit these writings as only authoritative, but to emphasize their importance and forbid their alteration when being hand copied: "You shall not add to the word which I command you, nor take from it . . ." (4:2).⁴ However this may be, from the recognized authority of the Book of the Covenant and then Deuteronomy's claim *also for its own religious and moral importance*, a dynamic expansion of the formal sources of authority would continue.

The book of Nehemiah tells of the priest-scribe Ezra's reading of the book of the law of Moses to the people (8:1–5, 13). The group of writings Nehemiah claimed was authoritative (but probably not demarcated) was likely an earlier version of the Pentateuch (the first five OT books), with the possible addition of Joshua.⁵ What should not be overlooked is that the *extra-pentateuchal claim* that the Pentateuch should be regarded as Mosaic law implicitly reflects widely recognized religious and moral written authority in Israel beyond the Pentateuch!

2. Judaism's Evolving Pre-Old Testament Scriptures

By 200 BC many Jewish people also looked to a group of prophetic writings. Most such books had existed before 400 BC, but had not been considered especially authoritative. That such earlier books came to be highly regarded by 200 BC was apparently linked to the emerging belief that the age of revelation and prophecy had ceased (1 Macc 9:27), that therefore no new prophetic literature could be written, and that the scope of accepted prophetic literature needed to be demarcated.⁶ In rabbinic

---

3. "The Book of the Covenant" phrase is also in Exod 24:7 and the contents are thought to be contained in Exod 21:1—23:33 and in parts of Deuteronomy, as discussed in the next paragraph.

4. The author of Revelation also warns against additions or deletions to his text (22:18–19), and this likely refers to a copyist making willful alterations. (For Paul's concern in this regard, see chap. 6, n123.)

5. Our current Pentateuch probably contains far more laws and regulations than did Ezra's. The earlier one likely continued to grow and develop, incorporating detailed laws from life in the promised land and regarding them as God's commands given to Moses on Mt. Sinai.

6. McDonald, *Formation/Canon*, 50–51. Writing in the first century CE, Josephus said that the age of prophetic inspiration in Israel was considered over by the time of Artaxerxes (465–424 BC). Not all rabbis agreed with Josephus's dating of the cessation of prophecy, but most agreed that it was over by the time of the writing of First Maccabees (between 200–100 BC). Hence any books that claimed to be based on direct prophetic inspiration that were written after such a date were not to be regarded as authoritative (same source, 61).

Judaism (Phariseeism) the movement toward authoritative writings seemed to link to a legalizing and formalizing of religion, the idea that God had no fresh Word for the present. Most Pharisees thought that God's present will was to be determined entirely by scribal analysis of the written testimonies concerning His revealed laws.

Childs and Blenkinsopp put an unjustifiably positive interpretation on the Jewish belief in the cessation of revelation and prophecy and the substitution of scribal interpretations of recognized texts. Certainly the formation of a collection of Jewish scriptures as a vehicle whereby past divine communication is actualized serves revelational purposes, as does the scholarly (scribal) interpretation of the same.[7] But the interpreting of sacred texts is not sufficient to make up for a sense of divine presence and guidance. The NT claims that with Christ and His resurrection the Spirit poured forth and that teaching/interpreting should be undertaken only by charismatic leading.

The Jews of the Dead Sea Scrolls (likely Essenes) were among the Jewish minority who did not confine revelation to the distant past, but saw it as continuing in their time and place, at least with their leader, the Teacher of Righteousness.[8] Furthermore, the pharisaic opinion that the time of revelation was past did not succeed in preventing new prophetic writings from being added to the authoritative (but not canonically demarcated) collection of OT scriptures.

Israel's scriptures were still developing during the NT period, and the third part ("the Writings") was still in flux. Thus when the NT refers to the OT scripture it usually mentions only the Law and the Prophets.[9] However, since the NT often alludes to particular psalms, many early Christians must have been familiar with some of those and attributed considerable authority to them. In line with the later recognition of the importance of the Psalms, Luke 24:44 goes beyond the two-part scripture to refer to those.

In spite of Judaism's developing formalism and legalism, in the last two centuries before Christ and in the first century after His birth, Judaism seems to have reached no verdict as to which writings were most authoritative. It is unlikely that the Jewish leaders who met at Jamnia in 90 CE—and it does not appear to have been a "council"—made a final decision concerning the Jewish canon.[10] Throughout the first century there did not seem to be even a recognized group of leaders who could speak on the behalf of all Jews.

However, even without a formal decision much consensus had emerged. Even before the destruction of the temple in 70 CE the pharisaic majority recognized the authority of the available parts of the Law and the Prophets. In a general way many Christians similarly regarded these as well as the available Psalms as important, but

---

7. Childs, *Biblical Theology OT/NT*, 172.
8. Vanderkam, "Canon/Dead Sea Scrolls," 92.
9. Matt 5:17; Luke 24:27; Acts 28:23.
10. If today's OT had been decided upon then, more of today's OT (such as its Wisdom traditions—Proverbs, Job, and Ecclesiastes) would likely be reflected in the NT.

(unlike the Jews) considered such scripture as having more to do with messianic prediction than legal prescription. Further variations existed. The Samaritans accepted only a slightly modified form of the parts of the Pentateuch that then existed, as did Sadducees; and the Essenes seem to have adopted an even wider body of sacred scripture than did the Pharisees. The NT alludes to such diverse groups' opinions concerning normative boundaries.

"We do not know how, when, or by whom the list of books now found in the Hebrew Bible was drawn up. All we have are hints over a considerable historical span suggesting that some books were regarded by certain writers as sufficiently authoritative that they could be cited to settle a dispute, explain a situation, provide an example, or predict what would happen."[11] Many of the books in today's OT enjoyed a lofty status for Jewish writers before 70 CE, but others not in today's OT were also deemed authoritative for some individuals and groups. In part because of such diversity canonical boundaries were not drawn.[12]

Some qualifying interpretive factors also need to be kept in mind when considering how the Jews have regarded their authoritative writings. Over the centuries Judaism has continued to regard the Pentateuch (understood primarily as Law) more highly than other parts of its OT.[13] Furthermore, Judaism has never been bound solely by her "canonical" writings—if indeed she has a "canon"—and has been much dependent on the traditions found in the Talmud, by which she has interpreted her scriptures. So also she has regarded specific interpretive methods as essential, especially midrash, which enabled non-historical and linguistically arbitrary meanings to be read into passages.[14]

3. Jewish Factors for Accepting Books as Authoritative Scripture

The Septuagint (LXX) was the earliest OT—*and likely contained only a fraction of today's OT*. It was created for Greek language speaking Hellenistic Jews in approximately 190 BC, probably from Hebrew fragments and partial versions. In contrast the Hebrew (Masoretic) version has been available only since approximately 700 CE, though, again, Hebrew fragments and partial versions were available earlier. Since its inception it has been regarded as most authoritative by most Jews. Like the Septuagint the Masoretic text was probably based on Hebrew segments and partial renditions. Only early Hebrew scriptural fragments have survived antiquity.

Reacting in part to the rise of Christianity and defeat by the Romans in 70 CE, Rabbinic Judaism reformulated its tradition. It may have eventually restricted the use

---

11. Vanderkam, "Canon/Dead Sea Scrolls," 91; my emphasis.

12. Ibid., 91–92.

13. To the contrary, NT Christians have tended to consider the prophetic writings (and Isaiah in particular) as of greater importance, though Genesis and the Psalms were also highly regarded.

14. See chap. 5, secs. 6–7.

of the apocalyptic content of its scriptures, utilized only its recent (Hebrew) version of scriptures, and elevated the legal aspects to preeminence.[15]

As with any historical religion, Judaism preserved and held in reverence her most authoritative writings because without those her memory would have become corrupted. Judaism, however, likely also developed her Hebrew Scriptures to compete with the new Christian writings and thereby to discourage Jews from reading those and having cause to convert to Christianity. The post-NT Jewish issuing of the Masoretic Old Testament was likely influenced by three interrelated beliefs with which Christians cannot agree: (1) That a new version of Old Covenant scriptures was needed to help defeat the new Christian religion, (2) that the age of the Spirit had ended, and (3) that hence the new scriptures (later canonized as the charismatically/prophetically influenced New Testament) were not authoritative.

Since Christians necessarily reject these assumptions, we are encouraged to reexamine the scope and meaning of the Masoretic-based, current OT's authority.[16] Since many of its apocryphal writings were apocalyptic,[17] they provide a history-of-ideas link between the primarily non-apocalyptic Hebrew OT and the considerably apocalyptic NT. Christians also need to consider the Christian importance of other intertestamental writings.[18]

4. Evidence for Christians' Use, Canonizing of Septuagint and Utilizing of Greek Language Testimony Books

Because Alexander the Great had required that conquered peoples adopt Greek culture and language, the writers of books later included in the NT likely read and quoted primarily from the Greek language pre-OT. They probably also employed their own Greek language testimony book selections and conflations (combinations) of Septuagint prophecies they highly regarded. Greek language testimony books and the Septuagint translation of then available writings likely had freer renderings than those later found in the Hebrew-based Masoretic version. Septuagint usage by pre-NT writers made it easier for them to interpret the OT as predicting Christ and pointing to eschatological meanings than did the later Masoretic version.

15. Childs, *Biblical Theology OT/NT*, 61, summarizing, but in my opinion unconvincingly disputing with Sundberg, *The Old Testament and the Early Church*.

16. See secs. 4, 5. Though only fragments of the Septuagint have survived antiquity, these can be compared with the post-NT, Hebrew-based Masoretic text.

17. Apocalyptic thinking contrasts this age with the coming eternal one and emphasizes the sinful and finite reality of this age.

18. The following changes occurred during the intertestamental period, the first three of which are reflected in the NT's interpretations of the OT: (1) A great increase in messianic expectation; (2) a heightened emphasis on the importance of OT predictive prophecy; (3) a tendency to regard predictive prophecies as pointing to eschatological events, rather than to those that had been in immediate proximity to those predictions; and, in considerable tension with the previous points, (4) the regarding of the OT as a repository of law (Barr, *Old/New Interpretation*, 118–27).

The presence of the Apocrypha in the Christian Bible until challenged by Protestantism in the sixteenth century is inexplicable unless early Christians canonized a Septuagint that included the Apocrypha. For the Hebrew, Masoretic text was not available until centuries later. The Christian use of Septuagint quotations of prophecies likely shaped the content of the NT[19] and provides this particular challenging of the Christian authority of the later *Hebrew OT*.

In addition the likely use of *Christian compiled* testimony books probably also helps to account for widespread discrepancies between NT passages and today's OT. "The availability of scriptural texts in [testimony book] format would go a long way toward making sense of features that characterize the quotations of scripture in early Christian literature: peculiar readings, similar groupings of texts, composite citations, misattributions of sources, and changes of application. Indeed, it is hard to find a satisfactory explanation of these phenomena without assuming the existence of primitive Christian collections of testimonies."[20]

Remember that the early Christians interpreted the pre-OT texts in highly figurative ways primarily to find messianic predictions.[21] By using Greek language Septuagint selections and/or testimony book derivations they could find the prediction that the Messiah would be born of a "virgin," rather than only of a young maiden (Isa 7:14). The post-NT church Fathers and Mothers probably utilized not only parts of the Septuagint's translation because it was available, but because it was easier to use for predictive purposes than pre-Masoretic Hebrew fragments. Jerome, however, thought early Christians' practice had been to use Hebrew pre-Masoretic scripture. As the person in charge of the Latin Vulgate translation of the OT that, against his judgment, came to include the Apocrypha, Jerome was aware of the looseness of the Septuagint translation, and unlike most early Christians, could compare the Septuagint with the Hebrew pre-OT fragments then available. Jerome translated directly from the latter source and relegated the Apocrypha to a collection with secondary status.[22] His theological principle concerning the latter, which was important for subsequent developments, "was that these books can and should be read 'for the edification of the people but not for establishing the authority of ecclesiastical doctrines.'"[23]

Augustine, however, disagreed with Jerome concerning the Apocrypha and the church of the day upheld Augustine's inclusion opinion, while accepting Jerome's Latin translation from the Hebrew non-apocryphal part of OT. Until the Protestant Reformation the entire church resisted Jerome's well-informed judgment concerning the Apocrypha and retained the broader OT canon, while recognizing that various books have varying value. In 1546, after the Protestants had opted for the smaller OT

---

19. McDonald, *Formation/Canon*, 65.
20. Gamble, *Books/Readers*, 27.
21. See next chapter.
22. Harrington, "Apocrypha/Early Church/Today," 204.
23. Ibid., 204.

canon, the Roman Catholic Church at the Council of Trent reaffirmed commitment to the Apocrypha.

5. Post–New Testament Church Opinions concerning Apocrypha

Luther appealed to Jerome's recognition that the Hebrew canonical listing did not include the Apocrypha. He also deferred to Jerome's principle that the Apocrypha should not be used for establishing church doctrines. Father Martin's attitude to individual apocryphal books depended on his judgment concerning what he regarded as normative in the NT and by that standard he agreed or disagreed theologically with them. "He said, in his vigorous way, that he would be happy to drop Second Esdras into the River Elbe, but on the other hand he respected the Letter of Manasseh." With the exception of First and Second Esdras, he included apocryphal books as an appendix in his German Bible and in his preface conceded that those he included "were useful and good to be read."[24] Calvin expressed respect for some of the apocryphal books (especially Ben Sira) and with caution and hesitation continued to use them in theological argument.

The Reformation helped to widen the distinction between the Apocrypha and canonical Scriptures. The position of the early Reformers was that the Apocrypha does not have full authority for establishing doctrine, yet parts are religiously instructive. Similarly, Article 6 of the Thirty-Nine Articles of the Church of England goes further by affirming that Christians should read such writings for examples of life and instruction in manners, yet should not derive doctrines from them. With Protestant orthodoxy, opinion hardened, as, for example, with the Westminster Confession's judgment that the Apocrypha is not divinely inspired and therefore has no authority in the church and no use should be made of it.[25]

Why did the Reformers demote these books from full biblical status and either place them in an appendix or eliminate them from the Bible? There were several interrelated issues on which the Reformers found false doctrine in the Apocrypha: These were the questions of atonement after death and prayers for the dead,[26] and closely linked to the latter was the belief in purgatory. Fourth Maccabees developed the atonement idea raised in Isaiah 53 and Second Maccabees 7, of the atoning value of martyrs'

24. Barr, *Concept/Biblical Theology*, 565.
25. Ibid.

26. Atonement concerns the way whereby God brings about reconciliation or at-one-ment. Barr misleadingly concludes that Paul's admittedly unfortunate words in 1 Cor 15:29 invokes baptism for the dead "as a reality upon which arguments may be based" (ibid., 573). Certainly Paul alludes to baptism for the dead, but Barr implies that Paul believed in this. Barr equates Paul's reference to baptism for the dead with the Second Maccabees advocacy of prayers for the dead and of atonement after death. To the contrary, surely Paul referred to the belief in the baptism of the dead only because some of the Corinthian Christians who disbelieved in eternal life illogically believed in the baptism of the dead. He argued that the practice they advocated (however faulty he regarded it) presupposed the resurrection of the dead, against whose denial he had been contending.

deaths for making renewal beyond death possible.[27] Against the latter, atonement has occurred once-and-for-all in Christ and therefore does not require churchly supplementation after people have died. The scope of grace may be broad, but churchly acts cannot make it so. The Reformers also discouraged prayers for the departed because the Reformers expected divine judgment to be rendered immediately after death.[28]

The apocryphal teaching concerning praying for the dead and making atoning offerings on their behalf is found in Second Maccabees 12, telling of a battle in which some Jewish soldiers had died. The next day Judas and his men "went to take up the bodies of the fallen and bring them back to lie with their kinsmen in the sepulchers of their fathers. Then under the tunic of every one of the dead they found sacred tokens of the idols of Jamnia, which the law forbids Jews to wear. And it became clear to all that this was why these men had fallen" (vv. 39–40 NRSV). Judas and his soldiers prayed that the sin that had been committed would be blotted out and Judas collected money for a sin offering. According to Second Maccabees, in doing these things Judas "acted very well and honorably, taking account of the resurrection. For if he were not expecting that those who had fallen would rise again, it would have been superfluous and foolish to pray for the dead. But if he was looking to the splendid reward that is laid up for those who fall asleep in godliness, it was a holy and pious thought. Therefore he made atonement for the dead that they might be delivered from their sin" (vv. 43b–45 NRSV).

"Nothing is more characteristic of traditional Protestantism than its negative view about prayers for the dead or atonement after death; nothing more seriously differentiates it from Catholic life and culture. It cannot be doubted that this passage, from Second Maccabees, which was widely used in arguments from the Catholic side, was a more important factor than any other single passage in the Protestant rejection of the Apocrypha." Luther's conflict over the sale of indulgences—whereby the Catholic Church raised money by encouraging people to pay to have their friends and relatives released from purgatory—also greatly influenced the Protestant reaction.

On the positive side, the Apocrypha contains two teachings that provide history of tradition background for NT instruction. Jesus's golden rule teaching (Matt 7:12; Luke 6:31) does not have an OT precedent, but only an apocryphal one. Such a perspective is found in Tobit 4:15 and relates to the well-known formulation of Hillel. Similarly, the NT emphasis on interpersonal forgiveness has only an apocryphal background. Only in Ben Sira do we find: "Forgive your neighbor the wrong he has done, and then your sins will be pardoned when you pray" (28:2).[29]

The difference between Protestants and Catholics concerning the books of the OT Scriptures may be slightly less than might appear. On the Protestant side, without regarding the apocryphal books as canonical, Lutherans have always held some of these in honor, and the Reformed Church's Synod of Dort argued that they should be

---

27. Harrington, "Apocrypha/Early Church/Today," 210.
28. Barr, *Concept/Biblical Theology*, 572.
29. Ibid., 572–73, 571–72.

Developments toward Old Testament Canon

translated and available for Christian consultation. Dort, however, thought that they should not to be supplied with annotations, but with warnings to compare the content "with the canonical books." Well into the nineteenth century Anglicans continued to print the Apocrypha together with the Old and New Testaments, and as an option the practice has now returned with many Protestant publishers. On the Catholic side, while regarding the Apocrypha as canonical, Catholics believe that Christians should be alert concerning differences between the Apocrypha and the books of the Jewish canon. The Roman Catholic *New Catechism* states that "The question is not as important as it may appear. The fact that these books, which are, incidentally, often very beautiful, are part of Scripture does not mean that they are as important as the rest. And they add no new message (47)."[30] But do they add no new message? I think, rather, that they do, and that we should not accept the parts of such teachings that conflict with the Word of God as we have come to hear that through Jesus Christ.

Only in the sixteenth century did Protestantism challenge the canonical authority of the Apocrypha and reject the Septuagint. The Christian decision concerning the canonicity of the OT, unlike the NT canonizing process, occurred with no vigorous debate about the validity of individual books.[31] When the fourth and fifth centuries' church affirmed the canonical authority of the NT scriptures, *in passing* she assumed the canonical authority of a total block of OT writings. The carelessness of this decision invites the church to reconsider the scope and authority of the OT canon. As the next chapter will show, the NT's figurative and cryptic way of interpreting the OT—that smoothed away conflicts with the NT—should also cause us to reconsider the authority of the OT.

---

30. Quoted in Berkhof, *Christian Faith*, 81.
31. See the next chapter.

Chapter 5

Authority of Old Testament for New Testament Christians and Christians Today

Part A

1. Introduction to Non-Historical, Non-Literary Ways Early Christian Writers Interpreted Old Covenant Texts

CHRISTIANS NEED TO BECOME familiar with the ways in which books *later included* in the NT[1] interpreted and used some of the books *later included in* the OT.[2] Such knowledge may help today's Christians think realistically concerning the OT's authority.

NT writings appropriated OT material in a variety of ways, such as agreeing, disagreeing, or creatively or fancifully using texts for prediction attribution. As for examples of disagreeing with OT tradition, Paul's epistles see much tension between the law and the gospel, and the Epistle to the Hebrews speaks of the "imperfection" of Israel's cultic institutions. Yet Hebrews is one of the strongest testimonies to the fact that aspects of the OT traditions are full of pointers to and predictions of the Christ event,[3] and Paul's writings often use the OT in similar ways (see below).

As for finding fanciful messianic predictions, consider Galatians 3:16a, and that Paul noticed that the word "offspring" from Genesis 12:7 is singular. Of course the singular in Genesis most naturally implies many people. But Paul regarded the accidental fact that Hebrew expresses descendants with a singular noun as providential, thereby indicating that the promises Abraham received would find their fulfillment in

---

1. In this chapter to avoid verbosity I will anachronistically often speak of NT writers and writings in reference to writers and writings of books later contained there. For the same reason I will speak of "biblical" and "NT" times.

2. This last phrase slightly oversimplifies, since a few late NT writings may have been written after the Septuagint was available. Again, to avoid verbosity I will often speak anachronistically of OT writings and writers to identify writings and writers of books later encompassed in the OT.

3. Rad, *OT Theology*, 2:330.

one man. Non-Christian Jews would have disputed Paul's specific application, but this kind of argumentation was fully acceptable within the first century Jewish context.[4]

Exegetical analysis shows that, like the Jews of the day, NT Christians primarily read meanings into OT texts (eisegesis), rather than in historically and literarily precise ways seeking to derive meanings from texts (exegesis) and their theological expansions. *The OT was thus not as authoritative for NT Christians as later Christians have usually assumed. Its supposed authority was largely dependent on and to a considerable extent a function of the figurative interpretive methods commonly employed.*[5]

Texts can be read as "sequences of words and sentences conveying a continuous semantic content," but in biblical times *ancient* passages were often regarded as "code[s] to be deciphered." At that time Judaism went further in this direction than Christianity, but both were familiar with a way of thinking about the OT "that makes it *a vast cryptogram*, from which meaning is extracted by methods quite different from those used in ordinary reading."[6]

As previously discussed[7] there were many differences between Hebrew passages from writings later incorporated into the Hebrew, Masoretic OT[8] (which is close to today's OT) and those Greek versions (whether directly from the Septuagint or indirectly from testimony books) that the NT writers were likely using. Even so, the main reason NT writers were shielded from the probable historical/literary meanings of OT texts is that they used textually disconnecting methods (see secs. 6–8) to interpret those documents. Surprisingly, as will be explained later, the early Christians read their NT writings more directly!

In conflict with the NT reading of the OT, *plain reading* strives to interpret the Bible in ways consistent with (but not limited to) honest awareness of the probable original meanings of texts accurately translated from their original languages. Antiochene theologians Theodore of Mopsuestia (350–426) and John Chrysostom (347–407) insisted on "literal" readings of texts, in contrast to the allegorizing of the Alexandrian school. Such plain reading was also promoted by the Protestant Reformation of the sixteenth century (especially by Calvin), but came to fruition in only the late seventeenth and following centuries.

The term "literal" does not exclude metaphorical or symbolic meanings if those accord with one's perception of a writing's intention. But normal linguistic procedures are seen to apply even to ancient Scripture—rather than requiring the importation of understandings not encouraged by language and context.[9] Interpretations involve

---

4. Barton, *Holy Writings*, 143.
5. See secs. 5–9.
6. Barton, *Holy Writings*, 145; my emphases.
7. Chap. 4, sec. 4.
8. Let us recall that this collection may have existed as a composite by 700 CE, long after the Christian canonizing of the Bible.
9. Thiselton, *Two Horizons*, 115.

expansions of textually contextual meanings—but those must not be new creations. Unless the spiritual significance of scriptural texts genuinely depends upon such direct meanings—interpretation in effect extends the canon, rather than interpreting it.

The modern literary-historical study of Scripture continued in the footsteps of the Antiochene and Protestant "plain reading" of texts in that it sought to understand the probable original meaning of scriptural passages—on the assumption that additional understandings need to be consistent with those. In taking account of historical significance the literary-historical approach isolated OT texts from the loosely connected meanings that the NT often read into such texts. When we seek a more straightforward sense of Scripture, as the Reformers desired, it is inevitable that the OT appears in a different light. Once it is no longer taken figuratively it demonstrates not only its own independent character, concealed over the ages, but to a considerable extent its *alien* nature.[10]

In recent decades much biblical theology has assumed that a plain reading of the OT is fully compatible with Christian Faith. The early church thought otherwise.[11] The OT read plainly had little influence upon NT understanding. Furthermore, the seldom admitted truth is that it has never been possible to be completely loyal to a plain or literal understanding of the OT and at the same time remain faithful to the essentials of Christian Faith.[12] *For NT writers and Paul in particular the OT heritage was "authoritative only insofar as it could be reinterpreted by and in relation to the new revelation in Jesus."* Concerning the NT's handling of OT scripture, the real question is not whether it regarded those as authoritative, but *"how their authority was understood in practice."*[13]

To the extent that NT authors used the Septuagint material directly[14] and not books of passages with selections made suitable for establishing predictions—they often considerably modified its *wording and meaning* to fit their christological commitment. Sometimes individual OT passages would be changed by being conflated (combined) with other OT texts to derive meanings not directly found in the contributing passages.[15] Most OT texts and traditions were in effect either abandoned because never utilized,[16] or not even known.

If Christians are today to largely agree with the content commitment of NT writers, the authority of our Hebrew-based OT needs to be evaluated in that context. But that does not mean that it has no authority. Such Christian agreement as is possible involves recognizing that the OT has to be used selectively in the light of perceptions

---

10. Gunneweg, *Understanding OT*, 4.
11. Barton, "Marcion Revisited," 350.
12. See secs. 12–13.
13. Dunn, *Unity/Diversity*, 101, 82; see also 78.
14. See sec. 2.
15. See sec. 6.
16. Dunn, *Unity/Diversity*, 94, 101. See sec. 12.

concerning the authority of Jesus Christ as attested by the NT. For the NT itself regards different parts of the OT as having varying degrees of authority. Even the NT must be relativized in the light of the Crucified and Risen One to whom Christians through the NT witness have become accountable.

2. Pre–New Testament Christian Message Determined What Would Be Creatively Utilized from Available Pre–Old Testament Traditions[17]

Since no testimony books and only fragments of the Septuagint survived antiquity, we must wrestle with the problem of the historical/literary disconnect between early Christian teachings that linked to such early Old Covenant sources and the major source available for comparison—the later Hebrew-based Masoretic OT.

Insofar as pre-NT writers referred to the available pre-OT books they likely did so in large part to commend early Christian convictions to Jews and to Jewish Christians who recognized the authority of such scriptures. Such NT writers apparently thought that if at many points they could show that fulfillments in Christ correlate closely with OT expectations or if they could interpret OT texts as direct statements about Christ—such evidence would help to convince Jews and edify Jewish Christians concerning Christian truth. Yet for early Christians, their effective commitment was to Christ—not to OT scriptures.[18]

Especially for Gentile Christians, the OT was not the basis of religious authority, having come to learn of the old scriptures only when they came to faith in Christ. For the first two centuries most Christians may have become familiar only with such Old Covenant passages as Genesis 1, some Psalms, and messianic testimonies from Isaiah.[19] What mattered were central passages that could be understood as pointing to Christ, who was recognized as the Redeemer on the basis of the kerygma (Christian preaching/message)—"not primarily because an already known scripture had been found to make more sense if read in the light of him."[20] This momentous shift in understanding the pre-history of the Christian biblical canon implies that *the contents of much of what would later constitute the NT became the datum—and the authority of the OT depended on that of the New.*[21]

Since few Christians are today preaching to Jews or Jewish Christians who find figurative eisegesis credible—the OT's predictive relevance lessens. Furthermore, as modern Christians pay attention to the historical and literary meanings of writings, and as neither Jews nor Christians any longer use translations based on the Septuagint, the

---

17. As n2 conceded, a few late pre-NT writings may have been written after the Septuagint was available.
18. Barr, *Scripture/Canon*, 14.
19. Barton, *Holy Writings*, 71.
20. Ibid., 71–72.
21. Ibid., 72.

OT's usefulness for preaching to Jews and Jewish Christians again diminishes. Historical study shows that most OT texts do not in their original historical/literary contexts convey meanings that point to the Christocentric ones the NT often attributes to them.[22]

The NT primarily offers interpretations of only those selected portions of the available OT scriptures that NT authors could interpret as shedding light on their messages. One biblical scholar thinks that nearly half of the explicit quotations in the NT come from Isaiah and the Psalms, which provided a backbone of material to which allusions were often made.[23] Furthermore, the NT ahistorically isolates snippits from the OT, rather than providing interpretations of full sequences of material. In line with midrash/pesher/allegorical interpretations,[24] the OT was used more to shed light upon the situations and events of the New than for interpreting the Old. In spite of the widespread use of some writings later included in the OT, the NT's utilization of the OT *is more like creative literature and illustration than exegesis.*[25]

3. Jesus's Use of Old Covenant Traditions

At the beginning of this section we should remind ourselves that NT interpreters and we ourselves only partially share Jesus's sense of authority, the difference being that Christians are sinners whose inner leading by the Spirit is imperfect, and who therefore require correction by and guidance from God's revelation in Jesus. This being so, we will necessarily need to be more dependent on the NT than was Jesus on pre-OT traditions.

Unlike the scribes' authority, Jesus's sense of authority was more direct—not based primarily on the exposition of texts. From His own sense of God's will Jesus was able to state the truth, whether in scripture or not. Unlike the rabbis He did not usually start from scriptural passages and interpret their meaning. Instead, they were brought in to help an argument, provide an illustration, establish a confirmation, or to indicate something omitted or overlooked in current thinking.[26] "Well did Isaiah prophesy of you hypocrites, as it was written . . ." (Mark 7:6). "Such a saying *is not so much an interpretation of Isaiah as an interpretation of the present situation through the use of Isaiah.*"[27] A similar situational use of scripture is seen in Jesus's response to the Pharisees' criticism of plucking grain on the Sabbath: "Have you never read what

22. See sec. 5.

23. Ibid., 61. Another such scholar regarded over 80 percent of Paul's citations as from the Pentateuch, Isaiah, and the Psalter, with Genesis and Isaiah being his favorites. Within the narrative material Paul focused on Adam and the Patriarchs, giving little attention to Israel's exodus or wilderness period, the conquest, the judges, or monarchy. If one includes allusions and not just explicit quotations, the prophets rather than the Pentateuch become the center of scripture for Paul (Childs, *Biblical Theology OT/NT*, 238).

24. See secs. 6–8.

25. Barr, *Scripture/Canon*, 70.

26. Ibid., 68.

27. Ibid., 68; my emphasis.

David did, when he was in need and hungry, he and those with him: how he entered the house of God . . . and ate the bread of the Presence . . . ?" (Mark 2:25a, 26a)

The use of *parables* is characteristic of Jesus's teaching,[28] which stands at the other end of the scale of literary types (*genres*) from the mere interpretation of texts. They depict life experience[29] illumined by scriptural perception and providing unexpected application twists.

Jesus asserted His freedom over against the law and the prophets and the religious practices of His day, and spoke with immediacy, directness, and spontaneity. Although His often indirect, highly figurative or metaphorical language was drawn from the world around Him, He did not have ordinary reality in mind. The parable of the leaven is not about baking, the mustard seed and sower not about gardening, and the admonition to lend to those unable to pay back not about banking practice. Jesus pointed to the kingdom by looking *through* daily existence to what lay beyond the everyday. He challenged everydayness by speaking of a Samaritan who cared for an enemy, a prodigal who returned home, and laborers granted undeserved wages. Of enemies to be loved and of those who save their lives by losing them.[30]

4. Old Testament Prophetic Hopes That Build toward New Testament Fulfillments and Beyond

The OT dynamic of promise and fulfillment took new forms in the proclamation of the classical prophets. They did not primarily interpret the present in the light of divine interaction in the past, but spoke of a future mainly characterized by catastrophic divine judgment that would expose as illusory claims to security based on Israel's election.[31] Yet beyond such judgment a definitive act of God on behalf of His people

---

28. See chap. 17, sec. 1. See chap. 2, sec. 6, for a related discussion concerning the use of analogical language.

29. Barr, *Scripture/Canon*, 69.

30. Funk, "Once and Future NT," 544, 550, 551.

31. In *Essays*, 193. Bultmann indicates that a contradiction is involved in speaking of a covenant with a historical people if within those people the covenant's validity depends on the individual's spiritual attitude and moral behavior. The natural thought that came from the idea of Israel's election was that the individual gained security from membership in the covenant people. Such a tribal viewpoint was the naive consciousness against which the prophets' protests were raised, and against which John the Baptist took issue: "'Do not presume to say to yourselves, "We have Abraham as our father"; I tell you, God is able from these stones to raise up children to Abraham'" (Matt 3:9). If John the Baptist was right, that the validity of the covenant depends on the individual's response, the idea of God's covenant with an entire people is done away with. That is exactly what Jesus said: "'I tell you, many will come from east and west and sit at table with Abraham, Isaac, and Jacob in the kingdom of heaven, while the sons of the kingdom will be thrown into the outer darkness . . .'" (Matt 8:11–12a).

With Christian faith the sign of the old covenant, circumcision, was abolished: "For a person is not a Jew who is one outwardly, nor is true circumcision something external and physical. Rather, a person is a Jew who is one inwardly, and real circumcision is a matter of the heart—it is spiritual and not literal. Such a person receives praise not from others but from God" (Rom 2:28-29 NRSV; cf. 1

was generally expected. The prophetic message thus differed from previous Israelite theology in that the prophets thought the decisive factor for Israel was to occur through future events.[32]

With the classical prophets God's revelation through visions, words and amid historical events awakened awe before the Holy God, before whom even the covenant people stood judged. This appeared most impressively with the vision of Isaiah's call (ch 6), which proclaimed ruin; but Amos, Micah, Hosea, Jeremiah and Ezekiel spoke similarly. For Jeremiah bad news was even characteristic of the truthfulness of prophetic messages (28:8).

Beyond divine judgment in the present, the classical prophets expected spiritual salvation in the future. Sometimes the expectation was that the people would serve Yahweh (Jehovah, the Lord) with whole heart (Jer 31:31–34; Ezek 36:26–27); or that God would dwell in Israel (Ezek 37:27; 48:35; Zech 2); or that the Lord's Spirit would descend upon everyone (Joel 2:28–29); or that all nations would share in God's feast, and that reproach, tears and death would be eliminated (Isa 25:6–8).

In focusing on OT prophetic hopes that built toward NT fulfillments and beyond we will look primarily, though not exclusively, at the book of *Isaiah*. Because of situational and content differences within that book scholars have long thought that it cannot convincingly be attributed to a single author and thus is a composite. The theory is that Isaiah of Jerusalem had students who, having learned from him, responded to the concrete realities of their day with somewhat different theological emphases. Many scholars think that only the first section was written by the original prophet/teacher/writer.

First Isaiah (chapters 1–23, 28–33, 36–39) expected ruin and only after that salvation. In-between he hoped for miraculous intervention by the "'Wonderful Counselor, Mighty God, Everlasting Father, Prince of Peace'" (9:6ef), who would be led in all things by the Lord's Spirit (11:1–3a) and who would bring about the new age (11:6–9).

According to this author, salvation, though received through Judah, would have universal effect and would fill the earth with the knowledge of God (11:9c). Such redemption would not be brought about by military victories, or result in the strengthening of a powerful state, but would bring world peace, even among the animals (11:6–8).

Because of his hope of worldwide spiritual renewal First Isaiah may be regarded as the initial preacher of *eschatological expectation*, perceiving salvation as transcending the historical plane. He looked upon the downfall of Judah as the dawning of the day of the Lord (2:10–18), as in later times the destruction of Jerusalem was viewed similarly (Lam 2:22). After Judah's predicted downfall Isaiah did not expect the old situation to return (2:4; 11:6–9), but hoped for more than historical restoration,

---

Cor 7:19; Gal 5:6; 6:15). "For we are the true circumcision, who worship God in spirit, and glory in Christ Jesus, and put no confidence in the flesh" (Phil 3:3) (same source, 196).

32. Rad, *OT Theology*, 2:117.

though enactment was expected on this earth. "The haughtiness of people shall be humbled, and the pride of everyone shall be brought low, and the Lord alone will be exalted in that day" (2:17 NRSV).

Second Isaiah (chapters 34–35, 40–55) had passed through the judgment his teacher (Isaiah) had predicted and he also expected the emergence of fulfillment in the near future. From the various terms and images he used it appears that the salvation he foresaw also far transcended the historical plane. He repeatedly used the verb "to create" (16 times), which indicates that the redemption of Israel would be no less than a new creation. God had said, "'Remember not the former things, nor consider the things of old. Behold, I am doing a new thing . . .'" (43:18–19). God would be glorified in the presence of all and unto Him every knee would bow; the Lord would reign again in Jerusalem (52:7–9; cf. 40:9b).

This writer prophesied that God would establish an everlasting covenant that would reveal all the faithful acts of grace granted to David, so that all the nations would run to Israel (55:3–5). God called her to be "a light to the Gentiles" and a "covenant to the people" to bring forth and to teach the world law and justice (42; 49). Israel's missionary vocation was hereby implied, a task viewed in the light of near eschatology.[33]

Second Isaiah believed that he stood at the end of the period of God's judgment of His people (40:1–2; 51:22–23) and at the beginning of that of salvation (40:3–5; 52:13–53:12). But he soon came to perceive even more deeply that his people were unbelieving, blind and deaf.[34] His changed perspective was due to a great spiritual disappointment he experienced because Israel did not believe in the reality of God's power. Because the author had and continued to have high hopes for his people and yet was called to confront them so decisively—he experienced much suffering (50:4–6). So amid his joyful hope for his people's deliverance we hear of the costly suffering of the servant of the Lord.[35]

Third Isaiah (chapters 56–66) reflects a *dualistic, apocalyptic eschatology*. Various causes influenced his development: Disappointment after the high hopes of Isaiah and Second Isaiah had not been fulfilled and a growing sense of distance from God, the latter influenced by Persian dualism. In his writings the divine is largely regarded as transcendent and this world is regarded as generally bound by demonic influence. The place where the new kingdom is to be fully realized is no longer on this earth—for this world is to be destroyed and a new one is to come. Though we can experience God now, the eternal kingdom is regarded as in the future.

Though chapters 60–62 of Third Isaiah place Jerusalem in the limelight the last few chapters (65–66) emphasize universal and supra-historical elements. In the time

---

33. Vriezen, *OT Theology*, 359–60, 354, 360, 361–62.

34. Isa 40:27; 42:18–20; 44:9–20; 48:8; 49:14; 50:1–2ab; 51:12–13.

35. Vriezen, *OT Theology*, 363, 362. See sec. 10 for a more comprehensive discussion of the suffering servant passages.

of this prophet people reveled in the signs of future salvation (chapter 65:20–25; cf. Zech 8:4–5).

With the "Little Apocalypse" of *Fourth Isaiah* (chapters 24–27) the cosmic element and personal salvation were increasingly emphasized, with expectation of resurrection from the dead (chapter 26; see also Joel 2).

Eschatology arose when people learned to rely on their own faith in God as the basis for life, and where highly critical attitudes toward Israel became possible. The coming upheaval was regarded as a just divine judgment, but faith also confessed that the Holy God remained unshakeable in His loyalty and love of Israel. Thus Israel's life came to have a double aspect: The sense that judgment was near and the belief that God would one day make a new beginning.[36] This perspective became possible as prophets so learned of God that they "experienced the discrepancy between what is and what should be. The final break in ancient Israelite totalitarian philosophy of life, which started from the unity of God, the world, the people and the compatriot, is the point where eschatology breaks through."[37]

Christians can believe that the eschatological hopes of the classical prophets have begun to be realized in Christ and through His resurrection from the dead and the outpouring of the Spirit that creates and energizes Christians. Yet the consummation has yet to occur.

5. Old Testament Prediction, Its New Testament Use, New Testament Prediction

(A) We begin by examining five types of primarily OT prophetic predictions. The first consists of what came to pass in the OT period. Included in this group was the forecast of the defeat of Israel under Jeroboam (Amos 7:9; see 2 Kgs 15:8–12 for its fulfillment); Hosea 3:4, who predicted that for many days Israel would be without many features of her life, whose prediction was shortly realized by the Assyrians' dismantling of the Northern Kingdom; and Jeremiah's prophecy (29:10), that after seventy years the Israelites would be released from Babylon, which Cyrus brought to completion by allowing the return home (Ezra 1:7–8).

The second category of prophecy did not come to pass and never will. For example, in Ezekiel 26–28:19 the prophet predicted the complete ruin of the city of Tyre. Then see Ezekiel 29:17–20 for attestation that Nebuchadnezzar failed in his campaign against Tyre.[38] Another way in which even a divine forecast cannot be accomplished is when God changes His plans. Even if Jonah does not describe a historical incident, the story indicates that God is capable of changing a declared intention. As the story goes, God convinced Jonah to proclaim judgment and condemnation to Nineveh, and

---

36. Ibid., 365, 368, 369–70. *John the Baptist and Jesus shared both convictions.*
37. Ibid., 370.
38. Roberts, *Prophetic Prediction*, 241–42.

Jonah eventually did so (Jonah 3:4b). Nonetheless, "when God saw what they did, how they turned from their evil way, God repented of the evil which he had said he would do to them; and he did not do it" (3:10).[39]

The third kind of prediction is yet to be fulfilled. For example, one can point to numerous OT passages that speak of an earth purified of evil (see, for example, Isa 11:6–9). To move to the NT, the promise of Jesus's second coming is an example of such a forecast yet to be realized. However, the second forecast's generally transcendent conception of the future conflicts with the first prediction's conception of the consummation as realized on this earth.[40]

The fourth type, like the immediately previous example, involves what will be attained in different ways than the OT expected. What can Christians make of Ezekiel 37–48, with its predictions of animal sacrifice, Zadokite priests, contemporary descendants of David, and parcels of land in Palestine, especially in view of the Book of Revelation's corrections and revisions of these texts? Since Revelation was written after Christ's coming, it expresses a new realization of how God deals with His people and what sacrifice is about.[41] Even with Revelation's clearer hope for the future, we yet see through a glass dimly (1 Cor 13:12a) and "it does not yet appear what we shall be, but we know that when he appears, we shall be like him" (1 John 3:2b).

As we have seen in Ezekiel, the language of prophecy often seems to imply one type of event, though the actual fulfillment or the NT's proposed fulfillment is different. Isaiah's prediction that the desert would bloom for Israelites returning home conflicts with Ezra's and Nehemiah's descriptions of the return from Babylonian captivity, where fulfillment consisted only of the joy of a safe return.[42] A related and often accompanying problem is well illustrated by the prediction in Haggai 2:20–22, that God was "*about to* shake the heavens and the earth and to overthrow the throne of kingdoms" (verses 21b–22a). God's shaking of the nations has proven to be more dis-

---

39. Though Christians can agree that God can change Her plans, we have NT reason for doubting that God would ever wish to destroy a city (cf. sec. 13), or would have tribal enemies She would undertake to destroy. Jesus tells us to love our enemies because we are to be like God, who is indiscriminate in Her benevolence (Matt 5:43–45; Luke 6:27, 35–36).

40. There are a few NT texts that speak of eschatological fulfilment on this earth. See, for example, Rev 21:2, as mentioned in the next note.

41. Roberts, "Prophetic Prediction," 244–45, 247. See Rev 20:4—22:5. According to Ezekiel God showed the prophet the new Jerusalem set on a high mountain, as it will be after the defeat of the nations (20:40). In Revelation, God revealed to John the new Jerusalem as it will be *when it comes down from heaven*, adorned as a bride for her husband (21:2), atop a high mountain (21:10). Unlike Ezekiel, in Revelation the angel will measure the *city*, not the *temple* (21:15–17), because Revelation's new Jerusalem will have no temple (21:22). Since God and the Lamb will themselves live with the people, there will be no need for temple mediation. Furthermore Revelation, unlike Ezekiel, makes *no mention of animal sacrifice*. The reason is that Jesus is the Lamb slain before the foundation of the world (Rev 13:8), in whose blood the saints cleanse their garments (7:14), and through whose blood they overcome the devil (12:11). Because the true sacrifice has now been offered there is no need for the animal variety (same source, 246).

42. Ibid., 252, 251.

tant than the prophet expected. A similar discrepancy is found in the NT. According to Mark 13 Jesus spoke of the Son of Man coming with the clouds of heaven, and verse 30 says, "'Truly, I say to you, this generation will not pass away before all these things take place.'"[43] There was an expectation among the earliest Christians that Jesus would return within their own lifetimes, a view consistent with many of Paul's statements.[44] Galatians and Second Corinthians do not write in these terms, nor does Colossians or Ephesians (the latter two of which may not have been written by Paul). Similarly, in Philippians 1:23 Paul weighs the advantages and disadvantages of departing to be with the Lord before the elapsing of his natural life span and before the consummation. He there implies that death may be the normal way whereby people enter the eternal kingdom.

The next sub-section will deal with the fifth type of OT prophecy, some of which to a large extent may have been fulfilled in Jesus Christ.

(B) We here not only examine how NT authors found some OT predictions fulfilled in Christ, but here and in the next three sections how more commonly they were able to *imaginatively redeploy non-predictive OT texts for predictive purposes*. Though NT authors utilized some texts that a "plain reading" can link to Christ,[45] such authors often attribute prediction where none is contained in texts' original historical and literary contexts.

First two provisos: The truthfulness of NT affirmations does not depend on being fulfillments of OT prophesies, so the absence of historically accurate prophesies linked to such affirmations only invalidates the few cases where NT factual claims seem to have been "created" by supposed OT predictions.[46] Generally[47] NT writers do not gain new knowledge from OT predictions, but read what they already know into them. This means that the OT "prophecies" often become clear as a result of "fulfillments." But what would have been the point of such a proceeding on God's part, since the foretelling would have had no meaning to the original recipients? And *"can the offence of the cross of Jesus be overcome by recognizing it as long-prophesied and decided upon by God—or only by grasping its meaning and significance?"*[48]

Another proviso: Though we must criticize ahistorical prediction attribution, with reference to this sub-section's exegetical criticisms and those in the next three sections we need to remind ourselves that the first century was not the nineteenth, twentieth or twenty-first. Historical science fully began only in the late seventeenth

---

43. For the more general problem that comes to expression in this paragraph, see chap. 8, sec. 3 concerning the dialectical traditioning process.

44. 1 Thess 4:15–17; 1 Cor 7:29–31; 15:51; Phil 4:5; Rom 13:11; 11:31.

45. See the following biblical quotations in nn49–52 just below, and this section's main text elaboration of the NT fulfillment of Jer 31:31–34.

46. See below in this same section.

47. Bultmann says "in all cases," which exaggerates.

48. Bultmann, *Essays*, 187; my emphasis.

century, and did not make steady progress even in the twentieth and twenty-first centuries, since late in the twentieth and even today purely literary approaches (as with many narrative theologies) have thumbed their noses at it and still do. Though I think the criticisms that will be made in this chapter are necessary for the sake of helping modern interpreters to read with precision, contextual sensitivity requires the humility that recognizes that first century Christians did not benefit from the historical-critical revolution of modern times.

NT writers found more than predictions of Christ in the OT, though many looked for those (see Luke 4:21). With a variety of nuances, prediction ascription occurred even in the pre-Pauline tradition, evidenced in Paul's quoting of the early belief that Christ's cross and resurrection are in accordance with the scriptures (1 Cor 15:3–5), and continued down to the latest NT strata. Some aspects of predictions applicable to God's eschatological act in Jesus Christ are genuinely contained in the OT, especially messianic ones like Isaiah 9:2, 6–7[49] and 11:1–3;[50] Micah 5:2;[51] and Zechariah 9:9.[52] But facets of even these texts conflict with historical/critical analysis of the Jesus tradition: Among other things, Jesus did not establish a Davidic government, nor by-and-large did the NT consider His Davidic ancestry important, nor is it likely that He was born in Bethlehem.[53] Even where prediction and fulfillment line up well they do not prove the truthfulness of NT claims, but provide only confirming testimony.

Since the old covenant had been shattered because of the people's guilt, God needed to conclude a new one:

> Behold, the days are coming, says the Lord, when I will make a new covenant with the house of Israel and the house of Judah, not like the covenant which I made with their fathers when I took them by the hand to bring them out of the land of Egypt, my covenant which they broke, though I was their husband, says the Lord. But this is the covenant which I will make with the house of Israel after those days, says the Lord: I will put my law within them, and I will

---

49. "The people who walked in darkness have seen a great light; those who dwelt in a land of deep darkness, on them has light shined . . . For to us a child is born, to us a son is given; and the government will be upon his shoulder, and his name will be called 'Wonderful Counselor, Mighty God, Everlasting Father, Prince of Peace.' Of the increase of his government and of peace there will be no end, upon the throne of David, and over his kingdom, to establish it, and to uphold it with justice and righteousness from this time forth and for evermore. The zeal of the Lord of hosts will do this."

50. "There shall come forth a shoot from the stump of Jesse, and a branch shall grow out of his roots. And the Spirit of the Lord shall rest upon him, the spirit of wisdom and understanding, the spirit of counsel and might, the spirit of knowledge and the fear of the Lord. And his delight shall be in the fear of the Lord."

51. "But you, O Bethlehem Eph'rathah, who are little to be among the clans of Judah, from you shall come forth for me one who is to be ruler in Israel, whose origin is from of old, from ancient days."

52. "Rejoice greatly, O daughter of Zion! Shout aloud, O daughter of Jerusalem! Lo, your king comes to you; triumphant and victorious is he, humble and riding on an ass, on a colt the foal of an ass."

53. Gunneweg, *Understanding OT*, 173, 174. For exposition on these matters, see below in this sec.

write it upon their hearts; and I will be their God, and they shall be my people. And no longer shall each person teach his neighbor and each his brother, saying, "Know the Lord," for they shall all know me, from the least of them to the greatest, says the Lord; for I will forgive their iniquity, and I will remember their sin no more (Jer 31:31–34).

The NT rightly believes that the promise of Jeremiah has been fulfilled through Christ and in the Christian community. Hebrews 8:8–12 repeats the Jeremiah prophecy and affirms that it has been fulfilled in Christ, and Hebrews 10:16–18 attests that Christ's once-and-for-all sacrifice abolished the need for repeated liturgical sacrifices.

Having emphasized the OT prophecies that Christians have good reason to believe were fulfilled with the new covenant, we can see that most of those that NT authors attribute to the OT are not grounded in a plain reading of the texts in question. Hebrews 2:6–8 cites Psalms 8:5–7 as predicting the temporary humiliation of the pre-existent Christ. The original text, however, describes the dignity of man. Hebrews 10:5–7 understands Psalms 40:6–9 as prophesying Christ's self-surrender as a sacrifice, which could only fulfill the Septuagint version,[54] which we do not possess. Contrary to multiple NT messianic references to Psalms 2 & 110, those celebrated the enthronement of a contemporary king.

Matthew develops the proof from prophecy thoroughly, seeing the OT as prophesying the work of Jesus Christ and His fate down to apparently unimportant details. "All this took place to fulfill what the Lord had spoken by the prophets" (Matt 1:22). Fulfillment quotations permeate Matthew's Gospel, reflecting a systematic attempt to depict the Christ event as a whole and in all its details as a fulfillment of OT prophecy. Yet Matthew seldom cites passages that were prophecies in their original sense.[55] For example, according to Matthew 8:17, Isaiah 53:4 predicted Jesus's miraculous healings, though the text obviously refers to atonement. Matthew 2:17–18 regards Jeremiah 31:15 as describing the murder of the children in Bethlehem, though "Rachel's weeping for her children" originally referred to the imprisonment of the exiles. The invitation in Psalms 78:1–2a to listen to the psalmist's parable is interpreted by Matthew in 13:34–35 as a prediction that Jesus would speak in parables. Matthew 27:9–10 says Jeremiah prophesied the thirty pieces of silver that Judas received as a reward, but the passage is from Zechariah 11:12 and originally had another reference. These are only a few examples of the way Matthew uses events from Jesus's life to locate passages in the OT that he imaginatively interprets as predicting Christ.[56]

Though rare, elements were sometimes even introduced into NT descriptions of events to establish correspondence with and fulfillment of what were regarded as OT

---

54. Bultmann, *Essays*, 186.

55. This unless Matthew used a book of testimonies that modified OT texts to predictively link more accurately or if the Septuagint differed from the Masoretic version at all these points and in all these ways.

56. Gunneweg, *Understanding OT*, 24, 25.

expectations. That is, the desire for "proofs from prophecy" seems in some cases to have led to the creation of a few NT "historical" traditions.[57] Matthew 21:5 regarded Zechariah 9:9 as predicting Jesus's triumphant entry into Jerusalem, and the OT passage did predict some kind of celebratory entry. But when Zechariah 9:9 described the animal ridden "as an ass, a colt the foal of an ass" he referred to a single beast. Matthew 21:5d, however, supposed that Zechariah 9:9 not only prophesied that Jesus would ride into Jerusalem, but on two animals, which strikes us as absurdly humorous. Having misunderstood his OT source Matthew felt obliged to alter his use of the Markan triumphant entry description to fit his understanding of the prediction. (Compare Mark 11:2–7 with Luke 19:30–36.)[58] More important but more contentious examples would be the location of Jesus's birth in Bethlehem and the virginal conception itself. Against the former, one notices that Jesus was habitually referred to as "Jesus of Nazareth" or "Jesus from Nazareth." The whole Bethlehem birth narrative may stem from the conviction that Jesus the Messiah should be shown as fulfilling Micah 5:2. More specifically, the virginal conception of Jesus may have originated in the apologetic desire to show Jesus as the fulfillment of Isaiah 7:14, using the likely Septuagint rendition of the Hebrew fragment "young maiden" as "virgin."[59] The notion of a virginal conception likely went beyond the available Hebrew, pre-Masoretic fragments, and definitely beyond the later Masoretic text.

Paul contrasted the spirit of the old and new covenants. Yet Paul believed that "all the promises of God find their Yes in him" (2 Cor 1:20a). Judged by historical and literary readings of current (Masoretic-based) versions, even Paul could treat OT texts with utter abandon: The words from Psalm 19:4 quoted in Romans 10:18 are not a prophecy of the mission to the Gentiles, but affirm that heaven and earth praise God's glory. Psalms 8 does not speak of Christ's eschatological Lordship (1 Cor 15:27), but of God's establishing of man's high estate.[60]

As we will see in the chapter 6, sec. 10, the choice of the codex (page book in contrast to the scroll) for bringing together the Pauline 10 book collection, the four Gospels, and then the NT shows that early Christians wanted such writings to be read straightforwardly. This practice is much in contrast with the fanciful ways many NT writers had often "found" OT predictions of Christ. Such usage differences indicate that the early Christians regarded the Christian narrative and message as more directly intelligible and more directly authoritative. Of course Christians also canonized the OT in codex form, but concerning it, figurative interpretation had long been established.

---

57. Dunn, *Unity/Diversity*, 99–100.
58. Gunneweg, *Understanding OT*, 25.
59. Dunn, *Unity/Diversity*, 99–100.
60. Bultmann, *Essays*, 186.

6. New Testament Midrashic Interpretation

If this section is over-documented that is because some readers may require that much evidence to convince them that the NT writers often read fanciful meanings *into* OT passages, rather than deriving meanings *from* those. To help readers who are already convinced or who require less persuading, here I pack a good deal of the evidence into footnotes, and use the body of the text to state only a moderate amount and to summarize conclusions.

The Jewish interpretive method called midrash sought the relevance of sacred texts by bringing together literarily and even topically disconnected texts. Such interpretation was usually achieved by modifying the OT text quoted.[61] The same interpretive tendency is found among midrash, pesher midrash and allegory—they all read ideas into texts.

The pre-NT writers did not generally utilize a plain reading/non-figurative approach in their use of the pre-OT, though they intended that their own writings be read that way. Therefore we should often regard NT quotations of OT texts "not against the context from which the quotations were taken"—which is what the modern literary approach encourages—"but against the context of what the early Christians were doing with them."[62]

I have two theological interests in discussing NT midrashic/pesher/allegorical interpretations. The first is hermeneutical: We will continue to see that those shunning the exegetical/theological use of hermeneutics have NT authors arrayed against them.[63] Though we often may not agree with the way the NT authors utilized the OT, they must have paid close attention to Jewish midrashic rules. By doing this they imply that scripture is not self-interpreting and requires some thoughtfulness concerning how it is understood.

My other practical interest concerning midrash, pesher midrash and allegory is this: Because these Jewish methods were generally used by most NT writers to imaginatively ascribe Christocentric meanings to OT texts that of themselves seldom convey such meanings—such usage challenges the common opinion that the OT has independent authority for Christians.[64] Much of the significance the OT has for NT authors was a function of interpretive methods that scientifically educated Christians with even slight knowledge of historical method can no longer countenance as helping to understand the OT. However, contrary to simplistic surmise, such early Christian interpretive methods do not challenge the NT's authority. Why not? Because that

---

61. Dunn, *Unity/Diversity*, 91. For example, compare Mic 5:2a: "You, Bethlehem, Eph'rathah who *are least* among clans of Judah . . ." with Matt 2:6a: "'You, O Bethlehem, who are *by no means* least among the rulers of Judah . . .'" (my emphases). See sec. 7 below.

62. Barr, *Old/New Interpretation*, 143. See secs. 3, 9–13 for areas where "plain readings" of the OT contribute to Christian understanding.

63. Also see this chap., secs. 5, 7–10; chap. 7, sec. 3.

64. See secs. 2 & 14.

authority does not depend on the historical accuracy of the claim that the Christ event is widely predicted in the OT. As related to the authority of the NT, the question is only whether or not we believe NT writers' conceptions of the significance of Jesus Christ from which they undertook to demonstrate that the OT predicted the same.

Midrashic interpretation often drew an association between a present event and isolated words from a text from the past. In the NT use of this first century Jewish interpretive method the starting point was some aspect of the Christ event. From this given the interpreter searched the available pre-OT writings to find a word or phrase that when isolated from its historical and literary context could be understood as predicting the Christ event or confirming it or (very occasionally) that could be used as the basis for a detail thereby attributed to Jesus's life.

Midrash technique is well illustrated in Galatians 3:8; 4:22–31; Second Corinthians 3:7–18 and Matthew 2:23. *Galatians 3:8*: "The scripture, foreseeing that God would justify the Gentiles by faith, preached the gospel beforehand to Abraham, saying, 'In you shall all the nations be blessed.'" Abraham did not hear such words as "gospel" in the sense of God demonstrating Her grace and empowerment, though there is parallelism between the new life the gospel enables and Abraham's new vocation. Paul likely perceived these words as gospel because he derived their meaning from God's redemptive activity in Jesus. *Galatians 4:22–31*: The significance Paul discerned in Isaac's and Ishmael's births is drawn from his allegory-like use of them to illustrate his categories "according to the Spirit" and "according to the flesh."[65] *Second Corinthians 3:7–18*: Paul contrasts the old and new covenants by his interpretation of Exodus 34:29–35. According to the OT text, Moses as mediator put a veil over his face when addressing the people to protect them from the "divine radiance" he had acquired from speaking with God. Paul supposed just the opposite, that the function of the veil was to conceal from the Israelites the fading splendor of the old covenant.[66] But for Paul the veil's true significance concerns the new dispensation—"the veil of Moses understood and interpreted as the veil over the hearts of the *Jews now* (3:14—it is the *same* veil)."[67] The significance Paul attaches to the veil is drawn from his understanding of the tension and conflict between the two dispensations. *Matthew 2:23c*: "He shall be called a Nazarene." Jesus would not have been called a "Nazarene" had He not come from Nazareth. Neither "Nazirite" nor *nezer* (branch) nor both together suggest "Nazarene."[68] The epitaph has more to do with the Gospel tradition than with the OT.

Though Christian midrash proceeds from the Christian message, it appeals to an OT "*text or often a single word; but . . . its meaning is extended and its implications drawn*

---

65. Dunn, *Unity/Diversity*, 94–95.
66. Childs, *Biblical Theology OT/NT*, 239.
67. Dunn, *Unity/Diversity*, 95.
68. Ibid., 95.

out with the help of every possible association of ideas."[69] Where the NT differs from Jewish uses of midrash only concerns the present beliefs and events to be interpreted.

To summarize much of this chapter to this point and to anticipate the remainder of this section and the next two: The common way the NT interprets OT texts is to reinterpret them in the light of the message concerning Jesus Christ and His work. The essential principle behind the NT use of such a hermeneutic is attested by Paul when he says that *OT texts were written for the sake of Christians.*[70] *A basic obstacle for the modern interpreter of Paul and others lies in their "not recognizing the Old Testament as having a voice separate from that of the New Testament.* Paul [and others] hear Israel's scripture as the voice of the gospel."[71] To achieve a Christian reading of OT texts, NT writers often change the sequence of verses, disregard the syntax[72] of sentences, drop words, add words, conflate passages or otherwise change wording.[73] The midrash in particular emerges from the bringing together of aspects of a given OT text or combination of texts and a given perspective concerning Jesus Christ. The importance of the interpreter's theology for interpretation is further illustrated by the fact that in some cases the same OT text is interpreted differently and even in opposite ways by different NT writers.[74]

---

69. Ibid., 84, quoting B. Gerhardsson; my emphasis. Consider two other NT midrashim. John 6:31–58 interprets Ps 78:24: He gave them "the grain of heaven to eat" (6:31). Against the historical reference of the OT text the Fourth Gospel has Jesus say that the "bread from heaven" was not manna, but the Son who came from heaven and gave His flesh for the life of the world. "And those who eat therefore are not the fathers in the desert eating manna and dying, but those who hear Jesus: if they eat his flesh and drink his blood, that is if they believe in him and receive his Spirit, they will never die" (same source, 87).

Rom 4:3–25 is a midrash on Genesis 15:6, "Abraham believed God, and it was counted to him for righteousness." Verses 4–8 explain that "counted" can be understood as receiving a *favor*, rather than earning a *reward*. Three arguments then attempt to show that Abraham's faith should be understood in the Pauline sense, not as faithfulness according to the rabbis (vv. 9–12, 13–17a, 17b–21) (same source, 87–88).

70. 1 Cor 9:10a; see also Rom 4:23–24; 15:4; 1 Cor 10:11.

71. Childs, *Biblical Theology OT/NT*, 242; my emphasis.

72. Rules for the formation of grammatical sentences. Paul's Galatians 3:16a interpretation of the promise of offspring as an intentional reference to a singular object is a classic example of distorting an original text's syntax (ibid., 239).

73. Ibid., 238. Childs mentions several examples of such inaccurate exegesis, and I summarize one: In Rom 10:5–13 Paul alludes to Deut 30:11–14 as testifying to a righteousness based on faith in God's self-giving in Christ. Yet according to the Deuteronomy passage it is the law that is the word that is near and that brings salvation (same source, 238–39). Christians should agree with Paul's affirmation, but recognize his use of Deuteronomy as flawed.

74. Dunn, *Unity/Diversity*, 95, 96. (1) Paul cites Gen 15:6 to prove that Abraham was justified by faith alone and not by works (Rom 4:3–5; Gal 3:6). James uses the same passage to indicate that Abraham was justified by works and not by faith alone (2:23; for context, see vv. 18–25). (2) Acts 13:33 has Paul use Psalm 2:7bc in Piscidia Antioch to refer to Jesus's risen reality and Hebrews employs the same psalm for the same purpose in 1:5; 5:5. But the Synoptic Gospels utilize that psalm to refer to Jesus's experience of the Spirit's descent upon Him at the Jordan river (Mark 1:11 & pars.). (3) John 12:37–40 says that the message summarized in Isa 6:9–10 is the reason that the response to the mission of Jesus was so small; in Acts 28:25b–28 the same text suggests why Paul turned from the Jews to

Like Paul, according to First Peter's midrashic hermeneutic the OT prophets' message did not concern their contemporaries, but the Christian church in general and the recipients of First Peter in particular (1:10–12). *The writer applies to Christians all the special images of the OT originally reserved for Israel:* "You are a chosen race, a royal priesthood, a holy nation, God's own people" (2:9a; compare Exod 19:5–6a; Deut 7:6). Christians were the "no people" of Hosea who are now God's people (2:10, 23c). The church as a spiritual house offers spiritual sacrifices to God through Jesus Christ (2:5). From a popular OT proof text the writer affirms that Christ the rejected stone has become "the head of the corner" (2:4–7ab; Isa 28:16; Ps 118:22).[75]

The Epistle of Hebrews was not concerned with the salvation-history problem as such, but *sought to give OT backing for contemporary faith.* The author wanted to justify the new revelation from old covenant scriptures, and thus to present its truth as already rooted in *aspects* of Israel's experience with God.[76] Yet the writer went "to great pains to contrast the incompleteness and frailty of the old covenant consisting of human priests, earthly sanctuary, and animal sacrifices with the true form of these realities (10:1)."[77]

Hebrews regarded the "law" as only the ceremonial law that failed to achieve expiation and sanctification. These goals are only attained through the perfect sacrifice of Christ, and in this sense the old law was but a shadow of the good things to come, not the actual reality (10:1). Because of their imperfection, the old obsolete arrangements were pointers to Christ's true atonement.[78] "Just why all this prefiguration of Christ's deed of salvation, which no one in the time before Christ could understand, should have been instituted at all, it would probably be fruitless to ask the author in his satisfaction over his interpretation."[79]

---

the Gentiles; and in Mark 4:11–12 and pars. it explains why Jesus taught in the intentionally cryptic form of parables. The two NT texts just listed explain responses in the face of disappointment, but do not refer to the same actor (same source, 96–97). The third understanding of the Isaiah text is said to explain a strategy *that determined* a negative response to Jesus, which considerably differs from the other readings of the Isaiah text, and is unlikely to be the reason that Jesus chose to speak in parables.

75. Childs, *Biblical Theology OT/NT*, 300. See sec. 10.

76. Campenhausen, *Formation/Christian Bible*, 69. The Epistle to the Hebrews's midrashic interpretive methods are similar to Paul's. Likely reading Ps 8 in Septuagint form, Heb 2:5–9 regarded the description of man's being made slightly lower than the angels as a description of Christ's incarnation, humiliation, and promise to put everything in subjection to Himself. Again, the writer described the figure of Melchizedek (5:6; 6:20; 7) by combining Ps 110 with Gen 14 to affirm that God through Christ brought salvation through a heavenly priest after the order of Melchizedek apart from the weak and imperfect law of Moses (7:19). More accurately, Hebrews understood Jeremiah's prophecy of the new covenant (31:31–34) as fulfilled by the Mediator who rendered the old covenant obsolete (8:8–13). Finally Hebrews rehearses the history of Israel to show examples of the faith of those who "suffered abuse for Christ" (11:26) and "endured as seeing him who is invisible" (11:27) (Childs, *Biblical Theology OT/NT*, 311).

77. Childs, *Biblical Theology OT/NT*, 310.

78. Campenhausen, *Formation/Christian Bible*, 68.

79. Ibid., 69.

7. New Testament Pesher "Translations" of Old Testament Texts as Sub-type of Midrashic Method

In the NT period both Jews and Christians used interpretive methods that read meaning into individual words, phrases or sentences, *though pesher was often more allegory-like than regular midrash*. For example, the relevance of the Zechariah prophecy to Matt 27:3-10 is a puzzle to be deciphered: In Zechariah 11 the shepherd fails and is rejected by the flock, and 30 shekels was his wage/price. Analogously, Israel rejected the Messiah and He was betrayed for 30 pieces of silver.[80] Because the Gospel writer decided that the story concerning Judas fulfilled the Zechariah prophecy, conflicting details between the prediction and fulfillment were ignored.

In agreement with the regular Christian use of midrashic method, the pesher/targumic type also *added words to old covenant quotations to provide Christocentric meaning*. The Dead Sea scrolls of Qumran well exhibit this tendency, as does Romans 10:6-9 and Hebrews 10:5-10, but I will discuss only the first text. Romans 10:6-9 is an interpretation of Deuteronomy 30:12-14, each verse being a very free "translation"[81] followed by a pesher explanation that drastically changes the meaning "The righteousness based on faith says, Do not say in your heart, 'Who will ascend unto heaven?' (that is, to bring Christ down) or 'Who will descend into the abyss?' (that is, to bring Christ up from the dead.) But what does it say? The word is near you, on your lips and in your heart (that is, the word of faith which we preach); because, if you confess with your lips that Jesus is Lord and believe in your heart that God raised him from the dead, you will be saved." Against this OT usage, the Deuteronomy passage made no reference to "the righteousness based on faith," but indicated that God's commandment is what is near, in the heart and on the lips. Since Paul believed in reconciliation through God's grace in Christ, and not by the law, he made that substitution, and went on to interject references to the Son's incarnation, resurrection and the preaching of this faith that leads to salvation. What Paul affirmed completely conflicts with the Deuteronomy 30:12-14 text he was "interpreting."

How conflicting the above Pesher "interpretation" is can be seen not only by comparing the OT and NT texts, but also by examining Paul's preceding verse. In Romans 10:5 Paul recognizes what Moses says in Deuteronomy 30:11-14: "Moses writes that the [person] who practices the righteousness which is based on the law shall live by it."[82] But Paul then proceeds to interpret away that text's meaning, as we have seen in the previous paragraph. Christians can well agree with the point Paul is making, but should not agree with the way he has used Deuteronomy 30:12-14 to make his point.

---

80. Dunn, *Unity/Diversity*, 95-96.
81. Ibid., 88.
82. Deut 30:11 even says: "For this commandment which I command you this day is not too hard for you, neither is it far off."

8. Direct Allegorizing

Though pesher and even regular midrash are allegory-like, the NT occasionally emphasizes more explicit allegory. Though arguments from prophecy or even typology (next sec.) were thought to discover a meaning at first hidden or a deeper meaning, allegory starts from the supposition that texts have two or more meanings, and claims that the immediate sense hides the true significance. With allegory even individual words are regarded as having hidden meanings. For example, the sower who goes out to sow is the proclaimer of the Word of God (Mark 4:14). Paul allegorizes when in First Corinthians 5:6–8 he understands old leaven as an image of malice and evil.[83] In Galatians 4:21–31 the apostle says that the OT text he quotes (Gen 16) must be understood allegorically (v. 24a), with Isaac, representing the believers in Christ who inherit salvation, and Ishmael depicting those who do not believe and are cast out. Though First Corinthians 10:1–4 recognizes a typological correspondence between the situations of the Israelites in the wilderness and the Corinthian Christians, it has allegorical features: the passage through the Red Sea is regarded as an allegory of baptism into Christ; manna from heaven and water from the rock are allegories of Christian's spiritual sustenance, with the rock as an allegory for Christ.[84]

I do not think Paul is allegorizing when he infers from the prohibition against muzzling an ox treading a threshing floor that preachers are entitled to earn their living from their preaching (1 Cor 9:8–10). This last example seems more like a far-fetched analogy, especially in view of the preceding discussion that includes the insistence that Paul and his fellow workers are entitled to receive food and drink (1 Cor 9:4).

From this discussion we can see that the line between pesher and allegory and even between midrash and allegory is thin: All of these methods conflict with either an Antiochene or Protestant plain reading of texts.

9. Typology

Typology looks for possible *parallels* and *analogies* between ideas, descriptions, events, persons, institutions, or patterns when comparing integrally connected periods of history, though the connection need not match exactly. For Paul some aspects of what the OT records are "typical" of what is happening in these last days (1 Cor 10:11). With this method we do not interpret words or sayings as predictions or promises, but as *prefigurations* of future fulfillments now dawning. Today's Bible readers may agree with many of the points where the NT finds connecting parallels with the OT, but may also find additional ones not explicitly noted in the NT but well-reflected there. We will examine both kinds.

---

83. Gunneweg, *Understanding OT*, 32–33.
84. Dunn, *Unity/Diversity*, 90.

Between the Old and New Testaments, a general and yet obvious "structural analogy" consists in the interconnection of revelation by *word* and *event* that characterize both Testaments, in contrast with all forms of mythological speculation that sacralize the past, rather than pointing toward the future.[85] "Within the orbit of the word of God addressed to Israel there are constant occurrences—promises, calls, acts of . . . judgment and guidance, of comfort and trial—which are absolutely without analogy in the religions and cultures of Israel's environment, but which correspond to the saving events of the New Testament."[86]

Another general but pervasive structural parallel between the Testaments concerns both God and Her way of disclosing Herself.[87] The NT depicts deep *hiddenness on God's part*, since in Her self-manifestation She divested Herself of Her power and glory. God's concealedness is also much emphasized in the OT, especially by the prophets. "Truly, you are a God who hides himself O God of Israel, the Savior" (Isa 45:15 NRSV). A range of extremely bold similes applied to God imply divine hiddenness: "Jahweh, the unsuccessful lover (Isa 5:1–7), Jahweh, the barber (Isa 7:20), Jahweh, the rock of stumbling for Israel (Isa 8:14), Jahweh, rottenness for Israel (Hos 5:12), Jahweh, the adoptive father of an adulterous foundling (Ezek 16:4–14), Jahweh, who searches the houses of Jerusalem with a lamp (Zeph 1:12)."[88]

The story of Joseph—his brothers' conspiracy against him and the hidden and mysterious way in which God used these events for His own good purpose—points beyond. The key verse in the story is Joseph's words, "You meant evil against me; but God meant it for good" (Gen 50:20). The theological reach of these words only becomes clear with their NT fulfillment in Christ's passion, that went far beyond the thought-world of the Joseph story, but parallels what occurred there and its interpretation.

With some OT descriptions of the calls and failures of charismatic leaders (Gideon, Samson, and Saul) we are dealing with literary compositions that show a typological trend, callings followed by speedy failures of the persons called. Such stories end with the reader feeling that, since Yahweh had so far been unable to find a suitable instrument, the commission remained unfulfilled until the coming of Christ.[89]

The people of Israel expected to realize rest in the promised land, but did not truly achieve it. Because after Israel had entered that land she forgot Yahweh and clung to the Baals, she had yet to come to the rest and inheritance that God willed to give (Deut 12:9). Without endorsing the "holy war" conquest tradition, the NT points to the eschatological fulfillment of the hope of sharing in God's Sabbath rest, which Israel

---

85. Radical openness to the future to be released by God is commonly reflected in both Testaments (Bultmann, *Primitive Christianity*, 183–86). In the OT we see this in the preaching of the prophets, but also in the Genesis creation stories that look to the historical future of God's saving action with Israel (Rad, *OT Theology*, 2:361).

86. Rad, *OT Theology*, 2:363.

87. See the next sec. and chap. 18, secs. 4–5, 7.

88. Rad, *OT Theology*, 2:375.

89. Ibid., 372, 369–70, 372–73.

had hoped to find in the promised land (Heb 11:13–16). Though this hope has been considerably realized through Christ, such OT hope had previously only been greeted from afar (Heb 11:13).

The main NT typological example is Paul's Adam Christology, where Adam is juxtaposed with Christ, who far surpassed him. Though accentuating the contrast, Paul nevertheless insisted that Adam, who represents us who are sinful and finite, can be usefully compared with Christ, who overcame these problems. In this way Paul found it instructive and edifying to compare Adam with Christ (Rom 5:12–14).

Paul also emphasized texts about Abraham and interpreted him as a believer to whom faith was reckoned as righteousness (Rom 4:3; Gal 3:6). Because Paul ignored most of OT history[90] his faith did not connect to a continuous OT salvation history. For Paul mere historical continuity between Abraham and the Jews (or anyone else) is spiritually and theologically irrelevant (Rom 4:13–25; 9:6–8; Gal 3:6–9).[91]

In Hebrews 3:7—4:13 an important typological correspondence is highlighted between Israel's wandering in the desert and the existence of the Christian community. Another NT employment of typology is where First Peter compares Noah and those in the ark with those being saved, as symbolized by water baptism (3:18–21).

10. Typology Illustrated: God's Servant Humiliated and Exalted (Isaiah 52:13–15; 53:1–12)[92]

This text is one of the most contested in the OT and is notoriously difficult to understand, yet it seems to many Christians to be one of the most important OT passages. Because it is seen as so important, piety may drive some to minimize the interpretive problems—but such dishonesty is no Christian virtue. We should also remember that everything essential that Christians need to believe pertaining to the meaning of Christ's life, death, and resurrection is well stated in the NT. Concerning reconciliation the NT affirms, for example, that "God shows His love for us in that while we were yet sinners Christ died for us" (Rom 5:8). We love because in and through Christ— God first loved us (1 John 4:19). Perhaps our suffering servant passage can provide Christians with poetic expressions that still inspire concerning the costly sacrifice of Christ for our salvation. This text is thus useful in this typological way, but is not the basis of our knowledge of Christ.

A lot of misunderstanding of this passage may occur because of a failure to appreciate the presence of multiple metaphors. "So often in Hebrew poetry (cf., e.g., Ps 23) the metaphors change rapidly, without explanation, and we are given an

---

90. See n23 where those omissions are stated.

91. Gunneweg, *Understanding OT*, 23, 214.

92. For a more general review of this author's writings, see the material on Second Isaiah in sec. 4 above.

impressionistic picture rather than an exact description."[93] In addition to metaphor imprecisions, our text seems intentionally cryptic. The more one studies this passage the more uncertain the suffering servant reference may become.

Let us remind ourselves of a few things. This poem describes an anonymous suffering servant who existed in Second Isaiah's time or previously. What is said in our passage is described in the past tense and stated nearly six centuries before Christ's death and resurrection. If you wish to regard this text as a direct prophecy of Christ you will need to regard past tense language as somehow intended to predict the future. I must confess that I take the language in a more conventional sense and regard the description as referring to what the author believed had already transpired. I do not see a direct prediction of Christ, but parallels or analogies that may help us to ponder the Christ event. Though the text seems to describe a past happening, Christians cannot hear these words without recognizing similarities between some—but only some—of what the author says of the suffering servant and what we believe concerning the Suffering Servant, Jesus Christ.

To whom might the passage refer? That's hard to say since the author gives conflicting answers. Earlier he seems to identify the servant with Israel (see 41:8–10; 42:1–9). However, just a few chapters before our texts he writes critically of Israel (49:14–15; 50:1–2a; 51:12–13). In 49:1–6 he refers to an individual (whom he confusingly calls "Israel") who was formed in the womb to bring the people of Israel back to the Lord. Along this later line, Second Isaiah writes that he no longer uses the servant title to refer to Israel as a nation, but has transferred that ascription to himself (49:3). Additional evidence against Israel as the suffering servant is that the poem says that a single individual was involved, though one entrusted with bearing sin and thereby setting people in right relationship with God (53:11d, 12ef). But the passage also says that the suffering servant died, an unlikely statement concerning Israel, but an impossible reference to the one doing the writing! *The author seems to wish to keep us puzzled.*

Since Second Isaiah was hoping for a new act of God that he figuratively called a New Exodus, he may have utilized an idealized notion of Moses. Moses is so regarded in Deuteronomy, being described as the servant of God who acted as a mediator between God and Israel and who died vicariously for the sins of his people, even absorbing God's anger against Israel (3:23–29; 4:21; 9:9, 18–21, 25–29). The Pentateuch, where theological nuances are very carefully indicated, shows Moses as the only person in Israel who was completely set apart to converse with God, and to be the great intercessor, who with representative suffering died alone outside the promised land.[94] Against the accuracy of the pentateuchal characterization, we know

---

93. Ackroyd, "Isaiah," 364. Within the first seven verses of Isa 53 the metaphors speak of griefs and sickness, sorrow and pain (v. 4ab), transgressions and iniquities (v. 5ab). Being oppressed and afflicted, the suffering servant is compared to a lamb being led to slaughter and a sheep being sheared (v. 7).

94. Rad, *OT Theology*, 2:260–61, 370.

that Moses was far from perfect, even having murdered someone. Though he never saw the promised land, and in that sense suffered, he did not die disgraced and disfigured. A Deuteronomic and pentateuchal idealized version of Moses conflicts with the "Moses of history." However it is with Moses's candidacy, Christians cannot agree that Moses or another sinner (such as Isaiah himself) or sinners (in the case of Israel) could have provided the needed atonement.

From Second Isaiah's words we are left with little more than a claim concerning an anonymous agent of atonement, which is little more than an atonement idea. For the only corroboration for the agent's existence or capacity to provide atonement is Second Isaiah's opinion. Atonement ideas apart from an event that convincingly establishes their reality are little more than wishful thoughts.

If reconciliation is really the once-and-for-all accomplishment in Christ that the NT claims, it is also not comparable to repeated acts of "atonement," as, for example, were thought to occur on the yearly Day of Atonement (Lev 16). From the perspective of Christ's atonement these seem merely to illustrate the general idea that the Holy God is willing to have dealings with penitent sinners. Again, a mere wishful thought unless there were action from God's side.

Furthermore, even if we were willing to forget that the text refers to an event from the past, Jesus does not provide a perfect fulfillment of our text's prediction. Contrary to a possible implication of the Isaiah text, maximal suffering does not equal atonement. Though Jesus Christ suffered much, many people may have suffered as much or more, as, for example, people who have had lifelong pain or even the suffering servant to whom Second Isaiah pointed. What makes the cross of Christ special is due to the One who suffered and died there, who, by God's choosing and Jesus's faithfulness, was alone qualified to be the Mediator to enact reconciliation.

Where are possible additional conflicts between the suffering servant text and the NT witness to Jesus Christ? The NT says that Christ as our representative stood in our place and in that sense bore our sin. It does not say that the Father punished the Son as the Father's required means for enabling reconciliation to occur, which is what we get if we use the suffering servant passage as the direct source for understanding reconciliation in Christ. Our OT text indeed says that an anonymous suffering servant centuries before Christ was "smitten by God," (53:4d), was "chastised" by Him (53:5c), and was "stricken for the transgressions of my people" (53:8d). It says unequivocally, "it was the Lord's will to bruise him" (53:10a). The only NT reconciliation text influenced by our OT passage seems to be First Peter 2:24–25, and that only slightly. The latter says that "by his wounds [we] have been healed," but does not talk of God's punishing the Son thereby. That passage probably attests only the costly love of God seen in Christ's willingness to suffer and die on our behalf.

Luther and Calvin unfortunately seem to have built an aspect of their atonement understanding directly on Isaiah 53, and taught that the Father imposed a representative punishment on the Son, thereby enabling the Father to forgive. Though I much respect Luther and Calvin, here their logic escapes me. Why would God need to punish Jesus in order to be able to reconcile us to Himself? The NT says nothing of the sort, though our OT passage could be used to contribute to something similar were we to apply it directly to the Christ event. Against such application, the NT affirms that from beginning to end God is the willing source of our salvation. As Paul insisted in Second Corinthians 5:18, reconciliation is directly from God, who through Christ reconciled us to Himself. Colossians 1:19–20 speaks similarly (cf. Eph 2:4–6). The NT attests the unity between the Father and Son, indicates that the entire Godhead is the source of salvation, and implies that the triune God suffered at Calvary. Thus any suffering endured by the Son was no punishment by the Father, unless we wish to argue that God was punishing Himself.

God did not have to be punitively satisfied in order to forgive, for She willed our redemption from all eternity. What happened with the substitution of Christ in our place was that Christ as God incarnate represented God in showing Her love, and Christ as truly human represented us before God, offering obedience on our behalf. The covenant was thereby fulfilled on both sides. God was actively involved in all of this and thereby laid Her own wrath aside.

In the face of such great, but hidden disclosure of divine love, we can dare to recognize how far we have gone astray (Isa 53:6a) and that everyone has turned to their own way (6b). Through God in Christ we experience the love that provides the security to see ourselves truthfully.

Anselm of Canterbury had developed an atonement understanding in the Middle Ages that (like Luther and Calvin) seems directly dependent upon Isaiah 53. Taking the feudal culture of his day too seriously, with its Big Man notions, he taught that God's honor first had to be satisfied before He could forgive. Anselm thought that all God could require of anyone was a life of sinless obedience, but Christ by His suffering went beyond God's requirement (supererogation). Jesus thereby established heavenly credit for us, and enabled the holy and just God to forgive us. Jesus's suffering and painful dying satisfied the reluctant God's honor, so that He was willing to be reconciled to us. According to this scheme God needed to be reconciled to us, not just us to God. Anselm's unhappy philosophical speculation much contrasts with the NT's confidence that the God of love (1 John 4:16b) is the source of reconciliation.

With these various critical comparisons between the OT servant passages and the NT witness, my more general insistence has been that we must use the OT with the selectivity that comes from our understanding of Jesus Christ as attested in the NT. Certainly the OT helps us to read the NT, and many times the two Testaments much agree[95]—but where the OT exhibits conflicting ideas we generally must side with the NT. I don't suppose many Christians keep kosher kitchens and that for the good reason that Jesus and Paul taught us to disregard such food laws because obedience to God is not concerned with such trivialities. When Jesus said that what goes

---

95. For example, see sec. 11.

into the mouth does not matter (Mark 7:15a; Matt 15:11), He rejected chapter after chapter of such OT regulations. Certainly Jesus was a Jew—but He was not uncritical of His Jewish heritage.

Instead of supposing that we should contrive prophecies concerning Christ where they do not exist—let us turn things around and start from the accomplished reconciliation in Christ. From such a perspective we can, for example, consider if what is said of an anonymous suffering servant may provide some parallel descriptions that help us to communicate concerning Calvary. It is interesting to note that according to Acts 8, when the Ethiopian eunuch asked about the identity of the suffering servant of our OT text, Philip did not say that Isaiah had predicted Christ. Rather, beginning with the OT scriptures he told the eunuch "the good news of Jesus" (Acts 8:35). What we may infer from Philip's response may be only that the description of the unknown suffering servant can shed light upon the meaning of Jesus's life, death, and resurrection. The church generally interpreted the OT suffering servant poem by drawing a parallel between the servant and Jesus's passion and death, not by seeing prophecy as fulfilled.[96]

To summarize to this point: Since our passage referred to the past, it did not likely intend to be a direct prophecy, but it nevertheless provides some useful comparisons with the Christ event, some negative, but most positive. We should not expect historical analogies to exactly match, and must reserve the right to disagree with even exact correspondences where those dishonor God's revelation in Jesus Christ—as, for example, Second Isaiah's seeming claim that an anonymous suffering servant previously established the needed atonement. As the NT book of Hebrews insists, the OT provides but shadows of what was realized in Jesus Christ (8:5a; 10:1).

Let us then briefly examine some of the remaining aspects of the suffering servant passage, noticing that *some of its poetic language beautifully articulates what God has enacted in Christ. Looking back from the Christ event, we are thus bold to take some of the words that in Second Isaiah's context already applied to the past and let them illumine the Christ event.* The preliminary verses in 52:13–15 depict God as speaking from the standpoint of His prior awareness that a suffering servant would act wisely and lead to the well-being of all. In NT terms, God's decision to share His life with a human creation and to come forth in the Son to call us to Himself was the guarantee of final victory. In and through the obedient Son, God remained faithful to that decision all the way to Calvary and beyond.

Chapter 53 provides testimony concerning a suffering servant from those who to their amazement have come to believe in God through him. Similarly, the NT "community hardly knew how it had come to believe, it was still so close to its own error and to its lack of understanding of what happened with the servant of God." He was despised, and they had esteemed him not (53:3d). Now they can only look back and marvel—about him, about themselves, and about others! "As contemporaries they

---

96. Childs, *Isaiah*, 423.

had not been equal to the task; no one watched with him. . . . In his solitude he was not even accompanied by the faith of his intimates."[97]

"Surely he has born our griefs and carried our sorrows" (v. 4a). "But he was wounded for our transgressions, he was bruised for our iniquities . . . and with his stripes we are healed" (v. 5abd). The servant suffered because of our sin. He was rejected, tortured, disfigured, and painfully killed because we humans so commonly turn away from God's disturbing grace and guiding power when God comes near. Yet well-being came to us because of who the Son was and what His redemptive life, death and resurrection mean. And as was said of Isaiah's suffering servant—Christ suffered much. We can even say that redemptive humiliation was and is willed by God. Our Eternal Mother chose the extraordinary humiliation of becoming a human being, and then the further extraordinary humiliation of going all the way to the cross in and through Her Son. Through such means God offered Her Son in our place and thereby Herself in our place. In these ways God laid upon Christ and upon Herself the iniquity of us all (see v. 6cd).

"Who has believed what we have heard? And to whom has the arm [or power] of the Lord been revealed?" (53:1) Second Isaiah had earlier (50:10–11) said that "the response to the servant would divide the people of Israel into two groups, those who believe and those who oppose."[98] The NT similarly says that some people will get the message concerning Christ and some will not.[99] Why this division occurs is baffling, since the God of power and love wills the salvation of all; nevertheless, at least for now the division is real.

Though many were only shocked by the apparent tragedy of the Servant-Son's dying, some were enabled to see beneath the surface and perceive God's gracious action amid the hiddenness of what had occurred (52:15). Though they had stood by and done nothing to help while the servant suffered and died, they are now overwhelmed with gratitude for the victory gained through him, and are thereby infused with power to rededicate their lives to God.

A cascade of OT servant images shed light: Though he was like a young plant that grew up straight, in the end people could not bear to look at his distorted form. At that point he indeed "had no form or comeliness that we should look at him, and no beauty that we should desire him. He was despised and rejected by people; a man of sorrows and acquainted with grief; and as one from whom people hide their faces he was despised, and we esteemed him not" (53:2c–3). It must have also been like that at Calvary.

The suffering Servant-Son also faced an unjust trial. "By oppression and judgment he was taken away" (v. 8a). "Although he had done no violence, and there was no deceit in his mouth" (v. 9cd), he was nevertheless condemned and killed. "He was cut

---

97. Rad, *Biblical Interpretations*, 88–89.

98. Childs, *Isaiah*, 414.

99. Matt 13:10–15, quoting Isa 6:9–10. For the same point, without the quotation from Isaiah, see Mark 4:10–12; Luke 8:9–10.

off from the land of the living, stricken for the transgressions of my people" (v. 8cd). The innocent sufferer willingly submitted to his destiny. "He was oppressed and he was afflicted, yet he opened not his mouth" (v. 7ab).

The NT somewhat corrects such Isaiahan language in the case of Christ, since (according to Mark 14:62) He did confess His authority at the Sanhedrin trial and said a few words at the civil trial, but not to find a way of escape. "He bore his sufferings differently from the way in which others suffer. He did not perish in proud resistance.... There was . . . a readiness, an inmost acquiescence in his suffering ([Isa] 53:7). Our concepts of activity or passivity fail us in the face of this event: 'It was a strange battle, when death and life wrestled.'"[100] This is what faith in retrospect can repeat: here God's judgment upon us is taken seriously, and Her holiness is exhibited. In the man of sorrows who suffered and died—though innocent (v. 9bc)—the true picture of faithful humanity is also held before us. We perceive the higher way to which God calls us—and our sin is thereby exposed. What we deserve falls upon Christ and upon God—that we might be reconciled.

Contrary to the Isaiah text, Christians must insist that it was Christ and no other human who made the offering for sin (v. 10c) and bore our iniquity (v. 11e). Through Christ the Righteous Servant, God overcame our guilt, accounted us righteous (v. 11cd) and thereby set us back in right relation with Her.

Part B

11. Ethical Similarities between Testaments

There are some theological and moral conceptions in which the NT much agrees with the OT and much depends on it. Many chapters of this work refer to these, but I hope to deal with these primarily when discussing specific doctrines in the future. Here I concentrate on some ethical aspects.

The NT morally presumes the *decalogue or ten commandments* (Exod 20:2-17; Deut 5:6-21),[101] plus other related OT moral counsel. The decalogue has received a central place in the disclosure of God purportedly revealed to Moses at Mount Sinai.[102]

---

100. Rad, *Biblical Interpretations*, 90.

101. All versions of the ten commandments exhibit some variations, with no literal doublet. Intermixed with other moral counsel, it has even been handed down in a shortened form in Lev 19:3-4, 11-12. That version seems to have been used with children, since v. 3 begins with the demand of respect for the parents, in which the mother is mentioned first! (Vriezen, *OT Theology*, 336)

102. William Johnstone summarizes some interpretations of the ten commandments. That two main versions are preserved with notable diversity (as, for example, concerning the reason for observing the Sabbath) suggests that a considerable history of development lies behind the two. Though these (especially Deuteronomy) claim that God spoke directly, even wrote on two tablets with Her finger (Deut 9:10), only the first two are in the first person. Commandments 3-5 communicate by someone speaking on God's behalf. Unlike the first and second, commandments 6-10, though direct statements, do not refer to God. *Such oddities suggest that the two texts are composites, secondary*

The Exodus version of the ten commandments is prefaced by a self-revelation formula in verse 2: "'I am the Lord your God, who brought you out of the land of Egypt, out of the house of bondage.'"[103] The laws quoted carry the authority of Israel's Savior, whose lordship involves moral claims.

The first commandment recognizes Yahweh as the exclusive basis for all spiritual and moral life in Israel: "'You shall have no other gods before me'" (Exod 20:3; Deut 5:7). Though theoretical monotheism developed only in the later OT period, the practical monotheism here exhibited, though not denying the existence of other gods, claims that the Lord alone has the right to complete allegiance, which is *morally* more monotheistic than forms of mere theoretical monotheism.

As for the second commandment (Exod 20:4–6; Deut 5:8–10): Because God alone is entitled to Israel's allegiance (God's "jealousy"), She will not share Her lordship with anything in this world. The prohibition against images opposes the belief that God's presence in Israel could be guaranteed by physical representation and thereby manipulated and controlled, thus weakening Her lordship. That God would punish to the third and fourth generations exhibits a primitive notion of collective guilt, corrected by the OT itself (Ezek 18:20).

The third commandment implies that because God's holiness was disclosed when She revealed Herself as Yahweh/Lord (Exod 3:14–15)—Her name must not be used unworthily, disrespectfully, or for manipulative purposes (Exod 20:7; Deut 5:11).

The fourth commandment (Exod 20:8–11; Deut 5:12–15) proclaims the holiness of the seventh day, which in Deuteronomy is understood as a day of rest from labor in thankfulness for redemption from Egypt. In contrast, in Exodus the day is described as sanctified at creation. The Sabbath is not merely one day, but according to the principle of the part for the total, the whole week is thereby to be dedicated to Yahweh. The Sabbath commandment is of great social importance because it applies to all,[104] even working animals.

The fifth commandment and the first of the so-called second table of the commandments (Exod 20:12–17 and Deut 5:16–21) concerns the demand to honor one's

---

compilations from diverse sources. Other evidence for such a conclusion is that the different commandments exhibit much variety. Some are short, some long; eight are negative, two positive; some offer explanations, inducements, or threats; others are mere prohibitions.

Prophets, priests, and wise men may all have had an influence in shaping the two versions. If this is so, not everything in these series reaches back to a single event from the remote past. What we now have to a considerable extent reflects a long and complex three-fold tradition from within Israelite theology. Because of some aspects of content, many scholars believe that the final editing of these commandments occurred only after the exile (Johnstone, "Ten Commandments," 453–56).

103. See the more expansive and different preface in Deut 5:1–5, but notice that the Exodus preface is in Deuteronomy found with the fourth commandment: "You shall remember that you were a servant in the land of Egypt, and the Lord your God brought you out thence with a mighty hand and an outstretched arm; therefore the Lord your God commanded you to keep the Sabbath day" (5:15).

104. Vriezen, *OT Theology*, 334. Early Christians moved the day of worship to the first of the week, since that was said to be the day of Jesus's resurrection. But until Constantine it was a regular working day.

parents, which implies the willingness to care for them in their old age. Since married daughters were joined to their husbands' families, caring for one's parents in old age would at that time have fallen upon the sons and their spouses.

The sixth commandment is against murder, the seventh against adultery (having sexual intercourse with a married woman), and the eighth against stealing. The ninth requires absolute truthfulness in human relationships.

The tenth forbids the inner sin that is prior to the above sins of stealing and committing adultery, namely, coveting what belongs to another. "'You shall not covet your neighbor's house; you shall not covet your neighbor's wife, or his manservant, or his maidservant,[105] or his ox, or his ass, or anything that is your neighbor's'" (Exod 20:17; see Deut 5:21).

The great importance of the decalogue is that it attempts to place all spheres of life under the rule of Yahweh, though, as Jesus and Paul emphasized, moral obligation cannot be encompassed within ten or multiple commandments. The extent to which the ten commandments form the basis of moral thought in Israel is indicated by Nathan's appearance before David after his adultery with Bathsheba, and David's repentant response to Nathan's reprimand (2 Sam 12:13).

The teaching of the prophets frequently makes use of partial summaries from the decalogue: "'Behold, you trust in deceptive words to no avail. Will you steal, murder, commit adultery, swear falsely, burn incense to Baal, and go after other gods that you have not known, and then come and stand before me in this house, which is called by my name, and say, "We are delivered!"—only to go on doing all these abominations?'" (Jer 7:8–10) "There is no faithfulness or kindness and no knowledge of God in the land; there is swearing, lying, killing, stealing, and committing adultery; they break all bounds and murder follows murder" (Hos 4:1d–2c).

Besides the two decalogue summaries of moral requirements and probably in imitation of them are several similar series of rules of life. The "mirror for judges" in Exodus 23, and the series of ethical and social commandments in Leviticus 19 are fine examples, particularly the Leviticus series, which concludes with the commandment the final part of which occupies a central position in the NT: "'You shall not hate your brother in your heart, but you shall reason with your neighbor, lest you bear sin because of him. You shall not take vengeance or bear any grudge against the sons of your own people, but you shall love your neighbor as yourself: I am the Lord'" (vv.

---

105. Though this commandment classifies women and workers as property (Exod 20:17), the fifth seems to imply marital equality: "Honor your father and mother . . ." (Exod 20:12a; Deut 5:16a). In line with the commandment against covetousness, Jesus rethought the one against adultery to include the thought prior to the adulterous act. It is doubtful that he was seeking to stifle the appreciation of beauty, but was condemning *the thought that would eventuate in the adulterous act if the opportunity arose*. "'You have heard it said, "You shall not commit adultery." But I say to you that everyone who looks at a woman lustfully has already committed adultery with her in his heart'" (Matt 5:27–28).

17–18).¹⁰⁶ Though the NT's teaching concerning love of neighbor¹⁰⁷ is not restricted as in the OT, it is not as high an expression of ethical thought as the further command to love even one's enemies (Matt 5:44; Luke 6:27, 35a).

Leviticus 19 incorporates some of the ten commandments into other equally important moral injunctions, with the much repeated motivational reminder: "I am the Lord your God." "And the Lord said to Moses, 'Say to all the congregation of the people of Israel, You shall be holy; for I the Lord your God am holy'" (vv. 1–2). From being holy and recognizing God's lordship, verses 3–4 expect some ten commandment results: revering father and mother and keeping Sabbaths, turning away from idols and not making molten gods. These fine commandments are succeeded by four verses of sacrificial regulations!

The following are additional Leviticus 19 results of honoring God's insistence that He alone is the Lord: A requirement allowing the gleaning of crops to help the poor (vv. 9–10), an injunction primarily concerning truthful speech (vv. 11–12), a stipulation that hired workers be paid promptly and that the handicapped be treated kindly (vv. 13–14). Justice is so important that judges are not only not to defer to the rich, but are not even to be partial to the poor, and no one is to slander their neighbors or threaten their lives (vv. 15–16). Judgments are to be fair, as are measurements, for God is not only the Lord, but the gracious one who brought deliverance from Egypt (vv. 35–37).¹⁰⁸

12. New Testament's Setting Aside or Abandoning Many Old Testament Traditions

Since some biblical teachings conflict with Christian Faith as determined by core NT teachings, refusing to criticize such teachings weakens faith and moral life. It is unfortunate that many Christians think it pious to claim to believe everything in the Bible, though, of course, no one can without contradicting oneself or using dubious interpretive methods.

---

106. Vriezen, *OT Theology*, 334–35. In the context of the immediate preceding verses that imply that one is free to bear grudges and to take revenge against non-Israelites, Leviticus's love of neighbor teaching seems limited to Israelites or to those strangers who lived permanently in Israel. (For the latter, see vv. 33–34 and see the more comprehensive discussion in sec. 13 below.) The NT use of the Leviticus 19:18b teaching about love of neighbor has no restriction as to who is to be treated as neighbor, nor does the parable of the Good Samaritan (Luke 10:29–37), nor the rest of the NT.

Unfortunately the Lev 19 moral commands just quoted are followed by regulations that were to be regarded as of equal importance: not letting cattle interbreed, not sowing a field with two kinds of seeds, not possessing a garment composed of two kinds of materials (v. 19), and not eating any flesh with blood in it (v. 26a). The second half of the next injunction could only apply to men: "'You shall not round off the hair on your temples or mar the edges of your beard'" (v. 27).

107. Matt 19:19; 22:39; Mark 12:31, 33; Luke 10:27b.

108. Though the book of Proverbs—much influenced by national and international popular wisdom—contains middle-class platitudes of dubious value, it also speaks of the fear of the Lord, warns against seductive women (why not seductive men?), emphasizes justice, instills reverence for one's parents, and warns against covetousness (Vriezen, *OT Theology*, 335–36).

Jesus set his own understanding of God's will over against much OT law. We should not base our view of Jesus's attitude to the authority of OT traditions on passages like John 10:35 ("'scripture cannot be broken'") and Matthew 5:17–18. With the latter text the position seems cut and dried: Not an iota or dot is to pass from the law until all has been accomplished. These extreme statements conflict with Jesus practice. Whatever "accomplish" and "fulfill" might mean, it seems that Matthew, no less than Mark, wants to present Jesus not only as interpreting the law, but as relativizing it by the higher norm of self-giving love. As in Mark, so in Matthew, loving your neighbor as yourself (Lev 19:18b) provides the Gospel writers with a governing principle by which other laws are to be evaluated. Mark cites this passage in only one place (12:31a, 33c), whereas Matthew quotes it in two (19:19b; 22:39),[109] and, like Luke (6:27a), refers to loving even one's enemies (5:44).

According to Matthew 5:21–48 Jesus was the determinative interpreter of the law, as when He expanded the sixth commandment against murder (5:21–23) and seventh against adultery (5:27–30).[110] In other Sermon on the Mount passages He annulled aspects of the law. In Matthew 5:33–37 in effect He abolished regulations about swearing[111] and in 5:38–42 did the same concerning the eye for an eye teaching.[112] In Matthew 19:3–9 (see also Mark 10:2–9) He repealed the Mosaic permission for divorce (Deut 24:1–4). And in 15:1–20 (see also Mark 7:1–23). He rejected pharisaic purity laws and repudiated the very basis of food laws (Mark 7:18b–19). His open table fellowship with the ritually unclean had the same effect. Because of such teachings and behavior pharisaic opposition arose.[113]

Though Jesus conserved much He evidenced considerable freedom. Similarly a *liberal—conservative* takes a caring and constructive attitude toward tradition, but exhibits much freedom with reference to traditional understandings. In contrast an *illiberal—*conservative will think that to abandon one part leads to abandoning all. What such people fail to see is that to claim to affirm inconsistencies only exhibits faulty logic and a superficial understanding of what affirmation entails.[114]

A liberal– conservative *biblical interpreter* takes a *constructive* attitude toward biblical tradition, but does not exempt the Bible from critical reflection, and thinks that only by making some distinction between essentials and non-essentials can the essentials be emphasized.

---

109. Dunn, *Living Word*, 47–48, 53.
110. See n105.
111. Lev 19:12; Num 30:2; Deut 23:21.
112. Exod 21:23–25; Lev 24:19–20; Deut 19:21.
113. Dunn, *Unity/Diversity*, 97–98.
114. Dunn, *Living Word*, 54. I have written of being liberal and conservative, whereas Dunn writes of polar choices between these. Part of the title of the book in hand is "Critical and Constructive," and Dunn proceeds similarly, but his terminological discussion about being liberal is unbalanced. Concerning the need for both emphases in all aspects of life, see chap. 8, sec. 3.

Jesus rejected some aspects of pre-OT tradition, and reinterpreted others. He distinguished between commandments, between what is important and what is unimportant, and also between essentials and non-essentials. For Jesus, the will of God was related to writings later incorporated into the OT, but He regarded God's will as reflected in only some portions of those traditions.

Consider Jesus's teaching concerning divorce. The OT allows easy divorce, but only on the part of the husband (Deut 24:1). Jesus cites different OT texts and interprets against divorce (Mark 10:2–12): Because "God made them male and female" (v. 6b, quoting Gen 1:27b), "a man shall leave his father and mother and be joined to his wife, and the two shall become one" (v. 7, quoting Gen 2:24). Then His application against divorce: "What therefore God has joined together, let not man put asunder" (Mark 10:9). That is, God wills indissoluble marriage, and divorce is but an emergency measure because of the hardness of human hearts (v. 5), and does not correspond with God's ideal.

Though Jesus sometimes made careful reference to pre-canonical scripture, its formal authority was not regarded as absolute. Here was the beginning of the distinction between letter and spirit,[115] made possible by the freedom to use some parts of scripture against other parts.

It is not surprising that Jesus rejected many pre-OT rules and regulations, for His ethical teaching and its basis differs much from what is widely taught in the OT. The ethical judgment and ethos of many parts of the OT contains a strong *eudaemonistic* element. There morally right actions are expected to bring earthly happiness and reward, and wrong behavior, earthly misery and punishment. The OT thus places much emphasis on the wealth and prosperity with which great men like Abraham and Job before and after their troubles are rewarded.

A *eudaemonistic* trait is particularly common within the wisdom literature. There the fear of evil consequences or retribution, hope of earthly reward, and the seeking of the approval of others are common motivations. Thus Proverbs often seems to suppose that riches and honor and long life are the greatest good and the highest purposes in life, though it also evidences concern for divine law and justice. Eudaemonism is found throughout the OT, as, for example, in the various promises in the opening words of Deuteronomy (among which is Israel's authorization to steal land occupied by others, 1:6–11). Notice also the motivation for following the fifth commandment—"that your days may be prolonged and that it may go well for you, in the land which the Lord your God gives you" (Deut 5:16b). The OT sanctified the earthly and material, which is why it tended to highly value prosperity and think that it is inseparable from divine blessing (see Job 42:10–17).[116] To the contrary Jesus taught

---

115. Gunneweg, *Understanding OT*, 15, 13. See chap. 7, sec. 5 for Paul's articulation of this distinction.

116. Vriezen, *OT Theology*, 341–42.

that material rewards should not be expected in this world, that riches are a danger and a temptation, and that the obedient will suffer and be persecuted,[117] as did He.

The OT emphasized the family and its cohesion, but Jesus perceived that the family is so often a threat to one's obedience to God that one has to relativize the relatives, as He certainly did, and which high church veneration of Mary fails to recognize concerning her. "And his mother and this brothers came; and standing outside they sent to him and called him. And a crowd was sitting about him; and they said to him, 'Your mother and your brothers are outside, asking for you.' And he replied, 'Who are my mother and my brothers?' And looking around on those who sat about him, he said, 'Here are my mother and my brothers! Whoever does the will of God is my brother, and sister, and mother'" (Mark 3:31–35; parallels in Matt 12:46–50; Luke 8:19–21). In spite of such warnings, Jesus clearly admonished disciples not to use religious tradition to avoid service to one's parents (Matt 15:1–9).

An instructive example of radical NT criticism of OT traditions is Stephen's attack on the temple (Acts 7, particularly vv. 44–50). It was likely inspired by Acts's claim that Jesus predicted the destruction and reconstitution of the temple (Acts 6:12–14), with Stephen having read the history of Israel's worship in the light of this saying. Using Isaiah 66:1–2, one of the few OT passages that completely denounced the temple, he argued (in contrast with Second Samuel 7:13 and numerous OT passages) that the building of the temple was a mark of Israel's apostasy from God. Stephen viewed the OT *in the light of Jesus's words and therefore quoted one part of OT tradition to justify abandoning the clear teaching of many other parts.*

Paul provides some of the clearest examples of first century Christianity that rejected and abandoned much OT tradition, particularly the dominating role of Jewish law. The law taken as a totality and easily used by sinners as a source of pride and autonomy was regarded by Paul as only a temporary "baby sitter" until the coming of faith (Gal 3:19–25). Since Christ had come, and Spirit-evoked, Christ-centered faith was possible, it had become clearer than in the OT that the law cannot provide salvation. Furthermore, Paul relativized the law as a moral guide (2 Cor 3:12–17; Eph 2:15). "In all these cases Christ and his followers evidently found themselves so at odds with the plain sense of certain key scriptural passages and themes that they had to abandon them."[118] For Christians the OT should continue to exercise authority only when critically evaluated in the light of God's disclosure in Jesus Christ.

13. Additional Examples of Specific Conflicts between Old and New Testament Convictions

The OT contains much that for good reason was not believed in nor practiced by NT Christians. For example, sacrificial and ceremonial laws were set aside by Christ's

---

117. Barr, *Holy Scripture*, 17.
118. Dunn, *Unity/Diversity*, 98.

perfect self-offering, as were rules about ritual cleanliness and uncleanliness, descriptions of the duties of the priests and of requirements affecting their support, and regulations concerning feasts and sacred occasions. Like Jesus, Paul in particular and the NT in general said that such rules and regulations have no authority for Christians.[119]

To affirm the unity of the two covenants is simplistic; one thinks, for example, of Psalm 109:6–20, 28b–29 with its implicit assumption that God is vengeful and unforgiving. A similar attitude was expressed by an embittered exile in Psalm 137:9, whose hatred of oppressors and whose desire for revenge was so extreme that he wished that someone might take opponents' babies and dash them against rocks.[120]

Holy War, Devoting the Enemy to Yahweh. Jesus told Christians to love even their enemies[121] because disciples are to be like God who is indiscriminate in His benevolence (Matt 5:44–45; Luke 6:35). Yet much of the OT says that God led Israel in holy wars against its enemies and His enemies—and fought and killed such people. Even the exodus tradition links to these notions.

Israel believed that God vehemently hated her enemies. An integral aspect of Yahweh's covenant with Israel was His supposed declaration, that if she would harken to His voice and do what He said, He would "be an enemy unto [her] enemies, and an adversary unto [her] adversaries" (Exod 23:22). The belief in "Yahweh's capacity for prolonged and violent hatred of Israel's foes is set down with unashamed emphasis, as in the traditions in the wilderness, where it is said that 'Yahweh will have war with Amalek from generation to generation' (Exod 17:16[b])."[122]

Influenced by Moab's practice, Israel slaughtered Canaanite populations because that had become part of her rules of warfare hallowed by her belief that God so commanded and by her desire to seize others' land.[123] "The book of Joshua describes the holy war of conquest and the *herem* or ban, God's supposed commanding of the butchery of the Canaanite population to the last thing that breathed. In this regard one reads of the prophet Samuel (1 Sam 15) who conveyed to Saul God's 'command

---

119. Bright, *Authority/OT*, 53. In cases of suspected adultery, should we require women to demonstrate their innocence by seeing what happens when they drink noxious potions, as Num 5:11–31 requires (same source, 54)? The requirement would be wrong for either sex, but it was obviously prejudicial that only women were singled out for this test.

120. Objections have often been raised against aspects of the historical books (for example, certain parts of the stories of Jacob and Samson), against Ps 45 on glorifying the king, and against particular writings, for example, Esther, the Song of Songs, and Ecclesiastes (Vriezen, *OT Theology*, 88).

121. Since Christians are to have no enemies, this teaching either recognizes the existence of what is forbidden, but challenges it, or means that Christians are to love even those who regard them as enemies.

122. Fosdick, *Guide/Bible*, 6, 6–7. The ascription "The Lord is a man of war; the Lord is his name" (Exod 15:3), is typical of the earliest traditions. Concerning the triumph of Joshua on the day when the sun was said to have stood still (Josh 10:13), we are told that "God fought for Israel" (Josh 10:14c). David defied Goliath, shouting, "I come to you in the name of the Lord of hosts, the God of the armies of Israel" (1 Sam 17:45b). Even the psalmist wrote, "He trains my hands for war, so that my arms can bend a bow of bronze" (18:34). Indeed, one compiler quotes from a writing that no longer exists, "the book of the Wars of the Lord" (Num 21:14a) (same source, 5–6).

123. Barr, *Biblical Faith/Natural Theology*, 217, 210.

to exterminate the Amalekites' (vs 3) and who, when Saul failed to carry this out completely, publicly rebuked him and himself hewed the Amalekite king to pieces 'before the Lord' (vs 33)."[124]

To try to avoid these issues by maintaining that biblical practices of warfare were time-bound seems to mean that, though genocidal massacre is wrong today, there was an earlier time when it was so right that God commanded it. Or, when interpretive difficulties arise one can retreat into talk of divine "mystery" and "inscrutability," or can remind oneself that as finite creatures one must live with "paradox," understood as "contradiction." Evasions of this kind are dishonest and disloyal to God. And in the twentieth and twenty-first centuries we have seen horrifying examples of genocide.[125] "The present situation in the Middle East demonstrates the results that follow when ancient ideologies of war, people, and land are allowed to survive and grow without adequate ethical evaluation."[126]

OT teachings concerning a warrior god cannot be reconciled with the NT's understanding of God. If the teaching and practice of our Lord and Savior are authoritative, the OT holy war tradition is not. Unless we are to revert to belief in an arbitrary and self-contradicting god—Christians cannot agree that God ever behaved in such ways. If we regard God as a holy warrior we have chosen divine power over divine love, and distorted the understanding of God revealed in Christ. Against a tribal warrior view of god leading his devotees to bloody triumph over their foes—First John concludes that "God is love, and those who abide in love abide in God, and God abides in them" (4:16b NRSV).

Love is to be Jesus's disciples' primary norm in dealing all people, and in Paul's thinking love is the fulfillment of the law (Rom 13:10b). Though many differences in situation and opinion separated Jesus and Paul, First Corinthians 13 attests great agreement between them. The OT also tells of God's demonstrated love. "The Lord, the Lord, a God merciful and gracious, slow to anger, and abounding in steadfast love and forgiveness, keeping steadfast love for thousands, forgiving iniquity and transgression and sin . . ." (Exod 34:6b–7a). Unfortunately verse 7b immediately goes on to say that "God will by no means clear the guilty, visiting the iniquity of the fathers upon the children and the children's children, to the third and fourth generation,"

---

124. Bright, *Authority/OT*, 56. English translations sometimes refer to the *harem* or ban with such terms as "utterly destroy," but in the margin correctly translate as "devote." When, for example, they utterly destroyed the Canaanites in Zephath (Judg 1:17) they regarded those killed as an offering given to God. As Num 21:1–3 reveals, Israel believed that one way to secure Yahweh's help in battle was to promise Him the complete "devotion" (via destruction) of all captured property and persons. They thought that God was so jealous of "devoted" loot that when, as at Jericho, tabooed property was secured, his wrath was ruinous (Josh 7). Or when as late as the ninth century, Ahab spared the life of the captured king of Syria, God is pictured as saying, "Because you have let go out of your hand the man whom I had devoted to destruction, therefore your life shall go for his life" (1 Kgs 20:42) (Fosdick, *Guide/Bible*, 7–8).

125. Barr, *Biblical Faith/Natural Theology*, 218, 219.

126. Ibid., 220.

i.e., corporate guilt! The Book of Esther discloses the narrow Jewish nationalism of the third century BC, calling for the dismissal of foreign wives. Yet against that the Book of Ruth opposes racial and national prejudice and the Book of Jonah encourages international reconciliation and the world-wide mission of Israel.

In line with the books of Ruth and Jonah, but against much OT tradition, Jesus's humane ethic involved the surpassing of national and racial restrictions. The parable of the Good Samaritan (Luke 10:29–37) was a deliberate attack on the limited range of moral responsibility in the Judaism of the day. The Law enjoined love of neighbor, but the question "who is my neighbor?" was hotly debated in the Rabbinical schools, and was answered in ever narrower ways. Jesus's Good Samaritan story indicated that no restrictions should be drawn.[127]

As previously implied, *a most obvious OT limitation was the narrowness of the area within which moral obligation was recognized.*[128] Thus we know of little provision for non-Israelites. There was a distinction between "strangers" (non-Israelites already established in Palestine) and most others. "Strangers" had a protected position and were included under the commandment of love,[129] and former allies were classified as "strangers." Non-allied foreigners were regarded as enemies, unless they lived too far away to have any contact. To real enemies or those regarded as enemies because of classification Israelites expressed little mercy.[130] "That is why Jesus's parable of the Good Samaritan"—which shows the goodness of a Samaritan, and implies that Jews should likewise care for them—"is so unprecedented, so entirely different from what the Old Testament taught (Luke 10)."[131] Though in Deuteronomy 21:10–14 a provision for non-Israelites is seen for female prisoners-of-war who were desired as wives,[132] here there would have been ulterior motives.

Another limitation of OT morality, especially in the beginning, concerned classes of people within the tribal group who were not regarded as entitled to full personal rights.

---

127. Fosdick, *Guide/Bible*, 138, 145.

128. An illustration of the moral limitations of certain laws is afforded by Deut 23:1–6: "He whose testicles are crushed or whose male member is cut off shall not enter the assembly of the Lord. No bastard shall enter the assembly of the Lord; even to the tenth generation none of his descendants shall enter the assembly of the Lord. No Ammonite or Moabite shall enter the assembly of the Lord; even to the tenth generation none belonging to them shall enter the assembly of the Lord, because they did not meet you with bread and water on the way, when you came forth out of Egypt, and because they hired against you Balaam . . . of Mesopotamia, to curse you. Nevertheless the Lord your God would not hearken to Balaam; but the Lord your God turned the curse into a blessing for you, because the Lord your God loved you. *You shall not seek their peace or their prosperity all your days forever*" (my emphasis). This is a religious recipe for tribalism.

129. "'When a stranger sojourns with you in your land, you shall not do him wrong. The stranger who sojourns with you shall be to you as a native among you, and you shall love him as yourself; for you were strangers in the land of Egypt: I am the Lord your God'" (Lev 19:33–34).

130. Vriezen, *OT Theology*, 337–38.

131. Ibid., 338.

132. Ibid.

Concerning Children. In the seventh century Jeremiah vehemently denied that *the command to slay the firstborn* had been given by Yahweh (7:31; 19:5; 32:35), something Jeremiah would not have said had there been no supposition of such a divine command and no such practice in Israel. As late as the eighth century BC the prophet Micah pictured a devotee supposedly appeasing Yahweh by offering up his son (6:7b). The Genesis 22:1–14 story of Abraham's willingness to sacrifice his son Isaac and his holding back of nothing that religious obligation was thought to require movingly portrays the meaning of child sacrifice. The story's obvious objective is reached when "Abraham lifted up his eyes, and looked, and behold behind him a ram caught in the thicket by his horns and Abraham went and took the ram, and offered him up for a burnt-offering instead of his son" (v. 13).[133] Perhaps the Abraham-Isaac legend was a narrative way of helping to end the child sacrifice practice,[134] a blatant denial of children's right to life.

What of the rights of women? Female inferiority was emphasized in the law.[135] Though, for example, it was possible for a man to have several wives (Deut 21:15–17), a woman could not have additional husbands. Furthermore, the right of divorce lay wholly with the husband (Deut 24:1–4).[136] Though he could divorce a wife for any reason—some unseemly thing in her of which he was the sole judge—no provision was made for a wife's escape from a cruel husband (cf. Deut 24:1–4).[137] Not surprisingly, a woman was valued between half and two-thirds of a man (Lev 27:1–7).

Especially in matters of religion women started with great disadvantages: Since blood was thought to cause ritual defilement, women were regarded as "unclean" for seven days after each menstruation (Lev 12:2). After the birth of a male child the mother was considered unclean for that same length of time; but after the birth of a female child she was regarded as unclean for twice as long (Lev 12:2–5). A healthy woman of childbearing age was for these reasons often prevented from taking part in religious services. Scrupulous men were much afraid that social contact with women could render them impure (Lev 15:19–31). Female inferiority was structured into the temple itself, with women's place of worship separated and with them not allowed into the inner court where sacrifices were offered.[138]

At marriage a daughter passed for a payment from her father's ownership to her husband's. Never did women escape the ownership of a proprietor—even finally to the clan patriarch if matters came to that—and against such men, women's rights were

---

133. Ibid., 102, 207.

134. See chap. 9, n68.

135. The Gen 2:18–25 recognition of male-female equality was not maintained in practice. Women were subordinate to men and this was justified as a permanent punishment in Gen 3:16 (Vriezen, *OT Theology*, 337).

136. Dunn, *Jesus' Call/Discipleship*, 81.

137. Fosdick, *Guide/Bible*, 106.

138. Dunn, *Jesus' Call/Discipleship*, 81–82.

meager. Even a woman's vow to Yahweh might be abrogated by a father or husband (Num 30:3–16) for, being the property of her family's head, she was not free to involve herself in oaths conflicting with his wishes.

This conception of woman as a possession led to grave abuses. For example, Lot felt free to offer his virgin daughters to the passions of the men of Sodom in order to save his male guests from those men's lust for his guests (Gen 19:8). A father could also sell his daughters into slavery (Exod 21:7) A father could do as he pleased with his women, even if, as in Jephthah's case, his vow involved the sacrifice of his daughter's life (Judg 11:30–40). His vow gave him the right and in some circumstances even the obligation to slay his daughter.[139]

Malachi's late protest against divorce bears eloquent testimony to Israel's developing conscience. "Let none be faithless to the wife of his youth. For I hate divorce, says the Lord..." (2:15c–16). Jesus challenged the injustice of husbands to wives when He stated a marriage ideal as involving a single indissoluble bond (Mark 10:2–12). The Markan text's legalistic insistence that divorce with remarriage always involves adultery (19:9) can be understood when seen in the historic context as a defense of women's rights.[140] The prerogative of the husband to sever the marriage tie and expel the wife from her home and children seemed to Jesus cruelly unjust, and against such misuse of power He denied this legal entitlement conferred on husbands by Deuteronomy 24:1–4.[141]

"All this is of one piece with Jesus's general attitude toward women. It is impossible to distinguish women from men in the personal respect with which Jesus treated them. Repeatedly he came to their defense as he came to the defense of children."[142] "Women were among his closest followers and friends (Mark 15:40–41; Luke 8:1–3; 10:38–42). The note in John 4:27, that Jesus's disciples were surprised to find him talking alone to a woman in a public place, catches something of the eyebrow-raising unconventionality of his conduct."[143] "*One understands the judgment that in Jesus women found the best friend they had ever had in the ancient world.*"[144]

Slavery. Slaves were another category of people denied full human rights in ancient Israel. Though effort was taken to make the system morally better, it remained inhumane. Early codes limiting the rights of masters concerned only Hebrew slaves.[145]

---

139. Verses 30–31 sounds as though the vow he took could also have been applied against a male who happened to be the first to come out of his house to greet him. But one wonders whether it would have been applied or that the male victim would have accepted being put to death. Of course, anyone's freedom to put any person to death to fulfill a vow is morally abhorrent.

140. Matthew's version attests that if the divorce and remarriage is due to the first spouses' infidelity, the second marriage does not entail adultery (19:9).

141. Fosdick, *Guide/Bible*, 102–3, 105, 103, 104, 125–26.

142. Ibid., 127.

143. Dunn, *Jesus' Call/Discipleship*, 82.

144. Fosdick, *Guide/Bible*, 127; my emphasis.

145. Dunn, *Jesus' Call/Discipleship*, 107.

Slavery as a kind of indentured servitude continued to exist even concerning Israelites, though in their case only because of debt and supposedly for only six years (Lev 25:39–41; see also Exod 21:1–11). According to Exodus 21:5–6, such a jubilee year requirement could be revoked only by the Israelite slave's permission. That slave owners often did not adhere to such restriction is apparent in Jeremiah 34:8–16.[146] OT humane consideration for slaves is most adequately expressed in Job's attitude: "If I have rejected the cause of my manservant or my maidservant, when they brought a complaint against me, what then shall I do when God rises up? When he makes inquiry, what shall I answer him?" (Job 31:13–14) "Did not he who made me in the womb make them?" (Job 31:15a NRSV)

Job's perspective continued and advanced in the NT. Jesus treated all people as loved and forgiven by God and therefore as of equal value. Though extending God's love to all types of people, Jesus seems to have assumed that the institution of slavery was inherent in the present evil age, and, as with Paul later, he was in no position to overturn that societal practice.

For Christians one of the first consequences of the sense that all people are loved by God was the admittance of slaves on equal terms with free people into the early churches. This represents the NT's great contribution in moving toward a solution to the problem of slavery. "There is neither . . . slave nor free . . .; for you are all one in Christ Jesus" (Gal 3:28). The Epistle to Philemon, far from deserving censure because it takes slavery for granted without protest, represented an indispensable forward step toward its elimination. It presents a plea that an "unprofitable slave" recently converted to Christ be regarded and treated "no longer as a slave, but more than a slave, a beloved brother" (v. 16a).[147]

It is no doubt true that particular OT convictions about God and God's relation to the world influenced Jesus and the writers of the NT. As indicated in some earlier sections of this chapter, specific OT beliefs helped to shape specific Christian ones. Nevertheless, many OT beliefs were ignored by the NT. And since many OT beliefs and practices conflict with NT ones, the Christian affirmation of particular OT convictions is not equivalent to affirming the whole OT as authoritative for Christians. Though Jesus was influenced by His Jewish heritage, He disagreed with many aspects of that. He was indeed *A Marginal Jew*.

---

146. Vriezen, *OT Theology*, 336.
147. Fosdick, *Modern Use/Bible*, 132, 132–33.

14. Marcion in the Context of Second-Century Christianity, His Rejection of Textually Disconnected Readings of Old Testament, His Christocentric/Soteriological Focus[148]

Marcion (who died in 160) was one of the first Christians to read the parts of the pre-OT then available in more historical and literarily precise ways.[149] Unfortunately, Marcion rejected the Old Covenant and its Creator God, from whom he thought the Redeemer frees us, and was docetic in his belief that Jesus only appeared to be human and to suffer. He shared these beliefs with the gnostics.[150] Otherwise Marcion's thought was similar to much second-century normative Christianity: As figurative methods were utilized less in that century the lack of fit between much of the OT and the emerging Christian literature had become more apparent.[151]

A key methodological text for Marcion is that "No one puts new wine into old wineskins; otherwise, the new wine will burst the skins, and will be spilled and the skins will be destroyed. But new wine must be put into fresh wineskins" (Luke 5:37–38). Marcion's surviving *Antitheses* show that, though overstated, his contrasts between available pre-OT traditions and Luke's Gospel generally reflect genuine differences: "(24) 'You shall love the one who loves you and hate your enemy.' But our Lord . . . says, 'Love your enemies and pray for those who persecute you.'" "(21) The Old Testament commands us to give to our brothers, but Christ simply says to give to all who ask." "(8) In the law it is said, 'An eye for an eye, a tooth for a tooth,' but the Lord, the Good, says in the gospel, 'If anyone strikes you on the cheek, turn to him the other also.'" "(26) The Old Testament rejects the publicans as non-Jewish and profane men; Christ accepts the publicans." "(7) The prophet . . ., when the people were locked in battle, climbed to the top of the mountain and stretched forth his hand to God, that he might kill as many as possible in the battle; our Lord, the Good, stretched forth his hands (on the cross) not to kill people but to save them." "(10) The prophet . . . in order to kill as many as possible in battle, had the sun stand still that it might not go down

---

148. Soteriology concerns the understanding of how salvation is attained. See chap. 7, sec. 7. For more material on Marcion, see chap. 6, secs. 8, 15; chap. 7, sec. 7.

149. Marcion's literarily careful reading of OT messianic texts was generally close to the Jewish perception of those. He held that often the Messiah predicted by the prophets was an earthly, purely human, royal figure who in their day was still to come. He, however, thought that, as attested in OT historical writings, some messianic predictions had already been fulfilled. He believed that the Messiah's role was to act as a savior of the Jewish people from their earthly enemies, as he simplistically supposed that Isaiah and Jeremiah had foretold. Marcion thought that Jesus was not the political/nationalistic messiah the Jews expected, but the heavenly Savior of the redeemed in every nation (Barton, *Holy Writings, Sacred Text*, 42–43).

What Nils Dahl says concerning why Jesus had long rejected the Messiah title much agrees with Marcion's analysis of OT messiahship. However, as Dahl supposes, Jesus may have finally accepted the title (Mark 14:61b–62) when it was apparent that the meaning of the term could be redefined by His death on the cross (*Crucified Messiah*, 33–35).

150. See chap. 6, sec. 8; chap. 7, sec. 7.

151. Barton, *Holy Writings*, 60.

until the adversaries of the people were utterly annihilated; but the Lord, the Good, says, 'Let not the sun go down upon your wrath.'" "(3) Joshua conquered the land with violence and cruelty, but Christ forbade all violence and preached mercy and peace." "(27) The law forbids the touching of a woman who has an issue of blood; Christ not only touched them but healed them as well." "(29) The Old Testament promised the Jews the restoration of the earlier state of things by the return of their land to them . . . Our Christ will establish the kingdom of God, an eternal and heavenly possession."[152] Harnack writes that beyond universal concern and unlimited forgiveness, the love of enemies was the characteristic emphasis of Marcionite Christianity because such behavior alone corresponds "to the great deed of the love of God, who redeems the 'strangers and foes.'"[153]

Beyond Marcion's appreciation of Lukan Gospel traditions, he regarded his own theology as the continuation of Paul's belief in the supersession of the law by the gospel. However, Marcion thought even Paul's epistles "spoiled" the novelty of this theme by continuing to quote the OT as though it were authoritative for Christians. Marcion accordingly purged OT material from the Pauline letters, eliminating difficulties by altering texts,[154] not by figurative interpretation.[155] He did similarly with Luke's Gospel. Once edited, he regarded these writings as alone authoritative, but these may have been the only writings known to him with indications of apostolic authorship.

In response to Marcion's renouncing of the Creator God and of the OT, third-century church leaders retaliated by rejecting his rejections—but did so by again beginning to read the OT in literarily inaccurate ways. (Such methods had been the means whereby pre-NT authors smoothed out difficulties by attaching Christocentric convictions to selected OT words or phrases.) Not surprisingly, Stuhlhofer's statistics indicate an *increase* in the citation of OT texts by Christian writers after Marcion, likely in reaction against him.[156]

Ironically Marcion became a factor influencing the continued retention of the OT as read imprecisely. The general church thought that Marcion, like many other "heretics," had drastically overstated himself both in regarding the Redeemer God as saving us from the evil creator god and in totally rejecting the OT.[157] The general Church was right in this regard, but wrong in rejecting a plain reading of the OT. Their uncritical attitude toward the OT was achieved by reading their own ideas into it.

---

152. Harnack, *Gospel/Alien God*, 61, 62, quoting from "Marcion's Antitheses."
153. Ibid., 85.
154. Marcion likely supposed that later editors had inserted such material into Paul's Epistles.
155. Barton, "Marcion Revisited," 351; *Holy Writings*, 170.
156. Barton, "Marcion Revisited," 351. See chap. 6, sec. 6.
157. Though like the gnostics Marcion had a disparaging attitude toward the Creator and creation, unlike them he straightforwardly read the texts he retained, and reduced the scope of scripture, rather than the opposite.

15. Proposals for Christian Use of Old Testament

In his witty and humorous way, James Barr points to a reason beyond all that I have indicated as to why Christians are impatient with the OT.

> The Hebrew Bible contains . . . a lot that is *not* thrilling to the average reader, who begins to skip passages as early as the fifth chapter of Genesis, when the first of the genealogical lists appears. Even less appetizing, from this point of view, are the first nine chapters of Chronicles, containing practically nothing but genealogies, or the latter part of Joshua, with its extensive lists of places and boundaries. These can by highly interesting for the meticulous scholar but they cannot be said to be, from the average reader's point of view, full of action, life, and personal involvement . . . Indeed, one of the main reasons why active apologetics on behalf of the Old Testament was necessary within Christianity [was that people] . . . found large stretches of it boring and unreadable. . . . How many readers find their pulse quickening when they read Ezekiel's nine chapters on his planned reconstruction of the temple, or the lists of the figures for the different tribal camps in Numbers? Are the lists of unclean birds and animals vitally filled with existential involvement?[158]

If we get beyond the tedium just mentioned, we notice that the OT calls for choice, for it manifests two streams of tradition, one that encourages acceptance of Christ and another that leads to the rejection of Christ. The line that proceeds from the OT to Christ *via* the recognition of sin and grace furthered the expectation of a Messianic Savior. But many other OT teachings promoted Phariseeism and drew people away from the Messiah.[159] The scribes and Pharisees represent the primary first-century form of tradition that grew out of the pre-OT. They were so influential that the NT depicts leading circles among the Jews as opposing Jesus. The tragedy of this opposition is entirely lost if we think that Rabbinic Judaism did not really emerge from the OT, but was the replacement of the OT position by something quite different.[160]

Even such a Reformed apologist for the Christian relevance of the OT as Brevard Childs had to admit that much OT tradition does not lead toward NT faith and that the Hebrew prophets do not simply foreshadow Christian teaching. Some chords from Jeremiah and Deutero-Isaiah resonate strongly in the NT: "new covenant, vicarious

---

158. Barr, *Concept/Biblical Theology*, 166.

159. Vriezen, *OT Theology*, 97. "The Church must always be willing to admit that 'from the historical point of view the Talmud is just as legitimate a continuation of the Old Testament as the Gospel' (H. W. Obbink), but the Church can never admit that, essentially and spiritually, the Talmud is the true continuation of the most profound elements of Old Testament preaching . . ." (same source, 98). There will always remain a fundamental difference between Judaism and Christianity as to which parts from the OT should be most highly valued (same source, 98).

160. Barr, *Old/New Interpretation*, 27–28.

suffering, new creation, suffering servant." Other prophetic notes were utilized by rabbinic Judaism to construct its faith: "temple, cult, priesthood, law."[161]

As can be seen at various places in the writing in hand, many normative Christian convictions build from OT insights, whereas others transcend or contradict those. Thus the NT exhibits both continuity and discontinuity with the OT. Though the Christian message had a Hebrew heritage, at particular points it burst the molds within which that heritage had found expression. In Pauline terms, this conflict is decisively—but not exclusively—between law and gospel. According to the Fourth Gospel, the center of the conflict is the Incarnation. That makes sense only on Jewish soil, where God and humans had been radically differentiated by a long tradition involving divine transcendence, monotheism, and a recognition of human sinfulness—requiring revelation for adequate knowledge of God. Though for these reasons Incarnation depends on OT background, the OT provides no adequate terms or conceptuality for it.[162]

Marcion was wrong in thinking that the OT should have no authority for Christians. Several books in the OT are surely of far greater value than several in the NT. For example, compare Isaiah, some of the Psalms or Genesis with Second Peter, Second and Third John, and Jude. But because many OT convictions conflict with NT ones and since the normative revelation in Christ is only attested in the NT, Christians must look primarily there. When equal importance is accorded to the Testaments, the church is tempted to smooth over theological conflicts between these via nonhistorical and literarily arbitrary reading of the OT. As for assessing the areas of agreement and disagreement, the NT witness to Jesus Christ should be the norm by which we evaluate OT teachings. Of course this is no simple standard, for the NT witness to Christ evidences much diversity.

The NT's literarily loose interpretive methods as applied to pre-OT traditions and the post-Marcion church's frequent use of the same prevented the church from honestly facing problems related to the OT's authority. In agreement with Marcion, the Protestant Reformers, and modern historical-literary study of Scripture, I regard it as intellectually dishonest to continue to read the NT message back into OT texts. For we live after the development and refinement of historical and literary methods for studying documents.

Not only should the NT in general take priority over the OT within Christianity, as it often has, but the functioning authority of some parts of the Old Testament has been and should be recognized as greater than others. Furthermore, the OT reflects two conflicting notions as to how truth claims are established. Though Proverbs teaches that the fear of the Lord is the beginning of wisdom (1:7), the wisdom writings in general, and Proverbs in particular, appeal to natural experience. Unfortunate for this approach, people seem to have conflicting "natural" experience. Furthermore, the rest of the OT and the NT do not regard this as the standard.

161. Childs, *Biblical Theology OT/NT*, 176.
162. Barr, *Old/New Interpretation*, 57.

Though Jews, Muslims, and Christians utilize the OT, none of these build directly on the whole of it as interpreted according to a "plain" and/or historical-literary reading. All three in effect abandon much of the OT because with the many centuries of history it depicts, it reflects diverse and highly conflicting theologies between which choices must be made.

I agree with the Biblical Theology Movement that careful descriptive study to perceive the OT's theological themes can help us to assess their Christian significance. However, merely descriptive theological exposition of OT topics cannot convincingly demonstrate wherein the OT should be regarded by Christians as normative. Modern Christians should try to read the Old and New Testaments with historical and literary precision, deal with each Testament's internal conflicts and with conflicts between the Testaments, and amid such homework seek to be faithful to what is consistent with well-considered understanding of God's disclosure in Jesus Christ. Theologians and ministers should be able to pursue such goals more directly than the laity, and should help them in this regard.

To discern the compatibility and incompatibility of various OT theological convictions with themselves and with NT ones requires that we make detailed OT and NT descriptions and comparisons. However, since not even everything attested in the NT is self-consistent nor valid for Christian Faith, there is no avoiding the risks involved in interpreting and evaluating. Christian Faith should be decisively informed by the NT and secondarily informed by the OT. But such faith is no mere product of descriptive biblical scholarship—but of spiritual sensitivity to the leading of the Risen Christ, having studied the biblical witness.

Chapter 6

Developments toward New Testament Canon, Their Theological Implications, General Canonical Conclusions

As CHAPTER FOUR ON developments toward the OT may have played its part in helping to encourage a realistic attitude toward that portion of the canon, this chapter should provide a parallel service concerning the NT. Without such recognitions of the Bible's humanity, as pointed to in these and various other chapters, Christians can fall prey to such ideologies and mythologies as that the Bible is inerrant—which distracts from accurately understanding God and faithfully serving Her. Like chapter 4, this one being primarily historical will be more straightforward than most, as only less theological chapters can be.

In the following we will see that, like OT canonical developments, NT ones were gradual and influenced by many factors. In a general way Christians can believe that God providentially guided this process, but should not use such an affirmation to encourage an uncritical attitude toward what is contained in either Testament.

1. Christian Faith in Earliest Period Primarily Communicated Orally, Pauline Exception, Pre-New Testament Book Dating and Composition

When the church in the late fourth and early fifth centuries finally canonized the NT, by the Spirit's leading she was seeking to honor God's disclosure in Jesus Christ and trying to prevent the latter from being misunderstood with the passing of years. For many previous decades much testimony had been primarily oral.

The existence of oral gospel traditions was likely a factor delaying the writing of gospels, and then postponing the acceptance of our four accounts. Another consideration that probably delayed their writing was the expectation that Christ would return in the near future. As long as the memory of oral tradition was recent and Christ was expected soon, there was little incentive to write gospel accounts for posterity.

Developments toward the Testaments, Authority of Each

The earliest writings that eventually became part of the NT were Paul's epistles. Though many of those indicate that he expected that Christ would soon return, communication required letters between a traveling apostle and the churches he founded and/or needed to visit. Thus eschatological expectation did not distract him from writing.

Determining the approximate dates of the writings of the various NT books depends on detailed analyses of their contents, and such analyses are beyond the scope of my purpose. Depending on Kummel's content analysis,[1] I will summarize only his conclusions concerning the approximate dating of writings to show the time-span between Jesus's death and resurrection, and the canonical writings interpreting the Christ event.

Most of Paul's authentic letters that survived were written during the 50s and (assuming that Jesus died when He was 35–39)[2] approximately 10–20 years after Jesus's death.[3] The Gospel of Mark, reckoned by most to be the earliest Gospel, is usually dated 65 to 70, so was 25–30 years after Jesus had died, and the Gospels of Matthew and Luke between 80 and 90, roughly 40–45 years after Jesus's death. As for the remaining NT books, all of which were written even later than the above, these are listed in highly approximate chronological order: Colossians: 65–90 (unless written by Paul, in which case 56–60); Hebrews: 80–96; Acts: near 90; First Peter and Revelation: 90–95; Ephesians: 80–100; John: 90–100; First, Second and Third John: much uncertainty, but possibly between 90–110; First and Second Timothy and Titus: 100–110; James:100–125; and Second Peter: 125–150. This chronology shows how distant many NT books were from the Christ event and how relatively close were Paul's own writings (in contrast with all else, including pseudonymous Pauline epistles).[4]

As we will discuss more fully in sections 6 and 7, the NT canon is comprised of three main collections: the four Gospels, Paul's authentic letters and those only attributed to him, and the catholic or general epistles. Beyond these collections are only Acts, Revelation and Hebrews, though the Eastern Church continues to classify Hebrews with the Pauline epistles. Each of the three collections, as well as the books contained therein, and the three other books had their own discrete histories prior to and independent of the history of the canon as a whole. *The canon is to a large extent a collection of collections of individual writings.*

---

1. *Introduction NT.*

2. Meier, *Marginal Jew*, 1:382.

3. Kummel regards Second Thessalonians as written by Paul and not long after First Thessalonians, which was likely composed in 50–51 (*Introduction NT*, 187–90).

4. In ancient times pseudonymous writings used well-known authors' names to entitle works to help secure acceptance, often implying that the writings were influenced by or in the spirit of the one named as the author.

2. Pre–New Testament Writings Crucial to Early Christians Though Many Illiterate in Greek

Because written documents—the NT's included—are composed for people's understanding, we may wonder how early Christians were able to benefit from pre-NT writings when many were illiterate in the language in which those were composed. In the multilingual context of early Christianity no more than ten percent, and far fewer in the provincial congregations where most Christians lived, would have been able *to read* Greek language literature. Christianity's linguistic pluralism was present from the beginning inasmuch as Christianity originated in an Aramaic-speaking environment and its earliest literature was in Greek.

Christians nevertheless placed high value on Christian texts and many *would have understood spoken Greek*. Because of the nature of Greco-Roman hand-copying all reading was aloud, and much of that occurred in public, quasi-public, and domestic settings where those who could not read Greek could listen and understand. And even among those literate in the language, it was as common to be read to as to read for oneself.[5] Even Christians who did not understand spoken Greek were not left out: With regular and lengthy congregational readings,[6] followed by their exposition in congregants' best known language, such Christians became knowledgeable concerning the substance of NT teaching. Also, before church membership Christians received important oral teaching in doctrine and ethics in their language. For these reasons limited Greek literacy or even incapacity to understand spoken Greek did not prevent Christians from gaining a close acquaintance with Christian teaching.[7]

In Greco-Roman culture when reading even to oneself the reader usually spoke the text aloud. The main reason for this was because texts were commonly written in "'continuous script'—with no division between words, sentences, or paragraphs and no punctuation." "A familiar passage in English becomes suddenly cryptic when deployed in this way:

> theearthisthelordsandthefulnessthereoftheworldandthosewhodwellthere-
> inforhehasfoundedituponttheseasandestablisheditupontheriverswhoshallas-
> cendtothehilloftheolordandwhoshallstandinhisholyplacehewhohascleanhand-

---

5. Gamble, *Books/Readers*, 5, 3, 39, 205. This was in part because of the scarcity of texts, where every rendition had to be hand copied, and because of the difficulty of deciphering such texts, as will be explored in the next paragraph.

6. Ibid., 8, citing Justin Martyr, *Apol.* 1.67. The length was perhaps in part because few had private copies.

7. Ibid., 8, 8–9. However, because of the importance of pre-NT writings to early Christians, literacy was a primary requirement for Christian leaders and teachers. Paul's literary abilities were important to his missionary work, as were Apollos's skills in explaining scripture (Acts 18:24). First Timothy affirmed that a church leader needed to be able to read "scripture," preach, and teach (4:13) (same source, 9).

sandapureheartanddoesnotliftuphissoultowhatisfalseanddoesnotsweardeceitfully.[8]

The best way to decipher a text written in this manner is by sounding the syllables and deciphering the pattern of meaning as much by hearing as by sight.[9]

Such texts demanded more interpretive decisions than required today. "When it is up to the reader to determine what groups of syllables form a word, what groups of words make up phrases and clauses and sentences, and to decide what group of sentences rounds up an idea into a paragraph, then the reader is obliged to constitute the sense of a text in a far more active and extensive way than we, who are assisted by word division, punctuation, capitalization, paragraph division, italicization, and other conventions of modern texts." "Good public reading required familiarity with the text. The initial reading of any text was inevitably experimental because it had to be decided, partly in retrospect, which of the possible construals of scriptio continua best rendered the sense. If public reading were not to be halting, tentative, or misleading, those decoding judgments had to be made in advance through rehearsals of the text."[10]

3. Paul's Epistles Understood to Carry More Authority Than Mere Letters

Paul's written communications contained more than *ad hoc* apostolic advice for individual congregations. Though his theology was situationally sensitive, and what we know of Paul comes from his actual letters,[11] he believed that what he said to one congregation had ongoing theological significance and ethical meaning for others. He sought to instruct, admonish, and advise concerning Christian beliefs and private and corporate morality. As epistles and not mere letters, Paul expected his writings to be read aloud in public worship services and shared by original recipient congregations with neighboring ones, who were also to read them aloud in such gatherings. At the close of First Thessalonians Paul enjoins that the letter "be read to all the brethren" (5:27), that is to members of each house church in the area.[12] Galatians is addressed "to the churches of Galatia" (1:2b). The letter to the Romans is to "all God's beloved in Rome" (1:7a), to the various churches in the city and to specific Christians well known to Paul (16:3–15). He also extends greetings from

---

8. Ibid., 203. One suspects that texts were written this way to save money on papyrus costs.

9. Ibid., 204. Our sons, who acquired knowledge of Pidgin English in Nigeria, sometimes write a few phrases to us in pidgin. The best procedure for deciphering such words is indeed to read them aloud.

10. Ibid., 204, 205.

11. I regard the Acts of the Apostles as an historically inaccurate secondary source for both knowledge of Paul and early Christianity, reflecting a late NT perspective. Concerning Acts see n16 below & sec. 7; chap. 7, nn49, 101, and sec. 8; chap. 10, sec. 6; chap. 13, n4.

12. Metzger, *Canon/NT*, 259.

all of the churches of Christ (16:16). The evidence summarized in this paragraph attests that the circulation of Paul's letters took place on the field in his lifetime and implies that early hand copying occurred there.[13]

As an apostle, Paul expected that his epistles would carry considerable weight in the churches (2 Thess 2:15; 3:14). Not only in the prescripts of his letters but throughout he emphasized his apostolic calling. As having encountered the Risen Lord and thereby having been called to proclaim and interpret the faith, Paul the Apostle's letters have an official character (Gal 1:1, 11–14). "Furthermore, in their length, their argumentative and expository development, and their rhetorical features, these letters more closely resemble the literary and philosophical letters of antiquity than any merely private correspondence." Paul's sophisticated opponents in Corinth recognized such features, considering them "weighty and strong" (2 Cor 10:10a). Though Paul's letters were occasional, they were not casual, but "composed and deployed as important instruments of his apostolic authority, teaching and administration among the churches of his mission field."[14]

Though Paul intended that his epistles have more influence than mere letters, as we will shortly see they were not likely written with the idea of inclusion in a broader Pauline corpus, let alone a canonical collection of definitive writings. Only from hindsight can we say that Paul's writings had sufficiently broad authority to become part of the trajectory heading toward later canonical inclusion.

4. Pauline Epistles, Pauline Corpus

Almost half of the books of the NT are ascribed to Paul. "However large Paul's influence may have been in earliest Christianity, his prominence in the NT canon is disproportionately large. The peculiarity of this fact should not be overlooked. Paul was not a historical disciple of Jesus, and even after he became a Christian apostle he stood in an oblique relationship with [Peter, James and other Jerusalem leaders]."[15]

Near the juncture of the first and second centuries, such Christian writers as Clement of Rome and Ignatius of Antioch were familiar with collections of Paul's

---

13. Gamble, *Books/Readers*, 97, 98. Though Romans and First Corinthians were originally written to particular communities (Rom 1:7a; 1 Cor 1:2a), the study of various early versions indicates that they also soon circulated in generalized forms with broad designations of recipients, as reflected in our texts: "Those who are beloved by God" (Rom 1:7a); and "those who are sanctified in Christ Jesus" (1 Cor 1:2b). As for the reverse historical development, the oldest and best manuscripts of Ephesians are not addressed to Ephesus, but widely and with grammatical peculiarity "to the saints who are also faithful" (1:16). Ephesians is commonly recognized as a pseudonymous letter relevant to a general historical situation, but not directly to a local one (same source, 98).

14. Ibid., 95.

15. Gamble, *NT Canon*, 35–36. Gamble says, "with the leading figures of the primitive church," but Paul was also a leading figure.

letters.¹⁶ Though we do not know how many epistles were in their collections, Rome and Antioch as the extreme poles of the Pauline mission prove breadth of circulation.¹⁷

Second Peter regarded *a collection* of Pauline letters as of equal authority with those books later to be included in the OT that were accessible to him, calling both types of writings "scripture." "So also our beloved brother Paul wrote to you according to the wisdom given to him, speaking of this as he does *in all his letters*. There are some things in them hard to understand, which the ignorant and unstable twist to their own destruction, as they do the *other scriptures*" (3:15–16, my emphases).

The collecting of ten Pauline epistles may have gradually arisen in different churches and regions within the Pauline mission field. More specifically, there is no better place to locate such effort than in a Pauline school that had its roots in the activities of Paul's circle of associates.¹⁸ The notion of a "Pauline school" is an inference supported by the production of pseudonymous Pauline letters demonstrating deep indebtedness to Paul, yet evidencing developments and applications to new circumstances. The written activities of Paul's associates in this period furthered, expanded, and at some points contradicted Paul.¹⁹ This could occur because they had been

---

16. However this may have been with others, the author of Acts—who wrote so much about Paul—seems to have had little historical information concerning him. Though he regarded Paul as a great hero of Christian Faith, the author of Acts, who must have written several decades after Paul's time, indicates no knowledge of any of Paul's letters and seems unaware that Paul even wrote letters. Acts's silence about Paul's writings may be because where Luke and Acts were composed (in about 90) neither the Pauline collection nor individual letters were known (ibid., 36–37, 39). Under such likely circumstances "Luke," however, still regarded himself as qualified to describe Paul's life and teaching!

As for Acts's minimal knowledge of Paul, it claims that he was a great preacher, who was never at a loss for the right word; Paul says otherwise. Compare Acts 17:22–34; 21:40; 22:1–2; 24:10–22 with 2 Cor 10:10, where Paul attests that Corinthians said his speech was of "no account." And see 1 Cor 2:4–8, where Paul concedes that he was not eloquent, though he made up for this by his wisdom, and I would add, by his writing abilities. Acts also regarded Paul as a great miracle worker (13:6–12; 14:8–10), whereas Paul thought that instead of regarding miracles as a means for overcoming obstacles, an Apostle must experience the help of Christ in the depth of suffering (2 Cor 12:10) (Haenchen, *Acts*, 114). See chap. 7, nn49, 101 for additional material on Acts's view of Paul as a great miracle worker. See also the current chap., sec. 7; chap. 7, sec. 8; chap. 10, sec. 6; and chap. 13, n4 for additional conflicts between the Acts account concerning Paul and what Paul's own writings say.

17. Gamble, *Books/Readers*, 100.

18. Gamble, "NT Canon/Research," 286. Paul customarily named others as co-senders of his letters. (See 1 Cor 1:1; 2 Cor 1:1; Phil 1:1; Col 1:1; Phlm 1; 1 Thess 1:1; 2 Thess 1:1; and Gal 1:2.) Naming other participants may have reflected particular people's involvement in the conception of the letters in question (Gamble, *Books/Readers*, 99, 284).

The impact of Paul's and his students' individual letters prior to the formation of the collection must have been diverse. Though we know that at least one of Paul's was lost (see Col 4:16b), others were preserved and circulated from early on. In the post-apostolic period Romans, First Corinthians and Ephesians were the most widely known and cited. Other letters came into later use, as would be expected of 2 Cor if it was assembled from smaller fragments of Paul's correspondence, which has long seemed probable because of the epistle's disjointedness (Gamble, *NT Canon*, 40).

19. Gamble, *Books/Readers*, 99.

involved in all aspects of Paul's work, were familiar with his thought, and in many cases pastored the churches he founded.[20]

By the late first century or early second the ten letter Pauline collection was likely available in various areas, but was first evidenced by Marcion near the middle of the second century, who, not coincidentally, was also the first second-century Christian thinker deeply indebted to Paul. Marcion's edition derived from one probably in existence by the beginning of the second century or earlier and did not contain the pseudonymous letters to Timothy and Titus.[21] The first explicit witness to their presence in a Pauline collection comes from Irenaeus late in the second century.[22]

Today's NT scholars agree that by the late second century Paul's letters had become widely established as apostolic scriptures. This conflicts with an earlier twentieth-century view that those were ignored by the broader church of the second century because use by heretics had discredited them.[23]

5. Oral, Written Gospel Traditions

It is unclear when traditions about Jesus, which were originally preserved by memory and transmitted orally, began to be committed to writing. The last half of the first century witnessed a rapid production and proliferation of documents embodying traditions about Jesus. The Gospel of Mark appears to have been the first comprehensive narrative, but its author may have drawn on written sources in addition to oral ones. The authors of Matthew and Luke besides making heavy use of Mark and a written collection of Jesus's sayings (Q), drew additionally from separate traditions, some parts of which may have been in written form. Other traditions were used by the author of John's Gospel, in addition to using a few found in the Synoptic Gospels.

Mark likely first decided upon his general narrative framework: John the Baptist and Jesus's baptism as inaugural happenings, the transfiguration and passion predictions as the turning point, and the passion and empty tomb stories as the climax.[24] In the first and second sections he then inserted oral units of tradition and possibly written ones, having theologically interpreted these. He linked these small units together

---

20. Gamble, *NT Canon*, 40.
21. Ibid., 41; Gamble, *Books/Readers*, 100.
22. Gamble, *NT Canon*, 42.
23. Gamble, "NT Canon/Research," 286–87. Because many of the Christian writings of the second century were addressed to outsiders, Paul's were among others that were not often quoted by apologists. However, had Paul's letters been disdained for most of the second century they could not have suddenly become well known and widely honored during the last two decades of that century. We know that his letters were highly regarded by Irenaeus, Tertullian, Clement of Alexandria, and the author of the Muratorian Fragment, and these scholars and their churches were widely separated geographically. Such facts imply that Paul's literary legacy had been continuously and broadly valued from the beginning (Gamble, *NT Canon*, 45–46).
24. Matthew and Luke incorporate this outline, and the Fourth Gospel to a lesser extent.

with brief connecting phrases concerning place and/or occasion. In these sections he groups narratives and sayings by type of story, form, or content, often using catchwords to join independent units. Aside from events related to Jesus's baptism, His rejection and crucifixion, and the empty tomb associated message that He had risen, Mark evidences little knowledge of the order of events.[25]

Some insights pertinent to the history of the formation of the canon can be gained from the very composition of the three later Gospels. Analysis of Matthew's and Luke's handling of Mark and of their other mutual, written source, plus their variable use of likely oral sources show that they regarded such as neither sacrosanct nor adequate, and tried to provide something better. Matthew, Luke and John may each have offered a comprehensive document to stand on its own, a purpose hinted at in Luke 1:1–4. A collection of Gospels may thus be at odds with a likely aim of these three Gospel writers.[26]

Although our canonical Gospels were among the earliest to be written, new gospels continued to be composed through the first half of the second century and Christian writers of the second century referred to many gospels besides our four. Another reality of the first half of the second century was indicated when Eusebius recorded that Papias did not assume that information from books would help as much as oral traditions. Furthermore, the utilization of oral traditions concerning Jesus was too well established to be completely displaced at that time by written materials. The persistent authority of the oral not only checked the popularity of our written Gospels, but furnished a rich resource for new gospel writings.[27]

With the passage of time as oral tradition became widely dispersed and distorted, written Gospels became more common. Originally only one Gospel document was treasured in a particular church. Evidence of this practice is found in scriptural manuscripts that contain only one. For example, Marcion employed only Luke or a form of it in his collection of Christian scriptures. Though this is often attributed to his theological bias, it is possible that he knew only of this written Gospel, or saw the need for only one.

"As each Gospel was composed in the first place with the aim of providing a sufficient and self-contained account, it was not easy for Christian communities to see why there should be more than one: a plurality of Gospels cast doubt on the adequacy of any. This problem was compounded by the fact that the Gospels differ significantly among themselves, an insight that was by no means lost on the early church. Though

---

25. See Funk, "Once and Future NT," 543.

26. Gamble, *NT Canon*, 24. The widest distribution was achieved by Matthew, which was regarded as an enlarged and improved version of Mark (Campenhausen, *Formation/Christian Bible*, 123).

27. Gamble, *NT Canon*, 25, 26, 27. The *Gospel of Thomas* and the *Unknown Gospel* as independent revisers of oral tradition owe neither form nor content to the canonical Gospels, which may be true also for the *Gospel of Peter* and the *Dialogue of the Savior* (same source, 27).

some accounting might be given for these differences, to accept more than one Gospel was to be burdened with justifying their divergences."[28]

Although the Gospels were originally and separately issued anonymously and without titles, in the first half of the second century they were called "Gospels" and their supposed apostolic authors named. Why did the two changes occur? The term *"gospel"* was long familiar as a designation of the Christian proclamation of the one message of salvation through Christ. It was probably subsequently applied to written narratives about Jesus because the author of the Gospel of Mark had introduced his work as "the beginning of the gospel of Jesus Christ" (1:1)[29] to indicate continuity with epistolary understandings of Jesus. In contrast, author attributing of Gospels achieved the purpose of distinguishing accounts and associating each with an apostle or one associated with an apostle.

Through the circulation of various Gospels churches gradually became acquainted with diverse interpretations of Jesus's life. The first evidence of knowledge and use of several Gospels comes from the middle of the second century in the writings of Justin Martyr. He was acquainted with Matthew and Luke, and probably with Mark, and highly regarded these. But like Papias, Justin continued to use oral tradition and written gospel accounts not known to us.[30]

Irenaeus, Bishop of Lyons in Gaul and writing about 180, promoted his collection of four Gospels—these four and no more. Noting the vigor and ingenuity of Irenaeus's arguments, many interpreters have concluded that the fourfold Gospel must have been a novelty at that time. Irenaeus did concede that many Christian groups were accustomed to using only one Gospel, and that others employed more than four. Even Irenaeus did not always seem to depend exclusively on written Gospels. The relative freedom of some of his citations and his reference to words of Jesus as distinct from Gospel reports reveals that he too may still have depended on oral traditions.[31]

Near Irenaeus's time a Syrian Christian named Tatian wrote his *Diatessaron, combining the four Gospels with some additional materials into one unified and continuous narrative.* Tatian is thus our first witness to the common availability and utilization of four Gospels, but his use of them shows that the fourfold Gospel contemporarily sponsored by Irenaeus was not broadly recognized. Furthermore we see that Gospels were not regarded as unalterable and that the multiplicity of Gospel documents was still regarded as problematic.[32] Tatian destroyed the literary integrity of his sources and freely recast their contents through transpositions—changes of the relative position of letters within words, words within sentences, or sentences within paragraphs—and

---

28. Ibid., 27, 29–30.
29. Gamble, *Books/Readers*, 153–4.
30. Gamble, *NT Canon*, 28–29.
31. Gamble, "NT Canon/Research," 280.
32. Ibid.

changes through additions and omissions. Obviously he did not value these documents as sacrosanct.[33]

Even when written Gospels came into customary use their texts were not beyond substantial alteration by copyists. For example, early manuscripts indicate that Mark originally ended at 16:8 and so lacked any narrative of post-resurrection appearances of Jesus. Probably in the first decades of the second century various longer endings were added to remedy what was regarded as a deficiency. The most common added verses, 9–20, were subsequently incorporated into most manuscripts and presented as integral to the text. Modern translations often put these verses in small print to indicate that they were not original to that Gospel. John 20:30–31 likely constituted the original conclusion of that Gospel, with the additional resurrection appearances of chapter 21 added later. Early manuscripts also indicate that the story of the woman taken in adultery, often found in John as 7:53—8:11, was not original. These three examples are instances where written Gospels have been expanded by the inclusion of pieces of oral tradition. These are but striking illustrations of the general second century tendency to regard the Gospels as subject to revisions.[34]

The Chester Beatty codex of the four Gospels and Acts from the first half of the third century is commonly regarded as the first *manuscript witness* for a collection of four Gospels.[35] At least by then the four canonical Gospels had acquired an authoritative status in the ancient church, replacing earlier local practices. Collecting four into a corpus limited the authority of other gospels as well as rejecting the option of reducing the four into one condensed and combined account.[36] Similarly any effort to critically sift the material, as Marcion had with the Gospel he used, had come to be regarded as a threat to the catholicity of the faith and was thus rejected. This though Matthew and Luke had done precisely that with Mark, and John had done even more drastically with Mark if he possessed a copy of it.

Once the church regarded the four Gospels as sacred texts of equal status—and having ruled out the imaginative interpretive methods that the Gospel writers and other NT witnesses used to interpret the OT—early Christian writers used one of two methods for sorting out the discrepancies. One was to practice careful and conscious harmonization, as exhibited by Augustine, but such a method is contrived, academically dubious, and must revert to eisegesis. The other technique was to interpret the Gospels the way extreme redaction critics treat discrepancies as pointers to evangelists' intentions, having become indifferent to the historical uncertainties that nevertheless exist. Clement's idea that John is a "spiritual Gospel" signifies this tendency's

---

33. Gamble, *NT Canon*, 30. "It is a telling fact that Tatian apparently encountered no criticism for his work; indeed, the *Diatessaron* enjoyed great popularity" (same source, 31).

34. Ibid., 28.

35. Gamble, "NT Canon/Research," 277.

36. Childs, *NT As Canon*, 145.

beginning, but Origen was its main articulator.[37] "The purely historical inconsistency of the Gospels is played down in the interests of the religious truths to be gained from their differing presentations. Thus Origen anticipates modern suggestions that the existence of four [considerably] incompatible accounts is really a good thing because it points us away from an attachment to mere historical proof and calls forth religious faith instead."[38] The problems are that some of the spiritual or theological teachings of the Fourth Gospel conflict significantly with the Synoptics, and the Synoptics exhibit theological incompatibilities among themselves. Both Origen's formula and redaction criticism by itself are dishonest, since we need to assess how particular theological affirmations agree or disagree, and in cases of disagreement, decide why we agree with one side or the other.

6. By Early Second Century the Following Were Used More Than Emerging Old Testament: Paul's Epistles Plus Ephesians and Colossians, Then Individual Synoptic Gospels, Later the Fourth Gospel

It is not surprising that the early Pauline corpus quickly became more important than the direct use of pre-OT writings. About the same time that the ten epistles Pauline corpus became well known and before a four Gospel corpus was available, individual pre-Synoptic Gospels also came to have higher authority than the emerging OT. By the early second century all but a few OT books, such as Isaiah and the Psalms, were utilized less than those pre-NT writings widely available. When in the early third century the Fourth Gospel was added to the other three to comprise a four Gospel corpus its prominence increased. However, soon thereafter and in likely reaction against Marcion's rejection of pre-OT scripture, citations of pre-NT and pre-OT scripture began to level out.[39]

7. Catholic or General Epistles, Acts, Hebrews, Revelation

To summarize and proceed: Though the Pauline Epistles were shaped into the first collection toward the end of the first or beginning of the second century, the Pastoral Epistles were added only toward the end of the second century and complete the first grouping. By the first half of the third century the four Gospels had likely been gathered into a second collection. The third major component of the NT canon, the Catholic or General Epistles, are theological essays in letter form, not closely tailored

---

37. Barton, *Holy Writings*, 95–96.
38. Ibid., 96.
39. Ibid., 64–68. Paul's writings and then the Gospels were received as more important than Jewish scriptures "*before* they were old enough to have a natural aura of sacred antiquity." An ascribing of authority to recent writings was consistent with the early Christian conviction that "a new and unprecedented era had arrived with Jesus and the apostolic Church" (same source, 67).

to the particular circumstances of addressees.[40] Some of these took much longer to be recognized as authoritative, though First Peter and First John were widely accepted individually at the end of the second century.

We do not see the term "catholic" applied to a *group* of letters until the fourth century, when Eusebius referred to the seven Catholic Epistles (James, First and Second Peter, First, Second and Third John, and Jude). Nevertheless, with the exception of First Peter and First John, Eusebius placed these in the "disputed" category.[41] The catholic letters had very diverse individual histories and were brought together in an artificial collection.[42]

As briefly indicated in section one, aside from the above three groupings only three additional documents were eventually included in the NT canon: Acts, Hebrews, and Revelation. Although composed as a companion piece to the Gospel of Luke, the Acts of the Apostles had a separate history and was not widely recognized until much later. Near the mid-second century Justin Martyr was the first writer to show any knowledge of Acts, but it was later that more importance was attached to it, possibly because its depiction of early church unity was useful in conflicts with Marcion and gnostic groups. Irenaeus appealed to Acts as a proof of the unity of the apostles and their preaching, a doubtful contention in view of Paul's accounts of his conflicts with the apostolic leaders of the Jerusalem Church.[43] Acts's authority for Irenaeus rested on the further dubious historical assumptions that its author was Paul's companion and a disciple of all of the apostles. Likely for these historically questionable reasons, by the end of the second century Acts's authority was confirmed by the Muratorian list, Tertullian, and Clement of Alexandria.

Because Hebrews was early associated with the Pauline epistles in the east, it was there accepted by the early third century. In the west it was neglected until late in the fourth century. This was due in large part to its teaching that a Christian who willfully persisted in sinning or fell away from faith (apostasy) would not be divinely forgiven (6:4–8; 10:26–31; 12:14–17).[44] In addition, the west was uncertain about authorship, and until the fifth century not willing to attribute it to Paul. (Few in the west today regard Hebrews as written by Paul.) As with Revelation in the east, the west's primary problem was content. In both cases theological reservations provoked authorship concerns.[45]

Revelation had a geographically opposite reception history than Hebrews, gaining some second-century recognition in the west. In reaction against Montanism's

---

40. Gamble, *Books/Readers*, 106.

41. Gamble, "NT Canon/Research," 271.

42. Gamble, *NT Canon*, 77.

43. See chap. 7, sec. 8.

44. This teaching was the reason many in the early church postponed baptism until near the time they thought they would die.

45. Gamble, *NT Canon*, 47, 52.

apocalyptic emphasis, Revelation in the east became suspect. There it was only in the late fourth century partially rehabilitated *on condition that it be interpreted allegorically*. Revelation furnishes perhaps the clearest example of "the interplay between the authority and use of writings and problems of interpretation."[46]

8. Marcion's New Testament Collecting, Editing in Context[47]

In 140 Marcion published his de-Judaized version[48] of Paul's ten letters,[49] and of Luke's Gospel, considering these as revisable and as forming a collection of historical and doctrinal material that Christians could further develop.[50] The true anticipators of Marcion's altering of his sources were the authors of Luke and John, and possibly of Matthew, though unlike Marcion they did not envision others modifying their writings. Luke 1:1–4 indicates the author's desire to provide the sole Gospel. Marcion may have thought he was merely restoring Luke's Gospel (possibly his sole Gospel source) and suppressing what he considered Jewish adulterations, while ignoring "spurious" Gospels, which may or may not have included our other three.[51]

Whatever sources the author of the Fourth Gospel may have had, he (like Marcion) must have handled very freely, omitting, rearranging, and making detailed corrections. Von Harnack suggested that the Fourth Evangelist was even bolder than Marcion, actually creating new historical incidents and long speeches.[52] But Marcion lived too late to convince the general church to agree with his massive alterations of Luke's and of Paul's writings or of his reduction of written Gospels to his own version. Because many people by mid-second century recognized our four Gospels as holy books, reduction was impossible, however difficult having four was in comparison

---

46. Gamble, "NT Canon/Research," 289.

47. See sec. 15; chap. 5, sec. 14; chap. 7, sec. 7.

48. McDonald, *Formation/Canon*, 89. As previously indicated, in agreement with gnostics, who regarded the material world as evil, Marcion regarded the Creator God of the OT as evil, and only had faith in the good Redeemer God seen in Jesus, who saves us from the wicked Creator God. The related new point is that these beliefs caused him to delete everything Jewish from the ten Pauline epistles and Luke, regarding such "additions" as due to Jewish Christian editors. Also in agreement with gnostics, Marcion believed that Jesus only appeared to have been born, and only seemed to have died—and thus he eliminated references to Jesus's resurrection (obviously a non-event if Jesus had neither been born nor died) (See Metzger, *Canon/NT*, 91, 93–94).

49. Not only the absence of the Pastorals from Marcion's and others' early lists of Paul's writings argues against Paul's authorship but evidence from some aspects of the Pastorals's content. Though these are valuable books worthy of study, it is not clear here that all Christians are recipients of spiritual gifts and that therefore females as well as males can be empowered for leadership in churches. See chap. 7, sec. 3 for a detailed discussion related to the second issue.

50. Barton, "Marcion Revisited," 347. We know that Marcion's students and successors felt free to use Matthew and Mark to supplement his "Luke" (same source, 347).

51. Ibid., 348; Barton, *Holy Writings*, 46–47.

52. Barton, *Holy Writings*, 47, quoting Harnack, *Marcion*, German ed., 67.

with possessing only a single, relatively consistent Gospel.[53] The creation of "critical" versions of the gospels ceased with the firm establishment of the four-Gospel collection early in the third century. As for Marcion's dejudaized version of Paul's writings, long before Marcion's time Paul's writings had widely circulated, and the large numbers of copies in circulation prevented such drastic modification as Marcion's from being generally accepted.

Surprisingly, Marcion's account of Paul's epistles and Luke's Gospel did not lead to an immediate effort by the general church to precisely indicate its own authoritative literature, and for a long while many writings not contained in the NT continued to be equally valued. The church drew boundaries around the NT two centuries later when Marcion's influences could not have been at work.

Marcion was rejected by the Church for three reasons, but only the first two are defensible. Firstly, patristic church leaders condemned Marcion for his total rejection of the OT as reflecting an alien religion, and secondly, for his belief that the OT Creator God is evil. Unfortunately the church thirdly also renounced his critique of the use of literarily inaccurate interpretative methods, such as allegory, to accommodate the OT to Christian beliefs.

Marcion had no direct influence on the formation of the NT.[54] But the early church's continued acceptance of literarily inexact interpretive methods guaranteed dishonest appraisal of the various writings of the OT and uncritical acceptance of the entire Septuagint into the Christian canon. Today we possess only fragments of the precise Septuagint texts to which early Christians responded.

9. Little Direct Canon-Determining Influence from Reactions against Montanist and Gnostic Direct Revelations and Their Proliferation of Writings

In the second half of the second century an emotional, intolerant, and apocalyptic kind of Christianity was popular in Asia Minor (now most of Turkey). Montanist leaders claimed such direct divine authorization for their messages as to regard their own words as God's words. Montanist "new revelations" threatened to undermine the very belief that Jesus Christ as a figure from the past is the definitive revelation of God.

Reactions against Montanism caused mainly the Eastern Church to became suspicious of those prophets who directly identified their words with God's words (as had OT ones and the author of the book of Revelation), and suspicious of apocalyptic writings in general and of the book of Revelation in particular.[55] More specifically, the Eastern Church became distrustful of those (like the Montanists) who not only

---

53. Barton, *Holy Writings*, 48, 59.
54. Barton, "Marcion Revisited," 354.
55. McDonald, "Identifying Scripture/Canon," 433.

continued to believe in the imminent end of the world, but who offered detailed predictions of the immediate preceding events.[56]

Von Campenhausen following Von Harnack claimed that Montanism's beliefs in continuing inspiration and new revelation provided the broader church with the decisive impetus toward reducing the scope of eventual authoritative scripture. To the contrary, though the differences were considerable, they did not lead to canonical disputes. This was in part because Montanists did not directly set their own oracles or writings in opposition to authoritative writings recognized by the broader church.[57] And the broader church agreed that we can and should be inspired by the Living God.

Unlike the gnostically influenced Marcion and like Montanism, though more extreme, gnostic Christianity in general tended to produce a vast and much conflicting literature, with teachers issuing forth what they regarded as independently authoritative writings based only on private revelations.[58] The general church countered that their speculative and otherworldly notions did not agree with the Gospels or Paul's epistles or the other Christian writings that were widely accepted, and therefore could not be considered as authoritative. In short, gnostic teaching was regarded as conflicting with the apostolic message. The gnostics agreed that many aspects of their teaching were unique, but insisted that the Lord had mystically communicated secret traditions to their leaders. In response to the latter presumption the general church may have been influenced to devalue oral tradition, though previously she had highly regarded that.

> Even though a special and determinative impact on the formation of the NT canon cannot be assigned to any one of these second century controversies, their *collective importance* ought not to be underestimated. The diverse conceptions of Christianity exemplified in these movements required their opponents to define more exactly the substance of the Christian confession, to specify its proper resources, and to safeguard it against criticism and deviation. The tendency to ascribe authority to certain traditional documents and to make argumentative theological appeals to them was an important part of this effort. But this was not effective apart from the concurrent tendencies to formulate Christian beliefs in concise and summary form and to lodge the prerogative of teaching and interpretation with authoritative ecclesiastical officers.[59]

---

56. Metzger, *Canon/NT*, 99, 102, 104, 106.
57. Gamble, "NT Canon/Research," 293.
58. See chap. 7, sec. 7 for many comparisons of NT normative Christianity with Gnosticism and for criticisms of the latter.
59. Gamble, *NT Canon*, 65; my emphasis.

10. Influence of the Codex Book-Making Technique on Development of the New Testament Canon

The history of the canon cannot even be completely separated from the issue of book forms in the ancient world and the one chosen by Christians for their NT. The roll book/scroll was the standard book form in Greco-Roman antiquity. Of the remains of non-Christian Greek books from the third century, more than 98 percent are scrolls, whereas in the same period the surviving Christian books are almost all page books/codices. This evidence shows that early Christianity widely preferred the codex as its writing medium and thus early departed from the established use of scrolls. To appreciate how odd was this development one must realize that in antiquity codices were for jotting notes for private or business use.[60]

We who have access to page books and even computer tablets and who live where many or most people are literate in the language of available literature easily attribute more significance to being able to read available writings than was possible when large manuscripts consisted of cumbersome piles of scrolls, and where most people were illiterate in the language of literature. (The maximum length of a roll convenient to handle was thirty-five feet—which was about the length of Luke's Gospel *or* the Acts of the Apostles.) Had Christians used the roll in the transmission of their sacred books, the four Gospels *or* the ten book Pauline Epistles could have been collected only by assembling several rolls in the same box or chest.[61]

"There must have been a decisive, precedent-setting development in the publication and circulation of early Christian literature that rapidly established the codex in Christian use, and it is likely that this development had to do with the religious authority accorded to whatever Christian documents first came to be known in codex form."[62] Based on available historical evidence, Paul's letters were not only the earliest Christian writings, but the earliest to be valued, imitated, circulated beyond their original recipients, and collected. These writings were also the earliest to be considered of apostolic authority and authorship, and likely formed a ten letter collection by the end of the first century. They were also the first Christians writings to receive the epithet of "scripture" (2 Pet 3:15b–16).[63]

What would have predisposed toward using the codex form for the Pauline collection? Because Paul's ten letters were too big for a single scroll, they could best be grouped together in a codex, rather than as several scrolls in a box. Furthermore, the

---

60. Gamble, *Books/Readers*, 49–50.

61. Metzger, *Canon/NT*, 109.

62. Gamble, *Books/Readers*, 58. Earlier Christians may have found the codex form handy for randomly accessing Christian compiled testimony books regarded as containing messianic predictions. But no such copies in any form have survived to prove or disprove this. Even if such usage occurred, it would not have marked a decisive step toward the use of codices for continuous literary texts (same source, 65).

63. Ibid., 58–59.

earliest recovered collection of Paul's letters emphasized the number of churches addressed, with the letters arrangement by decreasing length, of which neither feature "could have been established or sustained unless the letters were contained in a *single* book." Also a page book would have enabled the random access that was required for continual study of such complex documents. "On this hypothesis the adoption of the codex by early Christianity was neither circumstantial nor arbitrary, but a careful decision based on the advantages of the codex for the text at hand."[64] Not surprisingly, the first reference to parchment (papyrus) codices in a Greek writing occurred in Second Timothy 4:13c.

The codex development in book-making technique not only made it easier for Christians to early group Paul's writings together, but likely contributed to the eventual assembling of a four Gospel corpus by the first half of the third century. Christianity did not invent the codex, nor were Christians the first to use it for more than notes. The evidence only indicates that Christians adopted the codex sooner and more decisively for literature than their contemporaries and thus contributed to its popularity.[65]

"The appearance in the fourth century of very large . . . codices finally capable of containing the whole of Christian scriptures suggest that the technology of book production played a role in the delimitation of the canon, even as it did in the creation of early smaller collections. The aim of transcribing all scriptural documents in a single codex forced, in the most practical and unavoidable way, the question of precisely which books ought to be included, though it must be noted that whole Bibles . . . were a relative rarity in the ancient church."[66] "Once it was possible to produce and view (or visualize) 'the Bible' under one set of physical covers, the concept of 'canon' became concretized in a new way that shapes our thinking to the present day and makes it very difficult for us to recapture the perspectives of earlier times. 'The canon' in this sense is the product of fourth century technological developments. Before that things were less 'fixed,' and perceptions, accordingly, less concrete."[67]

11. Canon-Encouraging Indirect Effect of Diocletian Edict

The first of the two major attempts to establish conformity in the empire in the early fourth century was an edict of Diocletian in 303 to promote religious uniformity. This edict, which remained in effect until 313, led to the persecution of the church and required that Christians turn over their sacred books to the authorities to be burned. Christians tried to protect their own integrity and their sacred literature by

---

64. Ibid., 62, 62–63.
65. Ibid., 64, 65.
66. Gamble, "NT Canon/Research," 294.
67. Kraft, "Codex/Canon Consciousness," 230, 233, quoting James A. Sanders's discussion in the same volume.

surrendering texts not considered sacred.⁶⁸ Since no general church council had met to decide about normative scripture or any other matter, individual churches, regional ones and some leaders,⁶⁹ had to make their own judgments. Being in such a situation likely caused Christian leaders to anticipate the hard decision facing them and to conclude concerning what did and did not constitute authoritative Christian scripture.⁷⁰

12. Eusebius's Canonical Listing of Undisputed and Disputed New Testament Books[71]

Eusebius, Bishop of Caesarea in Palestine (265–340), wrote *Ecclesiastical History*, one of the most important resources for recovering the history leading to canonizing decisions. Writing in the early fourth century he provided a threefold classification of writings: acknowledged, disputed, or heretical. Under the category of "acknowledged books"—those received as authoritative though not delimited—Eusebius included the four Gospels, Acts, the letters of Paul (presumably including Hebrews, though it was widely disputed in the west), First John and First Peter. He also allowed that Revelation may be placed in this group "if it seems desirable." In the larger category of "disputed books" he placed James, Jude, Second Peter, Second and Third John and five books not included in our NT. Then he surprisingly added that Revelation *may* be placed among the disputed books "if this view prevails," and that some would position the *Gospel of Hebrews* "among the acknowledged books."[72]

Eusebius's division between disputed and undisputed books not merely summarizes the late third and early fourth century perspective, but *is similar* to that of the late second century's wide acceptance of the sixteen writings. Their recognition had come entirely from the grass roots, church usage being the decisive factor, with First John and First Peter not being widely regarded that early. In the late second century not only had no church council met, but no political pressure had been exerted.[73]

13. Constantinian Push toward New Testament Canonical Uniformity

As for the second major attempt to establish conformity in the empire: Under Constantine's sponsorship in the early fourth century the church became the official religion of the Roman Empire. As Constantine sought to consolidate and unify the Empire he also tried to do so with the church, also for the sake of unity in the empire.

68. McDonald, "Identifying Scripture/Canon," 417; Gamble, *NT Canon*, 66.
69. Most church members would not have possessed Christian writings.
70. McDonald, "Identifying Scripture/Canon," 106, 117, 110; Metzger, *Canon/NT*, 107.
71. See the church usage discussion in sec. 16.
72. Gamble, *NT Canon*, 53.
73. Ibid.

Because doctrine could not be separated from its primary source, agreement about scripture's scope could contribute to theological agreement. The theological dispute of the day—whether or not the Son had equal authority with the Father (which Arianism denied)—required concurrence between Eastern and Western Churches, which a consensus concerning NT composition could help to facilitate. The fourth century Athanasian-led interaction between eastern and western theological and scriptural traditions thus moved toward scriptural standardization.[74]

In approximately 332 Emperor Constantine asked Bishop Eusebius to supervise the production of fifty copies of "divine" scripture, to be used in the new capital city of Constantinople for churchly instruction. These were "'to be written on well-prepared parchment by copyists most skillful in the art of accurate and beautiful writings, which [copies] must be very legible and easily portable in order that they may be used. . . . This, then, shall be your responsibility, to see that the written copies be provided forthwith.'"[75]

Gamble in his 2002 essay in *The Canon Debate* emphasized Constantine's desire to use the copying to unify the empire by establishing "agreement about the scope of authoritative scripture . . ."[76] Gamble's view of seven years earlier (1995)—that Constantine only wanted the Gospels copied—would certainly not have achieved that.[77] Of course a NT had never before been transcribed, but Eusebius had already indicated those books that were widely utilized in church worship and those still disputed. As Emperor, Constantine would have had overriding interest in unifying the empire by having that dispute resolved by either the inclusion or exclusion of the disputed books. It seems likely that Constantine cleverly put the scope of the copying burden on Eusebius's shoulders ("shall be your responsibility"), thereby absolving himself of blame. A politically shrewd move *only* if the reference was to the transcribing of an entire New Testament, since the disputed matter concerned that.

It seems probable that Constantine forced a yes or no decision concerning the seven disputed NT books in the case of the fifty copies. Under imperial court pressure to decide one way or the other, Eusebius seems likely to have had the full twenty-seven pre-NT writings printed, and by so doing swayed future council resolutions regarding the composition of the NT. Was it not because Constantine demanded churchly uniformity in the case of the fifty copies for Constantinople that the canonical rosters from then onward became more precise?[78]

---

74. Gamble, "NT Canon/Research," 294.
75. Gamble, *Books/Readers*, 79, quoting Constantine's words.
76. Gamble, "NT Canon/Research," *The Canon Debate*, 294.
77. Gamble, *Books/Readers*, 80.
78. McDonald, *Formation/Canon*, 110, 114, 116, 117, 118.

14. Solidifying of Western Opinion by Athanasius, Augustine[79]

The final resolution began to take place in the late fourth and early fifth centuries, primarily through the actions of ecclesiastical councils. One of the earliest such pronouncements was that of the *Council of Laodicea*, held in 363, specifying only twenty-six of our NT books as suitable for reading in church worship services. Revelation's exclusion was probably due to Syrian and early Eusebian influences.[80]

In the thirty-ninth Festal Letter of Athanasius, bishop of Alexandria, issued in 367, he sought to regularize the scriptural usages of Churches in Egypt and to challenge heretical teachings supported from spurious documents. "Athanasius set forth a list of those writings 'handed on by tradition and believed to be divine' and 'in which *alone* the godly doctrine is proclaimed.'[81] His is the first list to name as *exclusively authoritative* exactly the twenty-seven books which make up our NT. Athanasius was the first eastern Christian writer since Origen to recognize Revelation . . ."[82] However, Athanasius's Egyptian canon was not binding on other eastern regions nor on the west.

Augustine, whose influence upon the Western Church was decisive, wrote most of his *Treatise On Christian Learning* in 396 and 397, but only completed it in 426. Though he there advocated Athanasius's twenty-seven book NT, he may have compromised that affirmation by (in early Eusebian fashion) candidly attesting that some of the books were accepted on weightier authority and were more widely used by churches than others.

Augustine in his role as Bishop largely influenced the council decisions in *Hippo* in 393 and in *Carthage* in 397,[83] both of which named the twenty-seven books of our NT, and accepted Hebrews without claiming it was written by Paul. The final council decision was a second one in *Carthage* in 418, at which the same twenty-seven books were accepted, but under eastern influence Jerome pressured the Western Church to assent to Paul's authorship of Hebrews.

We should remember that these fourth and early fifth century council decisions no longer reflected grass roots opinion, but were the Emperor-encouraged conclusions of prominent theologians/church leaders and the declarations of hierarchically structured councils.[84] Fanciful interpretative methods were also available to smooth away NT conflicts, especially for Revelation. Nevertheless, many churches continued to utilize the core books to a greater extent. Since some of the writings recognized as

---

79. Compare sec. 16 and specifically the church usage criterion for determining NT composition.

80. Gamble, *NT Canon*, 55. For the Syrian position, see n85.

81. My emphasis. Athanasius's perspective was obviously an oversimplification, since every sermon is supposed to proclaim godly doctrine.

82. Gamble, *NT Canon*, 54–55.

83. Metzger, *Canon/NT*, 236–38.

84. McDonald, *Formation/Canon*, 165, 132, 134.

canonical had not been widely used or commonly regarded as authoritative, in those cases bishops and councils *did not* ratify a status those writings had previously and broadly secured.

A closed canon of Scripture that closely approximates our NT cannot be dated before the second half of the fourth and beginning of the fifth centuries, and even then the Syrian Church dissented.[85] These consular concurrences were separate decisions of Eastern and Western Church assemblies that did not speak for all of the churches in their respective regions.

15. Scripture-Canon Distinction, Textual Versions and Variations, Necessity of Written Attestation, Then of Canonization

When referring to matters prior to the closing of the canon, *scriptures* were books that a community regarded as authoritative, but without implying that others had less authority. We can tell that a community regarded a writing as scriptural not only when it was mentioned, but when citations or allusions indicate its use to settle issues of faith, mission, disciplining, or when utilized in public worship.[86] Going beyond such narrower understandings, *a canon is an exclusive list of the books that are regarded as normative*. As Metzger cleverly described the distinction, "there is a difference between a collection of authoritative books and an authoritative collection of books."[87] That is, between an open-ended grouping of authoritative books and a relatively closed collection of books that alone has highest authority.

"All are in fact agreed that *we owe the present New Testament both to the inclusion of books (otherwise it would not exist at all) and to the exclusion of books (otherwise it would have gone on growing indefinitely)*."[88] A *closed* canon of authoritative writings *was* unique to the church, since when church councils were making definitive canonizing decisions the Jews had not closed their OT,[89] and there is no proof they ever have, and the Qur'an did not yet exist.[90] In part because early Christian decisions in

---

85. Though fourth century Syrian Christianity knew of separate written Gospels, Tatian's *Diatessaron* continued to be popular. Beyond what recognition was given to the Gospels, Syrian Christianity at that time recognized only Acts and Paul's letters. Only by the late fourth and early fifth centuries were James, 1 Pet, and 1 John accepted. Even well into the fifth century the Syrian Church recognized only twenty-two NT books (Gamble, *NT Canon*, 55).

86. McDonald, "Identifying Scripture/Canon," 420.

87. Barton, *Holy Writings*, 9, citing Metzger, *Canon/NT*, 282. Canon long signified a norm, standard or rule, and since the middle of the second century was employed to refer to the "rule of faith" (creed or summary of faith). The word was also used to describe a listing (Childs, *NT as Canon*, 24). It is in the combined senses that we use the term to mean *a definitive collection of books that in comparison with other books or collections is held to be normative*. Jesus Christ is, of course, a higher standard than the canonical books that to a lesser or greater extent point to Him.

88. Barton, *Holy Writings*, 15; my emphasis.

89. McDonald & Sanders, "Introduction," 13, referring to A. C. Sundberg's insight.

90. In contrast to many Christians' opinions concerning the Bible, Sunni Muslims regard the

this regard were regional ones, which were sometimes caused by theological conflicts with other regions,[91] even the Christian list is not absolutely closed.[92]

As there were no enumerations of canonical books until the fourth century, so there were no manuscripts that contained a complete Christian Bible before the fourth and early fifth centuries. The appearance at that time of four versions of the entire Christian Bible reflects the canonizing transition.[93]

Directly related to the issue of canonization is that concerning *versions and variations*. "Texts reproduced by hand, as all texts were before the invention of the printing press, were far less stable than modern printed texts because they were subject to accidental or deliberate modification in every new transcription."[94]

In the early period scribal mistakes occur as often in Christian as in other reproductions. Some early Christian texts even seemed to invite intentional revisions. The closely parallel and yet differing accounts among the Synoptic Gospels led many scribes to harmonize such related texts, and inexact quotations of Jewish scripture in Christian texts were often made to conform with the Septuagint. Some alterations were also made for theological reasons, with scribes revising texts they regarded as doctrinally problematic, on the assumption that those had been introduced by other scribes.[95]

Qur'an as absolutely closed.

91. See sec. 16.

92. See chap. 7, sec. 2.

93. Hahneman, "Muratorian Fragment/NT Canon," 415.

94. Gamble, *Books/Readers*, 30. In providing hand copies a writer surrendered further control and in effect the work became public property. The recipient could then make additional copies, and his recipients others. In this way a text spread beyond the author's acquaintances, and he had no influence concerning the carrying out of further renditions or possible revisions by others, nor over the number of copies in circulation, nor even about whether the work would be properly attributed (same source, 84–85). Copies were disseminated freely through informal networks of people who learned of a work and knew someone who had a copy and would permit it to be transcribed. In these ways texts quite haphazardly gained wider circulation from ever more numerous points where they were available for copying (same source, 84–85).

Though previous copies were already in circulation, a revised version could be made by an author who retained the original copy. But after each new copying, modifications beyond his control could again occur. For example, Paul likely retained originals of his epistles, and could have revised those, though we have no evidence that he did. We have much evidence that his students edited his epistles, possibly for the sake of inclusion in a broader Pauline corpus. That is, they introduced some intentional changes to Paul's writings and (under Paul's name) added their own Pauline writings to the collection, and (sometimes for better, sometimes for worse) their writings influenced the way Paul has been understood. See n49; also see chap. 7, sec. 3. Even if Paul's students had wished to only copy his writings, in all probability accidental changes would have been introduced. The Index indicates places where Acts and the Pastorals attempted to influence the way Paul is understood.

A biblical author's concern that his words not be distorted in future transcribings is expressed with a seemingly arrogant, presumptuous and even idolatrous threat/curse in Rev 22:18–19, as the author appears to confuse his powers with God's. "I warn everyone who hears the words of the prophecy of this book: if anyone adds to them, God will add to that person the plagues described in this book; if any one takes away from the words of the book of this prophecy, God will take away that person's share in the tree of life and in the holy city, which are described in this book" (NRSV). See chap. 4 above, n4.

95. Ibid., 71–74.

By the late second century Christians had learned from hard experience of the theological dangers latent in the malleability of texts, for *Marcion* was justly regarded as notorious for his recasting of texts.[96] He was among the first Christian writers to vest decisive theological authority exclusively in particular Christian texts, but did so only after excising and correcting his sources and in other ways making extensive revisions to the texts he held to be authoritative.[97]

> Marcion provides an exaggerated but not wholly misleading example of the extent to which Christians in the second century both invested authority in texts and revised texts with a view to their value in theological argument. The two concerns are closely correlative: the authoritative valuation of a document entails an interest in the accuracy and stability of the text. What is little recognized is that in antiquity the conscientious reader was always interested in the correction of textual corruptions since, given the conditions of production and transmission of texts, the accuracy of a text was necessarily an open question. *The irony is that the attribution of authority to a document did not necessarily confirm the received text and ensure its careful preservation but, by heightening interest in its accuracy, opened the way for critical emendation.* In the absence of controlled transmission, an ancient text acquired stability not in proportion to the extent of authority lodged in it, but by the broad circulation of enough copies to establish and sustain a consistent, self-reinforcing textual tradition.[98]

For the first two centuries Christians were so interested in making texts available that control over reproduction was lax, especially with reference to the Gospels.[99] No "particular collection, edition, or recension[100] of Gospels played a controlling role in the second century." This situation "evokes the startling, even paradoxical, question what it may have meant to value *documents* as authoritative apart from the availability of established, more or less standardized *texts* of those documents. As Parker puts it, '*while early Christianity may have come to make lists of authoritative books, there were no authoritative copies of them.*'"[101]

Only in the fourth century, as a result of the establishment of the Christian religion in the Roman Empire, did Christian books begin to be produced to a high standard. This was due to the utilization of professional resources made possible by the higher status Christianity came to more widely enjoy.[102] At this point some of the errors in earlier transcribings were corrected.

---

96. For more on Marcion, see sec. 8 above; chap. 5, sec. 14; chap. 7, sec. 7.
97. Gamble, *Books/Readers*, 125.
98. Ibid., 126; my emphasis.
99. Ibid., 74.
100. Editor's version based on a critical examination of a text and its sources.
101. Gamble, "NT Canon/Research," 282, quoting from *The Living Text of the Gospels*, 188; last emphasis mine.
102. Gamble, *Books/Readers*, 79.

Related to the issue of gaining access to the most accurate version, should we accept only the earliest texts available today, more likely reflecting the original hand of the authors? Or the later canonical form received from the apostolic community? Our choice in this matter may or may not be guided by the early church, which grounded its theology in the received form. In contrast, some may welcome the availability of versions that, for example, might come closer to showing the historical Paul, having eliminated some of the additions (as concerning a diminishing of women's rights) that likely came from his students as editors.

Consider an additional complexity: The United Bible Societies copyright each Nestle-Aland critical version, with its thousands of variants, and scholars buy these as though they were authoritative.[103] But no churchly body has ever declared any of these to be canonical. We of course have no copies of the fourth- and fifth century Greek NT that was originally canonized. Because we cannot agree on what version is authoritative, the NT may be canonical only in the sense of being a listing of particular books, whose contents are somewhat variable. Such an answer is adequate for those who do not require that the Bible be a legally precise and in no way contradicting source of authority, but distasteful medicine for those who believe in the non-biblical concept of inerrancy. Many such people find comfort not only in affirming belief in a lost, infallible original, but use that belief to endorse a chosen translation their group believes infallibly reflects the original. Both commitments are ideological and neither are supported by the Bible, nor open to analytical and comparative examination of the Bible's contents.[104]

Why were written documents and then a canon eventually seen as essential to Christian commitments centered upon divine revelation in Christ? Because in the absence of relevant writings and then a publically recognized scriptural canon, knowledge concerning what occurred and its meaning would have become greatly distorted *with the passage of many years.* As a historically grounded faith, Christianity would not have required written records if Jesus had returned as soon as many early Christians expected. But as years stretched on, only some agreement concerning foundational written boundaries could protect against vast intrusions of misinformation due either to lapses of memory or to intentional theological alterations.

Judaism, Christianity, and Islam as grounded in beliefs concerning divine action in history eventually had to develop written scriptures. Islam delimited theirs canonically to a great extent and Christianity did so to a lesser degree. Judaism may or may not have taken a formal canonizing decision. Christian fundamentalism excepted, Judaism and Christianity do not venerate their books the way Sunni Islam does. (Only Christian veneration of Christ should be analogous to the Sunni veneration of the Qur'an.) But all three faiths required considerably stable written form for the sake of relatively accurate remembrance.

---

103. Funk, "Once and Future NT," 546.

104. For more on inerrancy, see chap. 3, sec. 1; chap. 7, sec. 8.

Unlike the three historical communions just mentioned, nature religions (such as Traditional Religion/Animism, which regards nature as inhabited and largely controlled by conflicting spirits) and Mysticism (introspection as seen in Neoplatonism, Hinduism, and Buddhism) did not with the passing of years require written scriptures. This is because their religious truth claims are not directly connected with past historical events, thus requiring historical evidence.

Christian Faith believes that God's definitive self-manifestation occurred in Jesus Christ, and that God's further revelatory work as Spirit relates to and is consistent with Her once-and-for-all disclosure in Christ. Canon presupposes a situation in which revelation continues, but to a considerable extent as a history of interpretation.[105]

The Apostles' and the Nicene Creeds were written prior to the canonizing decisions of the early church, and summarize Christian beliefs without reference to scripture, for the canon was yet to be closed. One mid-fourth century council decision, two in the late fourth century and one in the early fifth called for commitment concerning the composition of the canon.[106] But these did not succeed in eliminating world church diversity concerning canonical composition.

Not only information concerning canonical history, but awareness of the varying standards used to determine inclusion in the NT help us avoid affirming docetically[107] unrealistic ideas as to what was meant and is meant by the New Testament's authority.

16. Criteria Used in Determining Composition of New Testament Canon

The criteria used for determining which books would be included in the NT canon were not uniformly applied. Sometimes one standard was emphasized and sometimes another, and even individual standards could be understood differently—good reasons for being skeptical of the supposition that everything in the NT is of equal value.

i. Church Usage

Whether a document had been utilized in the teaching, worship and life of many churches was likely the most important norm for determining inclusion in the NT. Thus authority was not intrinsic to individual writings, but depended on the church's recognition of their importance for its life. As applied to the NT there is an element of truth in H. Diem's one-sided and over-simplified characterization of this norm for canonization as that which "allows itself to be preached."[108] Many but not all writ-

---

105. Berkhof, *Christian Faith*, 83.

106. See sec. 14.

107. Docetism, as in Gnosticism, denied the humanity of Jesus and in doing so minimized the humanity of Scripture. See chap. 7, sec. 7, sub-sec.2 and sec. 8 for docetic aspects of the Fourth Gospel.

108. Cited in Childs, *NT as Canon*, 31–32. Such a notion in no way applied to the inclusion or

ings accorded NT canonical status well conveyed Christian Faith and greatly assisted Christians in living the Christian life. Furthermore, whether writings exhibited catholicity, that is, whether they were regarded as relevant to the whole church, was likely decided by wide church utilization.

Church usage can easily be misunderstood as implying that mere popularity was a criterion. To the contrary, it is likely that theological factors considerably underlay church usage, such as whether or not an early writing testifying to Christ served to draw Christians closer to the Crucified and Risen Lord and helped them become more responsible disciples.

Church usage consideration was particularly prominent in Origen and even more in Eusebius, who tried to ascertain whether a writing had been widely used from an early period.[109] Though the authorship of Hebrews was long questioned, it likely made it into the NT because the Eastern Church was reluctant to dismiss what it regarded as a useful and cherished document, though it had one very dubious teaching.[110]

Church utilization was an influential factor for the acceptance and eventual incorporation of eighteen of the twenty pre-NT books Eusebius reported as widely acknowledged. Though he included Acts, it was apparently not broadly used in preaching, though appealed to some who wanted a romanticized portrait of early church unity. If we add Acts to Eusebius's slate of books not extensively read in worship services we end up with seven: Acts, James, Second Peter, Second and Third John, Jude, and Revelation. For the Western Church Hebrews should be added, making eight that did not satisfy the church usage criterion. Furthermore, not all writings included in the NT were more extensively used in worship and church life than some non-included writings of the late first to mid second century.

The achievement of canonical status of the more disputed and less widely used books probably had more to do with the Constantinian command that fifty copies of scripture—surely New Testaments—be produced (sec.13), with the opinions of prominent theologians/church leaders (sec.14), and with the verdicts of hierarchically controlled church councils (sec.14).

ii. Temporal Proximity

In contrast to brilliant theological treatises written long after the apostolic period, books to be included in the NT had to have been written in closer proximity to the Christ event. So, for example, though Augustine's writings proved more helpful in

---

exclusion of particular OT writings—since council decisions seem merely to have validated Judaism's implicit canon.

109. Gamble, *NT Canon*, 70–71. Concerning the relationship between church use and canonical inclusion in the NT, Augustine preferred those writings favored by all Catholic Churches, but among those not everywhere received, he put more weight on the opinions of larger churches (McDonald, "Identifying Scripture/Canon," 433).

110. McDonald, "Identifying Scripture/Canon," 432. See sec. 7 above.

interpreting the meaning of Christian Faith than some NT books, his works could not have been considered for inclusion.

Because early Christians regarded the life, death and resurrection of Jesus as the normative Christian event, writings thought to be composed after the apostolic period were excluded from the NT canon. Therefore the author of the Muratorian Fragment (approximately 350) opposed accepting the *Shepherd of Hermas* as Scripture because it was written too late.[111] Because this criterion was not in all cases consistently applied—perhaps because the canonizers often did not know when books were written—some of the less significant writings included in the NT were written later than some significant ones that were excluded.[112]

iii. "Orthodoxy"[113]

A basic though usually only implicit criterion for NT canonicity was the agreement of a document's content with the Faith of the church. That particular writings could be appraised by the standard of "orthodoxy" may seem to imply that the tradition concerning the church's Faith was understood to be extrinsic to all books in today's NT. The matter is more complicated. Though some aspects of the early church's Faith were summarized in the pre-canon Apostles' and Nicene Creeds and in such condensed forms could be accessed there, Christian Faith had from early times been shaped by many of the same documents that later became the center of the NT canon. These writings helped to mold the tradition of faith, guaranteed their own inclusion, and influenced what else would be included.[114] "It is symptomatic of this interplay that the criterion of orthodoxy seems never to have been applied to such literature as the letters of Paul or the Synoptic Gospels. The reason is that these had been valued so long and used so widely that their orthodoxy could only be taken for granted: it would have been nonsensical for the church to have inquired, for example, into the orthodoxy of Paul!"[115] This criterion was used primarily in connection with writings whose authority on other counts remained uncertain, and was applied mainly as a final way of rejecting those. Incidentally, many highly orthodox Christian writings from the apostolic period did not become NT Scripture.[116]

---

111. Ibid., 431.

112. Today's more developed critical tools of investigation indicate that the Pastorals, James, 2 Peter and 1, 2, and 3 John were probably written later than such highly praised non-canonical books as the Didache, 1 Clement, the Epistles of Ignatius, Polycarp, Barnabas, and Hermas.

113. See chap. 7, sec. 7 for a more comprehensive summary of normative beliefs reflected in much of the NT.

114. Gamble, *NT Canon*, 69.

115. Ibid., 70. Though Paul's writings had been extensively recognized as authoritative much longer than the Gospels, the latter had been broadly accepted long enough to not be questioned by this criterion. But see chap. 7, sec. 7, sub-sec.2 for a problem within the Fourth Gospel.

116. Ibid., 70.

The ancient church had justifiable cause to reject the esoteric and ahistorical interpretation of Christian Faith in gnostic Christianity. Not all early Christian theologies were equally representative of the faith. Even in the first and second centuries there were emerging standards of normative theology, though those allowed considerable latitude. Though the NT by-in-large exhibits an underlying core of essential beliefs, it also manifests many theological differences,[117] and both are seen in many places in this work.

Paul's teaching that the death of Christ was for our sins conflicts with Acts's silence on the topic.[118] To suggest a correction in the other direction: Paul's requirement that Christians must be subject to governing authorities because they are all appointed by God (Rom 13:1–3) conflicts with Acts 4:19 and 5:29, which regarded direct obedience to God as taking precedent over the authority of governing officials. (Unfortunately Acts envisioned no such conflict in the case of the Jerusalem leaders' requirements!)[119] Paul's view here is even more difficult to reconcile with Revelation 13. Paul, however, did not always follow his teaching concerning uncritical obedience to governing authorities, since he fled Damascus upon learning that *the governor* was trying to seize him (2 Cor 11:32–33).[120]

The fourth and fifth centuries' church that canonized the NT did not think that the Bible by itself could establish orthodox belief. If the New Testament had been deemed a sufficient literary source for determining Christian Faith, many of the subsequent lengthy debates and difficult confessional decisions would likely have been unnecessary.[121]

iv. Apostolicity

Many may suppose that apostolicity as applied to a NT writing means that it was written by an apostle—one whose ministry of witness was authorized by extraordinary encounter with the Risen Christ. To the contrary, agreeing with what the church regarded as the Apostolic Faith was the most essential meaning concerning a writing's apostolicity.[122] Yet in some cases (to be discussed) where apostolic content was negligible and church usage minimal, *supposed*, but unconvincing, claims of apostolic authorship may have later helped a writing to gain acceptance into the NT.[123] When a

---

117. For example, see chap. 7, secs. 5 and 8.

118. In the speeches in Acts the death of Christ "for our sins" is not mentioned (2:22–39; 3:11–26, etc.), but is found frequently in Paul. See 1 Cor 1:17—2:2; 15:3; Rom 3:23–26; and Gal 2:20–21 (McDonald, "Identifying Scripture/Canon," 429).

119. See chap. 7, sec. 8.

120. Acts 9:23–25 puts the matter in terms of Jews wanting to kill him.

121. McDonald, *Formation/Canon*, 150.

122. Gamble, *NT Canon*, 68.

123. In NT times there were certainly many pseudonymous Christian writings, most of which were rejected, some of which form a worthy part of the NT, and some of which, though in the NT, may

writing gained acceptance because it was thought to have been written by an apostle, it would likely have referred to authorship by one of the eleven or Paul.[124]

Authorship by an apostle was so unimportant to *early recognition* of a writing's *authority* that names of apostles (Matthew and John) or names of people thought to be associated with apostles (Mark and Luke respectively with Peter and Paul) were only attached to the four Gospels at the beginning of the second century, after those had gained recognition primarily because of churchly appreciation of their content. Having studied the content of John and Matthew, historical-critical scholarship massively doubts that the Hellenistic Fourth Gospel was authored by the apostle John, and widely doubts that the First Gospel was written by the apostle Matthew. That the author of Mark was Peter's associate also seems unlikely, since that Gospel is very Hellenistic and Peter—according to both Acts and Paul—was highly Jewish. Similarly, that the author of Luke was Paul's companion is most improbable, since Acts's accounts concerning Paul conflict much with what Paul's epistles report. *Again, had any of the Gospels been written by apostles, why were their names attached so late?*[125] *Nor would apostle associates have been apostles!*

Look more closely at how apostolicity in the narrow sense of apostolic authorship was applied or not applied prior to canonizing and then with canonizing. The theology of First Peter is much influenced by Paul and is thus highly unlikely to have been written by the Apostle Peter! First Peter may have been attributed to Peter because of its impressive content recognized by church usage, but though Peter's name was put at the head of Second Peter, it was long disputed because of its mediocre content. It, however, may have been canonized because Peter's name had previously been added when Second Peter was listed after First Peter. After lengthy debate the Eastern Church concluded that Paul wrote the book of Hebrews, and Pauline attribution probably helped the Eastern Church to accept the book into the canon. The

---

cause more harm than good. Pseudonymous Pauline epistles were discussed in sec. 4; other such NT writings will be considered in the remainder of this sec. Paul affixed his unusual signature to his letters so those familiar with his signature could tell when a purported direct letter from him was a forgery. But copies could not have had an original author's signature.

124. That the "apostles" constituted the eleven plus Paul agrees with neither Luke nor Paul. Paul most certainly included himself as an apostle (1 Cor 15:5–8; Gal 2:8), which claim the author of Luke-Acts rejected in accepting only the eleven plus the post-resurrection selection of Matthias (Acts 1:21–26; 10:41; 13:30–31). Paul envisioned a much wider group of apostles, and Paul's broader concept of apostleship was likely the common early view. However, utilizing Paul's wide understanding of apostleship would have made the group impractically large as an authorship standard.

Matt 10:2–4 and Mark 3:14–19 agree in their listings of the original twelve apostles, except for slight variation in the order. Both disagree with Luke 6:13–16 and Acts 1:13 in mentioning Thaddaeus, rather than Judas, son of one of the James. Otherwise the three Synoptic writers agree concerning the following eleven: two Simons (Peter and another), two James, Andrew, John, Philip, Bartholomew, Thomas, Matthew, and Judas Iscariot. "It is surprising how little is known of the Twelve—of most of them, nothing at all; even the names are not entirely certain. They never functioned as a group, except perhaps in the very earliest days of the Jerusalem Church, after the resurrection. Except for Peter, they are the shadowiest of figures" (Beare, *Earliest Records*, 81).

125. See n4 above and sec. 7.

Western Church (under eastern pressure) agreed to the book's inclusion in the canon at the first council of Hippo and at Carthage apart from assent to Pauline authorship, though it finally acceded to that claim at the second council of Hippo. (Because of such variations as style, theology and vocabulary, most scholars today doubt that Paul wrote the work.)[126] From the above considerations one suspects that apostolic authorship was not required in the case of impressive writings, but that such attachment may have led to canonical acceptance of some books long questioned—James, Second Peter, Second and Third John, Jude, Revelation (in the case of the Eastern Church) and Hebrews (in that of the Western one).

Modern historical-critical scholarship concludes that Paul is the only apostle who wrote NT books and that only Romans, First and Second Corinthians, Galatians, Philippians, First Thessalonians, Philemon, and (likely) Second Thessalonians were written by him. Some scholars continue to think that Paul also wrote Colossians and even Ephesians. Whether or not the latter books were written by him, they manifest impressive Pauline content. Though some authentic traditions from Paul can be found in the Pastorals, the theology and polity represent a second generation Paulinism out of touch with some of Paul's most essential convictions.[127]

Apostolicity did not generally require authorship by an apostle but faithfulness to the apostolic witness concerning Jesus Christ. But such faithfulness was only one canonizing standard—and was not universally applied. Some of the marginal books that were included in the NT—though having the names of apostles attached—had content far removed from apostolic teaching concerning Jesus Christ as determined by the more central books of the NT.

v. Inspiredness Was Necessary but not Sufficient for Canonical Inclusion[128]

A writing had to be regarded as inspired if it were to be considered for incorporation into the NT, but being so regarded did not guarantee such inclusion. Contrary to later orthodox views that only the Bible is inspired,[129] early disciples believed that every Christian writing that truly attests the faith is inspired. The fourth century church regarded Augustine's writings as inspired by the same Spirit who inspired the NT authors—otherwise early Christians would have paid no attention to his writings. Clement of Rome said that First Corinthians was truly inspired, but claimed the same of his own letter. Even in writings dealing with the Montanists, who tended to equate their words with God's, the early church did not over-react by restricting inspiration to the

---

126. McDonald, "Identifying Scripture/Canon," 426.

127. See n49 above and chap. 7, sec. 3.

128. Cf. chap. 3, sec. 1.

129. Perhaps in reading that "all scripture is inspired . . ." (2 Tim 3:16–17) they wrongly concluded that only Scripture is inspired.

apostolic age nor to a collection of sacred writings. In fact the early church believed that the Spirit as God's gift to the whole church is not restricted to its writers of sacred literature nor to Christian verbal witness.[130]

"In the deliberations of the ancient church about the authority of its writings, we nowhere find an instance of inspiration being used as a criterion of discrimination. Of the literature current in the early church, only a few documents explicitly claimed to be inspired, most notably Revelation, *The Shepherd*, and the *Apocalypse of Peter*. Yet it is apparent in these cases how little consequence this claim had, for neither *The Shepherd*, nor the *Apocalypse of Peter* found its way into the canon, and Revelation did so only with difficulty." Because the church as a whole was believed to be inspired by the Spirit, the concept of inspiration "offered no leverage on the question of the authority of various writings." Heretical writings were not regarded as inspired, but that was because they stood apart from the inspired church and her beliefs. Inspiration was also not be used to differentiate non-heretical writings into canonical and non-canonical categories. "The NT writings did not become canonical because they were believed to be uniquely inspired; rather, they were judged to be inspired because they had previously commended themselves to the church for other, more particular and practical reasons."[131]

Conclusion Concerning Criteria. The ancient church's principles for canonizing were diverse, broadly defined and were used in various combinations. Though widespread usage over many years was the most important criterion, it did not prevail in all cases. Yet many of the other standards were often only the means for legitimizing the authority attached to a particular document in virtue of its long-standing and widespread use.[132]

Depending on the book in question, the early church sometimes omitted some of the criteria or applied the apostolicity criterion in different ways, and no single criterion was applied in all cases. The lack of consistently utilized canonical standards in determining NT composition discourages inflexible and uncritical attitudes toward NT Scripture.

17. Conclusions Concerning Canonizing Process, Historical Circumstances

Decisions leading toward the canonizing of the NT did not occur by heavenly command, but amid several centuries of history filled with uncertainty concerning some books later incorporated. "The crucible for the long process of canon formation was provided by a complex interplay of historical circumstances, theological controversies,

---

130. McDonald, *Formation/Canon*, 159; see 155–60; McDonald, "Identifying Scripture/Canon," 435, 437. See also Metzger, *Canon/NT*, 256.
131. Gamble, *NT Canon*, 72.
132. Ibid., 71.

traditions of interpretation, [and] regional usages."[133] In reaction against Montanism, many apocalyptic books and those claiming direct divine dictation were likely rejected and the Constantinian edict probably influenced the inclusion of seven disputed books. "The *opinions of respected theologians* (whether or not they happened also to be bishops) were often widely influential. Striking examples of this can be seen in such figures as Origen and Athanasius in the eastern church and Jerome and Augustine in the western. For the fortunes of some individual writings (e.g., Revelation, Hebrews) the judgments of such thinkers were crucial . . ."

> As far as canonization is understood strictly as the determination of a fixed and closed list of authoritative scriptures, *official ecclesiastical decisions* rendered by bishops or councils must be given their due. We do not know of any such decisions prior to the last half of the fourth century, by which time many documents had been in such long and wide use that an official decision could only confirm standing practice. But this was not true of all documents which found a place in the [NT] canon, and ecclesiastical pronouncements were instrumental in bringing some writings to full canonical recognition—for example, Hebrews in the west and Revelation in the east. The judgments of ecclesiastical authorities were more important than this, however, because they had the effect of concluding discussions about the authority of individual writings and of finalizing the scope of the canon. In this sense it is entirely legitimate to say that as a closed collection . . . the NT canon is contingent on official decisions of the church.[134]

But have the authority of particular writings and the scope of the canon been finalized? Perhaps in terms of Bible publishing it may seem to be. But as we will see in the next chapter, concerning the church's and individual Christian's variable use of biblical material, the canon is far from decided. And even in terms of Bible publishing the scope of the canon is being reconsidered, as with reference to the Protestant inclusion of the Apocrypha.

---

133. Ibid., 83.
134. Ibid., 65–66, 66–67.

Canon and Interpretation

Chapter 7

Canonical Interpretation Plus Its Perils and Promise

1. Primarily Concerning Long Existing Differences among Churches Regarding Precise Content of New Testament Canon

MANY PROTESTANTS HAVE AGREED with Catholics concerning the composition of the (twenty-seven book) NT and the (thirty-nine book) OT, but have disagreed concerning whether the (eighteen book) Apocrypha should be included in the Bible. Eastern Orthodoxy went its own way in having a larger OT than even the Catholics. Furthermore, the Ethiopian Church maintains a canon of eighty-one books, with forty-six in the OT and thirty-five in the NT—and has done so since the fourth century.[1]

Despite fourth and fifth century council decisions, diverse opinions concerning the scope of the NT canon have long existed. Prior to the Council of Trent's insistence upon the canonical authority of the twenty-seven book NT canon, Luther had denied full canonical status to James, Hebrews, Jude[2] and Revelation.[3] In the table of contents of his September Bible of 1522 Luther did not list these disputed NT books with the principle ones. He also (along similarly early Eusebian lines) placed the contested books in the back of his NT translation—thereby treating them as less than fully canonical. Before the Council of Trent's decision Erasmus and even Cardinal Cajetan had expressed doubts concerning the authority of Hebrews, James, Jude and 2 and 3 John. Zwingli thought Revelation should be rejected and Calvin omitted it from his otherwise complete commentary exposition of the NT. From his introductions to Second Peter and Second and Third John we can see that Calvin also had doubts concerning these.[4]

---

1. Metzger, *Canon/NT*, 144.

2. Luther regarded Jude as having copied ideas and phrasing from Second Peter, with both containing stories not found elsewhere in Scripture. Luther concluded that Jude should not be counted among the books that lay the foundation of faith (Kummel, *NT/History of Investigation*, 25).

3. McDonald, *Formation/Canon*, 144.

4. Barth, *CD*, 1/2:476–77.

Many of the NT books whose rights to be fully canonical were doubted by the early church were questioned by Luther and other Protestant Reformers. At both times James's lack of Christocentric focus and its emphasis on justification by works posed problems. Luther was also bothered by its incoherence and its essentially Jewish thinking. He thought that James mixes law and gospel in such disorderly fashion that it seemed to him that its author must have taken some sayings of the apostle's disciples and thrown them onto paper or perhaps someone else wrote them down from his preaching. James regarded the law as liberating (1:25a), though Paul considered it of itself as enslaving (Gal 3:23-24; Rom 7:9-11, 22-23)—since only the Risen Christ as Spirit can free from bondage to sin. Though the author refers to Christ several times, he describes only common faith in God and does not mention the passion, resurrection or Holy Spirit.[5]

In the fourth and sixteenth centuries many churches hesitated concerning the book of Revelation because of its apocalyptic emphases, its presumptuous claim concerning its own importance and its esoteric writing style.[6] Hebrews caused the Protestant Reformers difficulties mainly because of its teaching that if Christians apostatize they cannot repent a second time (6:4-6; 10:26-31; 12:14-17)—which implies that we need only repent once. They were also concerned because of its uncertain apostolic connection. First John's teaching (3:6) that perfection is to be attained in this life was seen as deeply problematic: "No one who abides in him sins; no one who sins has either seen him or knows him." Yet much of the other content and language of First John is not only noteworthy, but contradicts the perfection teaching. "If we say we have no sin we deceive ourselves and the truth is not in us . . ." (1:8).

Luther had emphasized that within the NT there are material differences that cannot be reconciled and that must be faced and decided upon—lest true Christian Faith be compromised.[7] As a result of the previous examples of critical discernment it became possible to observe the multiplicity of NT thinking. But such careful theological analysis stood in marked tension with the Reformation assumption that the Bible, explained by itself, is the sole and unambiguous means for learning of Christ. Thus Luther's discovery of conflicts was virtually stillborn and quickly forgotten by the church.[8] His critical insights were also ignored because the Protestant churches later

---

5. Kummel, *NT/History of Investigation*, 24-25. It was in the context of this concern that Luther made his famous statement, "'What does not teach Christ is not apostolic, even though St. Peter or Paul taught it; again, what preaches Christ would be apostolic, even though Judas, Annas, Pilate and Herod did it'" (same source, 25, quoting Luther).

See n60 for important theological points that in spite of the above criticisms are found in James.

6. Ibid., 26.

7. Calvin generally assumed that when passages seem to raise content conflicts it is not due to their essential teaching, but only to our ignorance in understanding them. Like later orthodoxy and then fundamentalism, Calvin often seemed to presume that all passages are reconcilable (Calvin, *Institutes*, 1:546), a teaching inconsistent with his doubts concerning whether some NT books should be in the canon. See par. 2 above and n7.

8. Kummel, *NT/History of Investigation*, 26.

became deferential toward church authorities and tradition, and these tended to blunt analytical and critical comparisons. Luther's critical insights were also in some tension with his (and later Calvin's) "perspicuity" doctrine that Scripture's central message is clear to Christian readers.

2. Canon's Scope in Principle Open to Revision

We have seen that the church's involvement in the development and delimiting of the canonical Scriptures was much greater than Protestants have traditionally assumed. The state's role was also more extensive than Christians usually recognized. For such reasons, because the standards for canonizing were unevenly applied, and because of content conflicts the precise boundary of the NT canon must remain open to critical churchly reexamination, as must that of the OT. "That the concrete form of the canon is not closed absolutely, but only very relatively, cannot be denied even with a view to the future."[9] Yet in today's much divided and theologically confused church—where canonicity is far from the most pressing issue—it is difficult to imagine how the whole church could achieve sufficient consensus to make major canonical revisions.

Even if the universal church does not rise to the occasion, individuals can and do, such as regarding some parts of the OT as less than canonical. For the ancient church apparently accepted all OT books without considering each book's merit, having merely canonized the available parts of the Septuagint—and then rescuing herself from much of its content by using figurative hermeneutics.[10] Today's OT, however, is not based on the Septuagint, but on the later, Hebrew based, Masoretic text.

While recognizing that a high degree of canonical firmness is essential for preserving the integrity of historically-based revelation, the working authority of Scripture in the lives of Christians has to do with their Spirit-inspired response to the Living Word as God utilizes the interpreted scriptural witness to Jesus Christ to draw people to Himself.

3. New Testament as Interpretation[11]

Although the NT requires interpretation, its writings are themselves interpretations. Paul's epistles interpret the Christian Faith for Hellenistic Gentile Christians, and Mark's author offers a particular understanding of the Jesus traditions, again for the same group. Such early writings in turn became the subjects of interpretation in other writings later included in the NT. Thus Matthew and Luke are interpretive revisions of Mark, supplemented by their creative use of the Q source and each one's separate source—with particular readers, listeners and congregations in mind. Matthew's

---

9. Barth, *CD*, 1/2:476.
10. Vriezen, *OT Theology*, 88.
11. For contemporary biblical hermeneutics, see secs. 4–6; chap. 3, sec. 3; chap. 15, sec. 5; chap. 17.

Gospel in particular relates to Christians of Jewish background and Luke's Gospel has an apologetic interest in showing the positive relationship of Christian Faith to the political order. Luke even begins his Gospel by addressing Theophilus (1:1–4). Similarly, the pseudonymous Pauline letters utilize, interpret, alter and sometimes distort Paul's teaching. These examples show that the NT incorporates various understandings that become further interpreted within the NT.

Even Paul's epistles as the oldest writings included in the NT were indebted to oral and/or written sources beyond pre-OT ones. That pre-NT authors interacted with such sources implies much concerning the old debate about the relationship between Scripture and tradition.[12] Though much of the NT as apostolic-influenced early tradition can and should be distinguished from later tradition, exegesis has undermined the simplistic distinction between Scripture and tradition by showing that canonical documents are themselves products of tradition. This is especially true of the Gospels, but the epistles also exhibit indebtedness to kerygmatic, liturgical, moral and exegetical traditions. *Historically, tradition precedes Scripture, is presumed by it, and persists in it.*[13] "Therefore it is increasingly common for Protestant scholars to characterize the canonical literature as 'a specific form of tradition' or as a 'freezing' or 'transcription' of tradition at a particular stage."[14]

As briefly alluded to earlier,[15] a four Gospel collection implies the importance of each Gospel, but also the relativizing of each by the others and by the gospel itself. The gospel message of salvation through Christ is not reducible to any one Gospel *document* or all four together. Nor those plus Paul and the rest of the NT. *The gospel transcends all NT sources as the subject to which they point.*[16]

Titles are a strong way of constraining texts' interpretations. That each of the four Gospels is to be read as *one version of the gospel* is conveyed more by the titles than by the texts themselves. If Matthew, Luke, and John each intended to eliminate the other Gospels (see Luke 1:1–3), the title appended to each book by some unknown editor thwarts such purpose more effectively in the words "according to" than textual alterations could have done.[17] "Titles can . . . subvert the works to which they are appended . . ."[18]

"At or near the inception of this collection its form was taken to be an essential correlate of its proper understanding (cf. Irenaeus), such that theological meaning and authority were vested in the collection rather than in the single documents taken by themselves. *Thus, the collection, by its very form, provides a critical principle for its*

---

12. See chap. 8.
13. Gamble, *NT Canon*, 73–74, 90.
14. Ibid., 90.
15. Chap. 6, sec. 5.
16. Gamble, *NT Canon*, 76.
17. Barton, *Holy Writings*, 193.
18. Ibid., 193.

interpretation."[19] Even so, Christians have tended to value some Gospels more highly than others. The Gospel of Mark early fell into disfavor for lacking the comprehensive teachings of Matthew and Luke, and the Fourth Gospel took longer to be accepted because of its divergent teachings, conflicting historical details, and popularity among gnostic Christians.

The Pauline pre-canonical corpus, even in its earliest known editions, incorporates pseudonymous letters that interpret and slightly alter Paul's teaching, as when Ephesians and Colossians expansively reinterpret without greatly distorting. However, the Pastoral Epistles seems to considerably alter Paul's teaching.[20] For example, concerning women's leadership in the church, Paul in First Corinthians 11:5 recognizes women's rights to pray aloud and prophesy in church, though they are to keep their heads covered; whereas First Timothy 2:11–12 insists that women must remain silent in church since they have no authority there. Their place of responsibility is said to be the home, and even there as subordinate to their husbands. And women are told that they "will be saved through childbearing," provided that they continue in faith, love, holiness, and modesty (1 Tim 2:15). Marriage is no longer a specific calling (Matt 19:10–12; 1 Cor 7:7), but—contrary to the teaching and example of Jesus and Paul—obligatory for women![21]

Having chosen the issue of women's rights to show an apparent difference between Paul's thinking and that of the Pastoral Epistles, one must concede that Paul's own writings seem sometimes to have been distorted by a later editorial hand that shared the view of the author of the Pastoral Epistles. In the same First Corinthian epistle where Paul defends women's right to speak in the church, we also read that they are to remain silent there and be so submissive that even if they only have questions, they are to wait and ask their husbands (assuming all are married!) when they get home (1 Cor 14:33b–35).[22]

Such editorial alterations as just mentioned and the Pastoral Epistles' distorting of aspects of Paul's thinking contributed to the post Constantinian church's loss of many authentic Christian notes. But let us not be defeated by this problem. The inclusion of editorial contradictions of Paul's thinking within some of Paul's epistles and the inclusion of the Pastorals in the NT canon does not require that Paul's direct witness should take second place. We can rather use that to critique the editorial revisions and the Pastorals at such points of conflict.[23] One thing should be obvious:

19. Gamble, "Scripture/Canon," 76; my emphasis.

20. See chap. 6, n49 for additional conflicts between Paul's thought and the Pastoral Epistles.

21. Aside from the dubious morality of such teachings, not all women are able to bear children. Also, sometimes there are more women than men, so that not every woman would be able to marry.

22. See also chap. 10, n13 for an analysis of 1 Cor 11:3, 7–13 that similarly attributes much to a later editor's distorting hand. Though granting women's rights to pray aloud in church—which likely goes back to Paul—the text denies that women are created in the image of God and therefore assumes their inferiority.

23. See sec. 5 below.

From these comparisons we can see that the canon has contributed to a hermeneutical conversation. *The canon's design promotes the possibility of interpreting texts with a view to other texts, but does not establish which texts are to normatively critique others.*

Like canonical interpretation, for the sake of thinking about what should be believed systematic theology has always insisted on the need to take account of the various writings within the canon and to compare what is said in one place with what is said elsewhere. This, however, should not involve indifference to each text's meaning in more original contexts nor imply that all biblical material is true and important for the church.

4. Evaluation of Brevard Childs's Canonical Approach

As can be seen at many places in this work, I have learned a good deal from Childs. Nevertheless, I disagree concerning some of his most basic points. From the insight that the Bible's documents intend to speak to new situations and different addressees Childs concludes that the search for the original historical context of biblical documents should be secondary and supplemental to the primary hermeneutical effort, which is to understand the final form of texts.[24] Contrary to a common historical-literary view, Childs is correct in insisting that theological interpretation does not depend upon one first being able to reconstruct original settings and probable meanings. He, however, so overextends that point as to become indifferent to the probable significance of original versions. He furthermore assumes that in cases of content conflicts between earlier and later forms one should always choose the teaching encased in the later account. To overemphasize the final form as Childs does is to avoid inquiry concerning the continuity of today's church with an earlier Israel and with the church that existed before there was a biblical canon,[25] and to abandon the effort to learn from Jesus's own life.

I cannot agree that it is advisable for Christians to turn aside from the historical Paul and accept instead "the canonical Paul" as of greater authority, i.e., Paul as softened and reinterpreted by the Acts of the Apostles,[26] the Pastorals,[27] and James![28] In spite of Childs's reverence for Barth, with Childs's methods Luther's and Barth's theological revolutions based on fresh encounters with Paul's own writings would never have happened. I think it more faithful to deal with the tensions between Paul and other NT views, and then to make Spirit-guided responsible choices. With such comparisons we still have the possibility of being influenced by the radicalness of the historical Paul. He should be allowed to stand in criticism of the canonical Paul, for

---

24. Childs, *NT as Canon*, 23, 247, 250.
25. Brown/Schneiders, "Hermeneutics," 1161.
26. See below nn49, 101 and sec. 8; chap. 6, n16; chap. 10, sec. 6; chap. 13, n4.
27. Concerning the Pastorals, see sec. 3 above and chap. 6, n49.
28. Concerning James, see secs. 1 and 7, especially n60.

whom, as in the Pastoral Epistles, the charismatic gifts were seen as distributed only upon the ordained clergy, and where (in those epistles, Second Peter, Jude and Second John) correct belief begins to replace relationship with the Living Christ. Childs's hermeneutic prevents him from recognizing substantial loss at such points.

Equally damaging is his unwillingness to probe beneath the canonical forms of the Gospels—and thus his rejection of quests for the historical Jesus. This position will either reinterpret in the light of the NT's latest Gospel witness (John) or will result in a biblical scholar/amateur systematic theologian's uncritical personal amalgam. With Childs Jesus's voice as recoverable through a literary-historical assessment of the sources has been silenced. As Käsemann long ago warned, if the church turns aside from historical assessment she is dishonest. She is content to leave the kerygma hanging in mid-air as a mere presupposition or myth. To the contrary, the tension between the historical Jesus's proclamation of the kingdom and the NT's proclamation of Jesus must be assessed—rather than such critical comparisons being disallowed in the name of churchly traditionalism.

Other basic criticisms can be raised. Because the meaning contained within writings included in the Bible was not circumscribed by the canon of Scripture—which did not exist when they were written[29]—Childs's canonical focus, though important for comparing individual books, "*does not thereby validate an extension to the point where the canon of the entire Scripture would define it as if it [were] a single text.*"[30]

The value in learning the different tradition-history levels is that we may profit theologically from each. This being so, we, unlike Childs, should not attribute unique inspiration to a particular level. "If anyone was 'more inspired' than others it would probably have been Moses who 'talked with God' and Jesus who alone 'knows the Father.' Yet we have their revelations at only one or more remove, through the inspiration of lesser people—do we not have to say through the qualitatively lesser inspiration of lesser people?"[31] Tradition-history investigation enables us to recognize the relativity of the final composition level.[32]

Childs's harmonizing proclivity interferes with hearing the distinctive witness each biblical author wished to make. It also minimizes the contribution of redaction criticism, which seeks to understand the viewpoints of editors. *In line with the historical evidence cited in chapters 4 and 6, the canon forming process was not as deliberate as might be inferred from the great theological emphasis placed on it by canonical apologists of Childs's type.* Some books likely perished through historical

---

29. Barr, "Biblical Theology," 110.
30. Ibid., 111; my emphasis.
31. Dunn, *Living Word*, 157–58.
32. Ibid., 169. James Sanders's interest in the historical depth of texts *and* his recognition of authority at the various historical levels is better able to handle the NT's *additional* levels than Childs's more limited conception of a single canonical context (same source, 187).

accidents;³³ some were preserved primarily because the canonizers supposed that they were written by the apostles whose names had been honorarily attached to previously anonymous works.³⁴ Even after the canon was completed some books (for example, Second and Third John, Jude, and Second Peter) played little or no role in church life. Furthermore, "versions have often been more influential than the canonical forms of the Hebrew Old Testament or the Greek NT, e.g., the Septuagint (LXX) on the early Christian church, the Vulgate on the western church, the KJV on English Protestantism. Increasingly, critically controlled translations that depart from both Masoretic Hebrew and *Textus Receptus* Greek become canonical Scripture for most churches."³⁵

5. New Testament as Whole not Source of Church Unity³⁶

Precise exegesis indicates that the NT manifests much unity and much diversity,³⁷ with some of the diversity conflicting with some of the unity. Remembering that not all aspects of the immediate following variations are discordant, nevertheless within the NT we find: Jewish Christianity (James and to an extent Matthew), various forms of Hellenistic Christianity (John, First John, Paul's relatively certain writings, Colossians, Ephesians, Hebrews, First Peter), apocalyptic Christianity (Revelation), and early catholic Christianity (the Pastorals, Second Peter, Second and Third John, and Jude). A theological point cannot now be vindicated by the simple claim that "the NT says . . .," not because it does not say that, but because it may say incompatible things. Therefore we are not able to use the NT as a clear and flawless theological standard.³⁸

To understand how this state of affairs came about we need to remember that the Bible not only discloses God's love but human fallibility and sin. Since even the biblical authors were both fallible and sinful, the history of Christianity and of its doctrinal tradition cannot honestly "be viewed and described purely in terms of continuity with Jesus. It is also a history of discontinuity between the Lord and the disciples. At the earliest stage in its life to which we can have access, the primitive community is already in part an apprehending, in part a misapprehending community. While it bears

---

33. Paul's letter to the Colossians not only refers to a letter he received from the Laodiceans, but asks that his letter to the Colossians be read to the Laodiceans (Col 4:16). It is thus reasonable to suspect that he had written to the Laodiceans.

34. I am not here referring to the Gospels, each of which, though nameless, had separately gained considerable reputation prior to inclusion in a foursome collection. There particular apostolic or apostolic-connected names were attached in large part to distinguish one from another.

35. Brown/Schneiders, "Hermeneutics," 1161.

36. The whole Bible is even less so, since the OT conflicts even more with itself than does the NT, and, as parts of chap. 5 summarize, contains many teachings that are incompatible with the NT.

37. This section's emphasis on NT diversity should be pondered in relationship with sec. 7's focus on NT unity.

38. Gamble, *NT Canon*, 86.

witness to the majesty of its Lord, at the same time it obscures it. Even its faith was hidden in the earthen vessel of its [fallible and sinful] humanity . . ."[39]

Once we recognize that like us the biblical authors were fallible servants it should not surprise us that opposing doctrinal viewpoints are found in the NT, some of which must be criticized. The phrases "the faith which was once for all delivered to the saints" (Jude 3) and "the truth that you have" (2 Pet 1:12) seem designed to play off the objective nature of church tradition against Spirit-guided new insight. With Second Peter, Second and Third John and Jude the current work of the Holy Spirit is so minimized that they often seem to dissolve the Spirit *into* tradition. Second John, can even speak of abiding "in the doctrine of Christ" (v. 9), rather than abiding in Christ, and of loving truth and following it, rather than loving Christ and following Him. In contrast stands the primitive Christian doctrine of the Spirit found in Paul and John and going back to Jesus.[40]

The conclusion that needs to be drawn from the incompatibility of some NT positions with others is that the NT in its totality does not constitute the foundation of the church's unity.[41] On the contrary, in its accessibility to the historian it not only attests much unity, but also provides a basis for the multiplicity of the confessions.[42]

In the face of theological incompatibilities, we should remember that the NT does not just articulate theological beliefs, but confronts us with the theological *task* of discerning the truth.[43] Toward achieving this goal, careful attention should be paid to the distinction between letter and spirit. What Paul said of the difference between these in Second Corinthians 3 concerning the OT equally applies to the NT. Because

---

39. Käsemann, *Essays/NT*, 102.

40. Ibid., 102–3. Third John writes only of loving truth and following it (vv. 1, 4), and does not mention Jesus Christ or the Holy Spirit. Equally unacceptable, Jude 9 reflects an alien and atypical NT tradition with its appeal to a Jewish legend about a fight between the archangel Michael and Satan for Moses's body. More positively, Jude criticizes people who are "devoid of Spirit" (v. 19c), in contrast with those who "pray in the Spirit" (v. 20b), and various times refers to Jesus Christ and God. Second Peter 1:21 asserts that *scriptural* prophecy came by the work of the Spirit, though says nothing of later prophecy (same source, 103).

41. Käsemann thinks that the notion of an original unity within the Christian community is the transference to the church of the myth of the "golden age" (Harrisville, *Bible/Modern Culture to Käsemann*, 260, summarizing Käsemann's perspective).

42. Orthodox theologies seldom worked according to the proportions found within the Bible, but commonly elevated or misinterpreted what had slight or marginal representation (Barr, *Holy Scripture*, 39): the virgin birth (two passages), predestination (very few), one passage on scriptural inspiration (which actually concerns the practical usefulness of then available pre-NT writings), and the book of Revelation's claim concerning its own inspiration. "In this sense traditional orthodoxy is a monumental example of the 'picking and choosing' that it deprecates in others" (same source, 40).

Theologies that claim to be built upon the equal inspiration of all Scripture are not less operations of selection and emphasis than are others. A church that supposedly takes the canon as one level piece must still make judgments concerning what is central and what peripheral (same source, 40, 41). It must do what it says it doesn't, since it does not and cannot regard everything as equally important. See sec. 8.

43. Also see chap. 3, sec. 4.

many Jews of Paul's day regarded the emerging OT as a static final authority, he said that, as so regarded, it is "the letter that kills." We are similarly reprehensible if we try to imprison God within the NT. If we equate biblical tradition with "the truth" we regard it apart from the Spirit who, according to John 16:13a, is always newly present to lead us into truth. This does not mean that as Spirit-guided we ignore tradition, for God has already "taken the field" in Her self-revelation. But at any moment Scripture can become "the letter" and does so as soon as we regard the Bible as the direct and immediate authority. The tension between Spirit and Scripture is essential, for Scripture is the witness to the Gospel concerning God's act in Jesus Christ, which can be grasped only through the Spirit, not by intellectual assent. Only with these limitations is the NT foundational for the church.[44]

6. Use of Intracanonical New Testament Norms— Canons within the Canon

At stake in the debate about canons within the canon is whether and then how the Bible can exercise a critical and corrective function over against the church and be the decisive literary means for coming to knowledge of God in Christ. Granted the multifaceted nature of Christian Faith, this belief/norm slogan put singularly is distortingly simplistic. But one's plural version must represent what one perceives to be the most essential aspects of biblically attested Christian Faith.

If the Bible is not to remain "unmanageably and meaninglessly diffuse" Christians must certainly use what they regard as most essential for helping to evaluate the rest. Furthermore, if God's revelation in Christ is the primary source for knowledge of God, the New Testament must be the highest written source for perceiving the intracanonical guiding beliefs and norms to be used to evaluate other biblical teachings, though the Old Testament should perform a supplementary role. And the existence of the Bible over against whatever summary convictions we prioritize resists an absolutizing of or reduction to our specially treasured biblical beliefs and norms. And so the canon maintains "the potentialities of interpretation against dogmatic foreclosures."[45]

Many Catholic scholars have criticized the quest for intracanonical norms, and see it as an admission of the inadequacy of the sixteenth century Protestant formula "Scripture alone." That statement was admittedly an oversimplification, for Christ is of higher authority than the primary literary means through which He is known. On this topic the main difference between typical Protestants and usual Catholics is that the former generally seek interpretive principles *within* the Bible, whereas the latter commonly appeal to the Catholic Church's *teaching authority*. Each view in its own way attests that the canon as a whole does not and cannot provide an effective theological standard.

---

44. Käsemann, *Essays/NT*, 103, 104, 105–6.
45. Gamble, *NT Canon*, 88, 89.

It should be noted that a strict division here between Protestants and Catholics oversimplifies, since there are Catholics who seek primarily to interpret Scripture, and Protestants who are guided mainly by what they suppose are denominational distinctives. For example, some emphasize Wesley's prevenient grace teaching as so presuppositional as to not require critical biblical inquiry. In emphasizing what one thinks are denominational distinctives, the hidden or not-so-hidden motives may be to hold or attract members by emphasizing ways in which one supposes that one's denomination is superior.

Intracanonical NT norms are like reference points, more personal than official. Canons within the canon can involve several different things, such as particular biblical books or group of books,[46] a number of favorite passages, key themes (like justification, sanctification or vocation), and particular christological or pneumatological emphases—or more likely a combination of such items. For many people a wide variety of NT witnesses to Christ help to measure and interpret the rest. Luther used mainly the Pauline testimony to Christ as a criterion to provide selectivity not only with reference to the OT, but also concerning the New. But he decisively interpreted that norm with reference to a more specific one—justification by God's grace in Jesus Christ received through faith.[47]

If we are to be consistent we have to question any biblical teaching that conflicts with the manifestation of God in Christ that we believe the Holy Spirit has impressed upon us. For example, if Paul's paradoxical way of understanding Christian strength amid weakness[48] has become an essential aspect of our faith, we will need to question the theology of glory and success that can be found in some parts of the book of Acts.[49]

---

46. "No Christian church or group has treated the NT writings as uniformly canonical . . . Anyone who uses his NT a great deal will at once acknowledge that some pages are more grubby with finger marks [or pen markings] than others" (Dunn, *Unity/Diversity*, 374).

47. Theological preferences still operate where no high points of Scripture are claimed to be particularly esteemed (Barr, *Concept/Biblical Theology*, 387). Maier protested vigorously against the idea of a canon within the canon (*Historical-Critical Method*, 49), but in the same work later acknowledged that "'every interpreter establishes for himself a more or less conscious total impression of Scripture, which in this or that manner usually comes through when he interprets individual portions' (88). Since this 'total impression of Scripture' will differ from individual to individual, or at least from tradition to tradition, it is in effect just another name for a 'canon within the canon'" (Barr, *Concept/Biblical Theology*, 180).

48. 2 Cor 12:1–10; see also 1:8–10; 4:7–11; 6:3–10.

49. The book of Acts raises as many or more interpretive problems as some of the seven books that faced even more difficulty getting accepted into the NT canon (Hebrews, James, 2 Peter, 2 and 3 John, Jude, and Revelation). Because the author of Luke-Acts regarded miracles and signs as providing demonstrable legitimacy, he saw them as playing a decisive role. Thus he portrayed Paul and Peter before him as great miracle-workers. The author of Luke-Acts apparently had no moral problem in claiming that Paul blinded Elymas (Acts 13:6–12); He also said that Paul gave the cripple at Lystra the power to walk (14:8–10) and, when Paul seemed to have been killed by stoning, just rose to continue his mission (14:19–20). In healings and exorcisms Paul's handkerchiefs are said to have been so full of miraculous power that they cured disease and drove out evil spirits (19:12). The author thought even a snake's venom left Paul unscathed (28:3–6) and that he returned Eutychus's corpse to life by laying

Though like Luther, Wesley emphasized justification by grace through faith, he (believing much in sanctification) also used a moral canon within the canon to critically evaluate Scripture by Scripture (and Liberal Theology much utilized this procedure). If God is concerned about holiness, texts or aspects of texts that negate holiness must be criticized.[50] Not all forms of NT faith are equally valid. Though the Gospels write of a faith that removes mountains, Wesley criticized such faith because he was decisively committed to NT "saving faith" that works by love. "Though I have all this 'faith, so as to remove mountains' (1 Cor 13:2e), yet if I have not the 'faith that works by love,' I am nothing."[51]

Christians today may need to admit that we cannot perceive how, even in highly indirect ways, some books of the Bible bear effective witness to Jesus Christ. But even such books may help us to understand biblical history. Furthermore, books that at one time seem to say little (as, for example, the book of Revelation during the Reformation) may come to be more sympathetically understood in another period, when the outward situation of the church may help her to understand in ways she was not able to earlier.[52]

7. Essential or Normative Beliefs

In recent times NT theologian Arland Hultgren has identified normative and widespread NT understandings and contrasted these with convictions shared by those that the NT and the early post-NT church regarded as heretical. Since "Christian" Gnosticism was a major threat to NT Christianity, we begin by examining Gnosticism in considerable detail. As we comprehend it and the other heresies that NT Christianity rejected, the contrasting Christian beliefs can be more clearly grasped and appreciated. This section should help us to realize that Christian substance can be eroded from within, and that it is necessary to emphasize the unity that exists within normative NT faith.[53]

---

on it (20:7–12), as Elijah and Elisha were said to have done (1 Kgs 17:21 and 2 Kgs 4:34).

These superstitious accounts are from one who was unfamiliar with Paul's writings and had never known him. Paul did claim to manifest the "signs of the Apostle" (2 Cor 12:12), but the exploits in question were so ordinary that his opponents denied his capacity to work miracles. Most certainly Paul did not regard the essence of his apostolate as residing in the performance of miraculous feats (Haenchen, *Acts*, 113–14). "Far from overcoming all obstacles by miraculous means, an Apostle must plunge into the depths of suffering and there experience the help of Christ (2 Cor 12:10)" (same source, 114). See chap. 6, n11 for additional comparisons between Acts's understanding of Paul as a great preacher and Paul's denial of the same. See also this chap., n101 and sec. 8; chap. 10, sec. 6; chap. 13, n4.

50. For moral reasons, in particular cases Wesley recommended using only portions of the Psalms in worship, since some parts of those conflict with God's nature and will as revealed in Christ.

51. Michalson, "Hermeneutics/Holiness/Wesley," 135, quoting from Wesley's *Notes On the New Testament* on Matt 17:20; 86.

52. Weber, *Dogmatics*, 1:266.

53. Gnosticism was a docetic and speculative heresy that in the first few centuries of Christianity infiltrated into much Christianity and competed with "normative" Christianity. Like Hultgren, I prefer the term "normative" to "orthodox," since NT and early church normative Christianity was much

There are indications of developing opposition to gnostic ideas in the Pastoral Epistles and in other later NT books. The 1 Timothy 6:20b reference to "what is falsely called knowledge" (*gnosis*, speculative knowledge) provided the word from which Irenaeus gave the movement its name. Mention of "myths and endless genealogies that promote speculations" (1 Tim 1:4; see also Titus 3:9) likely refer to the long successions of eons in gnostic systems. Second Timothy 4:4 and Second Peter 1:16 speak in this regard of myths that turn people away from the truth.[54] First John 4:2–3a opposes the gnostic denial that Jesus came in the flesh and thereby manifested God.

A major feature of gnostic thought is the extreme duality between God and world, people and world, and oneself with oneself. The deity is regarded as so completely transmundane as to be incapable of self-revelation in the universe it neither created nor in any way governs.[55] The world is regarded as the work of the demiurge (evil creator god) and of demonic or lesser powers that do not know the true God and yet obstruct knowledge of Him in the cosmos over which they rule.

Gnosticism regards people as composed of body, soul, and spirit, with body and soul considered products of the demiurge or lesser powers. Enclosed in soul and body is the spirit or *pneuma*, a portion of the divine that *somehow* fell to earth. But in most gnostic thought it is considered to be present within very few people, with the vast majority therefore incapable of salvation. "In its cosmic exile, the alien element is unconscious of itself, stupefied, asleep, or intoxicated by the poison of the world: in brief, it is 'ignorant.'"[56]

The goal of gnostic striving is the release of the spirit from bondage to the world and its eventual return to the realm of light. Saving *gnosis* is the means whereby some can be awakened to recognition of their true nature and heavenly origin and learn the potent formulas for overcoming the "gate-keepers" who otherwise bar ascent to reunion with the divine essence. This is a *self-contradicting salvation scheme*: If the spirit's return to its divine pre-temporal reality is because it is already by nature divine, could non-divine powers have the capacity to prevent reunion? And if they cannot, what is the need for knowledge of secret passwords to enable the spirit to safely pass through the heavens to the eternal realm?[57]

Gnosticism involves belief in a message that combines highly speculative and impersonal cosmological information with a call to wake up and be detached from the world.[58] Though normative Christianity understands detachment from the world as involving turning aside from sin and evil, it is not so regarded by gnostics, who

---

wider and more tolerant than seventeenth-century orthodoxy, and had no belief in biblical inerrancy.

54. Wilson, "Gnosticism," 229.
55. Jonas, "Gnosticism," 148–49.
56. Ibid., 149.
57. Wilson, "Gnosticism," 227. See sub-sec. 3 and especially n65.
58. Bultmann, *Primitive Christianity*, 168.

consider their inner essence as divine and who therefore merely wish to detach themselves from the non-divine creator and creation.

The general principle of gnostic ethics is hostility towards the world, but from this either ascetic or libertine conclusions can be drawn. The ascetic response deduces from such hostility the obligation to reduce contaminating contact with the world to a minimum. The libertine reaction draws the opposite conclusion, claiming the privilege of absolute freedom to do whatever. Both responses can be justified by the claim that the law as representing the will of the non-divine powers that created the world cannot constrain those who by their nature are in no way bound by the world or affected by world ruler retribution.[59]

Gnosticism and gnostic Christianity have incorrect understandings of how knowledge of God, self, and moral obligation are acquired. The NT insists that knowledge of God has been revealed in Christ, but is acquired through trust in Christ and morally influencing relationship with Christ, not by *secret gnosis*. The NT teaches that we are sinners, not divine, and that the very Creator God has come into this world to redeem us from sin and death.

Turning to Hultgren's analysis and synthesis of normative Christianity as standing against Christian heresies, though his summary is important, not every NT book is either consistent with or manifests the six beliefs he discusses. Much of the Synoptic Gospel testimony to the historical Jesus does not reflect Hultgren's christological or soteriological points. Also in conflict with these, James knows little of Jesus's saving significance and regards salvation as by works, to be supplemented only by general trust or confidence in God.[60] In spite of such criticisms of Hultgren's over-general-

---

59. Jonas, "Gnosticism," 150.

60. In spite of these criticisms and earlier ones in sec. 1, there is much in James that is valuable. James was one of Kierkegaard's favorite biblical books and for good reasons. He agreed with James that the inner reality that is prior to the act of turning away from God is wrong desire. "No one, when tempted, should say, 'I am being tempted by God'; for God cannot be tempted by evil and . . . tempts no one. But one is tempted by one's own desire, being lured and enticed by it; then when that desired has been conceived, it gives birth to sin . . ." (1:13–15a NRSV). In agreement with James SK had learned from his own experience that, for a Christian, suffering can be a great *Training In Christianity*. "Count it all joy, my brethren, when you meet various trials, for you know that the testing of your faith produces steadfastness. And let steadfastness have its full effect, that you may be perfect and complete, lacking in nothing" (1:2–4; see also 1:12). (SK, however, would have argued with the just mentioned belief that perfection can be attained in this life, if James is to be held to his literal words.) Both Kierkegaard and John Wesley endorsed James's criticism of double-mindedness (1:8; 4:8b), which Jesus challenged with His teaching that the pure in heart are blessed (Matt 5:8a). SK rephrased this as purity of heart as consisting in willing one thing—God's will.

Kierkegaard often criticized the hypocritical popular Christianity of his day, as when he told the parable of geese who Sunday after Sunday waddled to and from church, but delighted in sermons about the joy of flying. As James said, "Be doers of the word, and not merely hearers who deceive themselves. For if any are hearers of the word and not doers, they are like those who look at themselves in a mirror; for they look at themselves and, on going away, immediately forget what they were like. But those who look into the perfect law, the law of liberty, and persevere, being not hearers who forget but doers who act—they will be blessed in their doing" (1:22–25 NRSV). SK liked the moral activism encouraged by James, that faith must be active in love and show forth good works (2:15–18). In his

izations, his typology of normative NT Christianity encompasses much of the NT in contrast with early heresy.

The six affirmations Hultgren summarizes are not peculiar to any one Christian writer, but exhibit the basic expressions of Christianity found in much of the NT and among many extra-biblical first and second century writings, as well as in many later Christian reflections. Hultgren concedes only essentially non-contradicting NT variations within the six themes, but, as we will see, some NT differences entail flagrant dissension. Yet taking the various NT's expressions of Christianity into account as a whole—Theology, Christology, Soteriology, Ethics, and Local and then Universal Ecclesiology—they agree much more than with those of such figures as Marcion, Valentinus, or Montanus.

As for the six widespread convictions:

i. Theology

Normative Christianity attests with Jesus and Israel that the Creator can be loved and trusted as benevolent to humanity.[61] However, the Johannine witness (especially 1 John) does not reflect the backward look to the pre-OT to establish confidence in the Creator God.

ii. Christology

In speaking of Jesus as representing Israel's God, the NT and other early Christian writings either describe God or Christ as taking the initiative. Either they "theopractically"

---

later (though still young) years Kierkegaard would have appreciated James's criticism of the church's partiality toward and kowtowing to the rich (2:1–4), though would not have agreed with James's romanticizing of the poor (2:5) and vilifying of the non-poor (2:6b–7; 5:1–6).

SK recognized that living faith is different from mere intellectual assent to propositions, such as that God is one (2:19). A Christian should believe the latter and much more, but these must be affirmed as aspects of one's relationship with the Living God, who is at work morally transforming one's life. Kierkegaard would probably even have agreed to the importance of keeping control over one's words (1:26; 3:3–10; 4:11a), though would not have claimed to have well achieved this. SK would also have concurred with James's emphasis on keeping unstained from the world (1:27c). "Do you not know that friendship with the world is enmity with God? Therefore whoever wishes to be a friend of the world becomes an enemy of God" (4:4bc NRSV).

Kierkegaard might have concluded this footnote by quoting again from James: "'God opposes the proud, but gives grace to the humble.' Submit yourselves, therefore to God . . . Draw near to God and he will draw near to you. Cleanse your hands, you sinners, and purify your hearts, you people of double mind" (4:6b–7a, 8).

Though all legitimate criticisms of James and other problematic and less problematic biblical books need to be registered, we should not overlook the gems of divine wisdom present even in books subject to warranted criticism.

61. Hultgren, *Rise/Normative Christianity*, 86, 87. Neither Marcion nor stricter gnostics believed that the Redeemer God created the world (John 3:16; Acts 17:24; 2 Cor 5:19; Heb 1:2) or "all that is seen and unseen" (Council of Nicea, 325) (same source, 89–90).

write of *God* as redeeming humanity through Christ or "christopractically" of *Christ* as acting with redemption on God's behalf. A theopractic example: "God was in Christ reconciling the world to himself" (2 Cor 5:19a). A christopractic one: "Christ . . . died for sins once for all that he might bring us to God" (1 Pet 3:18ab).

Theopractic assertions concerning redemption more explicitly link Israel's God to redemption. In terms of salvation's motivation, the Son is described as being sent into the world, and then living obediently. With christopractic statements, the Son is depicted as having Himself come forth to rescue us and to bring us into a reconciled relationship with God. Though normative Christianity can affirm both perspectives, Hultgren supposes that earlier writers tend to stress the theopractic character of redemption, thereby preserving Jewish monotheism most clearly, whereas later ones bring the christopractic emphasis more to expression. He claims that as theological reflection developed, the epistles likely written by Paul's students ("Deutero-Pauline" ones, such as Ephesians, Colossians, First and Second Timothy and Titus), Hebrews, First Peter and First John accentuated the role of Christ in redemption, in line with the liturgical and creedal tendency to emphasize the Son.[62]

Though the theopractic-christopractic distinction is helpful, the division as to which writers use particular conceptuality often does not hold, as can be shown by a few examples. Paul himself, though likely quoting from elsewhere, also writes christopractically, regarding the Son as an initiator of salvation: He "did not count equality with God a thing to be grasped, but emptied himself . . ." (Phil 2:6b–7). Yet Ephesians as a late pseudonymous Pauline book can write theopractically (1:3–10, 15–23; 2:4–10). Theopractic-christopractic differences relate to understandings of Trinity and whether God is conceived as socially plural or whether that doctrine expresses only God's revelational relationships, whereby we learn of Him.

Hultgren claims that normative Christianity regards Jesus of Nazareth as sent by God to reveal God and to redeem humanity. This depends on what one means by "sent." At least from the time of His baptism Jesus seemed to have had a sense of being called by God for a mission to Israel and from Israel to the world. But the Synoptics reflect no knowledge of the Son being pre-temporally "sent." They do, however, indicate that Jesus had a unique sense of intimate fellowship with God, having the audacity to use the term *abba* (daddy) to refer to Him, which has many similar connotations to "mommy." Hultgren rightly claims that Jesus's sense of authority did not derive from his learning or cleverness in scriptural interpretation, but from His close relationship with God and obedience to His will. However, I cannot agree that Jesus's relationship with God is "the basis for" *later* christological affirmations.[63] Surely His resurrection is the foundation for those, but Jesus's experience is consistent with many resurrection-inspired later NT christological conclusions.

---

62. Ibid., 90.
63. Ibid., 79, 106–7, 107.

Hultgren rightly suspected that the Fourth Gospel manifests docetism, but then softened his criticism because not everything therein is docetic: "The Fourth Gospel, to be sure, portrays Jesus in [such] ways that his humanity is virtually lost, and so gnostics could make use of it, but even in that Gospel there are assertions of Jesus's humanity (particularly in its telling of his death). Neither Marcion nor gnostics could affirm that 'the Logos *became* flesh' (John 1:14)"[64] Though John was not as consistently docetic as the gnostics, he sometimes negated Jesus's humanity, which is why they loved his Gospel. For example according to John, Jesus had the power to resurrect himself (10:18b). The Fourth Gospel may not be consistently docetic, but . . .

iii. Soteriology

Normative Christianity affirms that in spite of human sinfulness, which would otherwise disqualify us from salvation, God's redemptive work in Christ provides access to salvation, which through trust in Christ and His work is begun in this life, but completed beyond it.[65] Though this understanding of salvation's outworking is widely taught in the NT, contrary to Hultgren it is not universally reflected there.[66]

Since Jesus regarded all people as sinful, He declared God's forgiveness of sins for all and in His earthly ministry engaged in a redemptive mission. Though answerable to God for carrying out this ministry, Jesus expected to be vindicated. Further, though during His ministry He did not likely refer to Himself as the Messiah (which concerned political power), He was no mere prophet of the coming kingdom. By word, deed and attitude He reflected that kingdom in anticipatory ways.[67] At His trial and

---

64. Ibid., 91. Excepting the Ebionites (Jewish Christians) the early sects represented extreme christopractic traditions, which separated the redeemer from Israel's God and denied Jesus's humanity. Such docetism was probably taught in the first century and was certainly taught in the second, since the author of First John opposed those who so believed (4:2–3a) (same source, 90–91). For the Ebionites see sub-sec. 5.

65. Ibid., 92. The soteriologies of the gnostic sects rest on other foundations. Like all gnostics, Basilides and his second-century gnostic followers held that salvation does not come by confessing Him who was crucified—which would not only require acceptance of Jesus's humanity, but repentance, that contrasts with the arrogance of consistently gnostic systems. Valentinian gnostics thought that they knew the secrets revealed to the one or two in ten thousand who by nature can receive them. According to Valentinus, humanity consists of three kinds of people: those who by nature are engrossed in the world and are incapable of salvation; Christians and non-Valentinian gnostics, who by faith and works can attain "salvation" with the demiurge (the artisan/fashioner of the physical universe); and Valentinian gnostics, who through perfect gnosis can alone enter the heavenly fullness (same source, 93). Since according to such thinking people are born into one of the three categories, salvation is by nature, though knowledge evokes the awareness of one's status. This scheme is based entirely on speculation.

66. Not only does James not center salvation on Christ, but 1 Tim 2:15 also fails to do so by teaching (as Mormons noticed) that women's salvation has a good deal to do with bearing children.

67. Hultgren, *Rise/Normative Christianity*, 107.

with His impending death looming He likely accepted the Messiah designation (Mark 14:62a)—for the final events of His life would redefine the term.[68]

As a result of Jesus's resurrection His disciples were able to believe that He—who during His earthly life had forgiven their sin in God's name—had provided atonement. Though the affirmation that Jesus is God's Revealer and humanity's Redeemer was foreshadowed in Jesus's words and deeds—such insight would have long been forgotten had God not reversed our rejection of Jesus by raising Him from death.

The means for appropriating the redemptive benefits of Christ in NT Christianity is experienced faith, not, as in Gnosticism, mere knowledge.[69] After Jesus's resurrection normative Christian Faith became grounded in Jesus's life, death and resurrection, and the experiences of conversion, repentance, and dying and rising with Christ that lead to belief in Him (John 3:16, 36; 5:24; 2 Tim 3:15c). Faith as a response to the interpretation of Jesus's life, death and resurrection is a post-resurrection possibility. Though such experienced faith is accompanied by knowledge—it is not mere knowledge. It involves a trusting relationship with God through Christ.

iv. Ethics

Normative Christianity affirms that those who respond to God's love in Christ are to love others. Christians' moral grounding includes some moral traditions of the OT, the example and teaching of Jesus and precepts from other parts of the NT. The traditions contained in the canonical Gospels affirm that the NT utilized major teachings from Israel's heritage—the Ten Commandments,[70] *the double commandments of love (though separated in the OT),*[71] and many injunctions concerning being responsible to others. He deepened, transformed and extended these, while rejecting many OT traditions.[72] Among other aspects of His life and its meaning, His self-giving service became in normative Christianity a model for Christian conduct.[73]

Although the gnostics gave some thought to ethics, and did not always promote either libertinism or asceticism, the contrasts with normative Christianity are striking. Moral exhortation in gnostic Christianity (Marcion excepted) is minimal. The many pages of the gnostic collection from Nag Hammadi contain only a page or two of exhortation to care for others and be trustworthy. Valentinian gnostic Christians

---

68. Dahl, *Crucified Messiah*, 33–35.

69. See chap. 19.

70. Exod 20:2–17; Deut 5:6–21; Mark 10:19; Rom 13:9.

71. Deut 6:4–5 and Lev 19:18b; Mark 12:29–31 and par.; cf. Rom 13:8–10; Gal 5:14.

72. See chap. 5, secs. 12–13.

73. Mark 10:42–45 and par.; John 13:15; Phil 2:1–11; Heb 12:1–2; 1 Pet 2:21 (Hultgren, *Rise/Normative Christianity*, 95–96). God's incarnational stooping, though incapable of imitation, is another moral paradigm that motivates the Christian life and helps to provide direction. Numerous other moral guidelines are present in the NT, such as the need to live as always prepared to die.

even thought that good works were not necessary, since pneumatics, as spiritual by nature, cannot perish.

v. The Church as Community

Normative Christianity affirms that those who trust in God through Jesus are to be involved with a local community of disciples. In the early centuries this stream of tradition was responsive to needed changes, and within widely set limits was able to hold people together who differed considerably concerning theology, piety and customs. In contrast the sects insisted on the separation of the "right minded" from others, though this occurred for varying reasons.

In the middle of the second century, Justin described Jewish Christians who, though placing their hope in Christ, practiced circumcision, observed the whole of the Mosaic law, and refused to converse or eat with Gentile Christians. This distortion of Christianity must have originated in the first century with James (Jesus's brother) and other like-minded Jewish Christians of Jerusalem who opposed table fellowship between Jewish and Gentile Christians (Gal 2:12). Later in the second century, the term *Ebionites* was applied to those who continued their separation, but by the early fourth century the Ebionites were a small tradition within Christianity. Their emphasis on Jewish-Gentile separation was incompatible with the normative Christian understanding of God's love for all and with the resulting practice that embraced Jews and Gentiles in one fellowship. Even such Jewish Christian documents as the Gospel of Matthew and the Epistle of James had moderate attitudes by comparison with Ebionites.[74]

As for a different kind of separatism, the gnostic Christian "stress on *gnosis* as the means of salvation—and the insistence that most persons are not capable of receiving it"—is an attitude that insofar as it gives shape to a community is one that "is exclusive and composed of persons who are primarily concerned about the cultivation of their own personal spirituality."[75] Marcion was an exception in this regard, but he was not a pure gnostic. He emphasized Christian love and redemptive grace through Christ, though distorted the latter because of his gnostic-influenced docetism.

In contrast with gnostic Christianity the sense of belonging in normative Christianity continued the legacy of the earthly ministry of Jesus. There is no reason to doubt the historicity of the claim that Jesus had disciples who formed a fellowship with Him and with one another. Furthermore the Synoptics attest that the fellowship around Jesus was characterized as familial,[76] with all as servants who were not to seek supremacy over the others.[77] Here and in later normative Christianity there is no agreement with such elitism as came to expression in various gnostic groups.

---

74. Ibid., 97, 93, 97–98, 103.
75. Ibid., 101, 99.
76. Matt 5:22–26 ; 18:15; 23:8; 12:46–50; pars. Mark 3:31–35; Luke 8:19–21.
77. Matt 20:20–28; pars. Mark 10:35–45; Luke 22:24–27.

vi. The Church as Extended Fellowship

Normative (and Marcionite) Christianity affirmed that Christians belong to a church that is larger than that provided by the local community. Though in Paul's writings the term *ekklesia* normally referred to a local gathering, he also applied it to the entire church, attesting that usage by the middle of the first century (1 Cor 12:28; 15:9; Gal 1:13; Phil 3:6). Further, a networking existed between congregations, apostles, other leaders, and between members of different congregations, as Paul's lists of greetings show. NT writings also tell of financial aid sent from one community to another, of intercessory prayers for congregations other than one's own, and of the wide extending of hospitality. Furthermore, the amount of correspondence among early Christian communities was unprecedented, which demonstrates that members of local churches had a sense of belonging to a wider fellowship. These developments can be traced to post-resurrection expansion much influenced by Paul's and others' missionary leadership and communication.[78]

8. Inerrancy's Errors Including Absence of Christian Freedom

Even in describing the normative doctrinal aspects of the NT, conflicting NT teachings have been indicated. I now extend that aspect of my concern by entering into a vigorous polemic against those who suppose that everything in Scripture agrees with everything else. Inerrancy[79] or verbal inerrancy is the doctrinaire insistence that the Bible contains no errors or contradictions of any kind and is authoritative on all subjects to which it refers, including history, geography and natural science (for example, involving the universe's physical structure and history). All of the Bible's statements are regarded as true in all respects because God is thought to have prevented its writers from erring. For example, since the Bible says that the sun stood still at Joshua's command (Josh 10:12b–13a), it must have done exactly that, which, of course, implies that the sun circles around the earth.

As largely a product of seventeenth century Protestant orthodoxy, the theory of verbal inerrancy lacks deeper roots in Christian tradition. In its most extreme form it taught not only the divine inspiration of all of the words and letters of Scripture, but also the inspired nature of the consonants and vowels of the Hebrew text. A robust debate ensued when Louis Cappel (1585–1658), French professor of Hebrew, demonstrated that the vowel vocalizations were added much later. His philological insight unhinged the inerrancy dogma, showing that these were not an original part of the supposedly inerrant text, but were products of the Christ-rejecting Jewish Masoretic version created long after the Christian canonizing of Scripture.[80]

---

78. Hultgren, *Rise/Normative Christianity*, 101–2, 108.
79. Compare chap. 3, sec. 1; chap. 6, sec. 15.
80. Gunneweg, *Understanding OT*, 67.

Aside from the above technical issue, the phenomenon of the Bible's diverse and sometimes contradicting teachings is made obvious by honest historical reading. The weakness of seventeenth century scholasticism's doctrine of authority was not that it took Scripture too seriously, but that it did not take it seriously enough: It imagined that the Bible required a rationalistic presupposition about its nature for external prop and proof.[81]

The intention behind scriptural inerrancy was the naturalistic postulate that Scripture must speak the Word of God with the same obviousness and directness as the plainest of human words or simple axioms.[82] It divorced "revelation" from the Living Word of God, thereby seeking to bring God under human control. It tried to divest revelation of its character as genuine revelation from God's side.[83] Such a teaching contradicts the NT insistence that the Holy Spirit is required for knowledge of the meaning of the Christ event.[84]

Why would the Bible need to be inerrant?[85] Is it really because such defenders are certain that two late passages of Scripture teach that? (2 Tim 3:16–17; 2 Pet 1:20–21) Isn't the real basis of such advocacy the fearful recognition that without this postulate faith is utterly dependent upon hearing the Word of the Living God speaking through Scripture, the awareness that without such personal encounter there can be no genuine sense of divine authority?

God revealed Herself amid hiddenness.[86] Since the Transcendent God cannot be seen, She veiled Herself in Jesus. She veiled Herself again amid the scriptural witness, whose writers were fallible and sinful human beings. A final aspect of hiddenness is that we fallible sinners can perceive the Bible's God-intended meanings only with the aid of the Spirit.

Since the NT teaches that—Christ excepted—all humans are sinful, it is inconsistent to assume that the biblical writers were infallible in their writing activities. If we recognize that sin affected the writers of books in Scripture we relate the acknowledged imperfections of some of the Bible's understandings of God not just to primitiveness or inadequate education, but to the profound NT teaching concerning universal sinfulness.[87]

Inerrancy defenders do not recognize that all theological expressions are but approximations. They believe that God miraculously immunized the biblical writers,

---

81. Barth, *Table Talk*, 26, 41; Barth, *Against Stream*, 223; Barth, *CD*, 1/2:519, 522–25. Johnson, *Authority/Protestant*, 184–85.

82. Barth, *CD*, 1/2:525.

83. Barth, *CD*, 4/1:368.

84. See chap. 3.

85. For implicit criticism of such a notion, see chap. 3, sec. 1; for an interpretation of the texts cited in the next sentence, see chap. 3, n4.

86. See chap. 18, secs. 4 and 5 for major discussions of this theme; see also chap. 9, sec. 4.

87. Barr, *Old/New Interpretation*, 163.

protecting them in their writing activities from the problems of sinfulness, fallibility, and cultural contamination. Disingenuously such advocates these days deny that God directly wrote the Bible, with Her finger so to speak. In effect they believe the equivalent. Recent inerrancy advocates still believe that God so perfectly guided the biblical writers that the Bible's words *are directly Her words*. Is this not the equivalent of claiming that the Bible's authors in their writing activities were incarnations of God—sinless—like our Lord Jesus Christ? This view seems to jeopardize the heart of the Gospel—that once only God incarnated Herself. We do not need a perfect book to learn of a perfect Savior. We can live with an imperfect book, since the perfect Savior, the Risen Christ as Holy Spirit can lead us into truth (John 16:12–15).

As Jesus can be regarded docetically (only seeming to be human), so Scripture can be considered docetically—only seeming to be comprised of human documents—since its authors were incapable of errors. "Those who hold the canon to be without error of any kind, perfectly evangelical, inspired in whole and parts alike, have a docetic understanding of it; this will necessarily lead them to a docetic understanding of Jesus; and then, like all docetics, they will no longer comprehend the [offensiveness of the] Cross, and thus they will make faith into mere intellectual assent. . . ."[88] Failing to perceive how offensive is the Christian belief in a Crucified Messiah, faith has no hurdle to overcome, and thus can be accepted by comfortably endorsing particular ideas. Part of Scripture's glory is that its truths stand out in spite of its human smudges, as the glory of Jesus Christ stands out amid the time-bound nature of His first century existence, with the limitations that placed on His perceptions. Consistent with the Incarnation, revelation comes *through* the contingent, rather than bypassing it.[89]

As for inerrancy advocates' insistence that the Bible's ancient science must be accepted: When the church confuses the offense of the cross with the offense first century science poses for modern people she drives intellectuals away. She confuses a less than ultimate offence with the ultimate one. No first century person had to accept what they regarded as scientifically absurd to become a Christian. Rather than sacrificing their intellects they needed only to recognize their sinfulness and gratefully respond to God's forgiveness in Christ.

Even if God had hurled the Bible directly from heaven, even if it were infallible from cover to cover, that would not enable us to interpret and apply it correctly. Even an infallible book in the hands of sinful and fallible interpreters would be a less than perfect resource. All biblical interpretation and application is fraught with the risk that one may misunderstand and misinterpret. The belief in inerrancy may encourage

---

88. Käsemann, *NT Questions*, 277.

89. Brown, "Good News/Barth," 97, describing Barth's perspective. Though Sunni Muslims reject the Christian incarnation claim concerning Jesus, their attitudes toward the Qur'an and its supposed authorship by the illiterate Mohammed make an implicit incarnation claim for both their book and their prophet. They say that God wrote the book and that Mohammed was only God's humble instrument. But a human believed to be sinless and infallible in respect to a particular activity is in that area regarded incarnationally.

pride and undue confidence that one's own group has *the correct understanding* of the Bible, and that the risk involved in interpreting has been transcended. This is bondage to tradition, not honest reading. Such proud inerrancy-encouraged confidence is an illusion. The Jehovah's Witnesses believe in biblical inerrancy, but that has not prevented them from developing an atrociously non-Christian theology. Also, Christians who affirm inerrancy often disagree at specific points of doctrine with others who so advocate, as, for example, concerning what one expects will occur just prior to the world's ending. Inerrancy cannot and does not resolve such disputes.

Every sermon, every teaching, and every commenting upon Scripture is an act of interpretation—by humans who are less than angelic. Even merely to quote the Bible in a particular context is an interpretive action whereby one who is fallible selects a specific passage that one regards as particularly applicable. The miracle is that God can use the biblical writers and even us in spite of our flaws.

A belief treasured by those who believe in inerrancy is justification by grace through faith. This is certainly a central Christian conviction. But is this belief valued by inerrantists more as a idea than as a continuing critical experience. With Paul the belief in justification led to freedom from authoritarian understandings of religious tradition. "For freedom Christ has set us free; stand fast therefore, and do not submit again to the yoke of slavery" (Gal 5:1). To the contrary, inerrantists seek to protect their members from exposure to diverse Christian viewpoints. Thus the life of Christian "freedom" becomes one demanding much conformity to human traditions and organizations.

We honor the Bible by seeking to understand what it says and by trying to be faithful to the Christ we have come to know through the scriptural witness. *We need to face the phenomenon of the Bible's content.* When we read Scripture carefully and without unnatural contortions we find some parts that conflict not only with other parts, but with the God we have come to know as God's Spirit has drawn us to Christ. *Traditions that conflict with our best comprehension of Jesus Christ must be criticized. Otherwise they compromise our understanding of and allegiance to Christ and weaken our discipleship.*

Particular scriptural traditions can be and have been used to defend sub-Christian practices,[90] such as slavery, racism, polygamy, the subservience of women, the lust for revenge, genocide, and a preference for dictatorships.[91] Saying that God once commanded harsh, loveless behavior, but would not do so now—solves no problem. To so affirm is to end up with a god whose commanding activities vary so much that His nature is contradictory. Let us avoid such theological acrobatics and freely admit that *Scripture reflects a developing history of thinking about God and about God's moral expectations.*

---

90. See chap. 5, secs. 12–13.

91. Barr, *Escaping Fundamentalism*, 111. Specific biblical traditions have also been used to justify treating unfairly those who dare to disagree with what the dominant group determines is orthodox Christian teaching.

Aspects of OT teaching and practice can be used to justify non-Christian traditions. By relying on those teachings people can remain in tribal and animistic Traditional Religion while imagining they are Christians. Those who claim to accept the whole of the Bible as equally authoritative in reality often empty much NT teaching of meaning—by subordinating it to the more tribal and ruthless aspects of the OT. We face precisely this interpretive danger in Africa and elsewhere.

The Bible exhibits theological diversity on many topics, and outright conflict on some. As for the latter, the OT moves from regarding all suffering as deserved punishment, to in some cases considering it a spiritual discipline, to sometimes thinking of it in terms of vicarious sacrifice. In Christ God utilized suffering in saving the world.[92] Another example concerns thinking about life after death. Though the hope of eternal life is resolutely proclaimed in the NT and began to be implied in some later portions of the OT, most of the OT envisioned no hope of personal immortality. "A living dog is better than a dead lion. For the living know that they will die, but the dead know nothing, and they have no more reward; but the memory of them is lost" (Eccl 9:4b–5). "All are from the dust and all turn to dust again" (Eccl 3:20b).

All Scripture should be read and studied, but the content of what is taught in some parts of the Bible "raises serious questions as to the propriety of . . . commending [those parts as] sources or standards of authentic Christian witness."[93]

Had the NT canonizers been committed to the Bible's infallibility they would not have left *four versions of the Gospels*—since they differ at many points. Also, had the early Christians been concerned about scriptural inerrancy they would not have sanctioned translations.[94] Every translator knows that translations are imperfect efforts to choose the closest proximate words in other languages, realizing there is seldom exact correspondence. That there was some infallible original document is a mere wishful thought of those who believe in inerrancy. But even if there had been, no later handwritten copy or translation would be a perfect rendition.

The inerrancy position may seem to respect scriptural texts, but bends them to support the presuppositional logic of the inerrancy position, denying the priority of careful exegesis and thoughtful interpretation. The inerrancy doctrine is not exegetically derived, but is a logical deduction based on a particular understanding of God—that a perfect and powerful God would not utilize an imperfect means for revealing His nature and will. Inerrancy advocacy in effect puts reason and later traditions above Scripture.[95]

---

92. Fosdick, *Modern Use/Bible*, 23–24.

93. Wood, *Formation/Christian Understanding*, 110–11, referring to Käsemann, "Kritische Analyse," in *Das Neue Testament als Kanon*, 366.

94. Islam takes a consistently inerrantist line in its negative attitude toward translations of the Qur'an, regarding those as mere interpretations.

95. Dunn, *Living Word*, 138, 186.

> Do inerrantists *take with sufficient seriousness even the most basic exegetical findings*, particularly with regard to the Synoptic Gospels? I refer here not to any particular theory of the relation between these Gospels, on which there is dispute, but to the fact of *literary dependence* between the material within these Gospels when that material was already in Greek, on which there is no dispute as far as I am aware. Where literary dependence at the level of the tradition in Greek is so clear, the sort of harmonizations which depend on postulating several incidents/sayings rather than different versions of the one incident/saying becomes increasingly improbable. Insistence on such harmonizations is one of the ways in which the character and text of scripture is not taken with sufficient seriousness. More important, it is one of the factors which cause greatest stress to students from an inerrancy background, when they find that the most self-evident character of the text is being ignored and denied as a way of escaping a "difficulty" or "error."[96]

Fourth Gospel. Inerrantists also suppose that the Fourth Gospel intended to give a verbal record of Jesus's daily life. They then smooth away its obvious discrepancies vis-a-vis the other Gospels. John, to the contrary, made what are essentially post-resurrection affirmations about Jesus by expressing those in narrative form, rather than more abstractly as did Paul. To a considerable extent "Mark retained the perspective of the pre-resurrection disciples for whom Jesus's real identity was hidden throughout most of his Gospel, whereas the Fourth Gospel was written consistently from the vantage point of Christ's mission as the Divine Son, who was sent from God."[97] In the Fourth Gospel when John the Baptist first saw Jesus (1:29) he recognized Him as "the lamb of God who takes away the sin of the world." Admittedly, the synoptic Gospels do *at this point* indicate that Jesus will baptize with the Holy Spirit (Matt 3:11c; Mark 1:8; Luke 3:16c). Like the Fourth Gospel, these parallel synoptic accounts likely reflect post-resurrection perspectives. However, Matthew 11:2–3 and Luke 7:19 later admit that from prison John sent *his disciples* to inquire whether Jesus is the Christ. And a Gospel writer would have had no motive for inventing such an incident.

Concerning Jesus' baptism, the writer of the Fourth Gospel had the Baptist proclaim the truth that we know and that the Baptist would have known had John and Christians of Jesus's day experienced Him from the post-resurrection perspective. The ultimate question is not whether John the Baptist said these words, which is doubtful in the extreme, but whether the essential message is true. It is not whether the narrative reflects the details of what was said and happened, but whether it reflects what we—instructed by the entire NT—believe to be the meaning of the Christ event.

Though many of the teachings of the Synoptics are reiterated in John's Gospel, the style of Jesus's teaching there is noticeably different from the others. No longer does Jesus speak in short sayings and parables, but in lengthy discourses that often

---

96. Ibid., 139–40; last emphasis mine.
97. Childs, *NT as Canon*, 51.

return to earlier sub-themes. The Fourth Gospel's christological points also become greatly amplified and highly explicit, as one would expect of a much later writing. The teaching about entering the kingdom of God as little children (Matt 18:3 & pars) becomes a long exposition on new birth (ch 3). Jesus's addressing God as *Abba* (Mark 14:36a) becomes a lengthy Father-Son discussion in John 5:17–47. And Jesus's parable of the Lost Sheep and the Caring Shepherd (Luke 15:3–7) becomes the chapter 10:1–18 elaborate discourse about Jesus as the Good Shepherd.

The Fourth Gospel discussions are probably best understood as extended meditations or reflections concerning the meaning of important events from Jesus's ministry and concerning some of His teachings as remembered within the late communities from which this Gospel came. Writing under the guidance of the Holy Spirit, John must have hoped that the Spirit would use his testimony to further God's purpose of re-proclaiming the truth of Jesus (16:13–15), indicating the significance of what He said (e.g., 2:21), and leading into fuller truth than when Jesus's disciples were able to hear or understand when He was with them (16:12–13).[98]

Acts. Beyond Fourth Gospel comparison with the Synoptics, we can also see how ill-founded is the belief in verbal inerrancy by noticing *how extensively Acts fails to understand Paul's theology and the events of his life in comparison with what we learn from Paul's own letters.*[99] Since Luke evidences no awareness that Paul wrote letters,[100] he must not have had access to any of those. Paul's speeches in Acts seem to reflect Lukan rather than Pauline theology.[101] Though centering on Christ, such speeches say nothing of being in Christ and under His new dominion, nor of Christ's atoning death and of our sharing in Christ by dying and rising with Him. Though Acts's speeches accentuate the Holy Spirit, they do so in non-Pauline ways, focusing on prophetic speech, rather than regarding life in the Spirit as equivalent to life in Christ. We hear nothing of the church as Christ's body, and the one mention of justification (13:38–39) says nothing of faith. Acts does not understand the nature of the conflict about the law nor of Paul's insistence that salvation has always been by grace alone. Peter's speech in Acts 10:34b–35 makes it clear that Luke even thought that people could be saved by works: "'Truly I perceive that God shows no partiality, but in every nation anyone who fears him and does what is right is acceptable to him.'" Acts depicts Paul as quarreling with Judaism more over resurrection (4:2; 23:6) than over the law, ascribing to Paul an astonishingly positive attitude to the latter.

Although Acts venerates Paul by devoting more than half of its length to him, it does not grant him the apostolic standing he so vehemently claimed from his

---

98. Dunn, *Living Word*, 41, 42.

99. See nn49, 101; chap. 6, n16 and sec. 7; chap. 10, sec. 6; chap. 13, n4.

100. See chap. 6, n16.

101. As a Gospel writer Luke had written sources, in particular Mark, Q, and another source. As a writer of Acts he apparently had no sources other than limited oral traditions from an area where Paul had done no mission work.

encounter with the Risen Christ (1 Cor 9:1; 15:1–11; Gal 1:15–17). At first when Acts describes Paul's call we might think that it depicts a meeting with the Risen Lord.[102] However in Acts 26:19 it becomes clear that, according to Luke's understanding, Paul's encounter was different in kind from what Luke regarded as resurrection encounters. This may be because, unlike Matthew's and Luke's descriptions of appearances of the Risen Christ,[103] Paul's encounter with the Risen Christ entailed no flesh and blood appearance, having occurred some years after Jesus' death and earlier resurrection disclosures. But Paul was the earliest NT writer and the only one who actually confronted the Risen Lord. His accounts are thus more historically credible.[104]

Luke/Acts defined apostleship in a further way that excluded Paul. When a replacement for Judas Iscariot was sought Acts had Peter declare that such a person must have accompanied Jesus during His ministry (1:21)—which ruled out Paul. Only two verses in Acts may seem to refer to Paul as an apostle; one is textually doubtful (14:14) and the other (14:4) is open to various interpretations. Perhaps the author only meant that Paul and Barnabas represented the apostles.

Acts represent Paul as an irenical, rather than a polemical figure, thus imagining that there were no conflicts between Paul and the original apostles. In this regard Acts 15 depicts a Jerusalem meeting that included Paul, Barnabas, Peter and James. It was purportedly held to discuss whether it was necessary for Gentile male converts to be circumcised and to observe the entire Mosaic law. Acts claims it was decided that though the circumcision aspect was not obligatory, Gentiles must abstain from food that had been sacrificed to idols, from eating meat with blood in it, from the meat of animals killed by strangulation, and (of course) from fornication (Acts 15:28–29). To these requirements Luke says that all present agreed, with Paul as an active agent in circulating these mainly Jewish obligations to the churches.[105] If the Acts's account were accurate, except for the rejection of fornication and the omission of the circumcision requirement people would in effect have had to become Jews to become Christians. The description of the outcome of this purported meeting conflicts significantly with Paul's attitude toward food regulations seen in First Corinthians 8, 10:23–33, Romans 14 and 15:1–6.

It's astonishing that according to Acts, Paul went even beyond the Jewishness required by Jerusalem and had Timothy circumcised (16:3), and proved his Jewish orthodoxy by having his hair cut as part of a vow (18:18b). We see the same picture of a pliant and accommodating Jewish Christian colleague in Acts's description of Paul's final return to Jerusalem (21:17). To test Paul's unswerving loyalty to the Jewish law, a member from the group of James and the Jerusalem elders commanded Paul: "Do

---

102. See the three accounts of Paul's heavenly vision in Acts (9:1–9; 22:6–10; 26:12–18), which exhibit conflicting details and clash with Paul's own accounts (1 Cor 9:1–2; 15:8–11; Gal 1:11–17).

103. Mark records no resurrection appearances.

104. Ziesler, *Pauline Christianity*, 129–30, 129.

105. Barrett, *Paul/Introduction*, 163–64.

therefore what we tell you. We have four men who are under vow; take these men and purify yourself along with them and pay their expenses, so that they may shave their heads. Thus all will know that there is nothing in what they have been told about you but that you yourself live in obedience of the law" (Acts 21:23–24). "Paul took the men, and the next day he purified himself with them and went into the temple, to give notice when the days of purification would be fulfilled and the offering presented for every one of them" (Acts 21:26). *Acts implies that other than circumcision, Paul agreed with the Jewish Christian leaders in Jerusalem to live according to the entire Jewish law.*

Was Paul such a dutiful servant of the Jerusalem leaders? Examine Gal 1:15–2:16. In particular note in 1:16–17 that after his encounter with the Risen Christ Paul said: "I did not confer with flesh and blood, nor did I go up to Jerusalem to those who were apostles before me . . ." He asserted that a full three years later he first went to Jerusalem and then only to visit Cephas, and otherwise met only the Lord's brother. Perhaps realizing that some would like to regard him as subservient to the Jerusalem apostles he emphasized that he did not lie (Gal 1:18–20). In chapter 2 he said that the next visit was a full fourteen years after the first, and its purpose was only to indicate in private to those of repute the gospel he preached to the Gentiles. He admitted that at that time some false brethren were secretly brought in to spy out his, Bartholomew's and Titus's freedom in Christ that they might bring them into bondage, but they "did not yield submission even for a moment" (v. 5a). Of a later visit Paul wrote that the Jerusalem leaders "added nothing to me" (v. 6c), and the reputed pillars gave the right hand of fellowship that "we should go to the Gentiles and they to the circumcised" (v. 9c).

Acts claims that when on trial in Jerusalem Paul said that his preaching of the resurrection was responsible for his predicament (23:6c; 26:6–8). This was the supposed cause of the trial! Not his teaching concerning salvation through God's grace in Christ, that rejected the saving value of the law (see Gal 3:10–12). Nor Christ's dying on the cross, that relativized the ethical role of OT law, that (among other things) said that anyone who so dies is condemned by God (Gal 3:13). Acts has Paul say that he remained a Pharisee (23:6b; 26:5b), mind boggling unless the author had never even heard a summary of Paul's thought. According to Acts, all Christians were to be so bound by numerous Jewish regulations that in effect Christianity would have been only a messianic sect within Judaism, not a separate religion. "Of course Acts is enthusiastically aware of the Gentile mission, but it seems unaware of the consequent agony and conflict even in Paul himself, for all is solved by the divine command to Peter (Acts 10:9–16; 11:1–18), and any problems are readily solved at the Jerusalem Council of Chapter 15."[106]

In spite of my historical and theological criticisms of the Acts portrait of Paul, the author reflects a few elements that seem historically accurate. Acts concedes that the Gentile mission was not bound by the circumcision requirement. More generally, Acts depicts Paul as a great "missionary, evangelist and pastor," who traveled and preached

---

106. Ziesler, *Pauline Christianity*, 130.

widely,[107] "founded churches, cared for their members, and did much to establish Christianity in the north-eastern quadrant of the Mediterranean. It represents him in particular as a [former] Jew who became the great missionary to the Gentiles . . ."[108]

I have offered these detailed analyses of the Fourth Gospel and Acts in the context of this section to show how intellectually dishonest is inerrancy doctrine. Such advocates cannot see the content conflicts here discussed and present elsewhere in Scripture because their doctrine prevents such perception. In contrast let us claim the freedom that is ours as adult children of God, as God's friends. As an aspect of our freedom and responsibility let us read and study the Bible carefully, comparing one part with another and looking to Jesus Christ as Scripture's norm and standard. And let us read and study our Bibles with the discretion provided by the Holy Spirit of the Living God, Immanuel, God with us even today.

---

107. Contrary to Acts, not brilliantly. See chap. 6, n16.
108. Barrett, *Paul/Introduction*, 164–65.

Chapter 8

Dynamic Traditioning Process in Scripture and beyond

WE HAVE SEEN THAT writers of material that became incorporated into the NT *regarded other such sources as malleable, though they wanted accurate transcribings of their own writings*. In their usage of their sources, such pre-NT writers embodied Jesus's recommendation in Matthew 13:52: "'Every scribe who has been trained for the kingdom of heaven is like a householder who brings out of his treasure what is new and what is old.'"

Because Scripture exhibits theological diversity it is no simple matter to use it to judge later traditions. Until one makes important decisions concerning which parts of Scripture have higher authority than others, one cannot effectively use Scripture to arbitrate concerning conflicts that occur in post-biblical traditions. In chapters 5 and 6 are indicated reasons for some of the decisions I have made in face of biblical diversity. More reasons will be offered here and in some of the following chapters.

1. A Preliminary Illustration: Biblical Reinterpretations to Take Account of Eschaton's Delay

The NT gospel, which from beginning to end was embodied in culturally conditioned forms, calls into question all cultures, "*including the one in which it was originally embodied.*"[1] Much of the NT assumed that the world would soon end, at least within the generation of those *then living*.[2] The NT writers who lived considerably beyond the early period in one way or another often reinterpreted eschatological hope to reconcile it with the world's continuing existence. They regarded as no longer credible the connecting of such hope with the expectation of a consummation in their lifetime. How could they have honestly done otherwise and how can we?

---

1. Newbigin, *Foolishness*, 4; my emphasis.
2. 1 Thess 4:16–17; 1 Pet 4:7; 1 Cor 15:51–52.

Luke, writing later than the author of Mark's Gospel or Paul, believed that the consummation was likely to be far distant and therefore made necessary textual adjustments in his use of Mark's Gospel. An obvious reference to the delay is Luke's introduction to the parable of the talents (19:11): "He proceeded to tell a parable . . . because they supposed that the kingdom of God was to appear immediately." As for another alteration: Mark 9:1 had written: "'There are some standing here who will not taste death before they see the kingdom of God *come with power.*'" Luke omitted the latter phrase and spoke only of "*seeing* the kingdom of God" (9:27, my emphases). To "see the kingdom" can easily be understood to mean only perceiving its inward and moral nature being realized apart from the ending of history. Luke thereby made Mark's text calendar independent.

Detailed comparison of Mark with Luke demonstrates that Luke disconnected belief in eternal life from linkage with the consummation of history. Mark attests that for the sake of the elect the days were shortened (13:20), and that "'this generation will not pass away before all these things take place'" (13:30). Mark 13:13b writes that "one who endures *to the end* will be saved" (NRSV, my emphasis). The parallel in Luke says, "By your endurance you will gain your lives" (21:19 NRSV), a calendar independent teaching. In place of Mark's assertion that false messianic claimants will say "I am he!" (13:6a), Luke records their saying "*the time is at hand!*" (Luke 21:8c, my emphasis)—the very words that Mark says Jesus used! (1:15a) What editorial freedom!

In the Acts of the Apostles the author of Luke-Acts tells the faithful not to link eschatological hope with the imminent coming of the kingdom nor try to figure out the sequence of events that would connect with the eschaton's arrival (Acts 1:6 –7). Second Peter rationalizes away the problem of its delay and is exegetically imprecise in assuming that early statements concerning the nearness of the end were not intended to be taken at face value (3:8). A thousand years may be as a day to the Lord, but those who expected Christ to return soon were not thinking in terms of thousands of years. As with the writer of Luke-Acts, the author of Second Peter assumes that the world's duration will likely be long. He affirms that the extension will be due to God's patience, which will provide more time for the world's repentance. Both authors nevertheless still believe that at some unexpected time God will bring history to fulfillment.[3]

Paul and Jesus seem to have believed in the nearness of the end, though according to Paul one could die and share in eternal life prior to the consummation (Phil 1:23b), and Jesus certainly expected the same for Himself. Yet the authors of Luke-Acts and Second Peter—aware that history had already endured longer than previously expected—supposed that it would continue to do so. They thus did not regard individual eternal life as linked to the consummation. From their later contexts to think otherwise could have jeopardized faith by tying eschatology to an ever lengthening calendar. The Fourth Gospel and the Johannine Epistles also disconnected the hope of eternal fellowship with God from the eschaton's arrival.

3. Barr, *Escaping Fundamentalism*, 105–6.

2. Scripture and Traditioning Process

The NT developed as the product of traditions *generated by* God's revelation in Jesus Christ. Only after the canonizing of the NT did the witness to God's disclosure in Christ lay embedded within the NT and could it be said that Christian Faith is born of the interpretation and proclamation of the NT.[4]

Schleiermacher's statement concerning the relationship of the NT to later traditions allows for the vital role of the NT, while recognizing that interpretive tradition continued to develop even after the canonizing of the NT: "The Holy Scriptures of the New Testament are, on the one hand, the first member in the series, ever since continued, of presentations of the Christian Faith; on the other hand, they are the norm for all succeeding presentations."[5] It would, however, be more precise not to claim that the NT is "the norm," but the most essential means for coming to know the norm—Jesus Christ.

3. Dialectical Traditioning Process

It is unfortunate that people often isolate biblical and/or post-biblical traditions from those traditions' own traditioning processes, thereby encouraging the sacralizing of set traditions. To the contrary, the present is intelligible only as a response to and interpretative commentary upon the past, whereby past ideas are to some extent corrected and to some extent transcended—and the process never stops. In the future—possibly even the next moment—present understanding will to a degree need to be revised.

Speaking more generally, because traditions can degenerate, later views (contrary to Hegel) are not necessarily superior to earlier ones. Yet when tradition is in good order there is a cumulative element in it and it will be progressing. Furthermore not every aspect of tradition is equally liable to be overthrown. Some aspects of a belief may be so essential that to abandon those would in effect involve rejecting an entire tradition.[6]

In formal logic contradiction signals defeat, but in the evolution of real knowledge the recognition of contradiction can mark the first step in progress towards victory.[7] To be vital, both theology and science must continue to develop and do so in part by critically evaluating their previous formulations. (To an extent, even exegesis works this way.) In all change, much is conserved—otherwise all would be continually erased. Yet in all living and vital conservation some amount of development must

---

4. See chap. 6.

5. Schleiermacher, *Christian Faith*, 2:594.

6. MacIntyre, *After Virtue*, 146–47. For example, one who does not in any sense regard Jesus Christ as Savior and Lord places oneself outside the Christian framework, as one who denies the reality of the natural world negates the essential premise presupposed by natural science.

7. Whitehead, *Science/Modern World*, 167.

occur. Both "conservative" and "liberal" emphases are thus essential in all aspects of life—and the debate should have to do entirely with the mixture of items of continuity and discontinuity. But "no generation can merely reproduce its ancestors."[8]

4. Critical Dialogue of Revisable Science with Revisable Theology

Since science and theology have different interests, they often *seem* to disagree. The best way to use such conflict is to let it help produce deeper understanding on both sides. Science, for example, can encourage theology to critically distinguish between what within its own tradition is merely yesterday's science and what is of essential religious importance. Scientific advances normally necessitate modifications in related theological statements, either through subtractions, expansions, explanations, or restatements. The changes required can help clarify the exact point of *theological importance*. The critical conversation of science with theology thus results in *theological* gain. In the absence of such dialogue, theology may think all kinds of miscellaneous information are of redemptive significance, and thus may lack discretion, making ultimate commitments to theologically irrelevant matters that happen to be found in the Bible. The clash between science and theology points to "wider truths and finer perspectives within which a reconciliation of a deeper religion and a more subtle science will be found."[9]

The slightest acquaintance with natural science will indicate how different the modern and even modern Christian understanding of nature is from that of biblical times, and that ancient world views need to be relativized. Most Christians today disagree with the ancient and thus biblical assumption that the earth is flat, with God's dwelling as "up" and hell as "down." Furthermore, "the older world-views had no idea of a world in which 'nature' could change, no idea of the fact 'that human agency through scientific and technological skill has the power, and also the duty, of molding to some extent what "nature" is to become.' The world was [regarded as] stable, except that in extreme cases God might destabilize it and reverse the process of creation; but human action, whether good or bad, did not have that power. Ecological theology becomes necessary today because we know that we do have that power."[10]

As for helping to achieve a more subtle science, theology can help rid it of nonscientific and ill-founded theological ideas that creep into some scientists' expressions because of hidden or overt commitments, such as the presumption that science can explain all there is to be explained. An example of that presumption is that in tracing

---

8. Ibid., 168; see also 179. See above, chap. 5, sec. 12. Liberal Theology sought to distinguish between essential theological kernels and mere cultural husks, a legitimate and necessary undertaking (see chap. 1, sec. 7), though Liberal Theology's own particular dividing is subject to criticism.

9. Ibid., 165; see also 162–63, 168–69.

10. Barr, *Concept/Biblical Theology*, 490, quoting himself.

the universe's development to a "big bang" science has accounted for why there is something and not nothing.

Science is even more developmental than theology. Unlike much theology, however, science does not consider the need for critical revision a sign of weakness or defeat. Neither should theology. In recent decades natural science has undergone profound transformations. Familiar examples are quantum theory, the awareness that all data are theory-laden, the realization of the role of interpretation in all scientific experiment, the recognition of the historical context of all scientific paradigms or models, and more generally the perception that all scientific arguments occur in historical contexts.[11] "A sense of wonder, even mystery, was once considered the skeleton in the family closet of the humanities. But now that wonder has surfaced in the natural sciences themselves." In contrast with positivism's preoccupation with supposed purely objective data, "reality is *constituted, not created or simply found* through the interpretations that have earned the right to be called relatively adequate or true." Language "inevitably influences *our understanding* of both data and facts, truth and reality. *Reality is neither out there nor in here. Reality is constituted by the interaction between a text, whether a book or world, and a questioning interpreter. The interaction called questioning can produce warranted assertions through relevant evidence.*"[12]

No modern scientist could without qualification endorse Galileo's views, or Newton's, or all of their own ideas from ten years previous. Even when the same assertions are made today as a thousand years ago they are interpreted with meaning subtractions or expansions not anticipated earlier.[13] "It is a general feature of our knowledge that we are insistently aware of important truth; and yet the only formulations of these truths which we are able to make presuppose a general standpoint of conceptions which may have to be modified."[14]

Theological understandings must undergo revisions not only because the horizons from which our interpretive dialogues proceed continue to develop, but because after a while the inherent ambiguities present in particular statements become apparent, necessitating reformulations. Because obscurities can affect essential meaning, the continuing work of interpretation is vital.

---

11. Tracy, *Plurality/Ambiguity*, 33. See below chap. 13, secs. 3, 5–9.

12. Ibid., 33, 48; my emphases. See below chap. 16, sec. 4. If these words of Tracy are carefully considered—especially the italicized ones—it is apparent that they do not disagree with Whitehead's comments on Realism-Objectivism, cited in chap. 12, sec. 12.

13. Whitehead, *Science/Modern World*, 163–64, 170.

14. Ibid., 164.

5. Need for Theological Restatements in Transmission of Biblical Tradition

Since God uniquely revealed Herself in Jesus Christ and since the NT contains the early traditions that attest the meaning of the Christ event, the NT has a normative role in relation to later traditions. Nevertheless, the NT cannot be such a contributory standard unless effectively understood. Because the Bible is a library full of heights and depths, central and peripheral aspects, and with some parts that conflict with others—the church has never been content merely to hand out Bibles and await the results. She has believed that Christians need help in gaining entrance into the Bible and in perceiving its central perspectives. Thus the church has offered sermons and teachings, introductory studies, commentaries, creeds, confessions and catechisms (and other types of explanatory summaries and abridgments), and full systematic theologies—as aids for perceiving the meaning of Scripture.

Because over the years the significance of words change and because churches confront new scientific understandings as well as particular cultural and theological insights and problems—theological reformulations and restatements are necessary if biblical meaning is to be preserved and the continuing relevance of the Bible's message is to be shown.[15]

---

15. Berkhof, *Christian Faith*, 93.

More Interaction With Related Disciplines

Chapter 9

Utilizing Christian Religious Experience, Reason/Apologetics, Historical and Biblical Theology in Systematics

1. Brief Discussion of Sources and Their Relationship

WE CANNOT CONSIDER SECONDARY sources without presupposing that the God decisively revealed in Jesus Christ is the primary source and standard for Christian Faith and for systematic theology, though the NT is the basis of knowledge of Jesus Christ, and the OT for contributing knowledge of God. Neither Testament, however, has meaning unless interpreted and applied, and to do that we need to employ reason and general human experience, take account of the church's understanding of the Bible over the centuries (tradition), and consider the ways in which Christian religious experience can authenticate Christian convictions. Though the extra-biblical sources do not provide independent access to the God revealed in Jesus Christ, without these we cannot comprehend the biblical witness.

The importance of *Scripture, post-biblical church tradition and reason* in the Christian learning process were long recognized by Anglicanism before Wesley, but Wesley's adding of Christian religious experience as a source established the Methodist "quadrilateral." The emphasis on *Christian religious experience* was also not an original contribution from Wesley, but one inherited from Pietism. Quite rightly, *general human experience* was later added, and this dimension came from the Liberal Protestant tradition. This aspect of experience should not be clustered with *uniquely Christian experience*, and thus constitutes a fifth standard.

The *sola scriptura* slogan of the early Lutheran and Reformed Churches seems less accurate, even to describe what actually occurred in those churches, than the insistence that Scripture (and especially the NT) is the highest norm for learning of God as decisively disclosed in Christ.[1] Following the practice of the early church (and

---

1. In Luther's initial challenging of the Catholic understanding of authority he appealed not only to the testimony of Scripture, but to *reason* and *conscience* as captive to the Living Word of God he had *experienced* through Scripture (Luther's defense at the Diet of Worms, repeated in the Smalcald

thus with possible exception of the human experience standard), today's ecumenical Protestants, including Lutheran and Reformed, tend to concede that the interpretation of the Bible requires the use of such additional tools as noted in the previous paragraphs. Remember, for example, that those Christians who established the canon did not isolate it from extra-scriptural creedal summaries of faith,[2] though admittedly those had been influenced by Paul's own writings and then by the four Gospel collection that had circulated before NT canonization.

It might have seemed more logical to briefly explain the ingredients of this discipline in the first chapter and I did make some concession to the more traditional format by there discussing the *nature and purposes* of systematic theology. But in my opinion it was important to first clarify particular *convictions* that Christian Faith assumes and that systematic theology must presuppose if it is to do its work. These convictions, of course, are acquired from the ingredients summarized in the first two paragraphs of this chapter. Some of these were discussed in previous chapters, and others will be considered here and in remaining chapters.[3]

If broadly understood, everything in this chapter can be squeezed under combinations of traditional source headings. For example, historical theology, though not manifesting reason in the philosophical sense, certainly employs historical and inductive kinds of reasoning. Biblical theology more directly falls under the Bible heading, while utilizing historical, inductive and deductive reasoning.

Source standards should often overlap. For example, Christian religious experience needs to be critically assessed by considering the Bible's teachings and comparing it with other claims concerning religious experience. Such activities employ reason in the service of understanding God's disclosure in Christ.

Merely to assert the importance of such standards and to insist on their interrelatedness says little theologically. When I was a pastor many pastors within my denomination seemed to think otherwise, as though spieling off four standards (the count at the time) said something particular about the content of Christian Faith or the living of the Christian life. And often such listings were not even prefaced by an insistence that the meaning of God's disclosure in the Son by the Spirit is what these standards should point toward. But even with such a goal and the four or five

---

Articles, cited in Kummel, *NT/History of Investigation*, 20–21).

2. Even before the NT canon existed the church looked for guidance to the Old Roman Symbol and then to the Apostles' and Nicene Creeds. The Old Roman Symbol, which existed in the late first or early second centuries, was the earliest known creed and was the archetype for all western and possibly eastern creeds. It had similar content to the Apostles' Creed, but significantly differed in two ways. "Creator of heaven and earth" and "descended into hell" of first and second articles were entirely missing. Less importantly, "the communion of saints" *phrase* (but not idea) of the third article was absent. Though in later western creeds the Old Roman Symbol's assertion of the forgiveness of sins, incorporation into the holy church, and the promise of resurrection/eternal life were attached to belief in the Holy Spirit, these benefits of faith *originally* and *more appropriately* were linked to the threefold name (Dahl, *Jesus the Christ*, 169, 174–75, 178).

3. Study the Table of Contents for particulars.

standards is not to do theology, but merely to take account of particular guidelines for proceeding. And, as I have done, one can have long since proceeded and shown relationships without systematically itemizing the various ingredients.

2. Christian Religious Experience and Wilhelm Herrmann's Understanding of Its Relation to Faith, Knowledge, Science

Christian religious experience is a vitally important ingredient of Christian Faith and of systematic theology, but one whose role has often been misinterpreted. Though I can and must attest from my own experience the help that I have received, my experience must not become the autonomous theme of what I say, lest my words lose the character of witness to Christ.[4] With this proviso, there is nothing objectionable in describing God's communication with people as involving Christian "religious experience." The problem is not with this terminology nor with what it denotes, namely the entry of the Word of God into people's lives. Unfortunately, religious experience is often burdened with the denotation or connotation that natural humankind apart from revelation can actualize this, and that it can become an independent norm.[5] Certainly when God reveals Herself to us we receive, understand, grasp and appropriate what She says to us with the same organs of perception that we use to know other things, yet *not in virtue of our own ability to use them in this regard, but because God provides the missing capacity*.[6]

Christian religious experience is a means through which Christ-centered biblical faith is validated, but is not an independent authority. Following the Fourth Gospel and Paul, Luther and Calvin insisted that the Spirit links us to the biblical witness to Jesus Christ. The event on which Christianity is based is derived from God's revelation in Christ, not personal experience. Though Christian religious experience is not an autonomous source for determining the content of Christian Faith, it is a vital medium through which its contents are received.[7] It is so vital in this respect that it transforms what it receives, and in this limited sense is a source.[8] *Experience as an ingredient of theology should not be so small that the result is a mere repetition of tradition (like handing on a baton), nor so large that the result is a new production*.[9]

The content of Christian Faith becomes effective through personal experience. What comes to us from the outside must live on the inside. "What is truly personal will ever be a secret of life."[10] For Wesley the way to recover the doctrinal tradition and

---

4. Barth, *CD*, 1/2:442.
5. Barth, *CD*, 1/1:220.
6. Barth, *CD*, 4/3.2:509. See below chap. 19, sec. 9.
7. Tillich, *ST*, 1:42.
8. McKelway, *ST/Tillich*, 54.
9. Tillich, *ST*, 1:46.
10. Troeltsch, *Christian Faith*, 38.

a motive for doing so is to experience its truth inwardly. Christian Faith is not to be founded on experience, but established by Scripture and confirmed by the inner and direct testimony of the Holy Spirit, the "inward impression in the soul whereby the Spirit of God immediately and directly witnesses to my spirit that I am reconciled to God."[11] Though the internalization of the truth is vital, its validity depends upon its agreement with one's interpretation of Scripture.

Herrmann realized that we of ourselves have no capacity to overcome our self-centeredness and that when we recognize our failure to live as we ought we can be crushed by a sense of guilt. Though such awareness does not of itself enable us to experience God, it is a common context in which that occurs. When that happens people can become aware that their moral failings are due to separation from God, can experience divine forgiveness, and can begin to be morally renewed. Herrmann believed that such encounters with God are so overwhelming that the experiences cannot be doubted. Such self-authenticating experiences provide religious assurances that scientific method can neither validate nor invalidate.

Herrmann regarded God as a life-giving Power who renews inner selves, often unexpectedly. However, he was critical of attempts to provide generic accounts of how faith arises—as though everyone's experience of Christ must be just like everyone else's—which ignores the individuality of religious experience. Furthermore, Herrmann regarded regeneration as something that begins at a point, but continues throughout life. In sum, he understood religious experience as individual and dynamic.

Hermann believed that *revelation-founded faith differs from scientific ways of knowing*: This is *first* because the Reality known by faith has to do with the Unique and Transcendent Being, who is radically different from anything that scientific method can uncover. Consistent with Herrmann's belief in God's transcendence was his suspicion of natural theology, believing that only those who had experienced God can find His genuine traces in nature. Thus Christian Faith must stand on its own feet and live from revelation alone.

As previously implied in this section, a *second* reason that Christian Faith differs from scientific knowing is that to know God is to experience faith as not due to our own created capacities.[12] In contrast scientific knowing depends precisely on such abilities.

A *third* reason for the differences is that the meaning of the historical facts to which faith responds must be supernaturally appropriated in the present. This was why Herrmann was critical of Schleiermacher, who defined religion as "the feeling of absolute dependence." Though Herrmann agreed that such a feeling is part of natural human consciousness, he did not regard such an intuition as either religious or

---

11. Outler, *John Wesley*, 211, quoting from the first Witness of the Spirit Discourse. Also see Welch, *Protestant Thought/Nineteenth Century*, 1:25.

12. McCormack, *Barth's Dialectical Theology*, 59–60, 60–61, 55–56.

Christian. The object of that feeling is the world on which our biological lives depend—fate—not the Christian God.[13]

Christian Faith derives from the appropriated meaning of biblically attested disclosures, and is thus hidden from direct observation. Historians can study biblical documents scientifically with methods that parallel the scientific study of nature, and such study can describe what others have believed and experienced. But historical methods cannot enable us to share in the spiritual reality depicted by such interpreted events. The latter is possible only as we inwardly participate in their effects.

Herrmann opposed historicism, which gave immanent explanations to all historical events. He also opposed the philosophical dominance of theology.[14] Barth seems to have continued to agree with the various aspects of Herrmann's ideas discussed in this section, but supplemented his inward emphasis with a Christocentric concentration, while rejecting his Kantian ethic.[15]

3. Interaction of Reason and Experiential Faith within Systematics

In systematic theology, reflection plays a larger role than in many other activities of Christian Faith. Systematic theologians must be willing to think deeply, be interested in systematizing, and committed to doing both concerning the meaning of Christian Faith. They themselves should be Christian participants, for systematics involves "believing thinking." Because this field does not entail the purely rational consideration of the truths of faith, openness of heart and mind to the Living God is essential. The systematician speaks of Christian beliefs in their interconnectedness—but apart from experiencing God's related impact one will fail to perceive many connections.

Though theological thinking involves a rational movement of thought, it requires the interaction of reason with personal faith, else a rationalistic and speculative theology develop that leads away from God. Only where rationality and faith intermesh do we have good dogmatics.[16] Since systematic theologians' believing reflections occur in ongoing relationship with God, such thinking can help to renew their own and others' faith. The relation between doctrine and faith is twofold: "Faith springs from doctrine insofar as doctrine springs from faith."[17]

---

13. See below chap. 11, sec. 6; chap. 19, sec. 5.
14. McCormack, *Barth's Dialectical Theology*, 57, 66.
15. See below, secs. 4 and 6; also see chap. 11, sec. 5; chap. 18, sec. 6.
16. Brunner, *God*, 73, 76.
17. Ibid., 41.

4. Christian Faith above Natural Reason but Interrelates with Rational and Empirical Truth[18]

Knowledge of God comes because God as active agent made Himself known in a particular history. It is one thing to receive and interpret God's disclosure in Jesus Christ and another to speculatively claim to be able to discover ultimate truth by oneself. We should have much confidence in the former, but no confidence in the latter. Though not contrary to natural reason, Christian Faith transcends the insights of natural reason. From an examination of natural reason, nature or general history it is not possible to discover the biblical claim that God chose to reveal Himself in the Son by the Spirit.[19]

Since God has so humbled Himself as to come into history and go to the cross, Christians must utilize the language of *paradox*,[20] which *witnesses to God's overturning of normal expectations*. The paradox seen in Jesus Christ is not just that God became a human to the point of lowly suffering, but that He revealed His *eternal glory through such an act of condescension*. Jesus's costly discipleship and humble death are the means for both the Son's and the Father's triumph and glorification—and for ours—as we follow Christ by carrying our daily crosses.

It was the limits and not any inherent untrustworthiness of reason that Kierkegaard exposed. For those who want to base everything on natural reason God's hidden revelation in Christ remains an offence (Matt 11:2–6/Luke 7:18–23).[21] SK regarded the incarnational stooping of God as of utmost importance and considered it as Christianity's defense against speculation.

As Christ was truly human and yet uniquely disclosed God, SK thought the offence was twofold: There is the offence against loftiness, that the exalted God humbled Himself; and the offence against lowliness, that one so humble was exalted by God.[22] Unfortunately SK did not go as far as Barth, who said that God's *glory* is revealed precisely in such incarnational humbling.

Christian paradoxes attest that God's ways overturn normal expectations. Such paradoxes have a major source in the NT witness to the Crucified and Risen One in whom we are called to participate. The death and resurrection of Jesus—while vindicating His life and teaching, which are also paradoxical—disclose much of the content of the Christian Faith and inform the Christian life. Such a life involves a continual mortification or putting to death of what is selfish and sinful (Col 3:3), as we struggle

---

18. See chap. 11, especially sec. 1.

19. Allen, *Christian Belief/Postmodern*, 150.

20. Paradoxes are ideas that when taken together seem to contradict each other, but upon closer examination can be seen to be compatible, though with polar tension or complexity (see also chap. 1, sec. 5).

21. For a major discussion of the hiddenness of revelation see chap. 18, secs. 4–5 and for a briefer one see chap. 7, sec. 8.

22. Croxall, *Kierkegaard*, 122, 123, 204–5.

to be concretely obedient (Gal 2:20; 5:24). Insofar as we are faithful, we will suffer for our witness, but in the process will learn to live from Christ's strength and power. God's grace is sufficient and God's power is made perfect in the weakness of dependence upon Christ (2 Cor 12:9a). "I will all the more gladly boast of my weaknesses, that the power of Christ may rest upon me. For the sake of Christ, then, I am content with weaknesses, insults, hardships, persecutions, and calamities; for when I am weak, then I am strong" (2 Cor 12:9b–10).

"We have this treasure in earthen vessels, to show that the transcendent power belongs to God and not to us. We are afflicted in every way, but not crushed; perplexed, but not driven to despair; persecuted, but not forsaken; struck down, but not destroyed; always carrying in the body the death of Jesus, so that the life of Jesus may also be manifested in our bodies. For while we live we are always being given up to death for Jesus's sake, so that the life of Jesus may be manifested in our mortal flesh" (2 Cor 4:7–11).

When Paul speaks of the paradox of the justification of the sinner, and when John affirms that the Word became flesh, neither wished to indulge in logical contradiction. But these affirmations imply that God's action transcends human expectations and preparations—surpassing but not destroying finite reason.[23]

Francois Wendel summarizes some of the paradoxes found in Calvin's thought: The unity of and distinction between the two natures of Christ; the tension between God's love and judgment; the immediate imputation of Christ's righteousness, though we nevertheless remain sinners; sanctification as beginning when we experience justification, and yet as requiring lifelong growth; the tension between humankind's greatness and misery; the law as in some respects abolished and in others as enduring; that we should be grateful for earthly goods and yet not cling to them too closely; and the church as both visible and invisible.[24]

God's transcending of common expectations is not recognized by the world. Platonic rationalism/idealism is naively confident that natural reason *independent of the senses* and uninfluenced by history can grasp ultimate reality. In contrast, Aristotelianism is certain that *by means of an analysis of sense experience* reason can perceive essential reality.[25] In believing that ultimate reality is disclosed in Christ, Paul and the NT as a whole *in effect* reject the speculative claim of each of these forms of Greek philosophy. Though Paul utilizes reason to articulate the meaning of Christian Faith, he does not think the latter could be established philosophically.[26] In First Corinthians 1:18–31 Paul draws a sharp distinction between the world's supposed rationalistic wisdom and the "word of the cross." Colossians 2:8a equates speculative philosophy with "empty deceit" incompatible with faith in Christ. That the eternal Logos (Word)

---

23. Tillich, *ST*, 1:57.
24. *Calvin*, 358–59.
25. For both understandings of all types of knowledge, see chap. 11, sec. 1.
26. Allen, *Christian Belief/Postmodern*, 151.

became a human being is also not something even Stoic rationalism (with its logos concept) could have deduced. Christ crucified seemed foolishness to the Greeks.[27]

As the final figure of the Enlightenment Kant exposed naive rationalism's overconfidence in what it supposed could be the dictates of pure reason uncontaminated by tradition and experience. He thought, however, that with speculative reason's decommissioning, practical reasoning could perform a useful role in evaluating insights largely generated by tradition and experience. He urged each person to claim the right to critically evaluate tradition and their own experience by using their powers of reason. When utilized in this way Kant still had much confidence in natural reason as the final arbiter concerning these matters. Kant expressed this viewpoint in his classic definition of Enlightenment as humankind's "release from self-incurred tutelage. Tutelage is the inability to use one's understanding without direction from another. Self-incurred is this tutelage when its cause lies not in lack of reason but in lack of resolution and courage . . . 'Have courage to use your own reason!'—that is the motto of enlightenment."[28]

Ernst Troeltsch, the liberal theologian/philosopher/sociologist reiterated this Kantian perspective when he wrote that "*Autonomy does not mean that everything must be self-produced. . . . [It] signifies a certain sort of consent*. It does not signify any unthinking [or thinking] cramming of something down someone's throat, but rather a person's grasping what it is that makes something so right. *Autonomy signifies not dead, passive reception, but understanding*."[29] *This is true enough as far as it goes, but it does not go far enough to be genuinely Christian.* Kant exhibited no awareness that the human mind can be truly influenced by the God who is with us, but who was decisively disclosed in Christ, who alone can bring the deliverance from the self-centeredness that Kant and the Kantians desired.[30]

Caveats concerning mere natural reason from Luther, Calvin, Brunner and Barth had to do with the way in which sinners use it to further their autonomy or independence over against God. (Like the thinkers just mentioned, Paul's sometimes negative words regarding reason likely came from the same concern.) When (like Kant) people rely only on reason to arbitrate between tradition and human experience they presumptuously understand themselves as their own masters, their own gods. *In contrast*

---

27. Watson, "Philosophy," 546.

28. Immanuel Kant, "What Is Enlightenment?," 132. After Kant Enlightenment thinking was no longer characterized by claims for reason's all-encompassing power as the basis of human understanding. Rather, its ability to critically evaluate came to prominence. This tendency linked with the political demand for the right to question everything, in the confidence that through such exercise reason would recognize its own limits and yet help to establish certainties (Welch, *Protestant Thought/ Nineteenth Century*, 1:32). Hegel broke with such Kantian limitations and from a romantic/rationalistic perspective once again *intentionally* deified natural reason. As the next four paragraphs explain, Kant had *unintentionally* done the same.

29. Troeltsch, *Christian Faith*, 80; my emphases.

30. See immediately below and sec. 6.

to such proud misuse of reason: *Receiving, perceiving, and interpreting reason can serve God and others if utilized through Christ and in His service.*[31]

As we will explore in section 6, Kant thought that his categorical imperative equivalent to the golden rule did not depend on recognizing the authority of the golden rule—though he had learned of this notion from the NT. He thought it could just as well be generated entirely by the moral logic of consistency as applied to morals. *But autonomous self-interested sinners do not have the will to so consistently perceive and the capacity to so consistently apply.*

Kant also *did not go far enough* with his insistence that reason must be reasonable about its own limitations. Because he did not believe in a God who had disclosed a good deal about Himself and yet is a Living Reality, he did not envision that God could seriously particularize one's sense of obligation. For example, leading one to choose between various legitimate vocations or influencing one to marry or not to marry a particular person. If Christian ethics were based only on the golden rule, it would be equally helpless in the face of what are far from neutral or simple choices.

Though critical of autonomy, Christian Faith nevertheless does not oppose a careful use of reason, but *requires such to understand and articulate the content of faith.*[32] Without employing reason it is not possible to comprehend even an experience as existential as repentance: As a mere emotional feeling devoid of rational consciousness of that of which one is repenting the experience lacks meaning. Repentance utilizes reason, but in such a way that reason renounces its autonomy.[33]

The gospel is not *personally* knowable in terms of general knowledge, but to a large extent is intelligible and explicable. Otherwise it would not be possible to proclaim Christian Faith to non-believers. SK thought that "the possibility of knowing what Christianity is without being a Christian must be affirmed," but that "it is a different question whether a person can know what it is to be a Christian without being one, which must be denied."[34] Against this latter claim, it is surely possible for non-Christians not only to know something of what Christianity is, but also to have a similarly limited knowledge concerning what it means to be a Christian—which is part of what Christianity is. Were either kind of knowledge incapable of degrees of communication to non-Christians, Christian witnessing to non-Christians would be to little point. However, in both cases explanations cannot enable the relationship with God through Christ that is essential to both.

Christian Faith's content and implications are rational,[35] but not provable. If Christian Faith could be proven its acceptance would be rationally compelling and

---

31. Weber, *Dogmatics*, 1:175.

32. "The Savoyard priest in Rousseau's *Emile* puts the same point: 'He who denies the right of reason must convince me without recourse to her aid' (Everyman ed., 265)" (cited by Chadwick, *Lessing*, 15).

33. Brunner, *Revelation/Reason*, 430.

34. Kierkegaard, *Philosophical Fragments*, 339, 332.

35. Barth, *CD*, 4/3.2:849.

not a matter of decision affecting the whole person. And all smart people would be Christian by virtue of their intelligence. When reason's autonomy has been shattered and the mind is receptive to truth that is qualitatively different from the merely rational or empirical, one can perceive that revelation possesses its own logic. One's mind can then be renewed (Rom 12:2), so that one can think God's thoughts after Her, discern Her will, begin to obey Her (2 Cor 10:5) and use reason in Her service.[36]

Truths of faith do not conflict with logic or with genuine sciences, but only with reason that claims the right to define all truth from a natural standpoint. Though faith conflicts only with such imperialism of reason, the illusion of autonomy is the natural standpoint. Conflicts between reason and faith occur when one or the other oversteps the limits of their competence, through autonomy's over-extension of what natural reason can perceive or through false claims that Christian Faith is rationally compelling.[37]

Systematic theology believes that one must consistently interrelate truths of various kinds because one *should not be intellectually schizophrenic*.[38] Thus systematics spends a good deal of time rethinking and restating Christian Faith's normative convictions so they do not conflict with what can be learned from careful and critical study of compelling extra-Christian sources. For the same reason theology interacts with general culture and learning by attempting to *relate* its Christian views concerning origins to concepts advanced by cosmology and evolution, its Christian understanding of human nature to what psychology teaches about human personality, and its beliefs about God's sovereignty to what philosophers of history assert.[39] Though systematics rethinks Christian Faith in dialogue with such insights, at many points it must criticize the explicit or implicit secular commitments found within the various varieties of worldly wisdom.

5. Sin's Corruption of Various Academic Disciplines' Use of Reason

Natural reason stands judged by Christian Faith to be an incompetent source for determining the nature of Ultimate Reality, since it manifests and encourages autonomy. Because of this way in which we tend to misuse reason, the potentially corrupting influence sin has upon the rationality of various academic enterprises can be assessed. The more any field depends upon *natural knowledge of human beings and/or supposes that it knows God naturally*, the greater will be sin's disruption of rational knowledge. Conversely, the less a field of study has such focuses, the less is such disturbance, and the less difference there will be between knowing as a Christian believer or as an

---

36. Brunner, *Revelation/Reason*, 212, 217, 429, 311.

37. Ibid., 213, 213–14, 217, 16–17.

38. See the chap. 1, sec. 11 discussion concerning truth's "coherence test."

39. Concerning dialogue with natural science see chap. 8, secs. 3–4 and chap. 13, with sec. 8 as related to one kind of psychology. Also see chap. 18 for discussions with historical science, and especially sec. 11.

unbeliever.[40] This disturbance is maximal in such fields as natural theology, in non-Christian religions, in philosophical types of metaphysics, and in similar kinds of ethics and anthropology; is less in theology and ethics that attempt to center in Jesus Christ; is minimal in the natural sciences if they have imported neither ideology nor theology (big "ifs"); and is near zero in logic and mathematics.[41]

We should also remember that though God as Creator is the principle of all truth, most human knowledge does not contribute to learning of God. Though mathematical and scientific capacities are creational gifts, these fields do not of themselves lead to knowledge of God.[42] Neither does Christian theology unless accompanied by faith. A difference between mathematical and scientific knowledge in comparison with theological learning is that it is hard to see how Christian Faith can interpenetrate math and science in the way it can theology.

6. Apologetics

Having discussed the general role of reason in systematic theology, we consider reason's apologetic use. Though systematicians must take seriously the concrete historical situation in which their communication occurs, they need to be particularly careful how they carry out apologetic activity. *They should not merely inquire about the voices of the day, but about the voice of God for the day,*[43] mindful that often the point of *contact is the point of conflict*. Even so "only one who has wrestled with the mind of his own day, and who knows the opposition between biblical [and much contemporary] thought, is in a position to make biblical doctrine intelligible to the person of the present day, without compromising . . ."[44]

Systematic theologians have often failed to faithfully interpret and articulate the meaning of Christian Faith, either because they have deified modern tendencies (as did those who tried and still try to modernize Jesus) or because they have suggested that if we are to be faithful disciples we must intellectually become first century people.[45] Concerning the first problem, since the present represents a change from the past, so also the future will be different from the present. A theology identified too closely with the present will become prematurely obsolete.[46] "He who marries the spirit of his age soon finds himself a widower" (W. R. Inge). Regarding the second

---

40. Brunner, *Revelation/Reason*, 383.

41. I have considerably modified Brunner's oversimplified description of the disturbances as "maximum in theology and minimum in the exact sciences, and zero in the sphere of the formal" (ibid.).

42. Ibid., 318.

43. Barth, *CD*, 1/2:843.

44. Thielicke, *Modern Faith*, 9.

45. Erickson, *Christian Theology*, 21–22, referring to the language of Henry J. Cadbury.

46. Ibid., 22.

problem, archaizing oneself is inevitable if one accepts the inerrancy of Scripture.[47] For that perspective mistakenly assumes that the Bible is entirely self-consistent and that in all respects today's Christians must agree with all views expressed in the Bible, even when those merely reflect ancient cultures.

Apologetics generally consists of the defense of the faith against attack, but in Brunner's and SK's cases involves what Brunner calls *"eristics," polemical theology entailing the intellectual critique of viewpoints and lifestyles contradicting Christian Faith.* Though Brunner sometimes utilizes the word "apologetics" he prefers the term "eristics" for two reasons. (1) "Apologetics" traditionally suggested an attempt to defend Christian Faith before the bar of natural reason, whereas we should challenge the idea that natural reason is the final court of appeal in all questions of truth. (2) The word "apologetics" tended to imply that the viewpoints under attack are only those of people outside the church, rather than of the unbeliever in everyone.[48]

Eristics and dogmatics cannot be separated, since every dogmatic statement asserts or implies polemical elements and every polemic implies normative convictions.[49] The biblical message is full of eristic aspects—as should be our proclamation of it—since the self-understanding of the natural person in everyone must be scrutinized and sometimes critiqued. Apologetic-polemical theology has been to the fore where the Christian message has been particularly threatened. The great theologians of the early church were also polemicists, and such works of the first four centuries— the greatest being Augustine's *City of God*—are as numerous and important as the dogmatic variety.

In the first half of the nineteenth century SK, while attacking the superficial Christianity of his day, critiqued current ideologies that opposed Christian Faith: Hegel's romantic idealism, preoccupation with immediate pleasure, complacent middle class morality, and the "mass spirit." SK discerned and articulated the contrast between Christian Faith and immanental possibilities. Unlike his thinking, polemical theology need not involve separate literary production, but can be incorporated within dogmatics, as Barth and Brunner often did.

In spite of Brunner's belief that eristics can clear away obstacles, he does not think we can reason people into faith. The success that attends all kinds of Christian instruction depends ultimately upon the Divine Teacher as Holy Spirit and human response to such leading.[50]

Part of Brunner's apologetic application concerns the Christian understanding of human sinfulness and how that recognition relates to the reception of the NT message of God's grace in Christ. Earlier we considered several Brunner-Kant differences

---

47. See chap. 7, sec. 8. Unfortunately Erickson falls prey to this aspect of the second tendency.
48. McCormack, *Barth's Dialectical Theology*, 403.
49. Brunner, "Intellectual Autobiography," 16.
50. Brunner, *God*, 100–101, 99, 100, 103.

that indirectly affect this issue.[51] Freedom, which formerly was a secondary element grounded in dependence on God, became primary with Kant, though only as it resolves to follow the rational dictates of duty. Though Kant claimed to recognize human selfishness, he thought that we could overcome self-centeredness through the mere exercise of will-power. In harmony with this understanding, though he was open to learning from tradition and experience, he founded ethics autonomously, rather than grounding it in divine forgiveness and empowerment. Kant thought that natural moral logic teaches all people the inconsistency of claiming rights for oneself that one does not grant to others. Unfortunately for this theory, we sinners specialize in making exceptions for ourselves, and no exercise of mere will-power is capable of overcoming such selfishness. Sinners approach moral issues with taints of self-interest (Reinhold Niebuhr), and thus assess moral choices in ways that misperceive and misapply the moral logic of consistency. We thus require continual deliverance from biased perceptions—we need a Redeemer, not a mere moral principle or rule.

Christian Faith agrees with Kant that we are responsible *for* ourselves, but not that we are responsible *to* ourselves—which annuls the very concept of responsibility.[52] Though Brunner formally paralleled Kant in emphasizing a command ethic, Brunner looked to biblical moral guidelines and believed that these must be utilized with the flexibility that comes from being directly obedient to the Living God.[53] In contrast, according to Kant all that is needed is that our more rational selves speak a formal, rationally-generated, general imperative to our lower selves.

Contrary to Kant, will-power cannot deliver us from self-centeredness. The NT knows of the desire to live from a self-generated ethic, and pictures that as resulting in moral ruin. The tenants of the vineyard, for example, assert that they are in charge of themselves and violently rebel against the master's rule (Matt 21:33–41). Similarly, after receiving his inheritance the prodigal son left his father's house, so that he also could live as he pleased (Luke 15:11–32).[54] The master and father in these parables symbolize God. Kant, of course, regarded his rational ethic as different from such hedonistic examples, but he also exhibited naturalism by believing that reason's call of duty was capable of generating moral renewal. Kant thus had an optimistic blind spot concerning the human will as bounded only by one's moral inner voice and one's wise use of experience and tradition. In this respect his thinking was controlled by the Enlightenment, and unenlightened by the NT teaching concerning human sinfulness and divine grace.

Having considered Brunner's eristics or polemical theology and its criticisms of Kant's autonomous and moralistic ethic, we now need to *critically examine the early Barth's supposed rejection of apologetics/eristics*. Because Barth had done and

---

51. See sec. 4.
52. Brunner, *Truth as Encounter*, 20; see also *Revelation and Reason*, 209.
53. Brunner and Barth agree concerning this, both having learned from SK.
54. Brunner, *Revelation/Reason*, 210.

continued to do the equivalent of eristics, it is surprising that he had an intense conflict in 1930 with other representatives of Dialectical Theology purportedly over this issue.[55] Barth's main target was Brunner, but included Bultmann and Gogarten because Barth thought all three regarded faith as a human possibility, rather than as a divine gift. Barth supposed that Brunner's and others' use of existentialism were forms of Pelagianism/Arminianism,[56] but this is a separate issue and should not stigmatize Brunner's defense of eristics. Furthermore, if everything were to rest upon the direct and unmediated Word from above, which Barth in an early article seemed to imply,[57] that would not merely delegitimatize eristics, but also render as ineffective regular dogmatics, preaching and other forms of Christian witnessing (whether oral, written or through life example).

Barth himself was highly polemical, as for example, when four years later he wrote the Barmen Confession advocating not only the required "Yes" to Jesus Christ as the sole Word of God, but "No" to totalitarian usurpers.[58] The *Church Dogmatics* is sprinkled with controversial polemics, as well it should be, since "yes" and "no" cannot be separated. Yes implies no, and the no is often best stated explicitly along with the yes. Of course the church is divided over the Pelagian/Arminian issue, but even if one stands on the Calvinist/Barthian side, that is no reason to reject polemics. *Surely part of the clarification of what the Christian Faith is and of what the choice for Christ entails is to indicate as best one can what is opposed to these.* Jacques Ellul, for example, seemed to be on Barth's side of the Pelagian issue, but spent much of his lifetime critiquing *The New Commonplaces* that interfere with allegiance to Christ, and by doing so promoted Christian Faith. My point is that the difference between Barth and Brunner presumably concerning eristics was not really over whether the activity is legitimate, even as an aspect of dogmatics, but concerns whether faith in Christ is entirely a gift.

Barth's *legitimate criticism* of Christian existentialism's apologetics can be seen concerning its reliance for coming to faith on situations of suffering where people recognize their limitations. Barth's problem with the apologetic use of these was that such awareness only leads to faith in Christ if the Holy Spirit enables that victory. To critique the well-worn example that there are no atheists in foxholes, there are not

---

55. See McCormack, *Barth's Dialectical Theology*, 404, 418–19.

56. The understanding of the decision of faith as within human creational capacities.

57. See McCormack, *Barth's Dialectical Theology*, 418–19, summarizing Barth's "Between the Times" article.

58. Inspired by Barth, Christopher Morse writes: "My thesis is that the truth in Christian doctrine harbors a lie whenever the . . . disbeliefs these doctrines [imply] go unrecognized" (*Not Every Spirit*, 13). The Barmen thesis was that "Jesus Christ, as he is attested in Holy Scripture, is the one Word of God which we have to hear and which we have to trust and obey in life and in death" (8.11) (*Book of Confessions* [1967], United Presbyterian Church, 8.08–.19). Consistent with this, Barmen rejected the false notion that the church has to acknowledge other powers and truths as God's revelation (8.12) and that there are areas of our lives in which we belong to other lords (8.15) (Book of Confessions, 8.08–.19).

only atheists and agnostics in the foxholes, but even more in less stressful situations upon return. Speaking more generally, some people may have been in desperate situations and amid such contexts been brought to dependence on Christ. Others have faced similar traumas and have not come to rely on Christ. Self-awareness in such situations does not lead directly or inevitably to faith in Christ. The Living Christ brings the victory, not the limit situations themselves. Otherwise every person who ever suffered or recognized that they were in a tough spot would be a Christian.

7. Some Aspects of Kierkegaard's Apologetics

SK develops an apologetic that takes account of the concrete ways of life that people cling to that prevent them from committing to Jesus Christ. He shows that many of the same words (such as happiness) carry different meanings, depending on whether people live with a primary quest for self-fulfillment or pleasure, follow a general sense of duty, *give highest allegiance to a religion of immanence* (with no source of authority beyond the self), *or are committed to the Transcendent God revealed in Christ.* As SK makes these phenomenological descriptions he also indicates that all ways of life apart from Christ have breaking points or limits, where their inadequacy can be seen.

SK's exposition of the first and seemingly natural way of living still appears to be considerably accurate for the western world, and thus is described below in some detail. However, if people are born into collectivist or tribally dominated cultures they will regard the natural state of affairs as having less to do with immediate individual self-fulfillment or pleasure and more with the tranquilizing effect of living in harmony with one's national or tribal culture. Even so, if people cling to such ways of thinking and living they likely do so either because they suppose that they will derive maximum well-being thereby or because they imagine that trying to challenge these would be too difficult, unpleasant or life-threatening.

As for SK's description of a western version of the first stage, the type of natural hedonism he focuses upon, and though later relativized never left, was the quest for high artistic fulfillment. In *Either/Or* SK explains that all forms of hedonism involve the "rotation method" because it is characterized by change upon change in pursuit of momentary pleasure.[59] It lacks the exercise of the moral will that lifts choice to the ethical sphere. The hedonist aesthete loses himself because he drifts and does not make moral choices.[60]

But "may it not be said that even an aesthete must at least choose his pleasure, and some may be good and some may be bad? Yes; but do we mean by that, aesthetically good

---

59. Because Traditional Religion links individual pleasure so directly to group fulfillment, it is more static and does not require recourse to the rotation method. The next three life-choice value systems SK lived through were his dedication to the general Kantianism of a secularized Protestantism, then his interest in the religion of Socrates, and finally his commitment to Christ.

60. Croxall, *Kierkegaard*, 23, 26, 24.

or bad? For, if so, we are still where we were. But if we mean ethically good or bad, then we have made the ethical distinction, wherein alone, if we choose good, we can integrate the personality."[61] To choose morally is the mark of the ethical person. In contrast, the character of the western aesthete either involves absorption in immediate pleasures or losing oneself in multifarious preferences.[62]

Those who center their lives in pursuit of individual self-fulfillment think in terms of fortune and misfortune, success and failure as outwardly determined. For the western aesthetic life, love is often viewed as a succession of first loves: it is experimental, uncertain, requires a series of finite justifications, is thought to affect only two persons and thus does not involve publically attested obligations. Engagement is for the aesthete more beautiful than marriage, and if one gets married and stays so, marriage has as its goals personal enjoyment and the continual avoidance of disappointment.[63]

If one's ultimate goal in life is self-fulfillment, enough will never be enough. "Ethics is a constant embarrassment to aesthetics, interposing its disquieting question at every turn—ought I to live so purposelessly, so selfishly?"[64]

Boredom can help lead people to opt for what SK regarded as an *ethic of "universal duty."* However, a hedonist who wishes to remain so, may concede that boredom is a problem, but not a sufficient one to move him toward living according to a different understanding of life. SK's analysis can only invite holistic decisions or "leaps" to what he regarded as the next higher way of living. *However, at the point of transcending hedonism one could surely commit directly to Jesus Christ, rather than starting on a journey that might go no further than the next stage.*

According to SK the choice of the ethical is the movement from the need for outward stimulation to inward determination in pursuit of the equivalent of golden rule justice. Marriage can become the natural example of the ethical life: here can be constancy and mutual sharing.[65]

SK agreed with Kant in regarding an ethic of duty as a universally available way of life, rather than as due to the cultural impact of a Christian norm. Against both thinkers, not only do people by nature not seem to have a sense of the propriety of some equivalent to the golden rule, but many people's senses of "right" and "wrong" are functions of tribal, national or other loyalties.

What of the place of talent in the lives of those who have moved beyond the aesthetic mode? Unlike morality or spirituality, aesthetic excellence in an artistic or intellectual sense depends upon possessing much ingenuity, which of itself does not lead to moral or spiritual heights. Yet no one should depreciate talent, which would be

---

61. Ibid., 25–26.

62. Ibid., 26.

63. Welch, *Protestant Thought/Nineteenth Century*, 1:299–300. See Kierkegaard, "Aesthetic Validity of Marriage," in *Either/Or*, 2:5–157.

64. Croxall, *Kierkegaard*, 23–24.

65. Welch, *Protestant Thought/Nineteenth Century*, 1:300–301. See Kierkegaard, *Stages*, 7–84.

contrary to Christ, who asks that we utilize our natural gifts in serving God and others (Matt 25:14–30; Luke 19:12–27). If we consider ability from that standpoint, we will not be puffed up by our possible endowments. We will also realize that whatever gifts we may possess do not make us morally or spiritually better.[66]

In spite of the superiority of SK's Kantian golden rule type of moral orientation over a pleasure-seeking one, an ethic of general duty is unstable. "If there is an 'ought,' i.e., a command, does not this imply a Commander? And who can that be but God? In other words religion, with its emphasis on the Divine, always hovers, however vaguely, in the background of ethics, embarrassing moralists by making them feel they ought to advance openly to the religious."[67]

The merely ethical way of life reaches its limit when people realize they have failed to live up to universal duty and/or when they sense that God's will is more specific than can be summarized by the golden rule. At such points they may search for the God who is only within. The *religion of immanence* SK called *Religion A* and called the *religion of transcendence (which he limited to Christian Faith) Religion B*.

Kierkegaard's claim that the story of Abraham's willingness to sacrifice his son exhibits a religion of immanence fails miserably. (1) Theologically, as a supposed transcendently personal Word of command it does not strike one as coming merely from the religious depths of one's self. (2) Morally, would the God revealed in Christ have defied His own nature as love—and as reflected in Christ's commandment to love neighbor and even enemy—to require that a father be willing to sacrifice a son for no reason other than to pass His testing?[68] This seems doubtful. Yet the broader point is true, that guidelines hold only generally, since the Living God revealed in Christ is able to give more specific directions to particular people in specific situations. God can ask something unique and this can constitute a "teleological suspension" of what is generally ethical, the goal-related, case-specific divine suspension of what would otherwise be one's duty.[69]

Religions of immanence may satisfy until people's experiences of moral guilt become senses of radical sinfulness, the awareness of the separation from God that resulted in the failure to fulfill God's will. The grace-led sense of sin and incapacity to cope with it by one's own strength is the starting point for the Christian life.[70] This final move toward *Christ-centered transcendent faith* is made possible by the fresh action of the Holy Spirit, evoking new experience and insight and enabling decision against self-reliance and for dependence on Jesus Christ as Savior and Lord.

By picturing genuinely existential ways of life—each of which makes sense only within one of four modes of self-understanding and living—SK shows that ultimate

---

66. Croxall, *Kierkegaard*, 26–27.

67. Ibid., 24.

68. See *Fear and Trembling* for SK's exposition of the story. Many scholars have long suspected that the passage was written as a way of justifying the abolition of child sacrifice, and thus should not be regarded as historical.

69. Welch, *Protestant Thought/Nineteenth Century*, 1:301.

70. Croxall, *Kierkegaard*, 37.

choices are not functions of abstract rationality. Experience makes the difference and in the case of Christianity, experience depends upon having heard proclamation or instruction concerning Jesus Christ, coming to an awareness of one's sinfulness and responding with gratitude.

SK's idea that the movement between the stages of life can be only via a "leap" (venture, decision) correlates with there being no single system of existence that all people find compelling. Each person must choose.[71] A leap is not irrational, but does involve an experience-based movement of the whole personality, not of reason alone.[72]

Because becoming a Christian is no mere intellectual decision, we cannot just think our way into being Christians. We also cannot just think our way out of life choices incompatible with Christ, for to realize their inadequacy also presupposes and requires holistic experience. Though people cannot be argued out of alternative commitments, problems with various non-Christian ways of thinking and living can be indicated, and genuinely Christian alternatives attested.

A further complexity is that those who look seriously to the Transcendent God revealed in Christ can still find pleasure, but are no longer aesthetes. They subordinate pleasure to higher obligations and find happiness in obeying the Living God. For example, SK continued to enjoy using his literary abilities, but integrated those into a sense of duty and into obedience to God.

When we understand Christian Faith properly we realize it does not conflict with reason or logic. But NT faith does insist on costly discipleship that entails a good deal of suffering. One, however, will be willing to carry the cross of Christian discipleship only if one believes in that strangely paradoxical revelation—that God was uniquely disclosed in a suffering human being who died on a cross. Insofar as Christians adhere to such faith, they accept this strange reversal both concerning God and what constitutes true human fulfillment. Insofar as people remain non-Christians they will not make either commitment, but might be helped to do so by Christian Faith being clearly articulated and by learning what Christians regard as the breaking points of conflicting ways of life.

---

71. Hegel was a monist, one who thinks that there is only one fundamental reality of which other beings—though having the semblance of separate selfhood and decision-making capacity—are but attributes or modes of the divine. SK was a pluralist, one who believes that reality consists of a genuine plurality of beings, having individual agency capacities. This being so, particularly in the human realm there continues to be genuine life alternatives, not just the semblance of choices. SK was also a relative dualist, one who draws a sharp distinction between God and world, regarding the latter as the battleground between good and evil, with God having supreme but not all-determining power.

72. Suppose people refuse to make the choice for the transcendent God revealed in Christ. Are they not free beings able to do as they please, possessed of free will, as Pelagius and Arminius said? In *The Concept of Dread*, but not consistently affirmed elsewhere, SK (like Luther) said that this is a false view of freedom. For, in the deepest sense, only when people choose the good are they truly free. Otherwise they are bound by sin as self-centeredness, autonomy, pride, disobedience. As the Fourth Gospel articulates and as Jesus shows, only by being God's obedient servant are we truly free (Croxall, *Kierkegaard*, 31–32). People have some freedom, but Christ grants the highest freedom, which enables a considerable degree of liberation from selfishness.

8. Christian Interpretation of Natural Experience

Within the Christian understanding we can distinguish between "faith *in* Christ and faith *from* Christ," with the first focused upon the person of Christ Himself, and the second surveying the world from the perspective of Christ. "In the second movement of faith Christ acts as the spiritual catalyst for a reinterpretation of the believer's experience as a whole."[73]

Systematics requires more than constructive, ethical, polemical and apologetic facets: Barth applied the dogmatic categories to elucidate our understanding of natural reality and general experience in the light of faith, showing the wider implications of explicitly Christian commitments.[74] Such expanded theological application is vital to systematic theology's concerns, but is not apologetics. Its conclusions will appeal only to those with Christian commitment and who are thus interested in thinking about such facets of its broader meanings. With this aspect of systematics Barth offered theological statements about wider and often more philosophical topics,[75] such as the meaning of time and history, the consideration of those aspects of human anthropology that transcend humankind as created good and yet as having given way to sin, and the understanding of religion.[76]

Systematic theology surely needs not only to develop a consistent doctrinal structure, but an understanding of the world that is congruent with that. One can see a major way Barth interrelated these two by looking at his examination of *"religion."*[77] At the level of Christian doctrinal convictions he was convinced that one's faith and life are pleasing to God only insofar as one is faithfully responsive to God. Because of his focus upon grace-full historical revelation in Jesus Christ, genuine Christian Faith (contrary to Liberal Theology's teaching) was seen as qualitatively different from the generic category of religion. Barth did not deny that most people are "religious," but from the Christian perspective regarded that as generally an effort to try to save

---

73. Hick, *Faith/Knowledge*, 217, 218.

74. If one is thinking of *comprehensive moral implications* of Christian faith one is in the area of Christian ethics. Like the Christian interpretation of natural experience, Christian ethics is explicitly theological, but unlike the former enterprise, does not involve merely reflecting about natural reality.

75. Barth regards this facet of systematizing work as a part of dogmatics proper, as does Brunner, but Brunner calls this second aspect "Christian philosophy." Thus Brunner affirms that every systematic theologian is both a theologian and a philosopher, a theologian as occupied with problems raised directly by the biblical message, a philosopher as concerned with those in the background of biblical revelation. A theologian, for example, who reflects on the understanding of what time means to us and to God is said to be working in the sub-discipline of Christian philosophy (*Revelation/Reaso*, 390). But would that be a *Christian* philosophy or would that involve Christian theological dialogue with philosophy, which Barth implies? (See chap. 12, sec. 2) I agree with the latter, except that more areas are involved than philosophy.

For systematics's indebtedness to the Hellenistic tradition, use of logic, and concerning the "coherence test of truth," see chap. 1, secs. 10 and 11.

76. Dalferth, "Barth's Eschatological Realism," 36.

77. See Barth, *CD*, 1/2:280–361.

oneself by one's own searching for God. From Christ-centered, grace-based faith, he critically evaluated religion—especially what often passes for the "Christian" religion—which has frequently been guilty of works righteousness. He went one step further and affirmed that insofar as Christians faithfully respond to God's revelation in Christ and live with gratitude for grace freely received, rather than merit earned, they can manifest true religion.

9. Differences, Relationships between Systematic Theology and Various Forms of Historical Theology[78]

Historical disciplines primarily say, "Thus it was." Systematic/dogmatic/doctrinal theology decisively says, "Thus it is." Dogmatics emphasizes truth more than historical accuracy. To the contrary, both biblical and post-biblical historical theology, though interested in truth, predominantly stress historical accuracy. Consistent with such differing emphases, historical disciplines allow us to keep considerable distance between ourselves and the subject matter—even insisting that we do so. In contrast in dogmatics personal involvement is paramount. Dogmatic theology must examine theologically relevant historical texts, but for the sake of establishing legitimate traditions.[79] It is one thing to quote a document like the Nicene Creed in terms of its probable original meaning and intent. It is something else to use it primarily to think about contemporary significance, or for expanding or illuminating a biblically-based theological point one is trying to make. Systematic theologians do these latter things and must, since their task is to articulate the normative meaning of faith today.[80]

Because all varieties of historical theology try to recreate the *theology* that lies behind texts, to do any type of historical theology one has to enter into the workings of theology. The historical theologian does not have to agree with the unit being studied, but must empathize sufficiently to summarize its theological content. Historical knowledge is essential and regulative for all historical theology, but not sufficient—for historical disciplines seek to know the kind of God the texts point toward, how such a being relates to humans, and what religious and ethical consequences are entailed. In these latter senses all historical theology disciplines are theological and directly contribute to systematics.[81]

Like the church historical theology that deals with post-biblical material, systematics spends much time examining such later interpretations of Christian Faith. Accurately understanding non-contemporary theological sources is of great

---

78. Post-biblical historical theology focuses upon those interpretations of Christian faith, whereas biblical historical theology studies the biblical basis of Christian Faith. See chap. 18, sec. 11 for discussions of the work of historians.
79. Ebeling, *Theology/Proclamation*, 23–26.
80. Barth, *Göttingen Dogmatics*, 294.
81. Barr, *Concept/Biblical Theology*, 211.

importance to theology itself,[82] for these in part provide commentary on the meaning of biblical faith. Because of the historical nature of its subject matter systematics did not remain unaltered while the new historical disciplines were being established. Systematics could no longer be taken seriously unless it engaged in historical reflection concerning its subject.[83]

10. More on Biblical Theology, Its Differences from, Relationships with Systematic Theology

Knowledge of God's manifestation in Christ is dependent on exegesis and the understanding provided by biblical theology. The main reason that biblical theology is justified is that it is a part of exegesis itself. Whether expressed or implicit, all exegesis of a small portion of Scripture implies some view of a wider totality. Biblical theology is a provisional attempt to express that wider perspective, taking as the totality the OT, the NT, both together, or major parts of either (such as the prophets, Paul's own writings or the Gospels). The systematician must critically assess biblical theology's input in the light of one's own exegetical understandings, one's knowledge of past and present biblical and post-biblical historical theology, and with openness to God.

To understand how biblical theology works and how it can provide valuable insight for systematics we should remember that biblical theology is a form of historical theology and that to do historical *theology* is to enter into the workings of theology. Biblical theology assists systematic theology in the same way that a theologically sensitive biblical commentary does, as it not only addresses the following preliminary questions, but also explores the later italicized ones: "A commentary may ask: What did the author (or redactors, or [early] readers) think? What part of their belief system was this? Or it may go farther and ask: *What if their thoughts were true? What if God is as they thought him to be, or depicted him to be? What are the consequences for the total religious picture of the world?* A Commentary becomes fully 'theological' when it enters into this second set of questions."[84]

Though scholars in both biblical and church historical types of historical theology need to think theologically about the meaning of the units studied, such fields are primarily descriptive. Yet both can take an emphasis from their sources and develop that into an important theme for modern theology and Christian life. Both such applications must be done in ways that accurately depict the ancient reality and disclose differences involved in the modern usage.[85]

The Bible does not provide organizing guidance for the construction of tightly coherent biblical theologies. To achieve these biblical theologians must recognize that

---

82. Ibid., 210.
83. Ebeling, *Theology/Proclamation*, 24.
84. Barr, *Concept/Biblical Theology*; my emphases.
85. Ibid., 212.

some things are more important than others,[86] such prioritizing being essential if one is to articulate a logically consistent view. In attempting to organize scriptural materials such scholars also interpret some elements literally and others figuratively or as mere illustrations. They attempt to emphasize what the Bible does, and have been relatively successful in doing so. Their analyses and syntheses of Scripture provide structured expressions that help biblical readers (including systematic theologians) better understand biblical materials related to particular themes. These various contributions are useful in part because the Bible—with its large and diverse contents—does not entirely generate its own theology. Of course the church worked at systematizing the Bible long before Gabler's 1787 essay mapped out the contours of the discipline of biblical theology. However imperfectly, dogmatics from the early centuries had been partially engaged in such activities.

In his preparatory essay of 1928 on OT theology Walther Eichrodt argued that it did not belong to the normative disciplines, such as doctrinal theology. He furthermore insisted that it did not appeal to faith, to particular modes of cognition or to special types of authority. *If systematics is subtle and didactic, similar in some ways to philosophy and in others to preaching, biblical theology is primarily descriptive. Systematics seeks to explain in relation to many disciplines; biblical theology deals only with the Bible and its scholarship.* Though systematics may interpret much of the Bible, unlike biblical theology it does so in more selective ways, and does not provide synthetic accounts of the Old or New Testaments.

In articulating an understanding of the Bible, systematics not only seeks to learn of God, but to influence the action and speech of the Christian community.[87] *Because this discipline involves* "the construction, criticism and refining of our concepts of God in Christ and in the church," "no amount of consideration of the biblical material, in whatever mode, will in itself perform [this] task." "Theology is a reflective activity in which the content of religious expressions is to some extent abstracted, contemplated, subjected to reflection and discussion, and deliberately reformulated."[88]

As a biblical scholar who has thought a lot about the differences between systematic and biblical theology, and who has written extensively in the latter area, James Barr gives an ironic warning, not to systematicians, but to biblical theologians like himself. "It should be clearly admitted by those working in biblical theology that the case in favor of their discipline, however it is defined, has not been satisfactorily established and remains precarious, and this from the most central *theological* point of view. Most important are the arguments of [those] doctrinal theologians, who see the enterprise as an amateurish attempt of pious biblical scholars to do the work of theology on the basis of their own biblical expertise alone, and thus as a fundamentally biblicistic illusion."[89]

---

86. See the "canon within the canon" discussion in chap. 7, sec. 6.

87. Barr, *Concept/Biblical Theology*, 38, 40, 6, 7, 524, 74.

88. Ibid., 73, 249; my emphases.

89. Ibid., 252. "I repeat . . . Childs's remark that 'Biblical theologians were forced to do their own theology'" (same source, 668).

11. Systematics' Social Context: Creative and Critical Dialogues with Yesterday's and Today's World Church, Possible to Extent of Its Obedience to the Living Christ

The social context in which systematic theology occurs should not be local or national culture, but the church universal, as it has existed over the centuries and around the world. But how can even a theologian who seeks to respond to such a broad churchly base transcend her culture and broader society, such as the western world or African culture? And if she could, would that not involve something equally unacceptable, imprisonment within the universal church's own autonomous culture, rather than openness to God? The answer to both questions is identical: The Living Word of God is the source of the church's freedom from both domination by society and imprisonment within her own autonomy. The church does not have cultural independence in and of herself, but only insofar as she remains the Body subject to the Head (Col 1:18; 2:10, 19). As sinners we Christians like everyone else tend to be conformists. Only insofar as we faithfully respond to the Living Christ can we be in the world, but not of it (Rom 12:1–2). The church discovers freedom and distancing from the world and herself only as she "seeks the things that are above, where Christ is, seated at the right hand of God" (Col 3:1b). Christian theology is a function of the church—but only to the extent that the church is responsive to the leading of the Living Christ. Inasmuch as the ecumenical church is so governed, it is the most essential social context for Christian theology. Insofar as she is thus faithful, the universal church is the school of faith, and systematic theology must learn from this school if it is to be *Christian*.

Most modern systematicians agree that the church is the essential social context for Christian theology, though the emphasis has seldom been placed so heavily on its universal dimensions. No less a theologian than Schleiermacher affirmed that dogmatics is a theological discipline pertaining solely to the Christian church.[90] Though critical of Schleiermacher at many points, Barth and Brunner followed him in insisting that dogmatics is a function of the church.[91]

All Christians must seek to be responsive to the guidance of the Living Lord. Within such a listening church, theological conversation occurs that is essential for understanding the faith. Penetrating perception of revelation's meaning requires constructive and critical dialogue; otherwise, Christians fall prey to individualistic or sectarian arbitrariness.

It is important that today's Christian theologians/teachers and church preachers/teachers actively participate in this worldwide intra-church conversation not only by teaching, but also by being taught. Even as theologians seek to provide content guidance for the church's preachers/teachers, theologians should learn from the church's preaching and more informal teaching—for systematic theology has no

---

90. Schleiermacher, *Christian Faith*, 2:3.
91. Barth, *CD*, 1/1:1; Brunner, *God*, 3.

norm unavailable to these others. Both the church's direct preaching/teaching and more formal theology seek to be responsive to the Living Christ attested by the NT and present with us today, especially amid the interpretive discussion provided by fellow Christians.

12. Critique of Biblicism's Illusions, Dialectical Attitude toward Early Post-Biblical Orthodoxy, Seventeenth Century and Modern Protestant Varieties[92]

If post-biblical tradition is understood as the voices of the church fathers and mothers, under no circumstances can this be regarded as a freestanding source of normative revelation. In contrast the Reformation Scripture principle placed the church *permanently* under the authority of the scriptural witness, believing that the distinction between the church and Scripture as the church's main teaching instrument helps to express the lasting difference between the *Lord* and the assembly of believers. However, even granted that the disclosure in Christ is normative and that Scripture is the original witness to that, a Christian can never overleap the centuries and, utilizing only one's own judgment, link up immediately with the Bible. Such biblicism appeared often in the eighteenth and nineteenth centuries with the claim that one can dismiss Nicea, orthodoxy, church Fathers and confessions and attend to the Bible alone.[93]

To the contrary the Bible is read and heard in the church, which means that individual Christians need to listen to what the church, as distinguished from themselves, has understood from the Bible. Though the church's great teachers and councils possess only human authority, what these sources have said needs to be understood, lest our interpreting of the Bible's meaning be only self-instruction. The commandment to honor father and mother applies to church tradition, which is also a limited authority, since we must obey God. But subject to our direct obedience to God we have also to honor[94] tradition. We are not bound or constrained by previous church judgments, but we should give the same respect[95] toward the church's past and its elders as we should pay to our fathers and mothers. Most certainly we cannot make an absolute

---

92. Chap. 7, sec. 5 critiqued the few places in the NT where correct belief is seen as taking the place of living relationship with Christ (Jude 3b; 2 Pet 1:12; 2 John 9). There is continuity between what was criticized there and will be here, but this sec. represents the varieties of such orthodoxy that developed within Protestantism.

93. Barth, *Credo*, 179, 180. "I am thinking of G. Menken, J. T. Beck, Hofman of Erlangen, Adolf Schlatter, all significantly gifted men. This proceeding that seems to maintain so logically the Scripture principle, always—strange to say—meant the emergence of a richly modern theology! For these determined 'Biblicists' had their contemporary philosophy in their heads, took it with them to the Bible and so most certainly read themselves into the Bible no less than church Fathers and Scholastics. They were no doubt free of church dogma but not of their own dogmas and conceptions. Luther and Calvin did not go to work on the Bible in this way. Neither should we" (same source, 180–81).

94. In scholastic mode Barth says "obey," but that overstates our allegiance to tradition.

95. Unfortunately, again in orthodox vein, Barth speaks of "obedience."

beginning today, carrying out a creation out of nothing! In honoring the church's past it is always possible to be a very *free* theologian. But it must be borne in mind that as members of the church we must hear before we speak. Along this line, the Protestant Reformers and their confessions appealed (as, for example, in their understanding of justification) to the christological and trinitarian verdicts of the early post-NT church. But they may have done so more uncritically than we should.

Agreeing with the fathers and mothers can never be an end in itself and *Living in the Past* is absurd: But where insights from orthodoxy are shunned, the rejection may spring from an "orthodoxy" connected with modes of modern thought. If people realized that in the latter instance there seems to be a strong tie, they might more appreciate the tie to the church's more distant past. As we break free from the illusion that the world began with us, we will discover that even the fathers of the seventeenth century were theologians of stature.[96] Nevertheless, "it cannot by any means be a matter of opening the gates wide and allowing whole wagon-loads of old doctrine to enter without discrimination! The past, too, had its mixture of pure and impure doctrine,"[97] and I would add, even concerning early christological and trinitarian conceptions. The norm that should determine our choice is Jesus Christ as attested in Scripture.

Barth's mainly orthodoxy defending statements in the 1935 *Credo* need to be further balanced against his later writings, and we begin by seeing his perspective in the 1951 preface to the original (German) edition of *Church Dogmatics*, III/4, in its 1961 English translation. There he insisted that bondage to ancient confessions or to particular theologians is wrong, and that looking to the future we must continually extend beyond those.[98] Elsewhere he even quoted Kant to the effect that Christians should "'have the courage to use their own intelligence.'"[99]

In a 1961 letter to Geoffrey Bromiley Barth explained why he was unwilling to respond to critical questions put by the American theologians Clark, Klooster and van Till:

> None of their questions leaves me with the impression that they want to seek with me the truth that is greater than us all. They take the stance of those who happily possess it already and who hope to enhance their happiness by succeeding in proving to themselves and the world that I do not share this happiness. Indeed they have long since decided and publicly proclaimed that I am a heretic, possibly (van Til) the worst heretic of all time. So be it! But they should not expect me to take the trouble to give them the satisfaction of offering explanations which they will simply use to confirm the judgment they have already passed on me.

---

96. Barth, *Credo*, 181–83.
97. Ibid., 183.
98. Barth, *CD*, 3/4:xiii.
99. Busch, *Karl Barth*, 354.

"These fundamentalists want to eat me up. They have not yet come to a 'better mind and attitude' as I once hoped. I can thus give them neither an angry or a gentle answer but instead no answer at all."[100]

Barth later also had a very critical attitude toward the Confessional Movement in Germany. He conceded that though he and they had common concerns, he did not support their "battle for the Bible," which in Bergmann's book he found "theology with a flail." There he perceived a judgmental spirit with little awareness that we are all sinners, and a failure to witness to the Gospel as "'a liberating, comforting, edifying, pleasing, and indeed glad word.'"[101]

More broadly put, anyone who desires to do the work of systematic theology "cannot proceed by building with complete confidence on the foundation of questions that are already settled, results that are already achieved, or conclusions that are already arrived at." This because "the theological center that comprehends and displays its manifold individual aspects is no blueprint available for the asking. It is, instead, Jesus Christ who, by the potency of the Holy Spirit, is risen, powerful, and speaking." "Only in the realm of the power of the Spirit can theology be realized as a humble, free, critical, and happy science of the God of the Gospel. Only in the courageous confidence that the Spirit is the truth does theology simultaneously pose and answer the question about truth."[102]

Orthodoxy confuses its descriptions of God with God Himself, virtually deifying its own theological traditions, and "*becomes coercive when it demands that people give up thinking and simply say yes to what they are told.*"[103] The theological formulations provided by the early post-biblical church concerning the meaning of scriptural teachings must—in the light of careful scriptural exegesis and interpretation—be rethought and restated afresh. Though we should respect the work of earlier theologians, "received dogmas are only preliminary stopping points in what is a continuing task of theological reflection within the church . . . Even the decisions of Nicea and Chalcedon are in principle open to correction."[104]

We should be receptive to what our church ancestors have said, realizing that though they have long since died, their written witness can still speak relevant words concerning the Bible's meaning.[105] However, we honor their interpretive insights by thinking seriously about what they said, and by striving diligently to restate matters in direct responsibility to the Living Christ whom we have come to know through our own fresh listening to Scripture.

---

100. Barth, *1961–1968 Letters*, 8.

101. Eberhard Busch quoting from Barth's comments to Pastor Dr. Gerhard Bergmann, found in ibid., 271.

102. Barth, *Evangelical Theology*, 165, 89, 55.

103. Daniel L. Migliore describing Barth's criticisms of orthodoxy, "Barth's First Lectures," *Göttingen Dogmatics*, xxviii; my emphasis.

104. Ibid., xxxv.

105. Barth, *Evangelical Theology*, 173.

Chapter 10

Question of General Revelation or Natural Theology

1. The Contemporary Context of This Discussion

THE ISSUE UNDER CONSIDERATION in this chapter is whether people can have a valid knowledge of God and relationship with Him without having responded to His revelation in Jesus Christ. Does the NT generally support such an assumption, and if it does, how needful is God's manifestation in Christ?

A historical sketch of the inroad of natural theology into Bible-centered Protestantism may help to set the stage for our discussion. Luther's social and political thought built from order of creation reasoning and Calvin also manifested some openness to natural theology.[1] For such reasons sixteenth century Protestantism's focus upon Jesus Christ as known through the Bible was only partial. Post-Reformation Protestant orthodoxy of the seventeenth century gave increasing prominence to natural theology, which prepared the way for its inrush in the eighteenth century.[2]

In the wake of Kant's eighteenth century *Critique of Pure Reason*, in the nineteenth century Schleiermacher and his successors no longer practiced traditional natural theology, which they understood as illegitimate metaphysics (philosophical speculation concerning the nature of reality). Because Schleiermacher's undertaking differed somewhat from previous natural theology, Barth did not at first accuse him of that, but of laying a foundation for Christian theology in an account of a general human capacity for religion knowable apart from revelation.[3] However for Barth the difference between the older natural theology and its modern basis in universal human religiousness is less important than what the two have in common: The attempt to establish a foundation for Christian Faith apart from that faith.

---

1. See sec. 7.
2. Barth, *CD*, 1/1:192; 1/2:123.
3. Watson, *Text/Truth*, 271.

After Brunner employed the term "natural theology" in 1934 for his own (in Barth's eyes dubious) theological apologetics, Barth reverted to using the "natural theology" label to refer even to Schleiermacher and those Barth supposed were his twentieth century descendants. By "natural theology" Barth by then—but this was still very early!—meant every positive or negative framework that claims to interpret revelation apart from the disclosure in Jesus Christ and that does not involve the exposition of Holy Scripture.[4] As for applying the first aspect of this conception of natural theology, though Schleiermacher tried to establish a foundation for Christian Faith that is prior to and independent of Jesus Christ, neither Kierkegaard nor Brunner were trying to do so, though at that time Barth thought they were.[5] As we have seen, SK's apologetic consisted only of exposing alternative life choices, that people may perceive how those differed from true faith in Christ, so they may be encouraged to decide for Christ. That was also the purpose of Brunner's critique of non-Christian thinking and behavior.

As for applying the second aspect of Barth's early conception of natural theology, that all theological activity short of exegesis is dubious: This limitation would not only ensnare much of the work of the church fathers, but would do the same to many aspects of Barth's activity. Though systematics needs to examine what the Bible says, it does not merely involve exegesis, but includes thinking along lines encouraged by one's understanding of God's disclosure in Jesus Christ. Such a distinguishing can be easily seen in this chapter by comparing sections 2–3 and 6, as more exegetical, with sections 4, 8–10, as more theologically expansionary, with 5 as mixed.

2. Mainly on Need to Here Discuss "Image of God" Teaching

The image of God topic needs to be dealt with in this context because many people assume that it endorses an innate sense of oneness with God, i.e., a type of general revelation or natural theology. As we will see, this teaching does nothing of the sort. To the contrary, as indicated in chapter 2, section 6, the OT and NT indications of our creation "in" or "after" God's image sharply differentiates us from God, since, unlike references to Jesus, we are *not* said "to be" the image of God.

The image of God terminology used in the OT describes existing humankind, and does not refer to a mode of being lost or diminished because of human sinfulness. (This characteristically OT sense of the phrase is also found in two passages in the NT, First Corinthians 11:7 and James 3:9.) In the OT meaning of image of God, human distinctiveness not only remains in spite of sin, but is presupposed as the possibility of being able to sin and for God to hold us accountable.

The OT's discussion of human creation in God's image or after Her likeness speaks of human uniqueness in contrast with animal creation. Unlike animals, most

---

4. "No!" Answer to Emil Brunner's "Natural Theology," in Brunner/Barth, *Nature/Grace*, 74–75; Watson, *Text/Truth*, 271.

5. See chap. 9, secs. 6 and 7.

humans are rational and capable of communicating at high levels verbally or with complex signs. *Such abilities indicate existing capacities that go some way in helping to qualify us to be God's deputies in relation to the rest of creation.* The OT image of God material does not concern how humans acquire faith in God, personal relationship with Her or knowledge of Her. What these texts imply[6] is that because God has created us with rational and symbolic communicative capacities, when She calls us into relationship with Herself She enlists our linguistic and rational abilities to understand and thereby relate to the animal kingdom.

The Bible is not self-interpreting and we cannot compel God to speak. But unless we utilize our creational ability to interpret, we will not understand Her when She does. The Living Word of God does not have to create our capacity for comprehending words or complex visual signs. We have never lost this; it is the presupposition of our power to intellectually grasp the Word of God. Salvation by grace alone through faith alone is not endangered by such limited "point of contact" recognition.[7] Our capacity for comprehending discourse is presupposed by belief in the Word of God,[8] but God speaking to our hearts is required for such a capacity to be utilized in relationship to God.

3. Old Testament Meanings of Human Creation in God's Image

Several OT passages use image of God or likeness to God terminology, though one avoids these words and only refers to the resulting function, and two mention the image of God or likeness to God phrase, while saying nothing of the resulting capacity. Two of the four OT texts on the image of God specifically contrast humankind as created in God's image with mere animal existence.[9]

(1) Perhaps the clearest passage is Genesis 1:26–28, which uses both the image of God terminology and refers to the deputyship function that flows from that. After God created the non-human aspects of the world He is thought to have said, "'Let us[10] make humankind in our *image*, according to our *likeness*;[11] and let them have dominion over the fish of the sea, and over the birds of the air, and over the cattle, and over all the earth, and over all the wild animals of the earth, and over every creeping thing

---

6. See below.
7. Brunner, in *Nature/Grace*, 31.
8. Cairns, *Image of God*, 162–3.
9. Barr, *Biblical Faith/Natural Theology*, 171.

10. The plural reference is unclear. Traditionalists assume that it is a reference to the Trinity. That is not only unlikely but such a plural understanding would imply that God's triune being is a composite of separate entities. Some exegetes regard the reference as to God's creational work as accompanied by angels, and that may be exegetically correct, but also is not theologically acceptable. Christians regard God alone as the Creator.

11. My emphases. Exegetical research concerning the relation between these two terms indicates that there is little difference between them, though "likeness" "limits to *mere likeness* the correspondence of the image to the original as it is present in the image" (Pannenberg, *ST*, 2:203; my emphasis).

that creeps upon the earth. So God created humankind in his image, in the image of God he created them; male and female he created them'" (NRSV).

(2) The deputyship *aspect* of the OT image of God is mentioned and clearly articulated in Psalm 8:4–8, but without terminological reference. "What is man that you are mindful of him, and the son of man that you do care for him? Yet you have made him little less than God, and crown him with glory and honor. You have given him dominion over the works of your hands; you have put all things under his feet . . ."[12] To be created "little less than God" does sound confident concerning human nature, but what immediately follows interprets the phrase as having to do with a deputyship function.

(3) Genesis 5:1b–2 uses "likeness to God" language, but does not mention the resulting function. "When God created humankind, he made them in the likeness of God. Male and female he created them, and he blessed them and named them Humankind when they were created" (NRSV). Because men and women are created in God's image both are responsible to God as trustees on behalf of the rest of creation.[13]

As for these first three kinds of OT texts referring to the image of God we can conclude that they refer to the *rational-linguistic-interpretive-supervisory* uniqueness of humans in contrast with animals.

(4) Another text uses the "image of God" phrase and draws a moral conclusion from that, but mentions no deputyship implication. After God is said to have given humans permission to kill animals for food, He forbade that we should kill one another. "'Whoever sheds the blood of a human, by a human shall that person's blood be shed, for in his own image God made humankind.[14] And you, be fruitful and multiply, abound on the earth and multiply in it'" (Gen 9:6 NRSV).[15]

---

12. Verses 4–6. Like Gen 1:26–28, Ps 8:6–8 also speaks of a deputyship function that is enabled by a likeness to God. If the divine likeness is a basis for a commission, the two meanings must be different (Pannenberg, *ST*, 2:204, having learned this point from Thielicke, *Theological Ethics*, 2).

13. Barth's claim that the man-woman relationship constitutes the OT image of God meaning is exegetically unconvincing. Maleness and femaleness are not human distinctives. "The reference to the creation of humankind as male and female is an addition to the statement that humankind is made in the image of God. It allows us to conclude that both man and woman are created equally in the divine image but not that the likeness consists of the relation between the sexes" (Pannenberg, *ST*, 2:205–6).

Contrary to Gen 1:27 (and the other OT image of God texts) and requiring much criticism is a problematic Pauline teaching that is likely a later editorial reworking, since it is much in conflict with Paul's acceptance of female leadership in his churches. Verse 7 of 1 Cor 11:3, 7–13 says that the man is the image and glory of God, but that the woman is only the glory of man. Regarding the Adam and Eve legend as literal history, the text concludes that "man [Adam] was not made from woman [Eve], but woman [Eve] from man [Adam]" (v. 8), and deduces that therefore man was not created for woman, but woman for man (v. 9). (See chap. 7, sec. 3 for the Pastoral Epistles' similar revision of Paul's thinking.) Yet verses 11–12a backtrack by recognizing that men and women are interdependent and concedes the obvious—that sons are born of mothers.

14. This verse does not reconcile with many others in the OT that justify non-retaliatory holy war.

15. Since the injunction to be fruitful was obviously written when the world was sparsely populated, it misinterpreted when applied directly today.

4. Theological Expansion of Old Testament Image of God Understandings

Moving from these specific texts to more general expository comments, we must not forget that sovereignty over the rest of creation is delegated to us by the Lord to whom we are accountable. Of the habitually misinterpreted text about subduing the earth and having dominion over it (Gen 1:26–28) Jacques Ellul writes: "The passage does not say that we can use the world however we like. In particular, since we are [in] the image of God, we must direct the earth *as* God directs creation. We must have dominion over the animals *as* God has dominion over the world. 'As' means 'imitating,' '*in the same manner,*' 'with the same restraint from doing all that could be done.'"[16]

As with the second creation account, which deals with Adam as gardener (Gen 2:15–17), deputyship excludes arbitrary control or exploitation. Though under our care, nature still belongs to God. This is why the misuse of our delegated power "rebounds upon ourselves and plunges us into ruin. In this sense we may view the ecological crisis at the end of the modern age of emancipation as a reminder that God is still the Lord of creation and that human arbitrariness in dealing with it is not without limits or consequences."[17]

Without isolating or glorifying reason by regarding it as what alone makes people uniquely human, the stewardship relationship of which Gen 1, 5, 9 and Psalm 8 speak presupposes rational capacities and communication abilities[18] sufficient to shepherd creation on God's behalf. The contrast of humans with other animals likely propelled the image of God notion into the *intellectual* realm. For humankind's dominion over the animals was not by strength alone, for many animals had advantages in strength and speed, and all were well adapted to their environment.[19] Human deputyship "*rested upon use of technology,*[20] however primitive then compared with now, *and technology rested upon human powers of thought, reason, language, and abstraction.*"[21]

---

16. Ellul, *Humiliation of Word*, 67.

17. Pannenberg, *ST*, 2:205. The criticism that regards the giving of dominion in Gen 1:28 as responsible for the unrestricted exploitation of nature by modern technology and industry and for the resulting ecological crisis is without merit. Industrial society had its basis in modern secular culture, which after the religious wars of the sixteenth and seventeenth centuries to a large extent cut itself off from Christian roots, leading to the autonomous development of economic life (same source, 204). "Contemporary secularism, while boasting of its emancipation from religious ties at the same time places responsibility for the consequences of its absolutizing of the striving for possessions on the religious origins from which it has broken free. Certainly faith in the one Transcendent God of the Bible has in fact de-divinized the world of nature and handed it over to us as a sphere over which to rule" (same source, 204). But for Christians this world is still the Creator's, to whom we as created in Her image are accountable (same source, 204–5).

18. Along these lines the Yahwist source refers to the human capacity to name the animals (Gen 2:19).

19. Barr, *Biblical Faith/Natural Theology*, 171–72.

20. Not that only human can use tools.

21. Barr, *Biblical Faith/Natural Theology*, 172; my emphases. An intellectual and linguistic

As for even broader theological and hermeneutical implications of what has been said: In spite of all dissimilarity, human communicating to a degree parallels the divine's. Unless there was some similarity between human and divine communication, we could not learn of God. Furthermore, that most humans can use and understand words is connected with being active subjects, which, with all our dissimilarity, parallels God as self-communicating Subject.[22] Though we learn of even God's transcendent reality through His revelation, we must utilize ordinary language to communicate concerning God and His ways. We can do this because by God's sustaining grace sin has not been able to efface our God-given intellectual and communicating capacities.

Granted that humans are sinful, it is doubtful that we can effectively fulfill our deputyship obligation until redeemed by Christ and enabled to share in relationship with Him who renews in us the image of God in the NT sense of the term. However, the point of these image of God OT texts does not directly concern personal dialogue with God, which only became possible in Israel's history, not from human creation onward. These passages speak only of being responsible to God to perform a task that assumes rational and communicative capacities. Though the creation accounts were likely written long after Israel had met God in covenant history, the Yahwist creation account does attest the importance of relationship with Him. But unless one interprets the Adam and Eve story as historically factual—rather than a mythological tale to account for an existing state of affairs—the OT regards such relationship as beginning with the calling of Abraham, not with creation.

The conclusion concerning OT image of God terminology is that though this implies much concerning our use of creational gifts as stewards of creation, the image of God term and the related stewardship obligation do not endorse a theology independent of God's revelation. These texts do *not* talk of coming to faith, but of human capacities required for deputyship over creation and presupposed for understanding God's disclosure in Christ.

5. Brief Reference to New Testament Image of God Usage

Though the NT also uses image of God terminology, the concept it *generally discusses* with such words has less to do with the *rational-linguistic-interpretive-supervisory* uniqueness of humans in contrast with animals and more with the reality of sinners redeemed and brought into relationship with God through Christ. The common NT meaning of the image of God language will be more thoroughly discussed when in a future volume human sinfulness and our resulting need for redemption is considered. Here I refer to that aspect only to clarify the differences between Old and New Testament image of God meanings.

---

understanding of the divine image in man is found also in the Book of Ben Sira (Ecclesiasticus), 17:3–8, which similarly links to the capacity for headship over animals (same source, 172).

22. Brunner, *Creation/Redemption*, 44, 177. See chap. 2, sec. 3 above.

As sinners we have broken relationship with God, and in this sense the image of God in its common NT meaning was lost only to begin to be restored through relationship with God through Christ. In the other frequent NT sense, the image of God is considerably defaced because of the considerable (but not total) immoral effects of separation from God. According to the NT meanings of the phrase, Christ alone is the image of God in terms of relationship with God and moral faithfulness. Only by redemption through Him can we sinners be renewed and enabled truly to reflect God's double-sided image realized in Him.

The efforts to harmonize Old and New Testament meanings of the image of God language introduced much confusion, such as concerning whether or not the image has been totally lost (Luther) or if a remnant remains (Calvin generally).[23] By and large the OT and NT are talking of different realities with image of God language.

6. Other Alleged Biblical Bases for General Revelation or Natural Theology

The Bible says little that can be interpreted as encouraging a belief in general revelation or a valid natural knowledge of God. Key NT passages to be considered in possible favor of non-revelational knowledge of God are Romans 1:18–25; 2:12–16 and Acts 17:16–33. The Romans passage deals with the manifestation of God's wrath against the ungodliness and wickedness of humankind. Verses 19–20a deliberately avoids the language of revelation and considerably limit what is supposedly perceivable through creation. Yet it does say that "what can be known about God is plain to them, because God has shown it to them. Ever since the creation of the world his invisible nature, namely, his eternal power and deity, has been clearly perceived in the things that have been made." These words seem to assert that some legitimate knowledge of God has been attained apart from historical revelation. But, appearing to contradict this, Paul immediately goes on to say that people have suppressed this God-given capacity, thereby becoming guilty. "They are without excuse; for although they knew God they did not honor him as God or give thanks to him, but they became futile in their thinking and their senseless minds were darkened. Claiming to be wise, they became fools, and exchanged the glory of the immortal God for images resembling mortal man or birds or animals or reptiles" (Rom 1:20–23). One wonders who Paul assumes truly learned of God through creation, since he concludes that all have "exchanged the truth of God for a lie and worshiped and served the creature rather than the Creator" (Rom 1: 25ab), and that "all have sinned and come short of the glory of God" (Rom 3:23).

---

23. Calvin confused matters by assuming that terminological similarities imply content identities between the Testaments. Yet at one point he admitted that he based his understanding entirely on the NT meaning. "The true nature of the image of God is to be derived from what Scripture says of its renewal through Christ" (*Institutes*, 1:189).

Most exegetes seem to think that Paul's extreme dialectic in Rom 1:18–25 is only a way of saying that *because we* "exchanged the truth about God for a lie" (vs 25a) our sin is our fault, in contrast with the notion that God made no creational provision for knowledge of Herself or that God caused, rather than merely permitted, our turning away. If this is the correct interpretation of this passage as a whole, verses 19–20a are not to be taken at face value.

Along such lines, many exegetes deliteralizingly interpret verses 19–20a[24] and assume that these are only intended as background for concluding that we are now guilty (vs 20b–23). Perhaps Paul believed that *God's creational disclosing went forth, but was not received—analogous to what largely occurred with God's revelation in Jesus prior to His resurrection.* Such an understanding interprets verses 19–20a in the context of those that follow, but may not do full justice to the earlier verses. But if we take the earlier verses more literally, we cannot do justice to the words that follow and the repeated message of Paul's epistles, that we come into relationship with and knowledge of God through faith in His act of redemption in Christ.

Verses 19–20a are preceded by the assertion that God's wrath against human sinfulness is to the point (vs 18), and are immediately followed by the statement that God's making Herself known through creation implies that everyone is without excuse (vs 20b). Therefore God gave them up (vs 24a, 26a) to the tragic results of their deeds. These verses do not promote natural theology nor encourage us to think that verses 19–20a endorse such.

I have found Brunner's ideas about Romans 1:18–25 particularly helpful, perhaps because in practical and spiritual ways he attempts to resolve the impasse posed by the polarity implied by Paul's words. But like many exegetes he slides over the explicit assertion "that what can be known of God is plain to them . . . namely, his eternal power and deity" (vss 19b, 20b). Brunner's interpretation: The accusation with which we are charged is that by our own unrighteousness we suppress the truth (Rom 1:18). Paul repeatedly asserts that we are accountable for this state and are without excuse.[25] The people "to whom the message of Jesus Christ is proclaimed are not merely ignorant, but are guilty in their ignorance; their lack of knowledge is due to the fact that they do not *want* to know."[26] It is an integral part of our sin that we suppress the creational knowledge of God and fall into idolatry and illusion. This being so, we are now living in opposition to ourselves, and this self-contradiction—*Man In Revolt*—is the fundamental tendency of our empirical nature. This is what went unchallenged before we were recreated by God's Spirit in response to the message concerning Jesus Christ.[27]

---

24. See below.
25. Brunner, *Revelation/Reason*, 63, 64.
26. Ibid., 64.
27. Ibid., 65, 74. Unfortunately Brunner links his view with Augustine's psychological assumption that we all have an innate sense of restlessness and guilt that neo-platonically pushes us toward God. Though many may begin the Christian journey in ways that seem well summarized by this theory, such

Romans 2:12–16 seems to imply the reality of natural *law*. "When the Gentiles, who have not the law, do by nature what the law requires, they are a law to themselves, even though they do not have the law. They show that what the law requires is written on their hearts, while their conscience also bears witness and their conflicting thoughts accuse or perhaps excuse them on that day when, according to my gospel, God judges the secrets of people by Christ Jesus" (vss 14–16). But chapter 3 concludes that "both Jews and Greeks are under the power of sin," and that "'none is righteous, no not one'" (9b, 10a).

Even if one regards natural theology/law as reflected in parts of Rom 1:18–25 and 2:12–16, are two short passages an adequate basis for concluding that Paul's theology presupposes such an enterprise? Much in conflict with reliance on natural theology or natural law, he says that "the god of this world has blinded the minds of unbelievers" (2 Cor 4:4a). Paul certainly does not build from natural theology, else he would not have written: "Since in the wisdom of God the world did not know God through wisdom, it pleased God through the folly of preaching to save those who believe (1 Cor 1:21)." "I determined not to know anything among you, save Jesus Christ and him crucified (1 Cor 2:2)." Though not likely written by Paul, Ephesians 2:12 likewise gives little encouragement to natural theology, since it assumes that prior to becoming Christians the author's readers had been without hope and without God in the world.

Acts 17:16–33 is more a reflection of Lucan than Pauline theology. Even so it offers scant support for natural theology or natural law. According to verse 16 the Athenian worship of idols provoked Paul, and verse 24 attests that "the God who made the world . . . does not live in shrines made by human hands" (NRSV). Against such background, the comment attributed to Paul (vs 22) as to how religious the Athenians were may seem more sarcastic than complimentary. No doubt in verses 27–28 Luke portrays Paul as quoting some Stoicism approvingly. Nevertheless, even the Lucan Paul is not said to have followed up such reasoning, but immediately asserted that God cannot be represented by stone, silver, or golden idols (vs 29). Luke claims that Paul astonished his hearers by speaking of Jesus's resurrection and they ridiculed him (vs 32). What is historical about these passages is Luke's theological understanding, not this incident's grounding in Paul's life. *But even by Luke's reckoning if this passage reflects natural theology it dies stillborn. Perhaps the same could be said of Romans 1:18–25 and 2:12–16.*

As for a possible source of natural theology from the OT, Psalm 104 does not truly reflect such a viewpoint, but affirms *faith* in God as Creator and Sustainer. This Psalm is based on experiential awareness made known through Israel's covenant history. "The Psalm is not concerned to perform the function that most normally and directly forms natural theology, namely to suggest that the nature of God can be known

---

a psychological framework contradicts Paul's and many others' experiences of being converted directly from proud self-righteousness. Brunner's linking of conversion with Neoplatonism may have been one reason for Barth's overreaction to Brunner's discussion of natural theology (same source, 74).

through contemplation of the universe and its workings. Taken in itself it seems to go in the opposite direction." It proceeds from God, telling that She "has set up the basic structures of the universe, provided the conditions for the fruitfulness of the earth, the changes of times and climate, day and night, under which beasts and humans live and die. It is all presented from the angle of [faith in] God as the Sustainer of the world and the life within it."[28]

Unlike the message of the prophets, the Book of Proverbs does not claim to be founded on revelation, but on what *according to it* is everyday wisdom or common sense. With its notion of gaining knowledge of God without revelation, Proverbs likely reflects a natural theology in the sense of uncritically endorsing the culture of the day. With even less awareness of divine revelation the Book of Ecclesiastes reaches highly skeptical conclusions about life and God. But these writings are on the fringe of the OT and neither of their supposedly natural ways of knowing can be harmonized with one another or with the thrust of either Testament. The proclamation and interpretation of the Christ events certainly places the emphasis elsewhere.

7. Calvin's Contradictory Views: Original Gift of Natural Awareness of God as Currently Implying Only Guilt and Accountability, Versus Idolatry and Impiety as Evidence of Sense of God's Presence

Calvin affirms that God had revealed Himself prior to and outside of His Israel/Christ disclosure, and that therefore all people are without excuse and accountable to Him. Yet Calvin also thought that every facet of natural human existence is now so depraved and knowledge of God so perverted that natural humankind has wrong knowledge of Him (Eph 2:10) and is in bondage to non-divine beings (Gal 4:8). Because he regarded the natural knowledge of God as so corrupted, it serves only to place humans under divine judgment, and can neither enlighten theologically nor save.[29] "Man, with all his acuteness, is as stupid in obtaining for himself a knowledge of the mysteries of God as an ass is unqualified for understanding musical harmonies."[30] Only trust in the Mediator has saving power (Rom 1:16).[31]

Though Calvin's view as just described seems in line with Paul's position as interpreted in the previous section, Calvin elsewhere contradicts that. Here Calvin manifests a complex and confusing attitude toward natural theology, with idolatry and impiety seen as ironic testimonies to the presence of God from whom people cannot escape. To cry out in despair or to blaspheme is here regarded as evidence that

---

28. Barr, *Biblical Faith/Natural Theology*, 82.

29. Calvin, *Institutes*, 1:43–44, 67–68, 63.

30. Calvin, commenting on 1 Cor 1:20 in his commentary on *The Epistle of Paul to the Corinthians*, cited in Johnson, *Authority/Protestant*, 200.

31. Calvin, *Institutes*, 1:341.

people are unable to live or think or act as though God did not exist.³² Though in this limited sense Calvin recognized natural theology, he did not regard it as a positive from which Christian Faith could build.

But is even this limited sense for natural theology convincing? Why does opposition to the true God indirectly indicate allegiance to Her? In trying to make this point Calvin insists (along the lines of philosophical idealism) that all people have the indelible mark of the presence of God in their minds. Is not such reasoning much in conflict with what he assumes in the first perspective summarized and when he discusses human sinfulness? What is the meaning of God's immediate presence to all people if the results are idolatry and impiety? Of course these are due to human sinfulness, but this obvious recognition is in line with Calvin's first perspective, not the second. If the point of God's immediate presence to all people is only that no one can avoid the God topic, this also is not true, unless it is just a reference to sub-conscious process. Many modern idolaters use no God or idolatry language. Nor is explicit rejection of God an ironic testimony to the existence of God, any more than Christian belief in God is an ironic testimony to atheism.

Beneath the Platonism of Calvin's second point may be the traditional reading of Romans 7:14-24 as autobiographical. Here Calvin may assume that all people have a natural awareness of their sinfulness, and from that self-consciousness live with degrees of despair that remind them of their need for God. Such an *interpretation* of that text is today regarded by many as exegetically dubious. Theologically it requires in all cases perception of failure under God's law as prior to experience of liberation by the Gospel—which is the opposite of Paul's experience: "As to zeal a persecutor of the church, as to righteousness under the law blameless" (Phil 3:6; see also Gal 1:13–17). Paul recognized his sinfulness only after encountering the Risen Christ.³³

8. Awareness of Our Own Deathwardness not Implying Natural Theology or General Revelation

Though humans (unlike other animals) are capable of pondering their own deathwardness, preoccupation with such does not guarantee belief in God nor openness to the gospel. Heidegger wrote much about the sense of finitude, but remained an atheist. Contrariwise, not being engrossed with this subject cannot block one from receiving grace. I suspect that most people will be willing truly to confront their own deathwardness only as they realize that God in Christ has forgiven their sin and wills

---

32. Calhoun, *Lectures*, 390. See Calvin, *Institutes*, 1:43–47.

33. Bultmann did not regard Rom 7:14–24 as Paul's confession of his pre-Christian subjective sense of inner division under the law, but as "that picture of the objective situation of [humankind]-under-the-law that became visible to him only after he had attained the viewpoint of faith" (*Existence/Faith*, 266). Bultmann's description is in line with Paul's pre-Christian sense of having a good conscience in doing what he believed the God of the Jewish religion required—such as persecuting those who believed that one who died on a cross is the Messiah.

to live in eternal fellowship with them. That is, most people will profoundly face their insecurity only as they experience security in God.

Revelation awakens new issues rather than merely dealing with questions and concerns people already have.[34] From a NT perspective death is a problem because we go to our deaths as guilty sinners who do not deserve eternal life. However, many people are not concerned about their sinfulness, though most would like to live eternally. We properly perceive the problem of our dying through awareness of our sinfulness, and since awareness of sinfulness is possible only through the gift of relationship with God, no more than finiteness can it furnish a *natural* point of contact for the receipt of grace.

More generally, the living God can open us to new insights, questions and concerns. Isaiah well knew that God's thoughts and ways are not our thoughts and ways (55:8–9). When revelation occurs we are confronted with "what no eye has seen nor ear heard nor heart of [humankind] conceived" (1 Cor 2:9). God's ways are so new and unexpected that Her truth is offensive to those who think they already know how God ought to act. Thus in the first century the Christian Gospel seemed to the Gentiles folly and to the Jews a stumbling block (1 Cor 1:23). As a Jew Paul had been taught that anyone who dies on a cross is cursed by God (Deut 21:23c, cited in Gal 3:13). Upon encountering the Risen Christ, Paul became convinced that the One who had died in such degrading circumstances was not only the Messiah—but the way of salvation.

Paralleling the uniquely Christian way of gaining fresh insight, the history of science indicates that great discoveries have often occurred when new insight has challenged some previous assumptions,[35] encouraging others to also ask new questions, think more deeply, and consider new ideas.[36]

9. Willingness to Learn from All Quarters Not Natural Theology

It is essential at all points of Christian theology to learn whatever we can from the knowledge available in the world. Doing so conflicts with revelation only if we claim to derive ultimate norms from secular sources or are unsuccessful in bringing such knowledge into consistent relationship with what we affirm on the basis of God's self-disclosure in Christ.

Thinking back over the chapters that have preceded, insights from various fields were utilized at many points, perhaps all. For example, the need to use historical-critical methods when studying the Bible, and the importance of knowledge of the history that led to the formation of the canon. Looking ahead, we will perceive that biblical interpreters can gain insights from some philosophers and philosophies.

---

34. Migliore, "Barth's First Lectures," xliv.

35. See chap. 13, sec. 9.

36. Migliore, *Faith Seeking*, 259, in an imagined dialogue stating matters as he thinks Barth would wish.

Looking beyond this volume: We will see that process philosophy/theology can add its confirming insights concerning God's involvement in the world and Her capacity for suffering. Furthermore, that a Christian understanding of human nature will gain insight from ethological (animal behavioral) studies, and that faith in God the Creator will be related to modern cosmological and evolutionary understandings.

"Natural theology" as often practiced is the opposite of an open-minded willingness to learn from all quarters and to struggle to discern how such knowledge can be integrated into genuinely Christian insights. Natural theology has frequently involved doctrinaire commitment to one philosophical viewpoint, as for example, Thomism (for traditional Roman Catholics).[37] Some Protestants have similarly canonized one philosopher, as for example, the early Heidegger (by Bultmann and much Christian Existentialism), or Whitehead (by Process Theology). In Africa many uncritically accommodate to African philosophies closely aligned with African Traditional Religion. And Liberation Theology has often uncritically accommodated to Marxist thinking. Utilizing various philosophies and philosophers here and there is one thing. Binding oneself to a particular philosophy or philosopher is something else, and misunderstands the open nature of philosophical inquiry and the need for Christian theology to utilize philosophies selectively, based in part on their helpfulness for illuminating theological themes.

10. Risen Christ's Word Spoken through Nature and amid Human Words and Events. This Also Not Natural Theology[38]

In a polite letter of response to Pope Paul's *Humanae Vitae* encyclical, sent to the Pope himself, Barth raised critical questions about the propriety of setting nature and conscience alongside revelation as equally authoritative: (1) Can we not agree that though there is no necessary antithesis there is a fundamental distinction between God's revelation and nature and conscience? (2) Can we not also agree that God's revelation is His personal Word disclosed in His Son and known through the Holy Spirit, whereas God's use of nature and conscience must be evaluated in the light of Son and Spirit if they are to be judged as fitting testimonies to God? (3) If these two assertions are true should nature and conscience be set alongside revelation as equally divine, as does the encyclical and letter? If so, where is convincing scriptural evidence?[39]

Divine disclosure "through natural mediums is not natural revelation."[40] Natural revelation is a contradiction in terms, since divine initiative is required to enable

---

37. If, as the Roman Catholic Church insists, natural law's moral implications are obvious to all rational people—if all such people can know the one true God and Creator by reason alone—such a claim can only be defended by convincing rational argument or similarly convincing empirical evidence. Thus Vatican 1 had no justifiable cause for invoking ecclesiastical authority concerning the matter. (See chap. 11 for critical appraisals of attempts to prove God's existence.)

38. See chap. 2, sec. 3; chap. 12, sec. 5; and chap. 18, sec. 7.

39. Barth, *1961–1968 Letters*, 334–35.

40. Tillich, *ST*, 1:119.

nature to point beyond itself.[41] Thus nature "cannot be an argumentative basis" for conclusions about God's existence.[42]

All Christians can agree that Jesus Christ is the sole Lord whom we are to honor and obey in all situations. All Christians can also agree that having received the Spirit of the Risen Christ, we should listen for any Word that Christ may wish to speak to us through the words of others (whether Christian or otherwise) or through personal or general events. Such mediations may also feature at the beginning of the Christian journey, when God may use human words and/or events to draw people to Herself. In such ways the world can and should from time to time *become* a means of grace. This point differs from the "general revelation" assumption that all people by virtue of a natural awareness of God (minimally dimmed by sinfulness) intuit God's nature and will.

"For Barth the world *in itself* is speechless; it is only from Christ that it receives the power of speech." To sum up Barth's "other lights" thought: "'The world *is not* a parable of the Kingdom of Heaven,'" but it can "'*become* one.'"[43] At issue is not whether God is active in general history or even whether She speaks forth Her Word, but how we experience God. If human words and events cannot *of themselves* be equated with God's Word, it is only through the Spirit's leading that we are we able to perceive what the Lord is saying.[44]

It will not do to criticize the Hitler-supporting "German Christians" for regarding "general history as revelation" if we uncritically conform to the societies in which we live or automatically endorse whatever theological or non-theological ideologies are "politically correct" or otherwise popular among our peers. If we deify western or African culture, or uncritically venerate popular viewpoints or movements—we lose our saltiness, our critical relevance to the world. But if Christ is our Standard, we can listen for His Living Word spoken amid the cultures in which we live, and among whatever movements are making impact. Insofar and only insofar as their concerns do not disagree with our best understanding of Christ can we agree with particular cultures and walk with specific movements for stretches of the road.

---

41. Ibid.

42. Ibid., 120.

43. Barr, *Biblical Faith/Natural Theology*, 189; first emphasis mine. See Barth, *CD*, 4/3.1:476–77.

44. At this point Barth's thought parallels Kierkegaard's. "In May, 1848, SK wrote in his Journal: 'How extraordinary that Socrates always spoke of having learnt from a woman. [We might ask why that should have been extraordinary!] I can also say, I owe what is best in me to a girl; but *I did not exactly learn it from her, but through her*.' SK believed that through Regina God had made him what he became—a poet at heart, and a writer of originality and power" (Gates, *Kierkegaard/Everyman*, 49, quoting from the Journals; my emphasis). Having had his passion thereby evoked, he used it in other ways.

Chapter 11

Evaluating Arguments That Attempt to Prove God's Existence[1]

Some Christians become nervous because they think Christianity is not intellectually respectable. More specifically some are disturbed because they think that if Christian Faith is important we should be able to prove God's existence by scholarly methods acceptable to all educated people. The existence of such concerns is the justification for the inclusion of this topic within systematics, rather than leaving it confined within the philosophy of religion, where less account is usually taken of Christian Faith.

Kant in his *Critique of Pure Reason* gave the deathblow to "proofs" for the existence of God. Nevertheless he said that he did not wish to discredit the belief in God, but hoped to "'create room' for it." Pascal, Kierkegaard and many others who emphasized the need for personal relationships with God regarded such "proofs" as arrogant and harmful to Christian Faith.[2] SK thought that to try to prove the existence of a person who is present is a shameless affront, since the attempt makes that person appear ridiculous. But as applied to God many people regard such an exercise as a pious undertaking. To the contrary, it is good that we cannot "know" God in a disinterested way, else we might see little need for personal encounter with and surrender of life to Him.

Since God wants relationship with us the NT generally portrays God's invitational ways, rather than God's trying to establish proof of His existence through outward displays of power.[3] Christ refused to perform miracles that simply exhibited His power, though Matthew's and Luke's versions of the wilderness temptations reflect the widespread expectation that He should have (Matt 4:1–11; Luke 4:1–13).

Christians should know that people cannot be intellectually coerced into belief. We trust that God has acted and spoken or we do not, but to reject God because there

---

1. See chap. 9, sec. 4.

2. Brunner, *Revelation/Reason*, 338, 340.

3. In contrast the author of Luke-Acts regarded miracles and signs as providing demonstrable legitimacy. See chap. 7, n49.

are no valid arguments that start from unbelief and end with belief is to reject God because the impossible cannot be achieved.

We do not learn about God from philosophy, but it can help to clear up misconceptions and thereby partly neutralize the acids of unwarranted skepticism. But a degree of skepticism is valuable to belief—helping to overthrow superstition, credulous faith, and intellectual fraud.[4]

1. Preliminary Conclusion: Existing Realities Convincingly Known and Experienced, but Providing No Argumentative Proof

Traditional philosophy recognizes two ways in which human beings may come to know whatever is to be known. As with Aristotelianism, one way is through experience, but "empiricism" is rationally doctrinaire in limiting experience to the senses. Furthermore, experience must be interpreted by the mind, and thus arises the second source of knowledge: Idealism/rationalism more directly utilizes the mind's powers for weighing evidence and drawing conclusions. But logic cannot demonstrate matters of fact nor prove existence. Factual realities either exist or do not, but thinking cannot make them so. If nothing were given through experience in its various modes we would have little to reason about. The reliance on experience is as true in religion as in other fields. In response to God's disclosure in Christ we rightly come to have many *ideas* about God's nature and will, but God is a self-existing *reality*. Therefore, if we are to gain confidence concerning His existence we must experience Him. Those who wish to speak of God but are doubtful and embarrassed by the need for personal encounter have not thought clearly as to how knowledge of personal agents is attained.[5] It would have seemed absurd to the biblical writers to use logical arguments to try to prove God's reality. For God was known to them as a Dynamic Interacting Will.

Christian Faith should not be criticized for being unable to prove that God exists, since no one can demonstrate their own existence. Hitting oneself or a wall might be thought to result only in the illusion of pain. Though most people presume their own and others reality, such cannot be rationally proven. The same holds for the existence of anything.

As the Descartian argument went, I can question my existence, but in that act cannot doubt my existence as one capable of such doubting. Why not? One could surely deny the reality of such an experience! Whole segments of people claim to disbelieve in the reality of the world, including their selfhood. For example, Buddhists and Christian Scientists suppose that the physical world is an illusion. Though this claim may seem nonsensical to most westerners and Africans, it cannot be disproven. We also cannot use the purported impossibility of self-doubt to prove *to others* that we are or that they are. Nevertheless, *people from their own experience have reason*

---

4. MacIntyre, *Difficulties/Belief*, 83, 79, 117, 118.
5. Kaufman, *ST/Historicist*, 112. See chap. 2, sec. 3 above.

to assume their own existence and that of others—unless philosophically or religiously schooled to deny the obvious.

Like everyone else, philosophers and scientists may recognize that whether or not God exists is an important question, and because of experience or lack of it may believe or disbelieve in God. But unless philosophers and scientists have imported theological convictions into their disciplines they are methodologically unable to answer positively or negatively as to whether a Transcendent God exists, nor say anything about Her nature.[6] Purely rational means cannot reach conclusions concerning God's existence in order subsequently to decide for Her. On the contrary, *we find the object of faith in the act of faith.* Christians certainly come to know the One in whom they believe, but do not know God and Her nature before believing.

The invalidity of arguments for God's existence precludes our drawing even limited encouragement from them. One occasionally hears theology teachers claiming that though the proofs do not provide a conclusive basis for belief in God, they are important pointers. "But a fallacious argument points nowhere (except to the lack of logical acumen on the part of those who accept it). And three fallacious arguments are no better than one."[7]

The defenders of proofs may regard these as only important in demonstrating experience-based Christian perspectives from which proving activity begins. But this is to concede that proofs do not prove. Consider two examples: (1) Christians who have experienced God may find themselves unshakably convinced of God's existence, so much so that they cannot envision His non-existence. Such people who wish to also defend the ontological argument (to be explained) may take their existential certitude and wrongly present it as a formal certainty of what cannot be denied without logical contradiction. *Doing this would be to tack a mistaken argument onto a legitimate experience.* (2) Christians know they have done nothing to deserve their own creation and that of the supporting world and are gratefully amazed by both. Similarly, nature's power and organization may evoke strong feelings of wonder and gratitude: "How Great Thou Art." Such people who also defend the cosmological and teleological arguments (to be explained) may mistakenly take such Christian experiences and present them as deductions or inferences from natural reason—which they are not.[8]

To focus the discussions in sections 2–4: Arguments for God's existence derive conclusions from something that is given concerning something that is sought. With the ontological argument, the mind's rationality is the given from which God's existence is supposedly deduced. With the cosmological and teleological arguments, some of the broader world are the givens from which God's existence is purportedly inferred.

---

6. Allen, *Christian Belief/Postmodern*, 52.
7. MacIntyre, *Difficulties/Belief*, 63.
8. Ibid., 63–64.

2. Ontological Argument

This argument claims that the very idea of God implies the fact of His existence. Anselm in the twelfth century and Descartes in the seventeenth argued that *the concept of a morally perfect being implied the existence of such a being*, and thus God's existence is logically undeniable. Since Immanuel Kant's refutation in the eighteenth century few philosophers have been convinced of the soundness of Anselm's and then of Descartes's arguments. The problem is that though a definition of God describes one's *concept* of God, it cannot prove that such a being *exists*.[9]

Archbishop (of Canterbury) Anselm reasoned that since a perfect and necessary being—whom he believed in because of his Christian Faith!—could not be perfect and necessary if non-existent, this being must exist. His argument is too good to be true, a kind of word magic. If we have biblically consistent, experiential reasons for believing in the God of Christian Faith, we will believe that She is morally perfect, and will believe that, in contrast with our contingent existence, She has always existed. But Anselm's rationalistic *argument* has nothing to do with such a confession of faith, other than that the same person held both a rationalistic and Christian view. His rationalistic deduction is that since we can conceive of a morally perfect being She must exist. Unfortunately for Anselm's contention, a fact either is or is not—but deduction cannot make it to be or not to be—which is the question.

Rene Descartes introduced a new and additionally mystifying factor into Anselm's already bewildering argument *by reasoning that existence is a characteristic or quality*. He appealed to a partial analogy: A triangle's internal angles have the characteristic of equaling two right angles; thus a triangle without this defining property would not be a triangle. Descartes thought this partial analogy concerning triangularity could show the similarity to and difference from natural reasoning concerning God. He thought that the similarity was that both triangles and God have qualities or properties. He considered the all-important difference to be that we cannot infer triangles' existence, since existence is not of their essence. But he thought that we can deduce God's existence, since existence is His very essence. For "existence is an essential attribute without which no being would be unlimitedly perfect."

Immanuel Kant entered into the logic of Descartes's argument, and accepted some aspects of what he said, but rejected his conclusion that this argument proves God's existence. Kant agreed that the *idea* of God's existence belongs analytically to the *concept* of God, as the idea of three angles belongs analytically to the concept of a three-sided plane figure. "What is analytically true is that *if* there is an infinitely perfect being, She must have existence." But this is merely to say that if such a God is, She is. "As Kant said, 'To posit a triangle, and yet to reject its three angles, is self-contradictory; but there is no self-contradiction in rejecting the triangle together with its three angles. The same

---

9. Hick, *Philosophy of Religion*, 20.

holds true of the concept of an absolutely necessary being."[10] If we had never seen a triangle, the triangle term and its definition would seem inapplicable to anything in reality. Similarly, if God had not impacted our experience no argument could elevate Her from conceptuality to reality. Like Anselm and Descartes, people who are convinced by such arguments were already convinced before they began trying to prove God's existence. Their conclusion was already posited as their starting point.

Kant showed also that Descartes's extension of Anselm's argument—that existence is a quality or characteristic—is false and only further confused already confused reasoning. *Existence is not a quality that something possesses, but the fact that something exists, rather than being merely an idea.* If I say that the man you are to meet at the airport will be tall, dark and handsome, will have a mustache, and be wearing a pith helmet with a tiny, solar powered fan—you will understand. If I add that he also will exist, you may think that I need a solar powered unit for my brain. That he exists is implied by the arrangement to meet him at the airport and is assumed in the entire description. The reason that the additional statement that he also exists seems absurd is that, contrary to Descartes, existence is not a characteristic or property. Saying that horses exist does not describe the characteristics of horses, but says that what we define as horses do exist and that horseness (unlike unicornness) is no mere concept. Likewise, affirming that God exists does not describe a characteristic He has, but only adds that the one called God is no mere concept.[11]

With deductive arguments, like the ontological one, conclusions follow from premises because they are already contained in the premises. "If from the premises that all men are mortal and that Socrates is a man I draw the conclusion that Socrates is mortal, my conclusion has nothing new in it."[12] As for deductive arguments for God's existence, the premises from which one undertakes to prove God's existence already contains the God-existing conclusion that is to be deduced from it—which is no proof, but a form of rationalistic presuppositionalism.

3. Cosmological Argument

The other two classical arguments for God's existence seek to prove only that He exists, not that His existence is logically undeniable. The Cosmological argument *begins with a distinction between contingent and necessary beings*. That contingent beings exist is justified by experience, since we confront such realities as tables, mountains, and people, whose non-existence we can conceive, and yet which "required other beings or events to bring them into existence—carpenters, geological upheavals, parents." The reasonableness of contingent beings' existence rests on the *principle of causation, that whatever begins to be owes its being to a cause, not to itself.* The minor premise

---

10. Ibid., 18, quoting from *Critique of Pure Reason*, no page reference.
11. MacIntyre, *Difficulties/Belief*, 56–57.
12. Ibid., 78–79.

is that finite beings begin to be. So far so good, but *the cosmological argument inappropriately extends the principle of causation, insisting "that the existence of contingent, finite beings points to the existence of a necessary non-finite being.* This thesis is often presented as simply the thesis that every being or event must have a cause, and that if we go back along the causal chain we must in the end arrive at the Great First Cause. To which the immediate and sufficient retort is: 'Why?' Why should we not go back, forever discovering an infinitely long chain of finite causes and *never* coming to the Great First Cause,"[13] the Uncaused Cause. Though an entire chain of causes without a first cause may seem improbable to many, such a suspicion does not constitute proof of an Uncaused Cause.

Though a supposed philosophical argument, the cosmological one presupposes the Jewish/Christian/Muslim belief that God as transcendent is not subject to our spatial-temporal limitations, and therefore did not require a cause. It furthermore assumes the Christian and Jewish conviction that as Creator and Reconciler, God though transcendent is yet involved in time. Certainly those who believe in the Creator revealed in the Redeemer thereby believe that a non-contingent Being called the world into existence, but such a revelation-based conviction has nothing to do with the idea that a non-contingent Uncaused Cause can be proven by rational deduction.

Extrapolating from current experience as Aquinas and others do is not as logical as it first appears. Arguments from effects to causes are sound only because daily experience has shown that when constant and repeated association between two things has been observed, they are often causally related. But the causal sequences we recognize within nature provide no basis for affirming a causal relation between God and the whole of nature (Hume).[14] Therefore the relationship between God as First Cause and the world cannot be proven. Again, this does not mean that God is not the world's Creator, only that the cosmological argument cannot prove this.

For the sake of showing how illogical the cosmological argument is, let's concede what is incorrect: The universe of itself requires a cause and natural humankind can perceive that cause is God. But "it could then be asked 'What caused God?' The response is usually 'God does not need a cause. He is a *necessary* being, whose cause is to be found within himself.' But he cosmological argument is founded on the assumption that everything requires a cause, yet ends in the conclusion that at least one thing (God) does not require a cause. The argument seems to be self-contradictory. Moreover, if one is prepared to concede that something—God—can exist without an external cause, why go that far along the chain? Why couldn't the universe exist without an external cause?"[15] Christians, of course, do not agree with this conclusion, but that is because we have revelational reasons for believing otherwise.

---

13. Ibid., 58; my emphasis.
14. Welch, *Protestant Thought/Nineteenth Century*, 1:43.
15. Davies, *God/New Physics*, 37–38.

Consider another problem: the cosmological argument for God's existence includes God with the universe only, though as its fundamental or constitutive component.[16] Against this, Christian Faith conceives of the entire cosmos as being created by a self-existing, transcendent God.

4. Design or Teleological Argument

The high degree of purposefulness in natural arrangements can suggest the existence of One who has ordained such. At all times it has found devoted advocates. No less a thinker than Kant, with his famous saying about the "starry heavens," might seem to have belonged to this group, but he may instead have been testifying to what he regarded as God's manifestation amid creation.[17] The difference between the teleological argument and the biblical witness is that the Bible never describes an argument leading to a conclusion, but is concerned about the "revelation of God in His works, which calls the whole person to adoring, obedient submission."[18]

The eighteenth century attempted to refurbish Aquinas's fifth argument—from evidence of purposiveness in nature to a divine designer—but in its optimism ignored the lack of purposiveness that nature also exhibits (see further below). Paley's analogy of the watch conveys the argument well, but also reflects its optimistic one-sidedness. If I happen upon a rock I can attribute its presence to the natural forces of "wind, rain, heat, frost and volcanic action." But a watch found lying on the ground cannot be accounted for in this way, for it consists of "a complex arrangement of wheels, cogs, axles, springs, and balances, all operating accurately together to provide a regular measurement of the lapse of time. It would be utterly implausible to attribute the formation and assembling of these metal parts into a functioning machine to the chance operation of such factors as wind and rain."[19] Paley was drawing a parallel between a watch's intricate and purposive design, which came from an intelligent mind, and the intricacies and purposiveness of nature, which also came from an even more Intelligent Mind.

Paley then argues that the natural world is a more complex mechanism and is more purposely designed than any watch. Design is suggested by the rotation of the planets in the solar system, the regular procession of the seasons on earth and the complex and generally well-functioning cooperative structures within living organisms, with their many backup systems. "In a human brain thousands of millions of cells function together in a coordinated system. The eye is a superb movie camera, with self-adjusting lenses, a high degree of accuracy, color-sensitivity, and the capacity to operate continuously for many hours at a time. Can such complex and efficient

---

16. As does Whitehead.
17. Brunner, *Revelation/Reason*, 346.
18. Ibid., 346–47.
19. Hick, *Philosophy of Religion*, 23–24.

mechanisms have come about by chance, as a stone might be formed by the random operation of natural forces?"[20]

A sense of wonder and gratitude to God is appropriate: "Thank you God for creation and for our own creation." But we also know that, even if well maintained, the human body does not work perfectly, else medical doctors and funeral directors would be unemployed. Christian Faith faces very directly the fact of human finiteness, namely, that at some point our bodies and minds stop working. We also realize that there are cruel anomalies in nature, as, for example, twins conjoined at birth or people born with some male and some female sexual organs.

Contrary to Paley's confidence, though we see degrees of purposiveness in the world, we have firsthand evidence that the world is not perfectly designed. Thus we cannot rationalistically infer from the world that its designer is perfectly wise and loving. New Testament Christians learned of God through His redemptive activity in Christ, and thereby became confident of His love in spite of the imperfection of this world. In contrast with Paley, the NT recognizes the existence of an evil force in the world and looks forward to a new age freed from sin, suffering and finiteness. Though the Bible exhibits wonder at and appreciation of creation, it is too realistic to have tried to deduce God's nature from creation. From divine revelation it affirms that God is the Creator and looks for signs of God's creative and redemptive activities—while well knowing that the world is neither perfect nor our final home.

The persistence of life in a relatively fixed environment presupposes order and adaptation, but aspects of this order can be understood to have come about otherwise than by conscious planning.[21] According to Darwin's theory of natural selection, animals are relatively well adapted to their environments because those less well suited have perished in the continual competition to survive and so have not perpetuated their species. (Against Darwin, different species sometimes survive through cooperative relationships, as between ants and butterflies.) Consider the ozone layer: The reason animal life on earth is so marvelously sheltered in this way is not because God first created the animals and then put the ozone layer in place for their protection, but because "the ozone layer was there first, and only those forms of life capable of existing in the precise level of ultraviolet radiation that penetrates this layer have developed on earth."[22] Christians, of course, will insist that God intended humans' eventual creation, but insofar as we take modern science seriously we will need to think of God's involvement with nature in more subtle terms than has often been conceived.

Among other factors discussed in this section, evolutionary understanding showed Paley's arguments to be incapable of proving God's existence. It should, however, also be said that narrowly antireligious Darwinism ignores such things as the way in which inanimate nature is in harmony with organic evolution, and has no understanding of the

20. Ibid., 24.
21. Ibid., 25.
22. Ibid.

transition from inanimate to animate nature upon which modern biology and physics shed some light. Furthermore, as Whitehead argued, the tendency in nature toward the development of increasingly complex organisms implies a degree of teleology and the existence of a dynamic creative force in the universe that has lured such advance forward. However, such a viewpoint does not prove that a Loving and Transcendent God has enabled this development, since much that occurs in this sinful and considerably tragic world conflicts with God's will as disclosed in Christ.

A recent approximation to the design argument is *the Anthropic Principle* in cosmology. Astrophysicists have concluded that life in the universe would have been impossible had some of the physical constants and other conditions in the early universe differed even slightly from what they were. "The universe seems to be 'fine-tuned' for the possibility of life." Though one doubts that Hawking knows the following with such precision, he writes: "'If the rate of expansion one second after the big bang had been smaller by even one part in a hundred thousand million million, the universe would have recollapsed before it even reached its present size.'" Freeman Dyson concludes from such theorizing "'that the universe is an unexpectedly hospitable place for living creatures to make their home in.'" He does not claim that the universe's structure proves God's existence, only that that structure "'is consistent with the hypothesis that mind plays an essential role in its functioning.'"[23] However, for those convinced of the Father's love disclosed in the Son by the Spirit, belief in God the Creator is no mere hypothesis, nor one needing to be propped up by semi-scientific arguments.

To refocus what was said in the cosmological and teleological sections: "If we derive God from the world, She cannot . . . transcend the world infinitely." With the cosmological arguments, a vague knowledge of God is found at the end of a "causal regression in answer to the question, 'Where from?' (Thomas Aquinas)." With the teleological argument, God is regarded as the "intelligence directing the meaningful processes of reality—if not identical with the processes (Whitehead)."[24] In both cases God is regarded as a missing part of the world, from which She is derived as a conclusion.[25]

From the massive evidence that Whitehead describes and analyzes (to be summarized in a later volume), his metaphysical arguments for a dynamic force of creativity seem reasonable. But such arguments cannot establish belief in a *Transcendent* God (One beyond Plato's demiurge). And Whitehead did not think they could. Christians have revelational reasons for believing in the transcendence of such a force, but cannot prove that by empirical or rationalistic persuasion.

---

23. From *Disturbing the Universe*, quoted by Barbour, *Religion/Science*, 25.
24. Tillich, *ST*, 1:205.
25. Ibid.

5. Moral Argument

Here we only briefly consider reason's confidence in God's reality based on the purported existence of a self-transcending, natural morality common to all people. Uncritically assuming that there are common moral standards among differing societies, logical inferences from societal moral laws to a divine law giver have been drawn; or from the presumed objectivity of such moral values to a transcendent ground of values; or from such understandings of conscience to God as its basis.[26]

The anthropological and sociological knowledge of the existence of moral diversity in different societies or in the same society at different times makes it doubtful that there are naturally knowable, common moral laws, identical values, or uniform understandings of the imperatives of conscience. The postulate behind the moral argument for God's existence encourages people to uncritically venerate their own culturally influenced moral laws, values, or senses of conscience. They suppose that those are transcendently based and are in common with those of other societies, whose moral guidance one assumes is also similarly based.

Even where Christian moral laws, values and sense of conscience have made indirect impact on particular societies, being satisfied with such minimal overlap with Christian norms can interfere with concrete obedience to Christ. People are thereby encouraged to imagine that they are capable of knowing what in God's eyes is truly moral or immoral without responding to divine revelation and without relationship with God. Such a supposition is synonymous with a Christian conception of sin (Gen 3:5).

Even the most sophisticated form of the moral argument is still unconvincing. Kant did not claim to prove God's existence, but insisted that people committed to naturally knowable moral values as exercising sovereign claims upon their lives "implicitly believe in the reality of a trans-human source and basis for these values, which religion calls God."[27] The presumed naturally knowable moral value Kant had in mind was the categorical imperative, which as a restatement of the golden rule even for him was derived from the Christian heritage and thus was not naturally known.

6. Religious Experience as Basis of Conviction[28]

Schleiermacher's non-argumentative apologetic needs to be mentioned with arguments for God's existence because he also seeks to persuade people of God's existence by building from a natural base. He rightly attests that as created and finite and having limited control over events that impact our lives, all people are considerably dependent, though for long stretches individuals may deny the obvious. Unfortunately he further supposes that a sense of absolute dependence is foundational for all religions.

---

26. Hick, *Philosophy of Religion*, 28.
27. Ibid., 29.
28. See chap. 9, secs. 2 and 3; chap. 19, sec. 6.

Evaluating Arguments That Attempt to Prove God's Existence

In criticism, even if people could be convinced that they are highly conditioned by what is beyond their control, they would not thereby have been persuaded of the existence of a Transcendent God, let alone the God disclosed in Christ.

Christians, of course, should object to Schleiermacher's equating of fatalism with God, and to regarding that awareness as the foundation on which Christian convictions should be built. To the contrary, the Christian recognition of divine forgiveness through Christ and new life in Him can help to free us from fatalism, as Ritschl's correction of Schleiermacher emphasized.

The NT teaches that even *Christian* religious experience cannot stand alone as an independent source of authority. It plays an important role in helping to bring people to faith in Christ and in the living of the Christian life, but must be critically scrutinized in the light of God's disclosure in Christ as reflected in the NT. If Christian religious experience evokes genuine trust in God through Christ and loyalty to Him it can and should be convincing.

Chapter 12

Relationship of Philosophy to Systematic Theology

WITH THE CHAPTER 10 challenging of natural theology and the chapter 11 critiquing of proofs for God's existence, it might seem that there is little place for philosophy in Christian theology. That, however, is not the case. Though systematics should focus upon knowledge of the Father through the Son by the Spirit, it can learn plenty from philosophy and from other fields of study.

Much philosophy is concerned with the universally human, whereas Christian theology is preoccupied with the specifically Christian.[1] Nevertheless, what is uniquely Christian needs to take account of the universally human, lest the Christian message fail to connect. Some types of philosophy focus primarily on hermeneutical aspects of the universally human, as we will see in chapter 16. Some others, such as Whitehead's, link the universally human to a general comprehension of world process, which can be related to such theological themes as faith in God the Creator and the meaning of divine sovereignty. Philosophy's variable interests cannot be fully identified by any list.[2] Systematics's concerns are similarly broad.

1. Natural Reason and Christian Faith

The Christian Faith involves the personal encounter between the God who reveals Himself in Jesus Christ and the person who is thereby delivered from bondage to sin

---

1. Stiver, *After Ricoeur*, 230.

2. I have learned especially from Michael Polanyi's hermeneutical insights (chap. 13, sec. 8) and his understanding of science, scientific discovery, and the non-scientific values required by science (chap. 13, secs. 7 and 9).. Kierkegaard's critique of Hegel's rationalism (chap. 18, sec. 7) and SK's existentialist apologetic (chap. 9, sec. 7) have been of particular help. So has Whitehead's conception of the dynamic and interactive process of all aspects of the universe (chap. 13, sec. 2)—especially concerning the workings of the human body—and his understanding of science and how it developed (chap. 13, sec. 3). See sec. 12 of this chap. for Whitehead on philosophical realism.

and self. It is thus fundamentally different from philosophy.[3] There seem to be three possible relations between the natural reason that philosophy utilizes and Christian Faith: *(1) That faith finds a place in natural reason, (2) that natural reason finds a place in faith, or (3) that they remain external to one another.* The widespread Christian use of Platonic-influenced idealism/rationalism exhibits the *first* of the three by attempting to so deepen the conception of reason that even the truth of Christian revelation may seem encompassed within its framework.[4] If theology accepts such an assumption—and it did to a large extent in the nineteenth and early twentieth centuries—it ceases to be an accurate expression of Christian Faith. Against such compromising, Paul insisted that Christ crucified is to mere rational thought a stumbling block and foolishness (1 Cor 1:23). Though no idealist, Thomas Aquinas's idealist-like belief that grace never sets aside but only completes natural reason is against what Christian Faith teaches concerning dying and rising with Christ, conversion, rebirth and new creation. Aquinas's "Christ of Culture" accommodation is challenged by Jesus's central teaching that we are to "repent, for the kingdom of God is at hand" (Matt 4:17b). Insofar as the *third* proposal implies no relation between reason and Christian Faith and makes no effort to critically examine inconsistencies between what Christians believe and what natural reason thinks, the result is an affirmation of contradictory truths. With this likely effect for the third proposal, the Christian reason/faith choice seems to be the *second*, that reason should find its place within the bounds of revelation, because only in that way can the legitimate claims and limits of natural reason be understood.[5]

2. Christian Theology's Unique Philosophical Contribution[6]

Concerning philosophical issues, Christians *should have* an advantage in thinking critically and realistically.[7] In recognizing universal sinfulness and that as affecting the exercise of all people's intellects, Christians can be (but often are not) fully *realistic* about themselves and the world. Furthermore, since Christians have encountered the God who transcends this world, they should be able to more easily recognize when reason oversteps its limits and becomes an idol.[8]

A cause of antagonism to faith from non-Christian philosophies is their all too common assumption that humankind is the measure of all things—which constitutes sin as autonomy. For the ultimate truth is not *in* us but must be disclosed *to* us in a singular historical event.[9]

---

3. Brunner, *Revelation/Reason*, 384.
4. See sec. 11.
5. Brunner, *Philosophy/Religion*, 55, 176, 56.
6. See Brunner, *Truth as Encounter, Revelation/Reason, Philosophy/Religion* and *Theology/Crisis*.
7. Brunner, *Revelation/Reason*, 393.
8. Schrader, "Brunner/Philosophy," 119, 120.
9. Brunner, *Theology/Crisis*, 43.

3. Rejection of Monism[10]

In the nineteenth and early twentieth centuries many "Christians" were committed to an optimistic and monistic Platonic rationalism. Against the latter's idea that we in our depth are divine stands the discontinuity that is basic to Christian Faith. For example, the concept of creation out of nothing draws a line of distinction between God and world, as does sinful separation and the belief that Jesus Christ is the Savior and Lord whom we must obey. The Christian distinguishing of God from creation and the recognition of human sinfulness links to awareness of God's transcendence and a relative dualism within God's lordship over the world. Monism is more closely related to Hindu mysticism than to the apostle Paul.

Those who have responded to Christ as Savior know themselves as sinners who cannot reconcile nor redeem themselves. To the contrary the Stoics, Pelagius, Erasmus, the Enlightenment, Schleiermacher, Ritschl and Hegel believed that sin only clings to us as barnacles to a ship's hull. Though monists see no need for a reconciling movement from beyond, "Christian" monists believe that a benevolent movement *initiated and sustained by us* is possible and helpful. But their minimizing of human sinfulness and guilt is inconsistent with the need for humanitarian efforts to lessen the results of human problems, since many of these are surely caused by human fault.[11] And if such help is required, does not humankind require much more than humans can provide?

In contrast with monism both Testaments affirm that this world is contingent and exists solely because the self-existing God continues to will its existence. Monism thinks the reverse, that "god" only "exists" as part of the universe, which, contrary to modern science, is regarded as never ending. A necessary connection of god with the universe is consistent with the monists' effort to reach the idea of god by concentrating only on knowledge of the world. Having said these things, it must nevertheless be emphasized that the radical distinguishing of God's being and nature from us and from the world must not be confused with a minimizing of God's activity in the world She created.

God's sole divinity is consistent with Her wanting to establish Her lordship over us and Her refusal to share Her glory with anyone or anything. Such ideas are reflected in what the Bible calls the kingship or kingdom of God. Two elements of this belief should be highlighted: (1) God wants to be recognized and honored as sole Lord and (2) humans have a God-given relative independence that in response to God's grace should be used to serve God and others.[12]

---

10. The belief that there is only one fundamental reality, of which other beings are but attributes or modes (also considered in chap. 9, sec. 7). For related definitions also listed in the glossary, see "relative dualism" and "philosophical pluralism."

11. Brunner, *Theology/Crisis*, 6, 12–13, 16–17.

12. Brunner, *Scandal/Christianity*, 37–39.

4. Existence as Relational

Moving to knowledge of fellow humans, we do not know whatever we know of others by inferring their existence. If that were so, their reality for us would be *hypothetical*. To the contrary, we are from the first involved with others and their participation with us is presupposed in all perceptions about them. Here as elsewhere existence is *given*, not deduced. Furthermore, we already receive from human relationships; that is, we do not take all the initiative in establishing our myriad relations, for we respond as much or more than we initiate. Our feelings are our own, but not merely so, for they refer beyond us and are related to those with whom we interact.[13]

Our lives occur in the social contexts whereby we become human. We would not recognize our own humanness if we did not already know that other people have self-consciousness as do we. Since we become human within a human society, children cut off from such fellowship, as for example, those few who grew up among wolves, lack *human* self-awareness. From socializing with other humans we know that they have minds akin to ours. We have relations with others through the medium of language and by observation. By what people say/sign and do we perceive something of what they are thinking.[14] The question how we know that other people have self-consciousness as do we is unreal, since we know this directly.[15] In short, Descartes was trying to prove intellectually and individualistically what must be experienced through relationships with others and through innate rather than deductive self-awareness.

"Language presupposes society and a realm of shared experience. Insofar as we ourselves do a great deal of our thinking in words or concepts closely related to language, even our own private thoughts presuppose the society in which our minds have been formed, and carry with them the built-in assumption that other people can share the same kind of experience."[16]

5. Exposition, Evaluation of Buber's "I-Thou" Personalism[17]

Martin Buber believed that God wishes to address us amid every event and wills to sanctify our everyday lives. Therefore we should seek to discern what He is saying, but this does not mean that God wills or causes everything that happens. Buber wrote of what he called an I-Thou relationship with God mediated through people, and belatedly wrote of that as also mediated through God directly.[18] He also recognized that detached (I-It) knowing is also part of life.

---

13. Schrader, "Brunner/Philosophy," 124, 125.
14. Habgood, "Minds/Machines," 305.
15. Ibid., 306.
16. Ibid., 305.
17. Cf. chap. 2, sec. 3; chap. 10, sec. 6; chap. 18, sec. 7.
18. Only in a later postscript to *I and Thou* did Buber clarify that God also speaks directly. I

In classifying human relationships as either highly personal or detached, Buber did not recognize that much knowing of other people is neither, but is of an "I-You" nature. For example, when we know people through less personal communication (such as a book), in groups, or by extending or receiving a helping hand from a distance. Similarly the Bible does not usually express direct address to God (prayer), nor describe direct words from God or through prophets, but more often speaks about God or concerning relationship with Him. Such words, however, are not detached I-It information.

Buber's understanding of personal relationships did not exclude having a considerably different relationship with nature and through it. He did not expect any aspect of nature to speak as a self or selves, as in the animistic belief of Traditional Religion that nature is inhabited by and much influenced by spirits. He understood nature's communion as "a presence with which we can enter into silent dialogue." "A tree is an object of experience which I can examine and classify and study scientifically, but at the same time, by virtue of what he calls 'grace,' the relationship may change: the tree becomes a presence 'and has to do with me, as I with it,' in a mutual relationship."[19]

6. Kierkegaard's Existentialist Philosophy in Criticism of Hegel's System[20]

The existentialists' experience is that the human situation is in many respects one of estrangement from the ideal. To the contrary, Hegel pantheistically believed that the divine-human unity only symbolized by the name "Jesus Christ" is directly realized in people and in world history. Existentialists regarded this as Hegel's fundamental error.[21] Though God was in Christ reconciling the world unto Himself (2 Cor 5:19a), we live at the overlap of the two ages, and only in eternity will our alienation from God be totally overcome. But even there we will only have relationship with God, not ourselves become divine. Here reconciliation is a matter of expectation and partial fulfillment, but not of full realization of our God-intended nature.

As in rationalism Hegel tended to equate reality with knowledge. Contrary to this, existentialists emphasized the importance of personal experience and heartfelt knowing, often involving suffering. For example, the recognition of finitude should not be merely cognitive. In this regard Kierkegaard pointed out that a person who

---

would add that the Living God also speaks through the Bible's written testimony concerning Him and through the written or verbal witness of others concerning the Bible's meaning, strange omissions by one who was Jewish

19. Hendry, *Theology/Nature*, 202, with no page reference to *I and Thou*.

20. I generally agree with only SK's existentialism, but, as will be seen, I do not disagree with all facets of other existentialists' thinking. Acceptance of the polarity between the social relationality seen in secs. 4–5 and the individual emphasis of secs. 6–7 indicates agreement with what H. Richard Niebuhr called "Social Existentialism" (*Christ/Culture*, 241–49).

21. Tillich, *ST*, 2:25.

knows that "all people are mortal" only knows an aspect of the universal essence of being human—but what is still needed is to experience the singular conclusion "I, too, must die." Kierkegaard's aim was to help people to experience the impact of truth in their lives and to draw conclusions that affect feeling and action, not mere knowledge.[22] Encouraging personal involvement, SK pointed out that when Socrates criticized the Sophists by saying that they were able to talk but not converse, he meant that though they said much on many subjects, because they personally appropriated nothing they were only acting. Appropriation is the secret of conversation.[23]

Hegel's system could provide no help for those crucial times (such as choosing a spouse or a profession) when one struggles for insight and gathers strength for a long-term decision. Hegel only cared about knowledge, not the guidance of the Living God. Against such a perspective, a person's thought must be the building in which he lives or all is madness. Though reality is full of chasms over which one must leap,[24] Hegel's map of reality reflected no precipices requiring decisions. Since existence comes before thought, the slogan cannot be Descartes's "I think or doubt, therefore I am," but "I am, therefore I think or doubt or whatever." The abstractions of philosophy must give way to a full-blooded experiential mode of thinking, deciding and acting. "First life, then philosophy," as the Latin adage has it.[25]

SK believed that even systematic expression that emphasizes the need for personal appropriation is not the final word, since God's speech and our response are needed. Yet in attacking philosophical systems (especially Hegel's), Kierkegaard did not reject systematizing. Though his thought is not systematic in the Hegelian sense and in some others, it is coherent and (largely) unified. He never depreciated thought or its systematic variety; he was too deep a thinker and too subtle a dialectician to do that. A dialectician must struggle with the polarities, tensions and paradoxes of complex thought, and that was part of what he did.

---

22. Smith, "Existentialist Philosophy," 126.

23. Kierkegaard, *Dread*, 15.

24. See chap. 9, sec. 7.

25. Croxall, *Kierkegaard*, 62, 63, 59, 63. Kierkegaard's understanding of truth, like Scripture's conception, involves the participation of the whole person (cf. chap. 19, secs. 1 and 3 below), and is unlike the impersonal and limited perspective of much of the older European philosophy. The latter as influenced by idealism/rationalism regarded truth as "'a relation between the thing and the conception, or between reality and thought, . . . passing as quickly as possible over the subject, the self, the individual, back to objects, things, and sensations'" (same source, 63, 64, quoting from Haecker).

Because Croxall uses only "op. cit." when apparently referring to several SK books, his references are imprecise.

7. Kierkegaard's Category: Individual as Responsible to God

Kierkegaard's individual is the opposite of a "proud, self-sufficing human being, living apart from or even defying God."[26] Not the individual as such, but as accountable to God is Kierkegaard's highest human category, for such a person through God's Spirit has been awakened for life in obedience to God. Pointing as Nathan did (2 Sam 12:7a) SK in effect says, "Thou art the person" to each of us, helping us to avoid hiding in such abstractions as the crowd or even the system. He insists that it is necessary to oppose such immoral confusions that would teach an ungodly contempt for the first condition of Christian religiousness—being an individual.[27]

Because the world is much influenced by evil (1 John 5:19) the Christian must to a considerable extent stand over against it. Jesus Christ "gave himself for our sins to deliver us from this present evil age . . ." (Gal 1:4a). Yet the Christian injunction to love one's neighbors and even one's enemies means that we must mix with people and try to understand them, being in the world but not of it. Insofar as we do not follow the masses, yet love those who do, we keep the right balance.[28]

8. Systematics's Dialectical Use of Philosophy: Evaluative, Selective, Eclectic[29]

Though Christians can and should gain degrees of freedom from bondage to the world, it is an illusion to imagine that anyone can or should completely escape from philosophical or other cultural influences.[30] This is not only because even Christians grow up within a culture or cultures and to an extent remain so conditioned, but because those influences are not all harmful. We do not get close to God by trying to empty our minds of all societal influences. Coming from whatever such mixtures of good, bad, or largely indifferent, God wills to challenge the unrighteous and corrupting cultural aspects and thereby transform us.

Though Jesus offered criticisms of the cultures in which He lived, He did not reject all facets of His Jewish heritage nor of His broader Hellenistic environment. With reference to philosophical and other societal influences, the biblical guideline is that though many things are lawful (1 Cor 6:12), we are to be captive only to Christ.[31] As long as we allow the Living Lord to critique and correct cultural impacts, positive lessons can be learned from such sources. Yet we should not cling tenaciously

---

26. Ibid., 72.

27. Ibid., 76, 66; see Kierkegaard, *Point of View*, 128. While emphasizing the individual's accountability to God, one should not minimize the importance of the church, which SK's corrective may have done. Yet a church composed of spiritually and morally weak individuals amounts to little.

28. Croxall, *Kierkegaard*, 70, 71.

29. For a general discussion of the meaning of dialectics, see chap. 1, sec. 5.

30. Barth, *CD*, 1/2:728.

31. Barth, *Credo*, 183.

to philosophical ideas in doctrinaire ways,[32] which also conflicts with the open and inquiring spirit that philosophy should encourage. An eclectic but consistent use of aspects from various philosophies can help to prevent doctrinaire philosophical (and perhaps even theological) bondage.[33]

Bultmann and other "philosophical police" for decades pressured Barth to bring his theology into line with Heidegger's existential philosophy, which had some similarity to the Kierkegaardian influences reflected in Barth's Second Edition of *The Epistle to the Romans*.[34] Though Barth sought to write coherently and non-contradictorily and though he had a modern understanding of science, he felt ultimately responsible to the Living God revealed in Christ[35] and thus opposed philosophical presumptuousness. "There is always the possibility that what is said may be 'not understood'; that possibility cannot be excluded. Even Holy Scripture is very often not understood. But no philosophy can deliver the key to us. The question of the 'proper' language of theology is *ultimately*[36] to be answered only with prayer and the life of faith." "Certainly we are responsible to speak so that we can be *understood*, but there is not the slightest chance that any philosophy could step forth to guarantee that we achieve this."[37]

Barth thought that Christian theologians should take special care to avoid venerating the latest philosophical fad. This was an error Barth early detected in Bultmann and other former members of the Dialectical Theology movement, and which (as the next note indicates) he came to detect in his earlier self. In 1928 Barth wrote to Bultmann, "It is a fact that I have come to abhor profoundly the spectacle of theology constantly trying above all to adjust to the philosophy of its age, thereby neglecting its own theme."[38]

---

32. Ibid., 184. Christians must have the freedom to let varied ways of thinking run through our heads. Barth, for example, learned something from Marxism, existentialism, and Hegel without becoming a Marxist, existentialist, or Hegelian. Barth confessed that he was "'fond of doing a bit of Hegeling'" (cited in Busch, *Karl Barth*, 387; see sec. 10 below). Though human presuppositions are always present, as theologians it is not our job to make a synthesis between Christian Faith and various philosophical notions, but to go from God speaking through Scripture to the form that serves, which can include philosophical terminology and conceptuality (Barth, *Credo*, 184).

33. Busch, *Karl Barth*, 387.

34. It seems that Barth continued to be influenced by SK, but increasingly expressed warnings against being enamored with his psychological tendencies. Kierkegaard suffered from what would today be called bipolar depression, but he did not wish his sometimes morose condition on others. Suffering with Christ as we carry the cross of discipleship is another matter. And SK regarded that as an essential part of the Christian life, as did Barth.

35. Barth, *Credo*, 185–86.

36. "Penultimately" hermeneutical philosophies can help (see chap. 16), as can historical-critical method (see chap. 18, sec. 11) and other intellectual tools.

37. Barth, *Credo*, 186.

38. Barth/Bultmann, *Letters*, 41. Writing to Bultmann in 1953 Barth explained that having been a Kantian and then a Schleiermachian romantic, he was unwilling *any longer* to regard a philosophy as the binding arbiter of theological utterances. Christians should not oppose philosophy as such, but the absoluteness of any philosophy. "Occasionally I may cheerfully make use of existential categories—not without going back again sometimes to father Plato and others—*but I simply do not summon up the ethical zeal to feel any consequent obligation to that philosophical approach* . . . Obviously I am no longer

9. Theological Method in Light of Kantian Philosophy

The only kind of reason Kant considered worthy of trust was that which had first become reasonable concerning itself, and his critique of reason attempted to bring such critical reason into prominence. From Kant onward a cogent theology could no longer formulate its convictions without a clear conception of the method it used in arriving at such.

Kant himself considered the possibility of a theology that *differed* much from the philosophical perspective he propounded. He called this other approach "*biblical theology*,"[39] and it was his wish that the affairs of this theology not in any way mingle with those of philosophy. He thought the discipline should be dedicated to the effort to understand the meaning of the Bible. For Kant the possibility for such a specifically theological discipline or faculty is given with the existence of the church that has its foundation in the Bible.[40]

Theology indeed needs to stand with considerable independence from philosophy, recognizing its point of departure in revelation, in contrast with philosophy, which has its starting point in reason or natural experience or some combination. Theology can conduct a dialogue with philosophy, but should not wrap "itself up in the mantle of philosophy," thereby evidencing "a quasi-philosophical monologue."[41] Contrary to Kant's recommendation, even a theology primarily dependent on biblical understanding should not cut off active engagement with other disciplines—including philosophy.

10. A Little "Hegeling"

George S. Hendry is correct that *Church Dogmatics* is cast in a more Hegelian way than Barth's previous writings. God's "wholly-otherness" is now overshadowed[42] by His concern for humanity. In this regard the Creator-creature relation is prefigured in the divine decision to distinguish Himself from Himself by coming forth in the Son, which manifested God's will for covenant fellowship with humankind. Since the end is foreshadowed in the beginning, even God's creating reflects a *Triumph of Grace*. Since such a God can negate the negation of sinful people and bring all safely home, theology is a most "happy science."[43] Having said these things, it is still true that Hegel's influence upon Barth primarily provoked theological discovery, helping him to recover overlooked aspects of the biblical heritage and encouraging the use of analogy in theology.

'existentially' captivated by it" (same source, 105–6, my emphasis).

39. What he likely meant was a biblically based theology, not a biblical theology in the modern sense of the term. See chap. 9, sec. 10.

40. Barth, *Protestant/Nineteenth*, 271, 273, 308.

41. Ibid., 307.

42. Hendry says "replaced," but this overstates the matter.

43. Hendry, "Barth/Philosopher," 214, 215.

11. Use of Critical Realism and Critical Idealism by Those Open to God's Transcending Word[44]

Though "realism" and "idealism" refer to ancient philosophical tendencies, in this section these terms are also employed to depict Christian theological dependence upon and use of such perspectives. Though philosophical realism (object-centered knowing, such as Aristotelianism and Thomism) and philosophical idealism (mind-centered knowing, such as Platonic rationalism and Hegelianism) represent conflicting ways of understanding, both have light to shed on reality and thought. Yet even in combination they cannot deliver final truth concerning God.

Here we will examine problems with some forms of philosophical realism and idealism and seek to perceive how Christian theology can make discerning use of both. (1) Naive realism uncritically accepts the reality of what the senses or other experience seem to disclose, without feeling the need to rationally scrutinize perceptions. Such realism is insufficiently aware that our experience often deceives us. Perceptual distortions occur because our experience must be processed through our minds, which are imperfect instruments of perception and understanding. Even what we think we see may not be there; the mirage is just that and hallucinations exist only in the mind.

Theological realism's confidence that God is easily knowable involves no dread before the fact that God not only discloses but hides Herself in Her disclosing, no awareness that God's self-giving involves free and dynamic revealing acts, rather than a static state of revealedness. Against naive realism, but compatible with critical realism, a theology of God's Word must ever presuppose the act character of divine disclosing—which expresses God's free will. God's activism is needed because not only our natural but our renewed will is sinful and of itself incapable of knowing God and of acting obediently toward Her.

Barth questions whether the realists really mean the Holy Spirit with their talk of experience of God. Since the Holy Spirit is no less God than the Father and the Son, we must respect God's otherness even concerning our inward experience of God.[45] In an early writing Barth overstated by writing that God's will is to be sought "in the Word spoken to us, not in the experience produced by the Word."[46] In contrast the later Barth, in critical and constructive dialogue with pietism and the charismatic movement, wrote more carefully.[47] He indicated that we are certainly not to minimize the experience of the Word, else we would have no way of validating that God has impressed Her Word upon us. But we must remain open to the Source of our experience, rather than preoccupied with our experience as an independent theme.

---

44. See chap. 9, sec. 4.
45. Barth, *Way of Theology*, 40–41.
46. Ibid., 41.
47. See *CD*, 4/3.2.

(2) With a discriminating and exacting perspective concerning what the senses and more general experience report, idealism starts from the opposite pole from philosophical realism. Idealism emphasizes the mind's quest for truth as not only enabling but conditioning every experience of knowing.[48] *Idealism understands knowledge primarily in terms of the subject who knows, rather than from confidence in impressions from experience.* But idealism is no more able to provide a way to God than realism. With idealism the accessibility of God to us is but our supposed natural and rational accessibility to Him, which assumes that we are holy enough to climb our way to God.

Idealism ought to have the purely critical function of helping to break through naive realism's undue confidence in outward appearances and concerning the supposed meaning of experience. If idealism seeks to do more, it forgets that (like realism) it has no criterion by which it can lay its hands on ultimate truth. Such must be given ever anew through revelation. *Idealism's equation of God with natural reason is just as intolerable as realism's equation of God with natural experience.*[49] For idealism's subject-centered understanding there is no common world to think about, so "what is perceived is not a partial vision of a complex of things generally independent of the act of cognition," but the expression of a common world of thought *we associate* with our perceptions.[50] As we will see in section 12, idealism's knower- or subject-centered understanding of perceiving furthermore depends upon an unconvincing mind-body and mind-world duality.

To summarize: Realism in theological mode takes uncritical confidence in natural "experience" and fails to emphasize God's ongoing revealing action. At the other extreme theological idealism is unduly confident concerning human rationality, which of itself cannot lead beyond the act of knowing. Such idealism not only fails to differentiate human discovery from God's revealing activity, but inevitably confuses anthropology with theology, knowing oneself deeply with knowing God.

Each of these approaches reflects but one side of the divide between what is known and the knowing subject. Even so, *realism can teach theology not to forget the givenness of objects and idealism can remind theology that objects are received by human minds.*[51] In contrast with philosophy, *systematics "reflects on the reality and truth of God's Word as spoken to [and received within]human existence,"* rather than "on the reality and truth of human existence" of itself.[52] Systematics is theocentrically based even in its anthropology.

---

48. See chap. 13, sec. 7 for my agreement with Polanyi's Platonic insights concerning scientific discovery, which shed light upon the activity of theological illumination and research, though being incapable of providing the requisite Christian ingredients.

49. McCormack, *Barth's Dialectical Theology*, 388, describing Barth's point.

50. Whitehead, *Science/Modern World*, 84.

51. McLelland, "Philosophy/Theology/Family Affair," 36.

52. Barth, *Way of Theology*, 54; my emphases.

What Barth says of the incapacity of either realism or idealism *to reach God* seems correct. Knowledge of the Father through the Son by the Spirit depends on God's initiative in history and in our lives, and corresponds to neither of the above ways of natural perceiving, though to an extent paralleling both.

> Real theology of God's Word . . . gets underway only . . . when God is underway "with his Spirit and gifts." But God's Spirit blows where it will. If I am called to do this theology, then so I am. Not because I found a way to God, but because God found a way to me. Not because I bind myself to God, but because God binds me to himself. Not because my dialectics are so great, but because God condescends to make use of me and this my doubtful tool. Therefore, not because I have unearthed the tablets of wisdom or squared the circle to discover the magic point at which reality and truth intersect. Not because I can demonstrate how [reality] is really idea, or idea really [reality], or how my synthesis of them is really God; but rather because it has pleased God, as the one superior to the contradiction of my existence and my thought, to step in for me as Revealer and Reconciler so that I should confess him; and therefore because it has pleased God to confess himself to me.
>
> In itself and as such how could my God-concept ever be a witness to God? It can, however, please God to make it to be that and to use it in that way. These then are the terms on which I may and must risk being a theologian—in obedience, equipped with these powers of my thought. It would simply be impossible to be a theologian, that is, from the standpoint of faith, if one were not allowed and in fact compelled to take risks on these terms.[53]

12. Whitehead Further on Realism-Objectivism[54]

Having argued that neither idealism nor realism are capable of providing knowledge of *God*, we now consider Whitehead's view that knowledge of the *natural world* implies the priority of objects over the minds that gain knowledge of them. Realism/objectivism holds that what is perceived by our senses with or without the aid of instruments reflects a common world, which includes our acts of cognition, but transcends these.[55] "*So far as there is dependence, the things pave the way for the cognition, rather than vice versa.*"[56]

We need to be especially careful not to over-interpret Whitehead's argument for realism; he was much influenced by Plato and, like Polanyi,[57] regarded the creative activity of mind as essential for scientific discovery and all other learning. Looking

---

53. Ibid., 59.
54. Whitehead's view was briefly alluded to in sec. 11.
55. Whitehead, *Science/Modern World*, 84.
56. Ibid.
57. See chap. 13, sec. 7.

at the total thrust of Whitehead's position, one would almost be inclined to see him agreeing with Barth that neither idealism nor realism should be given more weight. Yet because Whitehead seldom wrote of knowledge of God, though more of "religion," he would not have been interested in Barth's balancing between idealism and realism while emphasizing that God's revelation in Christ transcends both.

In spite of Whitehead's idealistic emphasis on the mind's cognitions, and in agreement with another aspect of Polanyi's thinking, Whitehead thought that the capacity of mind for scientific discovery presupposes the priority of a world external to our minds that awaits our discovery. In speaking of *knowledge of nature*, Whitehead showed that such knowledge must presuppose what is external to mind. Thus the world's existence cannot convincingly be attributed to human reason.

Mindful of science and of concrete experience and referring primarily to knowledge of the natural world, Whitehead provides *four defenses of realism/objectivism*. *First*, it appears from direct interrogation of perceived experience "that we are *within* a world of colors, and sounds . . . related in space and time to enduring objects such as stones, trees, and human bodies. We seem to be ourselves elements of this world . . . as are the other things which we perceive. But the subjectivist, even the moderate intermediate subjectivist [Kant], makes this world, as thus described, depend on us, in a way which directly traverses our naive experience."[58]

A *second defense* of realism/objectivism concerning knowledge of nature and a reason for distrusting subjectivism is based on the content of particular scientific insights. For example, we suppose that an ancient universe evolved independently of any human minds being present to observe its evolving, though humans can now postulate cosmological history by observing worldly evidence. Whitehead's doubts concerning pure idealism thus come from *the* impossibility of conceiving an original association of minds with what happened in bygone ages, "when the granite was formed or when our sun first blazed." *He thus denies "that some correlation with mentality can be proved to be essential for the very being of natural fact."*[59] Furthermore, from our equipment-assisted perceptions we infer that things are happening within the interior of the earth, and on the far side of the moon. And we suppose that in remote ages things were happening there, but those are either unknown in detail or must be reconstructed by inferential evidence. But well-founded deductions in such areas are incompatible with the notion that the experienced world is an attribute of our own mentality.[60]

---

58. Whitehead, *Science/Modern World*, 84, 85. Whitehead holds that the highest philosophical appeal is to naive experience, which is why he lays such stress on the evidence of poetry (same source, 85).

59. Whitehead, *Interpretation/Science*, 145, 142; my emphases.

60. Ibid., 85.

A *third argument* for realism/objectivism is that a particularly important part of nature that figures in the observation of any part of it is the body of the observer.[61] Nothing is more philosophically astonishing than the naive way we take our unity with our bodies for granted,[62] which argues against pure idealism's and subjectivism's mind-body split. Our intuition of bodily unity is so ingrained in our experience that we don't talk about it. "No one ever says, Here am I, and I have brought my body with me. In what does this intimacy of relationship consist? The body is the basis of our emotional and purposive experience."[63]

Mind-body unity is but an aspect of mind-body-universe unity. We can ask concerning where our bodies end and the external world begins, but if we wish to be scientifically precise our answer must be qualified. For our knowledge of our bodies occurs within the larger field of nature, and our bodies' demarcation from the rest of nature is imprecise. Among other things the body consists of the coordinated functioning of billions of molecules, in which we are continually losing and gaining molecules.[64] "Consider one definite molecule. It is part of nature. It has moved about for millions of years. Perhaps it started from a distant nebula. It enters the body; it may be as a factor in some edible vegetable; or it passes into the lungs as part of the air. At what exact point as it enters the mouth, or as it is absorbed through the skin, is it part of the body? At what exact moment, later on, does it cease to be part of the body? Exactness is out of the question." "When we consider the question with microscopic accuracy, there is no definite boundary to determine where the body begins and external nature ends. . . . The body requires the environment in order to exist. Thus there is a unity of the body with the environment, as well as a unity of body and soul into one person."[65]

Whitehead utilizes philosophical realism/objectivism to articulate the interrelatedness of all nature. The realist admits "that the simple proposition, 'the cloud is crimson,' is a meaningless statement about nature unless other items of nature are implicitly included in the proposition." "The crimson cloud is essentially connected with *every other item of nature* by the spatio-temporality of nature . . ."[66]

Whitehead's *fourth reason* for realism/objectivism (and this one does not pertain to knowledge of nature) relates to our instinct for action: As sense-perception seems to give knowledge of what lies beyond our minds, so our activities are directed toward purposes in the world that transcend ourselves and our complete cognizance.[67] Even the simplest vocational planning must take account of such external factors.

61. Whitehead, *Interpretation/Science*, 139.
62. Whitehead, *Modes*, 155–56.
63. Ibid., 156,;my emphasis.
64. Ibid., 155, 221.
65. Ibid., 30, 221.
66. Whitehead, *Interpretation/Science*, 139, 140; my emphasis.
67. Whitehead, *Science/Modern World*, 86.

Chapter 13

Dialogues, Meeting Points Involving Natural Science, Philosophy, Christian Theology

1. Preliminary Indications of Relationships

As we saw in the previous chapter, natural science could not exist without the conviction that the outer world is real, an idea that philosophical reflection concerning nature can help to supply. Christian Faith believes that a loving and rational God in His freedom created a world with a considerable amount of orderliness.[1] Such beliefs contributed much to the development of science[2] and it still depends upon extra-scientific values.[3]

Science and Christian Faith are relatively independent sources of ideas and activities, but have overlapping concerns that relate especially to creation and the understanding of nature, including human nature. Thus Christian theology and science can and should learn from each other.

Not only have there long been conflicts between diverse Christian understandings, but also between these and various scientific views. Since Christianity and science continue to develop, there is prospect that even fresh altercations can be faced and resolved. For this to happen hard thinking is required on both sides. Each has much to gain by learning from the other. Christian theology can help to protect scientific understandings from atheistic ideological contamination. Science can help to guard Christian Faith from ill-conceived endorsement of the Bible's various ancient world-views.

Science can and should critique expressions of Christian Faith that can be delegitimized by well-founded scientific evidence. An example is the ancient cosmology assumed in Acts's report of a literal ascension of Jesus as the way of affirming the Risen Christ's transition to the Father's presence.[4]

---

1. This in part means that the world's existence was not and is not necessary, that it was and is contingent.
2. See sec. 3.
3. See sec. 9.
4. Unlike Paul's understanding of Jesus's resurrection, Luke believed in the bodily aspect of the

One's scientific understanding of the general character of nature will affect one's conception of God's relation to it. Current science conceives nature as an evolutionary process with a long history of emerging novelty,[5] with ongoing tendencies that can change when nature does, and with elements of chance operating at all levels. However, science should not overstate the last point by denying all goal-directedness in nature, since science recognizes that more complex organisms have evolved from simpler ones.

Apart from the provision of factual knowledge to solve practical problems, science encourages the habit of deciphering causes and of classifying according to similarities. (Biblical and systematic theology and Christian ethics also classify in this way.) Science instills the habit of careful observation, which is also required by the disciplines just mentioned. Though many intellectuals assume that education consists primarily in developing the power of abstract thought,[6] even more important is that thought be linked to observation[7] and application.

Though Christian theology looks to God's disclosure in Jesus Christ and through prayer seeks God's guidance for its interpretations, theological activity largely parallels the creative aspect of scientific discovery.[8] In this respect and many others theology and science do not currently seem as dissimilar as many on both sides earlier thought. The opinion that Christian theology is purely subjective and science entirely objective is regarded today as gross distortion.

Though Christian Faith believes that the world was created by a rational God, theology and science have benefitted from the rationality that philosophy has often encouraged. Natural science was and is especially dependent upon the philosophical emphasis concerning the rationality *within nature*. Yet science and theology need to be critical of philosophy's tendency toward the rationalism criticized in the last chapter.

2. Commonalities, Differences between Science and Philosophy

Both science and philosophy wish to perceive natural facts that exemplify general principles capable of summation in abstraction from particular manifestations. Though animals recognize that things can fall to the ground, none likely supposes that

---

event, and thus visualized Jesus's transition. His account presupposes that God's dwelling is reachable by a short trip through the atmosphere. Luke is unlikely to have had any historical sources for his ascension descriptions and, consistent with his literary intention of linking his writings together, described ascension accounts at the end of his Gospel (24:50) and at the beginning of Acts (1:1–2, 9–11). See chap. 18, sec. 11 as related to Acts's world view. For additional material on the general perspective of the author of Luke-Acts, see chap. 6, nn11, 16, and sec. 7; chap. 7, nn49, 101, and sec. 8; chap. 10, sec. 6.

5. Barbour, *Religion/Science*, 26.
6. See chap. 1, sec. 11.
7. Whitehead, *Interpretation/Science*, 164.
8. See sec. 9.

a general principle can account for such effects. As early as Aristotle's theory that material bodies seek the center of the earth, western philosophy/science had produced a principle in this regard. Humans seem more curious than animals to understand the meaning of the facts of their experience and more capable of doing so. Human curiosity of the scientific and philosophical kind is dissatisfied with uninterpreted facts or unexplained routines of nature.[9] Stephen Toulman refers specifically to natural science as desiring to make the course of nature predictable and intelligible, doing this by looking for rational patterns of connections[10] that can make sense of the flux of natural events.

A chief connection and difference between natural science and philosophy is this: Science observes particular natural occurrences and either directly draws inferences or indirectly does so after observing related phenomena. These responses lead to classifications concerning the natural tendencies exhibited. In contrast, the emphasis of philosophy is upon generalizations that almost fail to classify because of their universal application. "For example, all things are involved in the creative advance of the universe, that is, in the general temporality which affects all things."[11]

3. History of Science

Urged on by human curiosity, a critical spirit, and freed from inherited superstitions, science had its birth in ancient Greece, with Thales as the earliest exponent known to us.[12] In attempting to account for the basis of every claim, in searching for principles with which to organize diverse phenomenon, and in prizing coherence—the Hellenic spirit influenced the development of modern science. Also contributing were the thoroughness with which the Greeks approached every subject and their conviction that reasonable structures exist within nature that can be discovered by the human mind.

Greek thought struggled to overcome cyclical and polytheistic thinking and was only partially successful. Insofar as they conquered such and inasmuch as their divine immanentism allowed for any goal-directedness, they tended to regard nature primarily in terms of the inherent teleology of each creaturely reality (Aristotle). Nature was conceived as a drama in which each thing plays its part, thereby exemplifying general ideas and converging toward a vague goal.

A world regarded as created by a Transcendent God disagrees with the Greeks' understanding of the forming of natural objects by analogy with the human creation of artifacts. The latter constructs are seen as designed by minds like our own and for specific purposes we understand. In contrast, if one believes in a Transcendent God

---

9. Whitehead, *Adventure/Ideas*, 179–81.
10. *Foresight/Understanding*, 99.
11. Whitehead, *Adventure/Ideas*, 183.
12. Ibid., 180.

an inherent purpose of earlier and current natural objects is far from clear.[13] However, Christians can agree that humans have come to exist for fellowship with God and others, and that the outer world provides the framework for this to occur. God surely treasures this outer framework, and so should we, and not just for its instrumental value.

Though Aristotle and Archimedes had more scientific minds than most Greek thinkers, Whitehead accuses even them of being overly theoretical and of regarding science as an offshoot of philosophy. Most Greek intellectuals sought answers to essentially philosophical questions, otherwise being strong only in mathematics and deductive reasoning. "Their minds were infected with an eager generality. They demanded clear, bold ideas, and strict reasoning from them. All this was excellent; it was genius; it was ideal preparatory work. But it was not science as we understand it. *The patience for minute observation was not nearly so prominent.* Their genius was not so apt for the state of *imaginative muddled suspense* which precedes successful inductive generalization."[14]

Western science and technology is as dependent on Roman know-how as on Greek curiosity. Though Hellenism included contributions from Greece and Rome, it was the Romans whose engineering concerns led to the building of aqueducts, an elaborate highway system and impressive buildings. Roman technical interests to a degree connect with our world, except that today's technology is grounded in greater scientific understanding. *But the Greco-Roman world did not lead directly to the modern world's scientific and technological developments.*

The Greeks believed in rationality, but faith in the world's rationality could contribute to the development of science only when the universe came to be regarded as *contingent rather than necessary*. Contingency implies that the world's orderliness cannot be deduced by reason, but requires the kind of investigation that natural science provides. In contrast to the Greek tendency to speak of God by speaking of this world, the world understood as created by the biblical God is sharply distinguished from its Creator. Since the world's Maker is regarded as rational, the world is seen as embodying regularities and patterns. But in contrast with Greek immanentism the Transcendent God of Jewish and Christian Faith is regarded as free, as is Her creating activity, and thus the particular regularities and patterns the world exhibits can be discovered only by examination, not by deduction.[15]

The beliefs in rationality and contingency are presuppositions of modern science—not products of it[16]*—and the Greeks only helped to contribute the former*. "If the world is not rational, science is not possible . . ." There are no rationally intelligible tendencies to be discovered. "If the world is not contingent, science is not necessary."[17] If everything is

13. Gilkey, *Maker*, 118.
14. Whitehead, *Science/Modern World*, 14; my emphases.
15. Hendry, *Theology/Nature*, 110.
16. Newbigin, *Foolishness*, 71.
17. Ibid., 70. Hindu philosophy regards the universe as non-contingent and as an outflowing and inflowing of Brahma (one of the gods), and believes that the only essential way to learn of Brahma

essentially divine, rational speculation is the best method for learning in every field, and nature as divine should not be interfered with. Christianity and Judaism agreed with the Greeks concerning nature's rationality, but made the additional, essential contribution to science concerning its contingency. So also the Romans—who challenged nature through their inventions—reflected a non-belief in nature's divinity.

Judaism and Christianity regarded the created world as *rational* because it is the creation of the God who is light and not darkness, and *contingent* because it is not an emanation or outflowing of God, but a genuine creation endowed by its Creator with a measure of autonomy. These faiths thought that though historical and spiritual revelation is required for understanding the Transcendent God and Her covenant purpose for humans, knowledge of natural objects can be learned only from direct study of them.[18]

Ancient Greece eventually reverted to the idea of a cyclical universe—the worlds most pervasive form of belief that nature is rational but not contingent. With the Greek philosophical theology of divine immanence (its emanation thinking), its lack of belief in a Creator and creation, and its failure to draw a distinction between the gods and the world, their science was subject to considerable religious constraint. They were not free to regard the world as non-divine—and therefore subject to human manipulation.

To the contrary, Jesus did not accept sickness's inevitability—but challenged it. Having learned methodological thoroughness from Hellenism, Christianity—following Jesus's example—wished to apply science in problem-solving ways to help improve humankind's material condition. Along this line the Benedictine Order was largely responsible for reinvigorating European agriculture in the Middle Ages and this technical expansion had a decisive influence upon the development of western science.

As implied by the earlier Roman and later Benedictine examples, western science and technology had long been more reciprocally related than is commonly supposed. The rise of modern science linked to progress that occurred in technology. For thousands of years there had been little change in the number and character of tools utilized by workers. But from the eleventh century onward, non-human energy rapidly replaced the human variety. In the late Middle Ages for the first time a complex civilization was built that did not rest on the backs of sweating slaves and unskilled laborers, but primarily on non-human power.[19]

Technological progress in Europe rose sharply from the thirteenth century onward, with increasing numbers of inventions that kept pace with scientific developments. Inventions were no longer stillborn, with little social application, but were quickly put to widespread use because of the economic advantages of replacing manual with non-manual labor.

---

is from within the recesses of the soul. Science's empirical and rational aspects are inconsistent with these premises and had to be imported. India's current scientific practice is inconsistent with Indian philosophy (same source, 71).

18. Newbigin, *Foolishness*, 14.

19. Van Leeuwen, *Christianity/World History*, 329, quoting Farrington.

The late Middle Ages form the essential link toward the development of modern science. The habit of definite and exact thought was implanted through the dominance of Christian scholastic philosophy and logic, which were highly influenced by Greek thinking. "The habit remained after the philosophy had been repudiated, *the priceless habit of looking for an exact point and of sticking to it when found.* Galileo owes more to Aristotle than appears on the surface of his *Dialogues*: he owes to him *his clear head and his analytic mind.*"[20]

The Middle Ages were a long training ground of the intellect. More particularly, at that time the idea arose that contingent, natural occurrences could be precisely correlated with antecedents, so as to exhibit order and constancy in nature and *rational general principles*. These convictions provided the final motivation for the development of natural science. Since the world is not an outflowing of its own divine Ground, it did not seem impious to seek to penetrate nature's secrets. Whitehead writes, "When we compare this tone of thought in Europe with the attitude of other civilizations when left to themselves, there seems but one source for its origin. It must come from the medieval insistence on the rationality of God, conceived as with the personal energy of Jehovah and with the rationality of a Greek philosopher."

"In Asia, the conceptions of God were of a being who was either too arbitrary[21] or too impersonal for such ideas to have much effect on instinctive habits of mind. Any definite occurrence might be due to the fiat of an irrational despot or might issue from some impersonal, inscrutable origin of things. There was not the same confidence in the intelligible rationality of a personal being."[22]

In the later Middle Ages Europe utilized the heritage of Greek science, but under the Christian and Jewish assumptions of a transcendent Creator and a contingent creation. There a new and more experimentally open mentality gradually began to emerge. However, we should not overstate the role of Judeo-Christian thought in the rise of science, since Arab science made significant contributions in the Middle Ages,[23] though those were in conflict with Islam's emphasis on fate. Also, when modern science developed in Europe it was aided by the Renaissance's humanistic interest, the growth of trade and commerce, and new patterns of education.[24]

A more experimentally open perspective was exhibited in the *fourteenth century*, when for the first time the theories concerning the circulation of blood and the functions of the heart, that had been accepted from the Roman physician, Galen since the second century AD!, were finally *subjected to empirical testing. Then for the first time a corpse was cut open to see what was actually inside!* However, it took three centuries before William Harvey, on the basis of anatomical observation, proved that Galen's

---

20. Whitehead, *Science/Modern World*, 19; my emphases.
21. Was this also not so in Africa as influenced by traditional religion?
22. Whitehead, *Science/Modern World*, 19.
23. Barbour, *Religion/Science*, 17.
24. Ibid.

theory about the circulation of blood was wrong. The threshold of modern science was crossed with that demonstration.

Immediately preceding the industrial revolution in England was a dramatic emigration. More efficient agricultural methods meant that fewer farm workers were needed than in the thirteenth century. Many laborers thus sought work in the towns, contributing to industrialization and providing additional consumers.[25]

Here the slave trade needs to be considered, since this was not only immoral, but might seem to provide evidence against the advancement of science and technology in some of the centuries we have been considering. The Americas and Caribbean leg of the trans-Atlantic trade involved the export of slave labor-harvested plantation crops primarily from less industrialized areas, such as the southern states of America. But the European segment entailed the factory-produced export of goods, many of which went to African rulers, who in turn provided the slaves for export to the Americas and Caribbean. (Brazil had its own direct network.) Because the European leg of the triangle involved machine-assisted production, the inhumane fifteenth to nineteenth century trade in human beings eventually presumed the technical advances previously described in this section, which having arisen in Britain, eventually involved those more industrialized states within America and elsewhere.

The most impressive scientific accomplishment of the nineteenth century was that science began more quickly to lead to technological applications. Whitehead puts it this way: "The greatest invention of the nineteenth century was the invention of the method of invention." An element in the new method was discovering how to bridge the gap between scientific ideas and practical application by "disciplined attack upon one problem after another."[26] What we see here is indeed Hellenic thoroughness, but now used to solve problems and thereby gain greater freedom in relation to nature.

Though the historical contribution of Judaism, Christianity, and the other sources to the rise of science is convincing, once science was established its own success satisfied many scientists. Today many scientists simplistically suppose that the contingency and intelligibility of nature are givens that require no intellectual defense.[27] *Insofar as scientists are content to do that they remain willfully ignorant of the presuppositional basis of their discipline and ungrateful for the historical ground on which they stand.*

4. Induction and "Laws of Nature"

The experimental and historical methods that began to develop in the seventeenth century turned aside from the scholastic emphasis on rational deduction, and focused on "irreducible and stubborn facts," seeking only to draw general inferences from

---

25. Whitehead, *Science/Modern World*, 316, 315.
26. Ibid., 91, 92.
27. Barbour, *Religion/Science*, 17.

particular occasions in the past to those in the future.[28] Though inductively generalizing from past occasions to future ones is important, its attempt to isolate such thought processes from rational deduction was an over-reaction. In reality their "facts" were not as uninterpreted as they imagined, but were understood in purely causal, rather than any teleological context.[29]

Since Bacon and Mill the inductive view has held that scientists begin with observations and formulate theories by merely generalizing from the patterns inherent in the data. This conception is not fully adequate because science increasingly refers to entities and relationships not directly observable, but recognized by inferences from other observations. Furthermore, there is no direct line of logical reasoning from data to theories—but only an indirect one representing "acts of *creative imagination*."[30]

Science seeks *explanatory* descriptions concerning ongoing natural tendencies beyond the particular instances observed.[31] Inasmuch as science utilizes direct induction it involves "the divinization of some characteristic of a particular future from a known characteristic of a particular past."[32] The wider assumption that "laws" based on deduction or otherwise founded hold for all cognizable occasions is an unsafe addendum to attach to such limited knowledge.[33] The laws of Newtonian physics do not hold at the atomic or astronomical levels, as quantum physics demonstrates for the first level and the theory of relativity for the second.[34]

Since tendencies within nature depend on the various characteristics of the elements constituting nature, as nature's composition alters, the tendencies change. For this reason we should conceive of nature's propensities as "evolving concurrently with the things constituting the environment. Thus the conception of the universe as evolving subject to fixed, eternal laws regulating all behavior should be abandoned."[35] "Why talk about 'the laws of nature' when what we mean is the characteristic behavior of phenomena within certain limits at a given stage of development in a given epoch—so far as these can be ascertained?"[36] Contrary to this Whiteheadian mouthful, the reason that "law of nature" terminology continues to be used is that we need a shorthand phrase, even if by that we now mean exactly what Whitehead stated. Perhaps, though, a somewhat more fitting terminology would be "tendencies of nature," which I have been using.

---

28. Whitehead, *Science/Modern World*, 22–23.
29. Newbigin, *Foolishness*, 76. See sec. 6 below.
30. Barbour, *Religion/Science*, 31, 32. See sec. 7 below.
31. Whitehead, *Adventure/Ideas*, 164.
32. Whitehead, *Science/Modern World*, 46.
33. Ibid.
34. See Appendix following this chapter.
35. Whitehead, *Adventure/Ideas*, 143.
36. Whitehead and Price, *Dialogues*, 346.

5. Newtonian Physics, Its Modifications

The separation of philosophy from natural science was much influenced by Newtonian materialism: From the seventeenth century until fairly recently science has been less than candid concerning its own presuppositions, especially its frequently held but quite insupportable philosophy concerning senseless and purposeless matter—which stands in conflict with the degree of teleology implicit in the evolution of the universe and of complex organisms from simpler life-forms. The above mechanistic understanding ("senseless and purposeless matter") was at the time inconsistently joined with an unwavering belief that people and higher animals are self-determining. Such inconsistencies at the foundation of modern thought account for much that is half-hearted and wavering in western civilization.[37] Newton's image of nature as a law-abiding machine long influenced scientific thinking; God was conceived deistically as a clockmaker who after creating the world left it to run by itself.

As for scientific changes since Newton's time, it is not just that many interpretations have changed, but also the understandings of what are the scientific facts being investigated.[38] Each generation not only confirms and applies aspects of the scientific results it has inherited, but must also critically evaluate and review its inheritance. With sensitive microscopes science has today probed a microscopic world and in other ways deduced the atomic world that even microscopes cannot perceive. With powerful telescopes it has discovered vast reaches of space. With knowledge of such worlds—unknown and unknowable to earlier centuries—we must now considerably qualify Newtonian physics. The latter investigated "the connections regulating the succession of obvious occurrences," reflecting "a triumph of organized common sense." "It grounded itself upon what every plain person could see with his own eyes, or with a microscope of moderate power. It measured the obvious things to be measured, and it generalized the obvious things to be generalized."[39]

Throughout the period of classical physics, space and time were regarded as separable, and time was considered to pass in a uniform way everywhere, with a simultaneous shared "now." Now here on Earth, now there on Mars. The mass of objects was regarded as unchanging, objective and entirely independent of the observer.[40] The Newtonian scheme has a large measure of applicability insofar as the focus is upon "bodies of some magnitude and upon motion of moderate velocity . . . These laws did not cease to be true when science passed beyond them to the investigation of elements in the universe to which they do not apply. What happened was that heretofore unrecognized limits of their truth came to light."[41]

---

37. Whitehead, *Science/Modern World*, 73.
38. Polanyi, *Science/Faith/Society*, 89.
39. Whitehead, *Science/Modern World*, 108, 106.
40. Barbour, *Religion/Science*, 108. See also Whitehead, *Adventure/Ideas*, 200–201.
41. Cobb, *Christian Natural Theology*, 272.

Though Newtonian physics is close to everyday experience and common-sense, scientific theory concerning the universe is today "outrunning common sense."[42] Relativity theory reflects "*a dynamic and interconnected universe*," with space and time as inseparable, and mass as a form of energy.[43] Empty space as the mere vehicle of spatial interconnections has been eliminated, with the universe now seen as a field of incessant activity, a theater for the transmission of light and sound.[44]

Even concerning this planet Newtonian physics is to a degree being challenged. In an organism the plan of the *whole* influences its subordinate organisms, even down to the smallest ones, such as electrons, so that subordinate organisms are not free standing and machine-like.[45] Due to the plan of the body an electron within a living body differs from one outside it.[46] "The electron blindly runs either within or without the body; but it runs within the body in accordance with the general plan of the body, and this plan includes the mental state. But the principle of modification is perfectly general throughout nature, and represents no property peculiar to living bodies."[47]

6. New Scientific Theories Needed to Interpret Direct or Indirect Evidence

It is a fact that a rock dropped from the leaning tower of Pisa took a certain number of seconds to reach the ground, but that observation had significance only when recognized as a particular exemplification of what came to be called the law of gravitation. Though science does take account of facts, it has much to do with understanding how to interpret those.

The matter is even more complicated, since what modern science regards as factual is often only indirectly based on observation. Today there is thought to be an elaborate hierarchy of fundamental particles from which all things in nature ultimately derived. "Yet if an inquirer be so bold as to ask whether anyone has ever *really* seen a single meson, the answer has to be 'No.' And the same is true of electrons . . . and almost all the dominant entities in modern physics." Much in agreement with Whitehead, Bertrand Russell says that "physics may have begun historically with a principle of naive realism—that things genuinely are what they seem to be—but its greatest triumphs are those associated with a leap beyond the [obvious] facts."[48]

---

42. Whitehead, *Science/Modern World*, 106.
43. Barbour, *Religion/Science*, 111.
44. Whitehead, *Modes*, 186, 182. See Appendix following this chapter.
45. Neither of course is the larger organism, since it interconnects and interacts with a broader nature.
46. Whitehead, *Science/Modern World*, 76.
47. Ibid., 76. Those geneticists who conceive of genes as the sole determinants of heredity promote the simplistic suppositions of the old common sense world (Whitehead, *Modes*, 189–90).
48. Coulson, "Science/Religion," 65–66, Russell source not provided.

More Interaction With Related Disciplines

In the 1960s Thomas Kuhn came to regard the sciences as similar to the humanities in being interpretive and shaped by history and context. He has been largely followed by contemporary philosophers of science,[49] many of whom in addition regard science as involving the imagination, utilizing metaphorical models,[50] and much reliant on theory.

All data seems theory-laden because the language used to report observations is theory dependent. Theories also influence the very selection of what is to be studied and the choice of variables to be measured.[51] That scientists randomly make observations uninfluenced by any theory until they finally succeed in establishing great new generalizations is mythology,[52] since such a procedure would be unfocused. The kinds of questions asked also contribute to the answers received. This account differs drastically from the empiricist one in which scientific knowledge was thought to be directly based on inferences drawn from unchanging, directly observable facts.

Science advances in two ways: By utilizing theories to help discover new facts and by using theories to recognize the meaning of what is already known. Jeans claimed that the landmarks in the progress of science have all been of the second type: Copernicus, Newton, Darwin, and Einstein.[53]

Consider a detail from scientific history that is consistent with the recognition that scientific discovery usually has to do with interpreting previously available evidence and the insistence on the priority of theory in understanding the world. With reference to understanding continental drift Gould demonstrated that the empirical facts had long pointed to continental movement. But typical of the way science progresses, until the hypothesis of "plate tectonics" was proposed, such evidence had not succeeded in dislodging the claim that the continents were immovable. "New facts, collected in old ways, under the guidance of old theories, rarely lead to any substantial revision of thought. Facts do not 'speak for themselves'; they are read in the light of theory. Creative thought, in science as much as in the arts, is the motor of changing opinion."[54]

As for the previous evidence concerning the movement of continents that had long been known, but had no influence until the recognition of a new theory: (1) Approximately 240 million years ago what is now South America, Antarctica, India, Africa, and Australia were covered by glaciers, which presents insuperable difficulties

---

49. Stiver, *After Ricoeur*, 225.

50. See chap. 2, sec. 6.

51. Barbour, *Religion/Science*, 33.

52. Polanyi, *Science/Faith/Society*, 28.

53. Ibid., 28; see also 13. Polanyi adds Dalton's atomic theory of chemical combination, de Broglie's wave theory of matter, Heisenberg and Schrodinger's quantum physics, and Dirac's theory of the electron and positron (same source, 28).

54. Gould, *Since Darwin*, 161.

if all continents have always been stable.[55] (2) From fossil records we know that "the Cambrian trilobites[56] of Europe and North America divided themselves into two rather different faunas[57] . . . It is devilishly difficult to make any sense of this distribution if the two continents always stood 3,000 miles apart."

Odd as it may seem only a new hypothesis as to how continental movements could have occurred caused science to regard the old evidence as convincing. Both examples just cited are widely regarded today as "proofs" of continental drift, but were soundly rejected previously, not because available data was less complete than ours, but "only because no one had devised an adequate mechanism to move continents." . . . "Drift triumphed only when it became the necessary consequence of a new theory."[58]

It had been assumed that if continents had plowed through the oceans they would have left huge holes in the surface beneath. In the absence of such evidence, continental drift did not seem credible. Now change the theory. Forget about continents plowing the ocean surface on their own. Suppose instead that the continents are attached to the oceanic crust and move passively as enormous pieces of ocean floor shift about. Assume also that what causes the movement is the rise of new material from the earth's interior, that covers the signs of crust movement, and thus large holes could not be expected. Such a new theory showed that the old evidence makes sense. Now the previous data could be appealed to as proving continental drift.[59] Such is the way science works!

Gould's impressive example should not be understood to mean that scientific theories have little concern for direct or indirect data. It is just that *until science can explain the evidence, it can do little with it*. Scientific explanations that over the long run survive are those successful in integrating and explaining the most data.

7. Understanding Problem Solving, Scientific Discovery

Examining the nature of scientific discovery is of interest to Christian theology because though the processes for the gaining of scientific and theological insights exhibit many differences, they also manifest many parallels. For example, both presuppose that current understandings are subject to revisions and that the procedures for making new discoveries, though related to guidelines, are not completely specifiable. Creative insights pull both science and theology ahead. Science primarily struggles with previous scientific evidence and theories and one's own probings. The considerations for Christian theology are different and more multifaceted. These include

55. Ibid., 162.
56. Three lobed ocean creatures that lived 521 million years ago and became extinct 250 million years ago.
57. The animal life of a particular region or time.
58. Gould, *Since Darwin*, 162–63, 163, 166.
59. Ibid., 165–66.

the Spirit-guided pondering of God's revelation in Christ, taking account of relevant biblical studies, pertinent insights from modern and historical theology, and germane historical-critical and other scientific insights. A Christian scientist may find inner divine guidance directly helpful for making discoveries; the Christian theologian certainly does. Even so, spiritual considerations also presuppose the more directly human dimensions of discovery to be here considered, and God can and does work in and through these as well.

To understand the creative act of discovery we first glance at *general problem solving*. No animal can be free of purposeful tension as it tries to make sense of a dangerous situation and retain self-control. This process involves *perplexity followed by perceiving and doing that dispels perplexity*. Similarly, human preoccupation with challenges imposes emotional strain and their solutions result in great joy. The story of Archimedes rushing from his bath into the Syracuse streets shouting "Eureka" attests to his happiness at the new insight. But so also do accounts of the way chimpanzees behave after solving problems.[60]

As with scientific work, the theological quest also involves tension and perplexity that with apprehension leads to the jubilant release of emotional strain, though the process soon begins anew. More paradoxically, even disquietude and bewilderment along the way have their enjoyable aspects because science and theology are so intellectually engrossing. Though Whitehead surely knew the anxiety and puzzlement of intellectual struggle, he highlighted only the fulfilling facets of scientific activity—perhaps supposing that even such tension and perplexity have pleasurable aspects. He thus affirmed that science is primarily the outgrowth of "pleasurable intellectual curiosity."[61]

Since creative scientific leaps involve modifications of existing interpretative frameworks, they do not follow strict rules, but are lured forward. In the absence of formal procedures on which one can rely, the investigator "senses the proximity of something unknown and strives passionately towards it." "'Illumination' is the leap by which the logical gap"—between antecedent knowledge and discovery—is crossed. "It is the plunge by which we gain a foothold at another shore of reality."[62]

Scientists exercise personal judgment in assessing evidence, for example, in deciding "whether an unexplained discrepancy disproves a theory or can be set aside as an anomaly or attributed to chance variation. Like a judge weighing ambiguous evidence or a doctor making a difficult diagnosis"[63] or a theologian appraising, interpreting and systematizing biblical and historical beliefs, the scientist must follow her own best judgment and use guidelines flexibly.

Not impersonal detachment, but commitment to rationality, openness to public scrutiny, and the intent to serve others protect scientific judgments from arbitrariness.

---

60. Polanyi, *Personal Knowledge*, 120, 122.
61. Whitehead, *Aims/Education*, 54.
62. Polanyi, *Personal Knowledge*, 395–96, 123.
63. Barbour, ed., "Science and Religion," 19, writing of Polanyi's views.

Though scientific and theological activity is personal it is not primarily subjective.[64] For science and theology participation in a community of inquiry is a safeguard against mere subjectivity, though such participation never removes the burden of individual responsibility.[65]

The process of gaining insight is more mysterious than is usually recognized. Speaking of illumination in general, Plato (in *Meno*) pointed out how the search for a solution to a conundrum already presupposes some apprehension concerning its solution, otherwise one would not know how to conduct the search. If a person is actively involved in trying to solve a problem, in effect there is only half of one to solve. Along similar lines, Polanyi insisted that in seeking a scientific solution, before you can ask intelligent questions you must have an intuition as to how you might proceed. Only if you have some hint concerning what you hope to find are you likely to find anything.[66]

Polanyi held an essentially Platonic/Stoic theory of general knowledge: "We acquire knowledge and hold it because our thoughts are moved by an innate affinity for making contact with reality and increasing our further hold upon it."[67] In general I don't disagree, but doubt that sinners can come to know the true God by such natural means. But what can be known in this way can be consistently interrelated with knowledge of God in Christ. Also the activity of theological interpretation in response to divine revelation in Christ, though responsive to divine guidance, can and should exhibit the creative process that Polanyi well describes here and below.

Polanyi's understanding of Plato's epistemological conundrum points to the role of implicit knowledge that lures toward the explicit kind. "We must have foreknowledge sufficient to guide our conjecture with reasonable probability in choosing a good problem and in choosing hunches that might solve the problem. A potential discovery may be thought to attract the mind which will reveal it—inflaming the scientist with creative desire and imparting to him intimations that guide him from clue to clue and from surmise to surmise. The testing hand, the straining eye, the ransacked brain, may all be thought to be laboring under the common spell of a potential discovery striving to emerge into actuality."[68]

---

64. In describing theological truth as involving subjectivity SK was not defending mere subjectivism, but insisting that we cannot know God while remaining disinterested. See chap. 18, sec. 8.

65. Barbour, *Religion/Science*, 22, describing Polanyi's perspective.

66. Polanyi, *Science/Faith/Society*, 14.

67. Polanyi, *Personal Knowledge*, 403.

68. Polanyi, *Science/Faith/Society*, 14. In spite of Polanyi's Platonism, he is a philosophical realist in regarding reason as but the means for discovering what waits to be found (same source, 6, 14, 35). "Great discovery is the realization of something obvious; a presence staring us in the face, waiting until we open our eyes" (same source, 35). After intellectual breakthroughs of all kinds, those involved often wonder why they had not seen much sooner what later became obvious. (See chap. 12, sec. 12 for Whitehead's argument for the priority of the natural world over our knowledge of it.)

Gifted, educated, and well-practiced scientific conjecturing is vital because it can guess "the several consecutive elements of a coherent sequence—even though each step guessed at a time can be justified only by the success of the further yet unguessed steps with which it will eventually combine to the final solution. . . . There must be a sufficient foreknowledge of the whole solution to guide conjecture with reasonable probability in making the right choice at each consecutive stage."[69]

Still in Platonic mode, Polanyi regards the intuition that guides creative guessing as lured on by intellectual eros, and considers the pursuit of science as motivated by a passion to understand, as more generally such a craving greatly influences our lives. In the search for understanding, the mind seeks to make itself more satisfying to itself by coming to appreciate the beauty of what it comprehends.[70] "The mind is attracted by beautiful problems promising beautiful solutions; it is fascinated by the clues to a beautiful discovery and pursues untiringly prospects of a beautiful invention."[71] Twentieth century physics and Einstein's theory of relativity in particular demonstrated that the recognition of scientific truth consists in part in the apprehension of a rationality that commands our respect, arouses our contemplative admiration, and that embraces a vision that guides us to ever deeper comprehending.[72]

Poincare notes that *final* discovery "does not usually occur at the culmination of mental effort—the way you reach the peak of a mountain by putting in your last ounce of strength—but more often comes in a flash after a period of rest or distraction" when our subconscious mind has worked on our behalf. "Our labors are spent as it were in an unsuccessful scramble among the rocks and in the gullies on the flanks of the hill and then when we would give up for the moment and settle down to tea we suddenly find ourselves transported to the top. All the efforts of the discoverer are but preparations for the main event of discovery, which eventually takes place—if at all—by a process of *spontaneous mental reorganization uncontrolled by conscious effort.*"[73] And such assembling processes can proceed even while sleeping.

Most that has been said about scientific discovery parallels aspects of the process of gaining theological understanding. In particular that theological insights also involve leaps from antecedent knowledge to new insight made possible by dissatisfaction with current perspectives. The cause of such dissatisfaction is either that some details currently regarded as normative should not be so considered or because important insights have not been recognized.

69. Ibid., 32.

70. Polanyi, *Study/Man*, 84, 34, 35–36.

71. Ibid., 37.

72. Polanyi, *Personal Knowledge*, 5–6. When sixteen Einstein had already speculated concerning the consequences that would occur if an observer kept pace with a light signal sent out by him, insight that later contributed to his theory of relativity (same source, 10).

73. Polanyi, *Science/Faith/Society*, 39, 30, 34; my emphasis.

Before we consider more general doubting or trusting attitudes as related to scientific discovery we need to understand how *implicit or temporary doubting and then trusting* contribute to general achievement. Doubting can be considered very widely, as when an animal briefly hesitates or a marksperson doubts the accuracy of aim until willing to pull the trigger. The repeated attempts of a poet or writer to get a line or a sentence just right are filled with such hesitations. Such kinds of doubting are required before actions can be well taken. Similarly, at a certain point well-founded confidence that one can accomplish a task or solve a problem can lead to success. The animal finds the confidence to pounce, the marksperson to pull the trigger, the writer to write the sentence, the spouse to correct it.

As for *skeptical or trustful longer term attitudes* contributing to intellectual leaps in science and other intellectual fields, either can be useful and neither can be recommended as a general rule. Some discoveries are prompted by the conviction that something is fundamentally lacking in an existing framework, others by the intuition that far more is implied in a perspective than has yet been realized. The first attitude may be regarded as more skeptical toward current opinion and the second more trusting. Furthermore, at the moment of deciding no rule can tell us whether the next step in research reflects mere recklessness or justified boldness, and no one can do our distinguishing between doubts that thwart boldness and reflect unimaginative dogmatism and those that curb recklessness and exhibit warranted caution.[74]

In spite of the justified use of skeptical or trusting attitudes in pursuit of discovery, the Descartian strategy of doubting everything that cannot be proven must not only be doubted but criticized.[75] Even by Descartes own logic his theory is discredited—since it cannot be proven.

Descartes had declared that universal doubt should purge our minds of all opinions held merely on trust and open them to knowledge firmly grounded in reason. Throughout the Descartian influenced critical period of philosophy it was taken for granted that the acceptance of unproven beliefs led to darkness, whereas truth was approached through systematic doubt. We were warned against hosts of unproven beliefs instilled from childhood and urged to pit the principle of philosophical doubt against traditional indoctrination.

Descartian doubt is the logical corollary of the extreme objectivism that presumes that the uprooting of beliefs enables the mind to be completely determined by objective evidence. Though Kant rejected this extreme, the Descartian critical thinkers unconditionally trusted this method for avoiding error and establishing truth. This is not to say that during the period of critical thought this procedure was ever rigorously practiced—which is impossible—but merely that its practice was avowed and emphasized, while its relaxation was acknowledged only in passing.[76]

74. Polanyi, *Personal Knowledge*, 272, 277.
75. See chap. 11, sec. 2; chap. 12, secs. 4 and 6.
76. Polanyi, *Personal Knowledge*, 269, 269–70.

Popular thought in the nineteenth century was dominated by writers who—with an eye on the then current objectivist understanding of the natural sciences—declared with complete assurance that they accepted no belief whatever that had not passed the test of unrestricted doubt. Though John Stewart Mill and others claimed that they strictly refrained from believing anything that could be disproven, they merely cloaked their own "will to believe" behind "a false pretense of self-critical severity."[77]

Philosophies of methodological doubt (Descartes, Locke, Mill and others) ignored the obvious, namely, that *"the doubting of any explicit statement merely implies an attempt to deny the belief expressed by the statement in favor of other beliefs which are not doubted for the time being."*[78] Because the basis of even methodological doubt is belief, viewpoints that venerate explicit doubt are misguided and dishonest. This is not to imply that everyone's opinion is equally good. It just means that people need to give their reasons for doubting or believing. But none will provide knock down proof that will convince everyone.[79] With fine post-critical irony Polanyi doubted the strategy of methodological doubting.

Theology can oppose the Bible at places where it is found to be subject to legitimate criticism when judged by convincing biblical disclosures of God in Christ or by well-founded scientific knowledge. Similarly science can reject aspects of its philosophical heritage (such as the Descartian doubt strategy), even as it reaffirms much of that heritage.[80] The "processes of creative renewal always imply an appeal from a tradition as it *is* to a tradition as it *ought to be*,"[81] *not the pretense of rejecting all tradition*.

8. Polanyi's Philosophical/Gestalt Psychological Understanding of Understanding

Presupposed in Polanyi's discussion of scientific discovery are his insights concerning the intuitive capacities of the human mind to grope toward and then to grasp previously hidden patterns of meaning. Once we come to know particulars or parts as helping to understand patterns or totalities we know them differently than previously. The difference is demonstrated in *gestalt* visual perceptions, where eyes/minds instantly move from focal awareness of particulars to using those to see the patterns to which they contribute. Once parts are seen in such contributory ways, it becomes difficult to see them in isolation. Similarly, because of the speed and complexity of tacit (merely

---

77. Ibid., 271. Polanyi gives examples of science's earlier irrational hypercriticism in denying meteorites, hypnotism, and painless amputations by the use of hypnotism (same source, 275).

78. Ibid., 272; my emphasis.

79. Ibid., 274.

80. Polanyi, *Science/Faith/Society*, 56.

81. Ibid.

implicit) integration, intuitive insights may arrive at unaccountable conclusions in flashes,[82] as, for example, with the final step of scientific discovery.

A similarly rapid shift from part to whole occurs when we hear or read words, but go beyond individual word meanings to the significance to which groups of words point. When this happens we are aware of words in a subsidiary or contributing manner.[83] In contrast, if we concentrate on individual words we lose the significance of groups of words. As with the use of words in subsidiary and contributing ways, we similarly use tools, machines, probes, and instruments. Polanyi concludes that "*no meaningful knowledge can be acquired, except by an act of comprehension which consists in merging our awareness of a set of particulars into our focal awareness of their joint significance.*"[84] "The skillful use of a tennis racket can be paralyzed by watching our racket instead of attending to the ball and the court in front of us."[85]

Related to the above *gestalt* insights, but shifting the focus slightly, the reason antecedent understandings cause us to ask important interpretive questions of texts, scientific problems, or other matters is because beneath the conscious surface of our minds we already faintly glimpse broader patterns of meaning in what is puzzling us. Thus to even perceive a scientific or theological problem is to have a hint concerning the coherence of hitherto uncomprehended particulars,[86] of how fragments may contribute to broader understanding. Such tacit knowledge is a source of interest-provoking intellectual eros, which lures interpretive passion toward finding a resolution.

The dominant role of tacit knowledge is evidenced in *subception*, where we are not only unaware of the knowledge we hold, but can never become conscious of how we know.[87] We recognize a person's face and can do so from among tens of thousands. Yet we usually cannot explain exactly how we recognize a face. We may say a few words about its appearance, but that information would usually be inadequate for identifying the person. From such words a computer simulation could progressively approximate the face, but a person's vision would have to confirm the correctness of the emerging portrait. Similarly we may quickly recognize a familiar voice or gait, though capable only vaguely of saying how we have done so.[88]

Tacit knowledge is exemplified in the way we accomplish a skill. If a person had read a book about music theory and learned all the mechanical movements involved in playing the piano one still would not be able to play. One has to learn that by practicing. In practicing a piano piece one disassembles the whole for the sake of analyzing and learning the parts. But one must then play using those holistically, else

---

82. Polanyi, *Knowing/Being*, 118, 144–45.
83. Polanyi, *Personal Knowledge*, 57.
84. Polanyi, *Study/Man*, 44.
85. Ibid., 31.
86. Polanyi, Tacit, 19. See also Polanyi, *Knowing/Being*, 118–19, 143; *The Study of Man*, 35.
87. Polanyi, *Knowing/Being*, 143.
88. Ibid., 141, 142; Polanyi, *Study/Man*, 45.

one's performance will not improve. A skillful performance involves an integration of all information into actual playing, and that depends upon previous learning and practicing that have been internalized. When performing, if one tried to remember the names and time values of the notes to be played and to recall the relationship of those to the muscular movements to be made, the performance would be sabotaged.

And reading about balance and forward movement would not get you riding down the road on a bicycle. It takes practice.[89] What has been said about learning to play the piano or to ride a bicycle applies to learning any skill or learning to play any sport.

A conclusion Polanyi draws from what has been summarized in this section is that because knowledge builds from tacit gropings to find meaningful patterns, knowledge integrally connects to the person who holds it—and this is a major aspect of what he means by "personal" knowledge. "Only the explicit, formulable core of knowledge can be transferred, neutrally, from person to person. Its implicit base (since it is not verbalized and cannot be formulated . . .) must be the groping of *someone*."[90] Such insight is as true in theology as it is in more directly scientific fields.

9. Non-Scientific Values Required by Science

Today scientists detect a hiss in the universe, interpret that as evidence that the universe continues to expand and regard the expansion as an indication of a creational "big bang." Natural science obviously does not just interpret evidence, but requires a goodly amount of deduction. Also commitment to *tolerance* and *fairness and respect for truth*.[91]

Tolerance involves listening carefully even to unfair and hostile statements, and struggling to separate truth from error. "It is irritating to open our mind wide to a spate of specious argument on the off-chance of catching a grain of truth in it; which, when acknowledged, would strengthen our opponent's position and be even unfairly exploited by him against us. It requires great strength of tolerance to go through with this."[92]

To be fair is to avoid stating points in the question-begging terms in which they first occur to the mind. It is to separate facts from opinions and emotions, and to welcome critical appraisal of what we say. It is to lay our entire position open even to opponents. It requires painful discipline, for it holds in check the tendency toward emotion-driven intellectual colonization. Fairness requires that even as we disagree we ascribe to our opponents their true points. It also necessitates that we acknowledge our own limitations and biases.

---

89. See Polanyi, *Study/Man*, 37; Polanyi, *Knowing/Being*, 141.

90. Marjorie Grene, "Introduction," in Polanyi, *Knowing/Being*, x.

91. "It is logically false to deny the existence of truth, since the very statement asserting this is based on the assumption that truth can be established" (Polanyi, *Science/Faith/Society*, 78).

92. Ibid., 68.

Fairness in argument involves preferring truth, even at the expense of losing argumentative force.[93] People will not practice this unless they believe that there is such a thing as truth. *Love of truth* is expressed in the give and take of free discussion, which is encouraged by democratic communal tradition. *In short, science embodies living tradition concerning the values that enable science and much else to occur.*

In creative response to evidence and to scientific tradition original judgments occur and new additions are made. *But science can continue only as long as scientists respect truth and care more about science than about pleasing their colleagues or fulfilling selfish desires.* If these latter become the norms, science will no longer pursue its proper task, and will soon collapse.[94]

One has only to substitute the words "theology," "theologians" and "theological" for "science," "scientists" and "scientific" in the above paragraph to see that practitioners in both fields face the temptations of careerism and the lure of advancement and popularity. And the same can be said for other professionals.

---

93. The Sophists were early exemplars of the opposite.

94. Polanyi, *Science/Faith/Society*, 68, 70–71, 54, 58, 62, 64, 65. In recent years some "scientists" have falsified evidence and experimental conclusions, thereby jeopardizing science.

Appendix

Highly Relative Summary Concerning Relativity, Quantum Theories[1]

1. Theory of Relativity

In 1905, at the age of twenty-six, Einstein ... postulated *the constancy of the velocity of light for all observers*. This hypothesis had unexpected and far-reaching implications. Imagine that an observer at the *middle of a moving railway train* sends light signals, which reach the equidistant front and rear of the train at the *same instance*. For an observer *on the ground*, the signals travel *different distances* to the two ends (since the train moves while the signals are traveling); therefore if the signals travel at constant velocity in this framework they must arrive at *different times*.[2] The two events are *simultaneous in one frame of reference but not in the other*. The effect would be very small with a train but would be large with[in] a space rocket ... approaching the velocity of light.[3]

EINSTEIN ALSO DEMONSTRATED THAT time can be slowed by speed. Consider another illustration: "An itinerant twin blasts off to a nearby star, nudging the light barrier. The stay-at-home twin waits for him to return ten years later. When the rocket returns, the earth-bound twin finds his brother has aged only one year to his ten."[4] The point of the example is clear, but seems to oversimplify. Though speed slows time, the reduction and then absence of gravity speeds it,[5] not to mention the wear and tear of space travel as affecting a traveler's health and therefore his longevity.

---

1. Real scientists are invited to critique this up one side and down the other. It will hurt my feelings only to a relative quantum degree, since it could help to ease my puzzlement. However, as was attributed to Max Planck: "Anyone who is not shocked by quantum theory has not understood it." This, of course, does not mean that anyone who has not understood it has understood it.

2. Would not the light also take less time to reach a passenger at the rear of the cabin, since she would be moving toward the light?

3. Barbour, *Religion/Science*, 109; emphases 2–4, 6–7 mine.

4. Davies, *God/New Physics*, 121.

5. See next paragraph.

Einstein's general theory of relativity incorporated gravity, not as a force (which it also is), but as a distortion of space-time, and this theory has been proven. That increased gravitational pressure slows time can be demonstrated, since a clock at the top of a tower gains time relative to one at the base, and this because the one at the top is subject to weaker gravitational force.[6]

2. Quantum Theory: Functioning of Atomic Components as Particles or Waves

Though the "components" of the atomic world can be described by statistical equations concerning what happens in experiments, they do not consistently behave in terms of space, time and general causality.[7] Problems arose when the atom was discovered to be composed of electrons and protons and empty space, though now there seem to be even more inhabitants. People tried at first to understand these new sub-atomic entities as particle-like, and sometimes this imagery seems accurate. However, at other times they behave more like waves of vibrations. (Scientists had long been puzzled by a similar duality in the function of light.) Furthermore, sub-atomic electrons and protons when particle-like are able to move in bursts or jerks from place to place without passing through intervening space. At such times, something happens here and then there with definite connections between the events, but without continuous movement between them. Further, electrons and protons do not carry electrical charges, as a material model would require, but *are* electrical charges.[8]

Here, as with the relativity theory, time is regarded as permeating the structure of nature in a more fundamental way in the new physics than in the classical one. When electrons vibrate/flow like musical sounds, time is required for the event to happen. Furthermore, the sub-atomic level is a world of dynamic flux in which as electrical waves come and go they become electrical particles and particles become waves. Such a world involves probability states, and only the passage of time can disclose which alternative potentiality was actualized.

Uncertainty as a fundamental aspect of quantum theory thus leads to *unpredictability*. For example, the image on the older type of television screen was produced as massive numbers of light pulses from electrons fired from the back of the set struck the florescent screen. The perceived picture was sharp because of the enormous numbers of electrons involved and because the cumulative effect of many electrons is predictable. However, particular electrons could go anywhere on the screen. The arrival of an electron at a particular place was uncertain and the minute part of the picture it produced could not be counted on. Though bullets from a

---

6. Davies, *God/New Physics*, 122.
7. Barbour, *Religion/Science*, 123, 97.
8. Cobb, *Christian Natural Theology*, 25–26.

normal gun follow a precise trajectory to their target, electrons from an electron gun cannot be guaranteed to turn up where expected, let alone hit the bull's eye.[9]

---

9. Davies, *God/New Physics*, 102, 103.

Service to Other Related Disciplines

Chapter 14

Proclamation and Teaching

1. Proclamation according to the New Testament

THE PROCLAMATION REFERRED TO in the first four sections of this chapter concern all Christian types, including NT house church congregational preaching by those having such charismatic gifts, as well as non-congregational missionary communication by those with that calling. According to Paul such interpretation and witness are vital. "For, 'everyone who calls upon the name of the Lord will be saved.' But how are they to call on one in whom they have not believed? And how are they to believe in one of whom they have never heard? And how are they to hear without someone to proclaim him?" (Rom 10:13–14 NRSV) "Since in the wisdom of God, the world did not know God through wisdom, it pleased God through the folly of what we preach to save those who believe" (1 Cor 1:21). "All this is from God, who through Christ reconciled the world to himself and gave us the ministry of reconciliation. . . . So we are ambassadors for Christ, God making his appeal through us" (2 Cor 5:18, 20a).

These texts certainly attest that faith is often evoked by Christian verbal communication. Yet Paul did not become a disciple in direct response to Christian exhortation (Gal 1:11–17), though as a persecutor of the Christian movement he surely was familiar with some Christian beliefs. His encounter with the Risen Christ must have convinced him of the truthfulness of the essential message about Christ.

Because Paul was the earliest writer of books later included in the NT, major aspects of the content of early missionary and congregational proclamation can best be determined by studying his understanding of Christian Faith as reflected in the epistles he likely wrote.[1] His teaching focuses upon the theological and moral meaning of Jesus Christ in the light of His death (1 Cor 1:23; 2:2), resurrection (1 Cor 15:1–8) and the outpouring of the Holy Spirit, rather than upon Jesus's example and teaching, of which Paul apparently knew little. Since the Gospels describe Jesus's life

---

1. See chap. 15, sec. 1 for a discussion of some possible theological patterns in early *congregational* preaching.

As a late writing the Acts of the Apostles is not a good indicator of the content of early witnessing.

and teachings, and since today's Christians have access to the entire NT, our exhortation can and should take close account of the Gospels, though Paul could not do so. Plus ours must respond to the rest of the NT and take some account of the OT.

2. Convincing Power Belongs to God

Present day oral communication has its own integrity and responsibility. Like prophetic teaching it does not merely repeat tradition. Though attesting and interpreting God's action in the past, it is a fresh testimony to Jesus Christ whereby God encounters and reclaims us here and now. The Living Word of God is neither Scripture nor exhortation in and of themselves. Only insofar as God speaks through these witnesses do they become the Word of God; God can use them to draw people into content-filled relationship with Christ and into participation in salvation. The Gospel "is the power of God for salvation to everyone who has faith . . . For in it the righteousness of God"—God's faithfulness that right-wises—"is revealed through faith and for faith" (Rom 1:16b–17a). Paul was confident that the Living Word of God is at work within and among believers (1 Thess 2:13), and this was in part because of his understanding of the role of Christian exhortation (Rom 10:17; 1 Cor 1:21).

Because God freely speaks amid Christian witnessing Her activity must be respected and we must risk our lives and ministries on God's faithfulness. The Spirit can and often does make impact as proclamation occurs (Gal 3:2); sometimes, however, Christian witnessing only contributes to that effect by later being remembered; and sometimes, for whatever reason, Christian attestation may not be utilized in either way. If we take seriously the Holy Spirit's freedom to utilize our testimony as She sees fit, we can gain freedom from preoccupation with results, and from the anxiety and arrogance of thinking that the convincing power belongs to us.

In preparation and even when proclaiming, we should listen for God's Word, and witness and apply what we learn, in the hope that the Living Christ will authenticate our testimony. If we are to communicate we must interpret, but we never perfectly hear or interpret. The miracle is that God can use proclaimers in spite of our imperfections! We should neither claim too much nor too little concerning the power of exhortation. On the one side, we claim too much if we identify every word that flows from a witness's mouth with God's Word. On the other, we avow too little if we think diligent and prayerful attentiveness to Christ is of little value. Certainly only God can speak Her Word—but She has chosen to use the imperfect words of sinful and fallible humans to help accomplish this purpose.

3. Divine Authorizing and Sustaining of Proclamatory Ministers

Though all Christians in word and deed are to witness to Jesus Christ, some Christians have been given particular grace-led vocations to interpret and attest Christian Faith.

Because the words of faithful proclamation require the guidance and correction of the Spirit (1 Cor 2:13), only by the calling and continuing empowerment of the Holy Spirit should one dare to undertake and continue such a ministry (1 Thess 1:5), whether within the church or primarily to outsiders. Paul felt that God had commissioned him to interpret and herald the gospel and specifically to outsiders (1 Cor 9:17), and that he would have been remiss had he not done so (1 Cor 9:16bc). His sense of authority came from his Spirit-grounded perception that he had been called, sent and continually sustained as Christ's representative,[2] and in his case, as an apostle.

Christian communicators must ever anew learn of their insufficiency and be renewed by the Holy Spirit. With Paul we need to realize that when we are weak, then we are strong (2 Cor 12:10b). Not that we are sufficient of ourselves to claim anything as coming from us; our sufficiency is from God who has qualified us to be ministers of a new covenant (2 Cor 12:9a).

Like Paul, the prophets' sense of authority came from their experiences of being authorized by the Living God for proclamatory mission and sustained in such work (Isa 6:1–13; 40:1–8; Jer 1:4–19). In studying the prophetic-apostolic tradition, one is impressed by the audacity of people who claim to have been directly called by God and likewise sent and sustained. They did not choose their vocation because of some natural capacity for their task or merely because a group authorized and supported their undertaking. "We may prescribe all kinds of academic, moral, ecclesiastical, psychological, and oratorical tests for would-be preachers in order to take some of the presumptuousness away from their 'call,' yet the audacious element in it can never be completely eliminated."[3]

In addition to being called, sent and sustained by God, proclaimers must do hard theological work in seeking to understand the meaning of God's self-communication. We dare not slander God by using our calling as an excuse for laziness.

As recipients of Christian communication should allow their preconceived ideas to be questioned by Jesus Christ, so should Christian interpreters. We must seek Christ's correction and then confirmation of our messages before we dare to attest such to others. Only the grace of Christ can raise our homework from death.

Hearers are less likely to encounter God if a proclaimer has not been guided by God in preparation, though it is not impossible through such a witness. I agree with the Catholic and Lutheran recognition that God can speak through unspiritual heralds—as He was once said to have spoken through the mouth of a jackass—but pietism and Wesleyanism express a legitimate counter concern. They recognize that a lack of spiritual depth and moral integrity tends to make effective Christian communication less likely. Nevertheless, God is free to speak both to proclaimers and to hearers, and this God cannot be mastered or domesticated.

---

2. See 1 Cor 2:4; 12:3.
3. Furnish, "Prophets/Apostles/Preachers," 57–58.

Though unnecessarily restricting his point to congregational preachers, Victor Paul Furnish rightly implies that those called and equipped by God are to be servants of the Living God, not slaves of those to whom they communicate. The prophets and apostles were representatives of the community and spoke from within it, and yet stood over against it as advocates of God. Indeed they most adequately "represented" the true community of God when they were able to stand far enough apart to ever again recall it to its true self. How can proclaimers be *in* the church and yet not *of* the church, not subservient to it?[4] Only when their testimony is rooted in and controlled by the biblical witness to God's disclosure in Jesus Christ.[5]

4. Evaluation of Proclamatory Witness

Christian exhortation should be thought out, digested, and evaluated in terms of how faithful it is to the essence of God's manifestation in Jesus Christ as attested in Scripture and made known through encounter with Christ. If the teachings or parts of them are unfaithful to this standard, listeners are legitimately free to disagree. The listeners' application of this criterion provides wide scope for critical thinking, but we should try to avoid the easier and natural question—whether we liked what was said.

Simon and Garfunkel sang that "a man hears what he wants to hear and disregards the rest." This may be naturally true, but in order to listen in a Christian spirit, we, to the contrary, must be ready to hear more than we want to hear. Many times what is hard to receive is true—and we dare not reject anything merely because it is challenging. The expounding of mere sermonic pleasantries is surely offensive to God and should not be appreciated by us.

It is equally true, however, that if we link Christian communication with discredited or absurd claims concerning nature or history—our witness is for that reason

---

4. A parallel problem exists in seminary teaching: How to be in a seminary, but not bound by its less Christian aspects. With *laissez faire* capitalism now in vogue, and with institutions intent on being financially at the top in competition with other institutions, even Christian theological teachers may be prone to provide their "clients" with whatever such teachers think students want—while such "consumers" true needs go unmet. The "flesh is weak" and Christian teachers also have the human desire to be popular. When evaluating students' performance, there is also the tendency to inflate marks in the hope of staying on best terms with them. And giving quick and easy marks allows teachers more time for the research and publishing that can help them to rise to the top of their profession. Even Christian administrators may have vested interests in encouraging these types of compromises.

More generally, the hard truth is that universities' financial goals often conflict with their educational purposes. The pressure on many such institutions is to continually "dumb down," as they pursue the short-term financial advantage of attracting many less than qualified students. (If the institution can first help such students to become *genuinely qualified* that is a different matter.) "Dumbing down" is to the detriment not only of high quality teaching and learning, but to that of such institutions' long-term financial well-being. But as with secular corporations, by the time disastrous institutional results are in, the administrators in question will likely have moved on to "bless" other institutions.

5. Furnish, "Prophets/Apostles/Preachers," 59. See chap. 15, sec. 4 for a more extensive discussion of this point.

subject to legitimate criticism. Christian affirmations need to consistently interrelate with other kinds of knowledge—lest we negate our God-given reasoning capacities.

5. Meaning, Purpose, Method of Christian Learning and thus of Christian Teaching[6]

In contrast with titles reserved for Jesus (such as Christ or Lord) the teacher designation has been and may be applied to persons other than Him without in any way infringing upon His preeminence. God came forth in Jesus and in this respect Jesus is unique. Yet here and elsewhere Christ's uniqueness requires the exercise of ecclesiastical tasks that derive from His uniqueness. Thus Matthew 23:8[7] needs to be corrected by such passages as First Corinthians 12:28–29 and Ephesians 4:11, which include teachers as among necessary charismatics within the church. The teaching ministry originates as one of the spiritual gifts bestowed by Christ (Eph 4:11) through the Spirit (1 Cor 12:4–11). Consistent with this, Acts 13:1–3 describes Barnabas and Paul as set aside and sent forth as teachers.[8]

Because all Christian proclamation involves teaching, NT Christians used the latter term in connection with all Christian witnessing. Because proclamation and teaching in the NT overlap and can be synonyms, much in this chapter that was said of Christian exhortation in general and that will be said of congregational preaching in the next can shed light upon Christian teaching.

Most of the writings that later came to be included in the NT were written for instructional purposes and were in the earliest period independently read and studied by Christian leaders. Within the small and informal house church worship services that were common, such writings were read aloud and then interpreted by those leaders. Though in NT times the consideration of pre-NT writings by the broader membership was limited primarily to worship settings, we can reflect biblically and theologically as to the dynamics of all types of Christian learning/teaching activity that seeks to interpret the biblically attested meaning of Christian Faith.[9]

The God to whom Christian instruction points establishes the ultimate goal of Christian teaching. Because this God is no inert datum, Christian witnesses hope that God by Her Spirit will convince learners of Her reality and significance—that they may enter into or deepen their Christ-informed relationship with Her and faithfulness to Her.

In interpreting Christianity, teachers begin "in a situation already alive with God's address to all persons . . ." Within this context, they are to place their "knowledge and

---

6. See chap. 1, sec. 9.

7. "You are not to be called rabbi, for you have one teacher, and you are all brethren."

8. Leuba, "Teaching," 415.

9. Though learning from direct reading is implied by the practice of early Christian leaders, this is not discussed here, since such kinds of learning are considered in chap. 15, sec. 5 & chaps. 16 & 17.

concern at the disposal of the learners, 'to cross over,' to become catalysts for the learners' responses."[10] The learners' initial responses may be to the teacher, to specific theological content or to the Living God, but response to any of these can and should lead to the others. Christian teaching and learning also soon entail interaction between student and student or parishioner and parishioner. Because the Christian learning-teaching situation is complex, a Christian teacher's method should not exclusively involve lecture/proclamation, or only discussion, or just relationships. Rather, Christian theological teachers should attempt to feel the situation whole.[11]

Because God is the key agent in divine-human dialogue, theology "is doomed to a certain degree of ineptitude." "In the service of theology words are strained to the breaking point and are forced to perform wonders no other discipline asks of them."[12] This is because we are pointing to a transcendent, free, and present Subject and because it is not within our power to enable encounter with Her.

In seeking to understand *the dogmatic and catechetical tasks* Barth refers to their similarities and differences, and to the thin line between them. Both dogmatics and catechetical instruction seek to enlighten concerning Christian doctrine primarily on the basis of Scripture. Both are constructive and evaluative and seek *pure doctrine*. *Doctrine*, for they are both constructive; and *pure* doctrine, for they are both evaluative. So the early church drew no fundamental distinction between dogmatic and catechetical tasks. The primary dogmatic of the Reformation period, (Calvin's *Institutes*) had been and to a degree always remained a catechetical work and the Heidelberg Catechism has often been used as a source for constructing dogmatic lectures.

Some differences, nevertheless, remain. Dogmatics instructs but is more occupied with investigation than is catechesis. Dogmatics is much concerned with raising questions, thinking things out, and seeking answers, and is largely teaching to those called to give different forms of Christian instruction to others. Yet the contrast is not great: Whereas dogmatics teaches primarily though not exclusively evangelists, congregational teachers and preachers—catechesis teaches those who would become Christians and helps general Christians to grow in their faith and discipleship. One side of a necessary partnership is that in their teaching, doctrinal theologians must be mindful of the whole range of Christian communicators. The other side of the partnership is that those engaged in congregational teaching will do well theologically only if they have been and continue to be instructed concerning Christian doctrine.[13]

As for the related topic of *theological writing*, it is first of all for the sake of helping writers to gain increased understanding, that they may help others to deepen their understanding. Similarly, sentences of philosophers are in large part intellectual exercises

---

10. Rood, *Teaching Christianity*, 25.
11. Ibid.
12. Ibid., 185.
13. Barth, *Credo*, 175–76.

that help them struggle to perceive what is true, that they may more effectively help others to know the truth.

As for the didactic role of *disputation*: The give and take between differing expressions is a way in which theologians are encouraged to think clearly and speak and write precisely. Not only did medieval university disputations and debate make formal use of this method, contemporary theologians similarly encourage discussion. Though such exchanges can become heated, when encompassed by mutual consideration, respect and eagerness to learn, it is an important tool for theological clarification.

The *argumentative process also occurs within one's own mind*, using the tools of logic: seeking coherence (Does it make sense?), consistency (Is it self-consistent and compatible with other knowledge?), and comprehensiveness (Has it taken account of all relevant material?).[14]

Christian Faith is harmed by insistence on conformity to rigid formulae. Orthodoxy's desire that correct answers be memorized and uncritically repeated inhibits genuine theological capacity. Its insistence on doctrinal uniformity can kill the spirit of adventure and discovery. Students, for example, might quickly "correct" their Christologies, but such reformulations may be made with little feeling and with even less awareness of moral implications. Pietism, a movement that began within German Lutheranism in the seventeenth century, rebelled against Protestant orthodoxy by insisting that theological convictions need to be internalized through struggle, lest affirmations make little religious and moral difference. Even committed Christians need to be encouraged to question, since one of the essential ways we learn of anything is by probing inquiry.[15] To gain Christian knowledge without raising questions conflicts with good pedagogy. *When knowledge is superficially acquired it will be similarly held.*

---

14. Rood, *Teaching Christianity*, 185, 188–89.

15. Such specific questioning does not involve Descartian doubt of everything excepting one's own existence as doubter.

Chapter 15

Congregational Preaching and Biblical Interpretation[1]

THE PREVIOUS CHAPTER CONCERNED various types of preaching, whereas this one focuses on congregational preaching to many who have already responded to the Christian message. Though such congregational communication went beyond the initial missionary message, such proclaiming must also have been conversion provoking, else such communities would not likely have continued to grow rapidly.

1. Some Possible Theological Patterns in Early Congregational Preaching

Though finding evidence primarily from the epistles, Bultmann and Dahl detect common theological patterns that they think may have been reflected in much early congregational proclamation. These scholars have performed an important service in showing how important these typologies are in the NT, and thus the likelihood that these patterns were important to the early Church. We can learn from these and may well choose to often use these to help structure our own congregational proclamation. But since we have no direct evidence of the connection of these with early preaching, and since the Gospels hardly feature in these typologies, we should not restrict our preaching to these.

Insofar as Paul's epistles and other parallel teachings shed light concerning the content of Christian Faith and thus of early congregational preaching, they took their bearings from what God in Christ had done, is doing and will do. Interlinked were moral instructions, consolations, exhortations and admonitions that would help to upbuild Christians and prepare them to meet the coming Lord.[2]

---

1. Concerning biblical interpretation see sec. 5. Also see chap. 3, sec. 3; chap. 7, secs. 3 and 6; chap. 17. For general hermeneutics or the understanding of how we interpret, see chap. 13, sec. 8 and for that as it relates to biblical hermeneutics, see chap. 16.

2. Dahl, *Jesus/Memory/Early Church*, 31.

The first theological patterning and possible preaching type that Bultmann identified within the Pauline and other teachings and that Dahl reiterated tell of an eternal mystery long hidden but now manifest.³ Here the newness and riches of the eternal kingdom are emphasized by focusing on the redemptive disclosure of God in Christ made contemporary by the Spirit. In the Pastoral Epistles, not likely written by Paul, and some others certainly not, the terms "mystery" and "hidden" are missing, but the point is still that what was promised before the foundation of the world has now been disclosed.⁴

Bultmann and Dahl's second theological classification is the contrast type dominated by the opposition between "once" and "now," and that exhibits saving action. Even within this theological structuring we find direct statements about God through Christ as the source of this transition⁵ and not preoccupation with human transformation (as in Christian pragmatism/existentialism/pietism). Though christologically grounded, the contrast in this form is anthropologically and soteriologically oriented. "Once you were, but now you are . . ."⁶

The difference between one's former existence estranged from God and one's new life is a dominant theme in Ephesians, Colossians, and First Peter.⁷ Also, in Romans the polarity between former ways of life in paganism or under the law (1:18—3:20) and after the revelation of God's righteousness, (3:21—8:39) is essential to the epistle's structure.

The divergence between once and now contains a call to thanksgiving rooted in knowledge of God in Christ (Eph 2; Col 1:12-29), to steadfastness against the temptations of pagan vice or Jewish legalism (Gal 4; Col 2—3), and to a new way of living corresponding to the renewal provided by Christ (Col 3:5-17; Titus 3:3-11; 1 Pet.).⁸

A third typology and one newly identified by Dahl, is "the conformity pattern," in which we are urged to *respond fittingly* to what God in Christ has done for us.⁹ Though we should behave in ways that to a considerable extent parallel Christ's *moral* example, Dahl's title is somewhat inaccurate because, as he attests, Christ's *saving* deeds are unique. Our fitting response to Christ is thus not synonymous with imitating Him. Most important about Christ, even morally, is His unique coming and saving life, death and victorious resurrection, which testify to God's gracious will, to which we are to respond with gratitude and dedication.¹⁰

---

3. 1 Cor 2:6–9; Col 1:26–27; Eph 3:4–7, 8–11.

4. 2 Tim 1:9–11; Titus 1:2–3; 1 Pet 1:18–21; 1 John 1:1–3.

5. Gal 4:3–5; Eph 2:5–9, 12–22; Col 2:13–15.

6. Gal 4:8–9; cf. 3:23–29; Eph 2:11–22; 5:8; Rom 6:17–22; 7:5–6; 11:30; 1 Pet 2:10.

7. Eph 1:15—2:22; Col 1:12–21; 2:8–15, 20; 3:17; 1 Pet 1:13—2:10.

8. Dahl, *Jesus/Memory/Early Church*, 32, 33–34.

9. Rom 15:1–9; Eph 4:32; 5:2, 25, 29; Col 3:13; cf. Eph 4:32; Mark 10:42–45; John 13:34–35; 1 John 4:7–12; 1 Pet 2:21–25. This pattern sometimes introduces detailed statements concerning Christ (Eph 5:25–27; 1 Pet 2:21–24; 3:18–22), which may include fragments of hymns (ibid., 34).

10. Dahl, *Jesus/Memory/Early Church*, 34.

Even in seeking to honor Christ's ethical teachings and moral example (best seen in the Gospels), it would be better to speak of "responding fittingly" or "being fittingly formed," and not of "conforming." For the latter's connotation is indistinguishable from mere imitation. And inflexible and uncreative repetition would not help us to live most faithfully in very different societies from those in which Jesus lived.

The teleological classification, the fourth and final one, is the second newly identified by Dahl. Here such terms as "so that" and "in order that" are essential connectors between christological/soteriological affirmations and goal statements based on those. In this structure the main emphasis is on the final clause—the behavioral or attitudinal effects of taking christological affirmations seriously.

We have access to the moral power of the coming kingdom because Christ came, lived, died and was raised in considerable part to empower us morally.[11] "And he died for all, that those who live might live no longer for themselves but for him who for their sake died and was raised."[12] The NT attests that (among other moral and spiritual effects) God's action in Christ was for the purpose of creating the church as a reconciled and reconciling community of Jews and Gentiles.[13] Other texts more generally affirm that God's purpose was that Christ's lordship would be realized both now and in eternity.[14] Such passages insist that we should learn to understand our own purposes from those of God in Christ.[15]

With the theological structuring summarized in this section, Paul and the other NT authors cited indicate a good deal concerning their understanding of Christian Faith. Such authors may indirectly reflect some of ways in which some essential and interrelated theological themes were elsewhere communicated in the early Church and encourage us to take account of such patterning in our proclamation. More general than the patterning described by Bultmann and Dahl, in highly variable ways congregational preaching should *often evidence what Scripture regards as the human problem, separation from God that leads to disregard for others. It should also proclaim and interpret God's related grace and guidance, and suggest ways in which Christians may faithfully respond.*[16] However our proclamation and its structuring can only be bounded by the God whom we perceive as speaking through the entire NT witness concerning the meaning of Her disclosure in Christ, and secondarily by Her disclosure in the OT.

---

11. Gal 1:4; 2 Cor 5:21; Heb 2:14–15.

12. 2 Cor 5:15; cf. Rom 8:3–4; Eph 5:27; Titus 2:14; 1 Pet 2:20–25.

13. Eph 2:15-16; 5:25–27; Titus 2:14; cf. Gal 3:13–14.

14. Rom 14:9; 1 Thess 5:9–11.

15. Dahl, *Jesus/Memory/Early Church*, 35, 36.

16. Such general aspects of our faith should be implicit within sermons, but emphases can and often should be disproportionate.

2. Homily as a Form of Congregational Preaching

In the NT only Acts uses the word "homily" to refer to Christian interpretive communication within a worship service (20:11). With Ignatius, who died in 110, this word came to be widely used with reference to congregational preaching by those charismatically led and delegated with special responsibilities. This was in contrast to early NT period mission proclamation and the more informal house church preaching. Certainly congregational preachers and all others should have a sense of divine calling and exemplify high moral standards and good self-discipline. These last two requirements are helpfully, but imperfectly described in First Timothy 3:1–7; 4:6–10 and Second Timothy 4:1–5.

Like the personal dialogues ancient philosophers had with their students, and from which the word came, homilies are to be dialogical in style. "The congregational sermon was given as a form of instruction from the Scriptures . . . in a way that the listeners became involved as much as possible."[17] Furthermore, the homily is not truly conversational if it does not lead to churchly discussion—within the worship service or soon afterward.[18]

3. Christ—not Congregation or Preacher—Source of Authority

As there is tension between Christ and us sinners, there necessarily is tension between the scriptural testimony to Christ upon whom the homily is based and us sinners, congregants and preachers alike. Though sinners, preachers are called and can be equipped to witness to God's disclosure in Christ. Contrary to Schleiermacher (who at this point was close to traditional Roman Catholicism), proclaimers' authority does not well up from the "Spirit-possessing congregation"—but from God's scriptural and presently attesting revelation. Because of the tension between sinful humans and the Holy God, neither the congregation nor the preacher of herself is in a position to generate norms. The Living Word does not come *from* the congregation, but *to* the congregation, though faithful preaching can facilitate this occurrence.

For a preacher merely to articulate the pious (or otherwise) feelings of the assembly is not to preach,[19] but to conform to the other sinners who comprise the congregation. The preacher is primarily to be a servant of the Word, not an articulator of one's own piety nor of that of the congregation. The preacher, who most certainly is also a sinner, must come before the congregation as one who has been pierced by God's Word and led to repentance in the face of God's judgment, but also

---

17. Berkhof, *Christian* Faith, 357. "Through the centuries the sermon reflects rather accurately the different cultures and rhetorical styles . . . And that is how it should be if this medium is to maintain its mediating character" (same source, 357). This does not imply that methodological issues are matters of theological indifference. See sec. 5.

18. Ibid.

19. Barth, *Homiletics*, 23–24.

as one who has thankfully received God's forgiveness and guidance in the sermon's preparation.[20] "Only in this progression through judgment and grace can preaching become genuinely original."[21]

Those of us who are preachers should be concerned to communicate effectively with our congregants, but must struggle even more to be faithful to Christ, lest we have little to live by or to communicate. We must not compromise the Christian message for the sake of worldly success. God does not will that proclaimers "stoop to overcome resistance with bargain counter methods."[22] . . . "For we are not, like so many, peddlers of God's word; but as people of sincerity, as commissioned by God, in the sight of God we speak in Christ" (2 Cor 2:17).

Paul certainly pointed to Christ, rather than to the inherent authority of preachers or congregations. "When I came to you, brothers and sisters, I did not come proclaiming the mystery of God to you in lofty words [of] wisdom. For I decided to know nothing among you except Jesus Christ, and him crucified. And I came to you in weakness and in fear and much trembling. My speech and my proclamation were not with plausible words of wisdom, but with a demonstration of the Spirit and of power, so that your faith might rest not on human wisdom but on the power of God" (1Cor 2:1–5 NRSV). Though recognizing that preachers are unworthy, Paul yet affirmed that God calls and equips them for their task.

> For since, in the wisdom of God, the world did not know God through wisdom, God decided, through the foolishness of our proclamation, to save those who believe. For Jews demand signs and Greeks desire wisdom, but we proclaim Christ crucified, a stumbling block to Jews and foolishness to Gentiles, but to those who are called, both Jews and Greeks, Christ the power of God and the wisdom of God. For God's foolishness is wiser than human wisdom, and God's weakness is stronger than human strength.
>
> Consider your own call, brothers and sisters: not many of you were wise by human standards, not many were powerful, not many were of noble birth. But God chose what is foolish in the world to shame the wise; God chose what is weak in the world to shame the strong; God chose what is low and despised in the world, things that are not, to reduce to nothing things that are, so that no one might boast in the presence of God. He is the source of your life in Christ Jesus, who became for us wisdom from God, and righteousness and sanctification and redemption, in order that, as it is written, "Let the one who boasts, boast of the Lord" (1 Cor 1:21–31 NRSV).

---

20. Barth, *Preaching*, 51.
21. Ibid.
22. Barth/Thurneysen, *Come Holy Spirit*, 220.

4. Congregational Preaching Method

Each proclaimer must witness to Christ as the unique person God has called her or him to be. Each should proclaim the faith in ways that take account of one's own characteristics and history, rather than try to adapt roles or imitate others.[23] "Even the best things, when taken over from others, are no longer what they were when spoken by those others. We must not slip into comedy in borrowed robes."[24]

Should sermons normally focus on single passages or be biblically topical, drawing together a variety of scriptural passages that relate to the theme of the sermon?[25] Scripture does not answer this methodological question. Of course it doesn't! Since the writings contained in the Bible were written before there was a canon, canonical Scripture is in no position to instruct us concerning how it should be utilized in preaching.

Karl Barth in his later sermons approximated a single text pattern of preaching[26] and John Wesley demonstrated a biblically topical approach. Lectionary preaching that utilizes two or three passages is a third type. It lacks the comprehensiveness of fully topical preaching, but has moved from single text toward biblically topical preaching. Each way of utilizing scriptural passages faces particular pitfalls that preachers must surmount if they are to use any of these methods responsibly and effectively. An advocate of the single text method admits that if such preaching is not to become a Sunday by Sunday fragmented "exposition of scattered documents one must have a view of the interrelatedness of the various passages of Scripture."[27] But if one indeed has such a connected perspective one should surely demonstrate this. This would move single text preaching toward the biblically topical.[28]

The thematic use of a variety of scriptural texts must also be used carefully, for it can easily convey meanings contrary to what individual texts say in their scriptural contexts. Furthermore such sermons easily become academic discourses, lacking personal quality. To avoid textual dishonesty, one should use individual passages

---

23. Barth, *Homiletics*, 81, 83.

24. Ibid., 83.

25. Occasionally a faithful biblical sermon might *not* be directly based on either a single text or multiple ones. Biblical preaching need not in all cases be explicitly expository, but occurs where Jesus Christ is proclaimed in agreement with the scriptural witness. Even Luther often preached without expounding a definite biblical text, as with his fast-day sermons of 1522 or his travel sermons (W. A., 10, III, *Abt*, cited in Brunner, *Revelation/Reason*, 142–43).

26. Barth's early sermons seem to be less tied to single texts, but because he always considered individual texts in canonical context, even his later sermons are somewhat broader than his words concerning preaching seem to envision. Nevertheless, his later, single text-based prison sermons (*Deliverance to the Captives*) took little account of broader biblical contexts or of his own systematics reflections. However this may be, I agree with Bultmann that Barth's best "sermons" were within the *Church Dogmatics*.

27. Randolph, *Renewal/Preaching*, 30.

28. Biblically topical preaching differs from general topical preaching, which is preoccupied with subjects of particular current interest. However, since biblically topical preaching can deal with the same, the difference is not absolute. But biblically topical preaching would always pay much attention to scriptural themes and texts.

conscientiously and not create syntheses that conflict with the contributing individual passages. Methodological imbalance can be redressed by preaching from time to time more directly expository sermons or series of sermons (as, for example, on the Lord's Prayer, the Sermon on the Mount, or the parables). With any method concrete applications are vital for understanding and for helping people to integrate and apply the message to their own lives.

If one can avert the problems just mentioned, using a variety of biblical texts thematically has the advantage of enabling one to explore subjects with greatest thoroughness and clarity, since one can freely pool the available biblical material on topics, and systematics can help in the process. With this method, over an extended period one's preaching is also more likely to be consistent, since each sermon must come to terms with a wide variety of texts that relate positively or negatively to a theme. Because biblically topical preparation for preaching necessarily involves systematic reflection, it has the advantage of being able to discover content conflicts that are often unrecognized or easily ignored by individual text or lectionary preparations. If preaching does not help Christians face and come to terms with biblical conflicts, lay people's surprising discovery of those can damage their faith and weaken discipleship.

If preachers are to utilize their unique gifts, most will likely decide on their preferred form.[29] Nevertheless, to keep freshness in preaching, preachers can allow themselves to vary their approach.

5. Interpreting Related to Congregational Preaching[30]

Whatever method of text usage employed, congregational preachers and other biblical interpreters should not think about passages merely in terms of understanding their past meanings, but consider them as points on moving lines from the past into the present. Interpreters should thus seek to show present meanings and possible applications. Preaching has not accomplished its purpose until hearers come to *understand themselves anew* through the Bible's texts and messages.[31] Thus sermons should not be merely *on* biblical verses, but also *from* those,[32] helping to set them in motion in peo-

---

29. Catholics, Anglicans, and Lutherans also face denominational pressure toward lectionary preaching—but need they succumb?

30. See chap. 17 for a more thorough discussion of biblical hermeneutics; see additional references in n1 of the current chapter.

31. At one point Ebeling concedes that we cannot speak accurately of human nature if we abstract from relationship with God (*Theology/Proclamation*, 141). Yet in his words concerning the power of biblical texts as word-events affecting lives and enabling new self-understanding, he says nothing of the Holy Spirit as the force that causes this to happen. With Ebeling texts of themselves are often seen to do the job (same source, 27–28).

32. Decades before Ebeling's "New Hermeneutic" had developed, Barth similarly insisted that preaching should talk *from* rather than *about* Scripture and use it to address people's hearts and lives. He also maintained that the consideration of the present significance of passages is essential for understanding those, not just for proclamation (Barth, *Homiletics*, 49, 81). Barth's present tense biblical

ple's lives.[33] Unlike a purely existentialistic "New Hermeneutic," I am not indifferent to theological content nor solely concerned with achieving new self-understanding. It is agreed, however, that we must not take people back to Bible Land and leave them there. Toward avoiding this effect, application should not be *habitually* delayed until a late part of the sermon—thereby calling attention to the gap between the biblical past and present meaning.

The contemporary reference concerning texts helps preachers to discover what a particular sermon should try to accomplish. Thus the linking to the present is not something to be added to already complete understandings of passages. We may perceive some of our most significant insights as we juxtapose texts in relationship to our life and times.[34]

We should not misunderstand contemporary application as the need for novelty, but for *fresh* restatements and applications. To achieve such, reflection and imagination should be utilized. "A fresh study may lead us only to say what we and others have said before. But the conclusions, whether new or not, must have been freshly arrived at and thought through. The possibility of communication depends on the extent to which the minister himself learns; and this in turn depends on his involvement in exegetical study (and many other kinds). . . ."[35]

Systematic theology can help preachers discern texts' present meanings, since it also stands at the point of transition from understanding texts to understanding by means of texts.[36] A vital purpose of both kinds of interpretations is to discover what God requires of us, God's Word becoming a lamp to our feet and light to our path (Ps 119:105).

Congregational preachers ponder the current meaning of a text or texts or of a textually grounded biblical theme by considering significance for themselves,[37] for their cultural contemporaries, and for the particular people to whom they are

---

hermeneutic was part of what many scholars found so offensive about the Second Edition of his commentary on *The Epistle to the Romans*.

33. Randolph, *Renewal/Preaching*, 37–38, 49, 1, 97; along similar lines, see Barth, *CD*, 4/3.2:868–69. I put more emphasis on biblical content than does Randolph, whose one-sided obsession with current effects is similar to Ebeling's.

34. Randolph, *Renewal/Preaching*, 44; my emphasis. This insight agrees with that of Hans-Georg Gadamer (see chap. 16, sec. 4).

35. Barr, *Old/New Interpretation*, 197.

36. Ebeling, *Word/Faith*, 431.

37. Randolph, *Renewal/Preaching*, 47–48. There is a place not only for personal questions that we in preaching share with others, but also for one's own purely personal ones. At a certain stage of sermon preparation, the preacher "should let his imagination float freely over what may be of exclusively private interest to him. The result of this may appear not in *what* he says, but in *how* he says it: in the tone of conviction which issues from one who has felt a text [or texts] applied to his life like a sharp sword or a healing balm" (same source, 48). The preacher must first perceive how texts relate to him or her before preaching from them to others.

preaching.[38] Preaching certainly has much to do with rhetoric if the latter "consists of putting oneself into others' shoes and so identifying with their innermost being as to be able to speak [to] them."[39]

The sermon is the communicative word utilizing biblical texts. "Therefore there is an inherent tension in the preacher's task. It is not merely some generalized uneasiness; it is a tension which arises every time the preacher preaches"[40]—a tension between the way biblical texts communicate and the way we do.[41] "Preaching is a creative process, because the tension cannot be relieved . . . Every sermon is an adventure."[42] There is nothing that can be memorized that can relieve this tension—including this general warning.

---

38. Ibid., 44–45. Though we should not refer to individuals from the congregation in sermons, "the people to whom one preaches should 'occur' in the sermons. Their needs and longings, hopes and aspirations should, from the beginning, be part of the stuff of the sermon . . . It was a turning point in the history of art when artists began painting portraits against landscapes. It is a turning point in preaching when the preacher begins to preach to faces, to particular persons and problems, seen against the landscape of modernity" or of other contexts from which people come (same source, 45).

39. Barth, *Homiletics*, 25, 42.

40. Randolph, *Renewal/Preaching*, 105.

41. Randolph refers to the different "structure" of each of these, which sounds highly abstract. An example of what he means is seen earlier on the same page where he indicates that a clear propositional summary may help to communicate today, but is not the way the Bible communicates (ibid.). To the contrary, the Bible sometimes communicates in that way—such as when it affirms that "God is love"—but often communicates less abstractly, as should we.

42. Ibid.

General Interpretation And Additional Biblical Interpretation

Chapter 16

General Hermeneutics, Its Relationship to Biblical Hermeneutics

1. Need for Hermeneutics

"Hermeneutics" is the understanding of how we understand.[1] The word contains a reference to Hermes, the supposed messenger of the gods in Greek mythology. Hermes's task was to explain to humans the decisions and plans of their gods, thereby bridging the gap between the divine and human realms. Though rejecting polytheism, biblical hermeneutics reflects a related concern: That God through the Holy Spirit may help us to learn of Him through the interpreting of biblical texts. In contrast to the biblical variety, general hermeneutics unfortunately today examines only how humans of themselves are able to understand this-worldly realities, such as texts, works of art, events and experiences.

Why is any hermeneutic necessary? Do not we understand matters to be interpreted? Where is the problem that hermeneutics wishes to solve?

The interpretive problem can be illustrated by the experience of rereading a book. A second reading may bring so many new insights that we may think that we see with different eyes, but our eyes and the book are the same. What changes is the perspective we bring to the activity, which means that *we have changed*. One obvious way in which this occurs is through the remembering of some things from the first reading, and thus being able to concentrate on aspects not carefully pondered earlier. Events have also happened in the meantime, influencing who we are and what we bring to the interpretive task. Because understanding is not automatic and unproblematic, our active participation is required. All interpreting requires that at least two realities meet: A *current* reader or hearer or experiencer and what is to be understood.[2]

Hermeneutical processes related to literature involve interaction between interpreters with their historical relatedness and texts with their historical relatedness.

---

1. See chap. 7; chap. 13, sec. 8; chap. 17.
2. Jeanrond, *Theological Hermeneutics*, 1–2.

Christian interpretation as applied to biblical texts is furthermore conditioned by our opinions concerning what are Scripture's clear teachings, and our experience or lack of experience of God's grace.[3] Furthermore, we may or may not think that God has illuminated our understanding of a particular text or theme.

2. Role of Philosophical and Theological Presuppositions

We all come from various influencing contexts and no one is context free. As those who encounter the Living God through Scripture and its interpretation, we are not blank slates, but those who have made specific commitments, who hold definite values, and who are influenced by particular ways of thinking.[4]

Concerning the philosophical presuppositions we bring to interpretation:

> None of us has any right to boast that *we* do not intermingle the New Testament with our own world view but simply let the thoughts of scripture speak for themselves.[5] . . . I set myself wholly in the same group. I do not pretend to be any better than the rest. . . . *Of none of us is it true that we do not mix the gospel with philosophy.* Luther and Calvin had their philosophy. So far as I can see they were both Platonists, although of different schools. By the cozily pragmatic and unreflecting way in which we work we may show that we are naive followers of Aristotle, or by the manner in which we stay aloof from the content of the text . . . we may give evidence that we are modern agnostics or by the dialectical movement in which alone the texts gain vitality for us we may show that we are [students] of Plato, Kant [or Hegel].[6]

A lack of self-awareness is exhibited by some scholars who advise that interpreters should clear their minds prior to interpreting—as though those scholars could do anything of the kind. Like other investigations, scriptural study is not purely objective or value free. People study the Bible only if they have reason to. One's perspective enables one to approach Scripture with questions and expectations, and conditions one's hearing of God's Word, since God speaks to human beings *who already think in particular ways*. If, however, our theological thinking is to become truly Christian we must listen attentively for what God wishes to say through the scriptural witness concerning Jesus Christ, and not take up permanent and uncritical residence within a prior standpoint. Insofar as a theology is normed by God's manifestation in Christ, it should be able to critique and improve one's philosophy. Yet for Christians

---

3. Dunn, *Living Word*, 134.

4. "Even the old peasant has some philosophy—and perhaps not the worst" (Barth, *Göttingen Dogmatics*, 258).

5. We, of course, may not be conscious of many influences and of many aspects of our world-view.

6. Barth, *Göttingen Dogmatics*, 258–59; second emphasis mine.

the question is not *primarily* whether philosophy shall serve Christian theology, but *whether both shall serve the God to whom Scripture testifies.*[7]

No neutral or disinterested scriptural exegesis is possible. The church over the centuries and around the world cannot provide infallible hermeneutical guidance, but its exegetical insights, doctrinal reflections and decisions help Christians hear God's Word through the scriptural witness.[8] Such guidance can help to orient us and to hold our exegetical caprice in check.[9]

Though imperfect, insights from past and present systematic theology are important aspects of church tradition that enable Christians to ask important interpretive questions and encourage active listening to Scripture. Pre-understanding is not simply a matter of one's non-theological attitudes or experiences of life. Systematic theology might be said to represent the end-process to date of that long growth of tradition in which the Christian community has struggled to arrive at an interpretation of biblical texts, that does justice to the Christian community's present place within biblically normed tradition and that seeks to discard those false pre-judgments that have proved unfruitful.

Lest we fall into doctrinal traditionalism we should recognize that theological tradition can also inhibit biblical understanding. When we look at the history of biblical interpretation, we can see that too often a theological pre-understanding has brought about a premature and uncritical perspective concerning a biblical text or author, forcing the Bible to say what was required by an interpreter or a doctrinal tradition. Against such tendencies, doctrines often have to be revised in the light of fresh and scientifically honest, biblical exegesis and interpretation. But this challenging of doctrinal tradition cannot spring from the exposition of one particular biblical passage, but only from a broader survey[10] that also takes account of scientific understandings of the world.

3. Hermeneutical Circle

To comprehend the role of presupposition in biblical interpretation we need to further understand the process involved in interpreting any written text or anything else. The most general issue concerns *the relationship between what people think they already know and what they hope to learn.* Here is the paradox: Unless people already know

---

7. Johnson, *Authority/Protestant*, 180–81. In using the word "primarily" I have modified Johnson's thought by supposing that a major way in which philosophy can serve the God to whom Scripture testifies is by being useful within Christian theology itself, which attempts to serve God.

8. See chap. 3, sec. 3; chap. 9, sec11. Unlike many biblical interpreters, James Barr is aware of the role of church tradition in biblical interpretation. He thus thinks that biblical interpretation has more to do with reappraising previous interpretations than with the discovery of completely new meanings (*Old/New Interpretation*, 186).

9. Barth, *Göttingen Dogmatics*, 260.

10. Thiselton, *Two Horizons*, 314, 315, 323, referring to H Diem, *Dogmatics*, 304.

something that provides an interest in studying texts or other subjects, they would see no point to specific interpretive labor. However, were they entirely satisfied with their prior understandings they would have no deep and personal reason for wanting to study ancient or modern writings or anything else,[11] since they could not expect to learn anything. An aspect of what has been called "the hermeneutical circle" is thus that *our antecedent understandings cause us to put questions to texts, experiences, objects, or events and help to enable the dialogue required for further understanding. But what texts, experiences, objects, or events say back to us can expand, modify, or call previous views into question.*[12]

To focus on interpreting a particular biblical text, account should be taken of the surrounding verses and chapter or chapters and of the book of which it is a part. But the matter is more complicated, since a person's grasp of a book should also be informed and corrected by their perception of the text's particular contribution. Then the relationship of the text to other thematically related ones by the same author can be considered. Delving into thematically related passages by other biblical authors may also be needed. Finally, the text being interpreted may be better understood by being compared with ones that seem to say otherwise.

For example, we should interpret a text by Paul in the context of knowledge of the particular epistle and chapter in which it occurs, but should take account of what Paul taught on that topic in the other epistles we have good reasons to think he wrote. We should also compare ours broadened understanding of the text with other related and even conflicting teachings beyond Paul's own writings, doing this in pursuit of truth, not to melt away the perspective of the text being exposited.

4. Cultural Context for Hermeneutical Endeavour

Contrary to the relativistic tendencies of some post-modern philosophies,[13] Hans-Georg Gadamer's still allows for considered judgments based on convincing evidence and reasons.[14] However, against rationalistic presumptuousness, Gadamer's post-modern hermeneutical philosophy recognizes tradition as an often constructive factor in gaining knowledge and regards interpretation as required for all knowledge.[15]

---

11. Doing so merely because one gets paid or wishes to pass a course involves a functional "commitment," but not dedication to the subject studied, and leads to limited comprehension.

12. Experience of Christ's present impact can provoke interest in learning more concerning Jesus, and vice versa. See chap. 18, sec. 3.

13. Consistent with this paragraph is a glossary item defining postmodern philosophy.

14. Stiver, *After Ricoeur*, 53.

15. Gadamer agrees that traditions and present interpretations can be oppressive and can interfere with accurately understanding texts. Nevertheless, he insists that voices from the past—and most especially from the texts themselves—can help to liberate us from bondage to current patterns of conformity (Placher, *Unapologetic*, 113). If, for example, we assume that Augustine and Luther represent only the dead hand of tradition we are deprived of their questioning (same source, 113).

General Hermeneutics, Its Relationship to Biblical Hermeneutics

Yet the understanding that reason's use of tradition and interpretation makes possible, can be and often is contested.

It is a common experience in expositing a text for people to differ in their interpretations; yet their views are not considered purely subjective. We and they can offer reasons and evidence—even the text itself—but our perspectives are also influenced by our training and traditions. Discussion can occur and opinions can change. Though assumptions can become deformed into prejudices, we should not deceive ourselves into supposing we can rid ourselves of influences from our past. Instead we should strive to be aware of our preconceptions and biases, but open to new insight over against prior conditioning.[16]

To limit our discussion for a moment to understanding texts, as those who live in history we cannot view culturally received writings solely in terms of their original contexts. The meaning such writings have for us is shaped partly by our place within text-influenced traditions that reach into the present. These do not provide infallible interpretive perspectives, but can help questioning to begin and critical dialogue to occur.[17]

Critical judgment arises not from the futile effort to free oneself from one's background in order to be totally objective, but to a large extent as traditions "set horizons in critical dialogue with one another."[18] All interpreters begin at particular points in

---

16. Stiver, *After Ricoeur*, 44, 49. Gadamer, *Truth/Method*, 269.

17. Gadamer, *Truth/Method*, 268–69.

18. Stiver, *After Ricoeur*, 53. The ironic *presupposition of presuppositionless understanding* was the Enlightenment dream that continued to live in many twentieth century understandings of scientific method, the illusion that we can remove ourselves so that knowledge can be objective and thus true. Gadamer terms this the Enlightenment "prejudice against prejudice itself" (Gadamer, *Truth/Method*, 270), which blinded its enthusiasts "to assumptions that continued to exert their influence, whether acknowledged or not" (Stiver, *After Ricoeur*, 47).

Gadamer regarded all knowledge, even highly precise and assured types, as finally based on practical wisdom (Stiver, *After Ricoeur*, 43), a perspective similar to Whitehead's (See chap. 12, sec. 12). Moving from grounding in Gadamer's above insight, Stiver rightly assumes that Gadamer's perspective encourages a sea change for theology vis-a-vis other disciplines. Seeing theology as a kind of practical knowledge, which is neither subjective nor impervious to evidence, Stiver regards it as broadly akin to other types of knowledge. While conceding that theology is not science (though is in many respects scientific) and that disciplines differ, he thinks that the difference is only relative, whereas "modernity" regarded the difference as absolute. He concludes that theology should reenter the public sphere (Stiver, *After Ricoeur*, 44), seeming to imply that disciplines such as Christian theology and Christian ethics may be directly taught in American public universities' "departments of religion."

Being allowed to enter the public sphere in this way seems too good to be true. And is! Though there is much truth in what Stiver says, he oversimplifies by ignoring the fact that the basis of practical wisdom for normative Christian disciplines, such as Christian dogmatics and Christian ethics, depends upon continual openness to the impact of the Risen Christ. Secular universities become considerably uncomfortable with such a premise, and thus these disciplines have difficulties finding homes there, unless they are content to sign on as types of historical theology. Stiver's useful book is an example of a descriptive and evaluative kind of historical theology dealing with Christian hermeneutics, requiring no dependence upon the very premise essential to Christian systematic theology and Christian ethics. For a related discussion concerning whether systematics is a science see chap. 1, sec. 13.

history and with assumptions. "The horizon is the range of vision that includes everything that can be seen from a particular vantage point. Applying this to the thinking mind, we speak of narrowness of horizon, of the possible expansion of horizon, of the opening up of new horizons."[19]

Gadamer makes a claim about the necessary interplay of horizons, not about the predominance of one over another or the capacity to totally separate these. His work implies that one's perspective can and should be expanded by encounter with other horizons, though we understand the others *through interaction with our own*. Even if after careful consideration we reject what was considered, we have been affected. Another possibility is that our horizon may need to be altered. A further option is that we may creatively appropriate aspects of what we have pondered, as Aquinas substantially altered Aristotle's thought in the process of using it. In each case, a "dialogue"[20] between horizons occurs.[21]

No interpreter can jump out of their own skin. Because interpreters must relate texts to their situation if they want to understand them, Gadamer concludes that the meaning of texts always go beyond their authors' intentions.[22] His *dialogical understanding* is far removed both from traditional text-centered minimizing of the interpreter's perspective and from modern "reader-response" monological deafness to what God through Scripture may wish to say that challenges our prior assumptions.

Gadamer thinks that interpretation is much like translation, which is similar to conversation. In conversation/translation/interpretation people must become actively involved, give of themselves, dare to recreate what has been said, and not try to merely repeat or reproduce it. Otherwise they will not understand. If one is unwilling to highlight aspects and to try to restate in clearer ways, one is not conversing, translating, or interpreting. Translators must enter into active dialogue, and are able to only if they respect their own language and thought. Because the meanings interpreters perceive in texts always go beyond those intended by authors, understanding is never a merely reproductive activity.[23]

Gadamer is critical of the traditional historical-critical notion, as seen in Krister Stendahl, that we can in an isolated way first access what the text "meant," which involves "exegesis," and only then consider what it "means," which is "interpretation." Rather, at the first moment access to what a text "meant" involves creative interplay with what we think it "means." This is because *thinking about application* is already at

---

19. Gadamer, *Truth/Method*, 269; see also 238, 475.

20. My chosen term. Gadamer's preferred term, "fusion," which Stiver seems to endorse, causes much "confusion," since it normally implies that two or more perspectives melt together, fuse. No response Gadamer summarizes fits his terminology of "fusion." The need to evaluate every text discourages unrealistic hopes of often fusing completely with viewpoints of texts (Jeanrond, *Theological Hermeneutics*, 115, reflecting Ricoeur's perspective).

21. Stiver, *After Ricoeur*, 47.

22. Gadamer, *Truth/Method*, 289, 264.

23. Ibid., 345, 347–79, 264.

work at the first stage of understanding a text.[24] Gadamer compares the work of legal historians with that of lawyers and concludes that both must be decisively concerned about the applied meaning of law. Otherwise neither understands it.[25] Gadamer draws the unusual conclusion that since all reading involves application, the reader "is himself part of the meaning he apprehends."[26]

In tension with Gadamer's usual blurring of the distinction between what a text meant and what it means, in his studies of Plato and Aristotle he accepts *a relative distinction between our interpretation of what a text meant and our interpretation of what it means*. Does Gadamer at such points in effect agree with Stendahl? Not really. In opposition to Stendahl, Gadamer insists that an understanding of Aristotle *already involves* a sense of his continuing value or lack of value.[27] Perhaps here and concerning early consideration of application are where he actually disagrees with Stendahl.[28]

Gadamer's emphasis on dialogue or conversation between horizons accords with *truth as manifestation*.[29] Truth concerns the object's power to disclose, which evokes "truth as an experience of recognition on the side of the [receiving] subject." "Anyone who has experienced even one such moment—in watching a film, in listening to music, in looking at a painting, in participating in a religious ritual, in reading a classic text, in conversation with friends, or in finding oneself in love—knows that

---

24. Stiver, *After Ricoeur*, 46. See chap. 17, sec. 2 below, where we see that the pietists and Barth had earlier made the same point.

25. Gadamer, *Truth/Method*, xx, 274, 289–90, 303.

26. Ibid., 304.

27. Ibid., 48.

28. Gadamer's student Wolfhart Pannenberg emphasizes the distance between past and present understandings, much in agreement with Stendahl. In particular Pannenberg insists that *before* a new horizon based on a relating of viewpoints can emerge, the interpreter must grasp "the strange object to be understood precisely in its *distance* from the total horizon the interpreter brings with him." Pannenberg quotes Gadamer to support his point, but at no stage does Gadamer isolate historical understanding from present meaning. Gadamer only insists that "'the hermeneutical task consists not in concealing the tension by a naive assimilation, but rather of deliberately developing it.'" Directly following this quoting of Gadamer Pannenberg writes, "In this way there is some prospect of overcoming any constriction of viewpoint which might be lodged *in the very formulation of the question a person brings with him*." Gadamer would agree that the interpreter should try to be open to what the text is saying, however strange it may seem to be, but he did not think it was possible to lay aside who we are. Instead, we can strive to use evidence fairly and to be willing to learn from perspectives very different from our current one. Pannenberg's misapplication of the quotation from Gadamer helps Pannenberg to return to a sharp distinction at the beginning of interpretation between what was "meant" and what it "means," which Gadamer challenged repeatedly in *Truth and Method*. Pannenberg, however, does concede to Gadamer that "The comprehensive horizon is formed in every case only in the course of the process of understanding itself. It is precisely what understanding consists of." (Pannenberg, *Basic Questions*, 1:118–19, my emphasis, quoting from *Wahrheit und Methode*, 290. See chap. 17, sec. 2 below.)

29. Tracy, *Plurality/Ambiguity*, 28. "Gadamer resists defining truth despite his title *Truth and Method*. The reason seems obvious: Truth for Gadamer, as for Heidegger and, in a different way, for Ricoeur, is fundamentally an event that happens to a subject and is not under the control of any subject" (same source, 28). Here Gadamer parallels Barth's theological emphasis on divine revelation in the present.

truth as manifestation is real.... Without such truth, life is indeed nasty, brutish, and short. Without manifestation, thought is too thin. Truth, in its primordial sense, is manifestation."[30]

When interpreters recognize any manifestation, they also imply the relative adequacy of their interpretation of that disclosure. Since others may disagree, discussion and even argument may ensue, and horizon may influence horizon.[31]

5. Understanding Truth amid Ambiguity of Spoken,[32] Written Communication

Like Jacques Ellul, who is the major focus of this section, Alfred North Whitehead gives priority to spoken communication and sharply differentiates between the way we use oral and written language. In particular he regards vocal language as the triumph of human ingenuity and as old as human nature itself. Though speech would be impossible apart from the evolution of the requisite throat structure, Whitehead regards speaking as a leading creative factor in the emergence of humankind.[33] "Speech is humanity itself, with none of the artificialities of written language." Of spoken communication he says that "the mentality of mankind and the language of mankind created each other."

Oral language arose with the immediate situation as its focus. For example, what such language primarily conveyed with reference to seeing birds was "the direction of attention to these birds, here, now, amid these surroundings."[34] Another example showing that verbal language is highly situational is the phrase "a warm day," which means inbetween hot and cold. But what is regarded as neither a hot nor cold day varies between speakers in Nigeria and those in Scotland. Spoken language generally refers to particular environments and the immediacies of social connections. In contrast written language is intended to be opened and read wherever and whenever.[35]

Though babies are capable of thinking though they cannot communicate with words,[36] and though adults can think without having learned vocal or signed language, the conclusion that spoken or signed communication is the essence of thought is nearly true. However, though the next quotation refers to oral communication,

---

30. Ibid., 28, 29. "This primordial understanding of truth-as-manifestation seems historically true of the origin of all the religions" (same source, 121).

31. Ibid., 29. See chap. 17, sec. 3 for culture critical insights that help to counterbalance Gadamer's culture appreciative emphasis.

32. Much that is written below concerning verbal communication would also apply to signed communication.

33. Whitehead, *Modes*, 44, 51.

34. Ibid., 53.

35. Ibid., 54–55.

36. Most babies, however, communicate with sounds, facial expressions and motions from their earliest moments.

written language contributes to some of these achievements. "Apart from language, the retention of thought, the easy recall of thought, the interweaving of thought into higher complexity, the communication of thought, are all gravely limited. Human civilization is an outgrowth of language, and [the refinement of][37] language is the product of advancing civilization. Freedom of thought is made possible by language: we are thereby released from complete bondage to the immediacies of mood and circumstance."

In contrast with spoken communication, writing is very modern. "Writing as an effective instrument of thought, with widespread influence, may be given about five or six thousand years at the most." Many today "so habitually intermingle writing and speech in daily experience that, when we discuss language, we hardly know whether we are referring to speech, or to writing, or to the mixture of both. But this final mixture is very modern." "Writing as a factor in human experience is comparable to the steam engine. It is important, modern, and artificial."[38]

We move from Whitehead's to Jacques Ellul's compatible, but more expansive understanding of the subject of this section.[39] We need to recall that the OT image of God texts teach that the contrast between human and animal existence concerns the human deputyship calling with reference to the world—which presupposes the uniquely human capacity to gain complex understanding through verbal or signed interchange.[40] We could not engage in such deputyship had we not the capacities just mentioned.

High level communication capacity[41] "constitutes human specificity, just as it constitutes the specificity of God. . . ."[42] Had not God given humankind the rational and communicative abilities implied by OT image of God passages, She would not have revealed Herself so subtly, amid history and requiring interpretation through words or signs. Under the Spirit's directing, we have some prospect of learning of God's revelation in Christ by using our rational and language capacities to interpret biblical interpretations, some possibility of understanding truth amid the ambiguity of verbal and written communication.

---

37. Without the bracketed interpretive aid Whitehead's statement is contradictory.

38. Whitehead, *Modes*, 49–50, 51, 52, 51.

39. Though in *The Humiliation of the Word* Ellul discusses primarily general hermeneutics, he thinks that the Bible exemplifies these kinds of problems. For example, the Bible also exhibits ambiguities, especially when read in intertextual/canonical context. Ironically and puzzlingly, Ellul, who was highly informed by the Bible and who wrote so much, on hermeneutics referred mainly to spoken communication. More specifically, he wrote of the contrast between interpreting spoken language and responding to pictures. Because he said less about written communication, biblical or otherwise, I have sometimes had to intuit what he seems to imply.

40. See chap. 10, sec. 3.

41. Ellul says "speech," but concerning humans and God Ellul surely means their entire communication capacity.

42. Ellul, *Humiliation of Word*, 63.

The dialogue required for interpreting can provoke self-discovery. "There is always a margin around our conversation. More precisely, conversation is like this printed page, framed on all sides by white margins, without words, but which can be filled in with any word at all. The margins situate a conversation and give it the possibility of rebounding and beginning again. They allow the other person to participate with his marginal comments. I am aware of this possibility, but I do not know what marginal comments are going to appear beside what I say, changing it. Here we are dealing with the unexpected."[43]

Dialogue is possible because other people are both like and unlike us. Like us, they have the reasoning and communicating capacities to use words to gain understanding, and some of their views may be similar to our own. Unlike us, they do not use language exactly as we do, nor are their thought processes precisely like ours, nor are their perspectives indistinguishable. People communicate not only because they have something to say, but because they desire to convey something they think others lack. Similarly, people receive communication because they think they have something to gain. Though people try to communicate in understandable ways, there would be little point to such sharing if people's ideas were identical.

Speech fills the gap separating us, but discourse must begin ever again in part because the distance between us remains. We must also sometimes restate what we have said because it is seldom exactly what we wished to communicate. Our words contain a fuzziness that is less precise than mere information.

Part of the reason words are hard to interpret is that they not only denote (explicitly state), but connote, and communicate both thoughts and feelings intermixed. The interpretive difficulty is also because language is filled with the rich complexity of things left unexpressed, where the communicator lays the message between the lines. Another reason words are hard to interpret is that what is said sometimes hides something else that could be said, and sometimes reveals what is not said. The most explicit and best-explained speaking or writing still leaves me with the mystery of the other person, whom I cannot fully understand, and whose communication provides me with only an echo of their person and thought.[44]

Truth is transmitted and discerned through highly uncertain and fragile methods. Our Christ-centered revelation occurred amid the ambiguities of history, where God not only condescended to come forth, but to go the way of the cross. Consistent with these facts is that God allowed fallible biblical writers to interpret this event. God further humbled Himself by permitting His revelation and its biblical interpretation to be subjected to our additional interpretations. "The God who reveals himself by His Word accepts entering into this game and its symbolism, into this flexibility of human relationships, as he accepts the limitations of the human condition in the Incarnation."[45] God

---

43. Ibid., 25.
44. Ibid., 16, 17, 16, 25.
45. Ibid., 57.

acts toward human beings through proposal and discretion, and is seldom obvious.[46] He speaks and we are to respond by listening and interpreting and following. Perhaps we wish things were different, but interpretive obviousness would be worse.[47] "What would become of us if we could grasp truth with unvarying precision and express it without the slightest imperfection or without any uncertainty? What would happen if the means were perfectly adequate for expressing truth? Such a situation would be dreadful and completely unlivable. We would be pinned down once and for all in a butterfly museum. We would be there in all our splendor, unable to move anymore, because everything would be said, closed up, and finished: perfect."[48] With interpretive obviousness we would be alive, but would lack freedom, spontaneity.

In contrast to the rationality and subtlety required for interpreting spoken or written communication, including the Bible, Ellul bemoans that many people no longer have these requisite interpretive qualities. And this because they primarily "think" in terms of the direct impact of pictorial images. These tendencies inhibit our ability to respond to God's hidden disclosure in Christ and thwart our discipleship and the carrying out of our rationally informed deputyship responsibility. For such reasons pictorial impressions must be understood (by comparing with linear learning), critiqued, and their dominance resisted.

The linear thinking of verbal or written communication is rational in that the incomplete thought of the first part of the sentence must be kept in mind until the second completes it. And the sentences that comprise a group of sentences must be rationally integrated, and then that group must be kept in mind when hearing or reading additional statements. Unlike the utilization of words, envisioning communicates non-sequentially, non-linearly, and in ways that do not *require* rational and critical reflection.

Through language we learn truth by learning to separate truth from falsehood, and the same applies in coming to terms with the Bible. Only if we are willing to critique aspects of our previous thinking can we proceed with language-based learning. In contrast, instantaneous visual impressions tends to short circuit the rational and critical process.[49] We live in such a world, with its overabundance of pictorial depictions from TV and TV advertising, films, the internet and internet advertising. And advertising is generally manipulative, since it bypasses rational reflection.

Visualizing tends to "prevent me from taking my distance. And if I cannot establish a certain distance, I can neither judge nor criticize. Of course, I can feel pleasure

---

46. Unlike some non-Christian religions, such as Hinduism, theophany or God being directly on display is foreign to biblical faith (ibid., 72). The Gospels attest that God's unique disclosure in Jesus was not obvious (same source, 83). What God offered were signs and invitations, awaiting response and acceptance.

47. Ibid., 99.

48. Ibid., 41.

49. Ibid., 34, 14, 214.

or displeasure in what I see. I can find it beautiful or ugly."[50] But only with the aid of language can this become a critical process. Shapes and sights perceived by the eye seem incontestable. *Only people experienced in critical reasoning and language usage will pause to evaluate these to determine their meaning.*[51]

In short, the intellectual process based on visualizing tends to conflict with one utilizing words.[52] People much impacted by visual impressions become less and less capable of reasoning and using language. "The overall and unconscious perception of a whole 'package' of information which does not follow the slow and arduous path of language also explains why we are naturally, through laziness, inclined to watch images rather than to read a long book or listen to a demonstration. Intellectual laziness automatically causes the image to win out over the word, and we observe its victory on every hand."[53] Image impacting predominates in societies that highly value comfort and ease, since interpretation is an laborious process.

Verbal communication cannot reach those uncritically oriented toward visual images,[54] because such people partition their feelings and emotional impulses from rational appraisal.[55] Though such people lack coherent arguments for their opinions, they yet hold those all the more inflexibly.

Our failure to rationally process information is not only due to our tendency to think pictorially. Such a breakdown is also worsened by the massive amounts of lightly interpreted information received from the mass media. In this additional way words increasingly lose meaning.[56] In "a wasteland of empty verbiage . . . we suffer from an excess of information broadcast everywhere about everything, so that its quality is utterly destroyed." Having "been exposed to too many words and too much information, I must defend myself against these invasions; my mind closes up spontaneously, to keep me from being torn to pieces. . . . I have stopped listening. I refuse to hear (without even realizing it)."[57]

When written and spoken communication is depreciated, as is occurring in our time, human rational specificity diminishes, and thus it becomes increasingly difficult to understand God's revelation in Jesus Christ. The capacity to use words to gain understanding and to find meaning does not guarantee that one will encounter God through

---

50. Ibid., 37. Generally, spoken words are more emotionally hot than written ones, but both, more emotionally cool than pictures.

51. A picture is not "worth a thousand words," because apart from previous or current interpretation pictures exhibit limited meaning.

52. Ibid., 8, 214.

53. Ibid., 37. TV, films and the internet utilize both images and words, but images often so dominate that words make little impression.

54. Ellul does not mean visualizable verbal images or analogies.

55. Ibid., 217.

56. Ibid., 211, 155. Such short written expressions of *opinion* as currently Trumpeted about, with equally short and fallacious supporting "evidence" is propaganda and does not exhibit linear thinking.

57. Ibid., 156–7.

Christ, but a diminishing of such capacities makes it more difficult to understand the meaning of biblically depicted revelation and later verbal and written witnessing. Though a renewal of challenging attestation does not guarantee Christian revival, its absence all but ensures the opposite. So, penultimately, for what linguistic sharing can contribute to understanding Jesus Christ, Christians need to rediscover and reaffirm the importance of thoughtful and serious written and oral communication.

Chapter 17

Biblical Hermeneutics[1]

IN THE PREVIOUS CHAPTER and chapter 13, section 8 we recognized the creative, dialogical, cultural and linguistic nature of interpreting and have seen that no one can approach such a task as a blank slate. Christians must nevertheless strive to be faithful to Christ and claim the freedom from bondage to this world and to ourselves that Christ enables.

1. Jesus's Parables as Hermeneutically Challenging[2]

Some types of liberal theology thought that the teachings of Jesus (and the parables in particular) are simple and easily accessible. This is far from the case. Though much of Jesus's teaching appealed to everyday experience, His thinking was determined by His convictions about God and conditioned by His expectation of the coming of an eternal kingdom in the lifetime of those then living. Because of these factors He often used metaphors from daily life in highly unusual ways. Thus interpretive labor is required even concerning Jesus's teachings, not just with other parts of the Bible.[3]

Certainly there are common elements in the teachings of Jesus, including His parables:

> The lilies of the field, the patches on the garment, the women sweeping the house or putting leaven in bread, the fishermen separating the good fish from the bad; but other elements are far from commonplace and seem, on the contrary, to be colossal exaggerations: the man digging a hole in the garden to keep a huge sum of money, or the king who, when guests did not turn up at his son's wedding, sent his forces and destroyed the whole lot, burning their city. This suggests something more like poetry or unrealistic fiction than like

---

1. See chap. 3, sec. 3; chap. 7, sec. 3; chap. 15, sec. 5.

2. See chap. 5, sec. 3 for another discussion of Jesus' use of parables. See chap. 2, sec. 6 concerning analogical language.

3. One should not assume that all aspects of Jesus' parables or even all of His parables came from Him.

everyday experience.... The basis is not so much experience but notions that, whether familiar or rather fantastic, as they often are, can make contact with common experience ... or can be seen to enlarge it or enrich it [or challenge it]. It is well stated by Sallie McFague. "[The parables] work on a pattern of *orientation, disorientation, and reorientation*: the parable begins in the ordinary world with its conventional standards and expectations, but in the course of the story a radically different perspective is introduced, often by means of a surrealistic extravagance, that disorients the listener, and, finally, through the interaction of the two competing viewpoints tension is created that results in a reorientation, a redescription of life in the world."[4]

The theologically based unexpected twists of Jesus's parables cause His description of everyday experience to seem strange and unexpected. Ricoeur emphasizes the extravagant nature of many of Jesus's parables. They speak of small seeds growing into unusually large plants, or of "workers being paid far beyond what they have earned, of a prodigal son being welcomed home [with no repentance required], and so on." These represent a metaphorical "intensification" or "transgression," that "point beyond their immediate signification toward the Wholly Other."[5]

Ricoeur argued that metaphorical language in general and, like McFague, that parables in particular utilize a dynamic, complex, and elusive is/is not framework that implies that a point may be culturally common at one level and uncommon at another.[6] It may be that we cannot reach the new apart from metaphorical language's linguistic innovation and capacity to project new worlds.[7] "Metaphor's potency also lies in the focused way in which it can frame an entire discourse. It is in this sense that it is now more commonly recognized that neither science nor philosophy nor theology ... can do without metaphor."

Having learned from NT parable interpretation, Ricoeur (contrary to Schleiermacher) concluded that Christian hermeneutics is not only a subcategory of hermeneutics, but, while sharing many characteristics with the latter, stretches general hermeneutics "to the breaking point as it attempts to interpret discourse about God."[8]

---

4. Barr, *Biblical Faith/Natural Theology*, 191; my emphasis, quoting from *Models of God*.

5. Stiver, *After Ricoeur*, 119, describing Ricoeur's perspective.

6. Ibid., 107, citing Ricoeur, *Biblical Hermeneutics*, 88. Parables are extended metaphors, and "a good metaphor implies an intuitive perception of the similarity in dissimilars" (Aristotle) (Stiver, *After Ricoeur*, 109).

7. Stiver, *After Ricoeur*, 108.

8. Ibid., 108, 120.

2. Facets of Christian Hermeneutical Activity with Reference to Scripture

No carrying out of specific procedures can guarantee that Christian interpreters will hear God speaking through Scripture, understand Her correctly, and be claimed by Her. However, as *an exercise of Christian freedom and responsibility in listening attentively*, Christian expositors can and should engage in specific interpretive activity. We are most likely to understand the scriptural message if, in addition to reading Scripture and praying for understanding, we study biblical texts in the following ways, while being careful not to play one or more of these off against one or more of the others.

First, we should take seriously the historical and literary particularity of biblical verses. Historically and literarily precise reading may affect the understanding of different texts in varying ways. (a) When read in such ways, some passages may seem to speak directly today. For example, the double love commandments or the teaching that we are to love God because He in Christ first loved us. Yet our understanding of even such verses is not identical to that of the author or the first readers or hearers. (b) Other texts at a historically accurate plain reading level may reflect legitimate principles capable of wider application than was envisioned by their authors or was possible at that time. For example, though Paul said that in Christ there is neither Jew nor Greek, slave nor free, male nor female (Gal 3:28), we should extend this principle more widely than he did. Paul worked out the broad implication of equality only in the case of the relationship of Jew and Greek. Though in the churches he founded, slaves apparently had equal standing with others (see Philemon), Paul did not challenge societal slavery. (Had he done so the Roman empire would likely have sought to crush the emerging church.) Nor did Paul in a general way develop an egalitarian understanding of the relationship between men and women, as in marriage, though he, unlike his redactor, apparently welcomed women as preachers and teachers and in the exercise of other charismatically guided leadership roles. (c) With historically and literarily precise readings some texts need to be critiqued in the light of conflicting biblical teachings whose truth has won our acceptance. For example, the holy war tradition of the OT as incompatible with Jesus's insistence that we are to love even "enemies."

To read biblical passages intelligibly we need to take some account of the probable historical environment in which they were written, which for the Synoptics was preceded by an oral period. For parts of books that seem to have had earlier oral and/or literary forms, we do well to consider what such utterances would likely have meant in such contexts, as well as try to develop historically informed opinions as to the nature of the events to which such texts originally referred. Toward achieving these ends expositors should seek grammatical understandings of the meaning of Scripture, and utilize historical-critical procedures.[9] "The historical-critical method of biblical

---

9. Barth, *CD*, 1/2:723; Barth, *Göttingen Dogmatics*, 257.

investigation has its rightful place.[10] . . . : it is concerned with the preparation of the intelligence—and this can never be superfluous."[11]

> The witness of the prophets and apostles is a collection of records of concrete historical situations. As I study these, I unavoidably try to reconstruct these situations. On the basis of what is in the text I try to establish how things were then, what the authors had in mind when they said this or that, and apart from the authors and the texts how the events took place which they record. I combine these findings with other things that the same author might have said about the same [or related] subjects. . . . When the text is silent, I try to supplement its thoughts with cautious conjectures so as to form them into a whole. I try to understand them on the basis of what earlier or contemporary authors [of their time] say on whom they might be dependent or with whom they might share a common legacy.[12]

This quotation and the one in note 10 show that Barth did encourage us to look *behind* texts and narratives, however little we may see evidence of his doing so.

Though Barth sought to establish probable "authorial intent" and even to reach opinions that could lead to historical reconstructions, unlike most advocates of historical-critical method he regarded this activity as but *one procedure for attentively listening to Scripture. He did not think that the meaning or meanings in original historical/literary contexts reflect the final or full canonical significance, or the significance for today.* Barth's criticism was not directed at historical-critical study as such, but at the historicist assumption of the then current guild of biblical scholars, "in accordance with which the meaning of the text was reduced to its historical sense."[13]

Historicism assumed that Scripture and all other historical texts can and should be read in purely historical ways. It was foreshadowed in the fifteenth and sixteenth centuries' humanist confidence that by the impartiality of pure objectivity we could "return to the sources." Such humanists as Erasmus (and to a degree Zwingli and Calvin) were also naive in failing to recognize the historical conditionedness of biblical writers' views and of the exegetes—and in under-emphasizing the hermeneutically significant role of tradition for both. Though Zwingli and Calvin were much influenced by the humanist concern to get back to the sources, their Christian need for present theological meaning prevented them from looking only backward. [14]

---

10. Early in his career, when Barth was particularly concerned about the misuse of historical-critical method, he nevertheless wrote, "I have nothing whatever to say against historical criticism. I recognize it, and once more state quite definitely that it is both necessary and justified" (Barth, *Romans*, "Preface," 2nd ed., 6).

11. Barth, *Romans*, "Preface," 1st ed., 1. The next two methods Barth advocates are also but tools to prepare the intellect.

12. Barth, *Göttingen Dogmatics*, 256.

13. McCormack, *Barth's Dialectical Theology*, 232.

14. Historicism in purer form began with Herder in the eighteenth century with the advent of more refined historical methods, and was reflected in Hegel in the eighteenth and nineteenth centuries

Historicists' careful textual and literary reading of Scripture was the means by which unjustified claims on behalf of later church tradition could be exposed and challenged. Insofar as later traditions were historically unjustified they needed to be challenged, but the process of criticism could not rest on the illusory objectivism of historicism.

Lest we have no sympathy with historicism's reaction, we should recognize that until the fifteenth and sixteenth centuries, "a historical phenomenon [was] always seen in indissoluble and ultimately unproblematic fusion with the history of its effects."[15] Though such an uncritical fusion is illegitimate, so also is it hermeneutically impossible to separate events from the effects by which they are still remembered (Gadamer).

By itself the historically focused critical method manifests an oversimplified and distorted view of what exegesis entails. When taken in isolation such a method conflicts with the fact that the books of the Bible were written to help bring us to God—as Zwingli and Calvin recognized—not primarily to provide information about the past.[16] Because historically focused critics tended to look only backward they caused past events to seem strange, distant and devoid of transcendent reference.[17]

Without being guilty of imprisonment in the past, *Schleiermacher's hermeneutic* rightly built from the fact that historical texts were first addressed to original recipients. Therefore, only historical interpretation does justice to the Bible's authors' rootedness in their own time and place.[18] What interpreters learn concerning historical meanings can help them perceive present meanings, and present meanings need to be corrected by historical meanings, lest the Bible become like a wax nose that can be bent as interpreters choose. Even so, trying to empathize fully with a writer or writing,

---

and Troeltsch in the nineteenth and twentieth centuries. Purer historicism is inherently deterministic, since it regards "any person, event, culture, institution, or philosophy as capable of being explained solely in terms of its historical antecedents" (Harvey, *Historian/Believer*, 119). Tracing the variations among these and numerous other later exemplars is beyond the scope of my purpose, since I am referring to a continuity going back to the fifteenth and sixteenth centuries.

15. Hahn, *Historical Investigation*, 15.

16. Ibid., 26–29. "The distancing and objectifying procedure of historical criticism does not do justice to the tendency and the explicit aims of the texts that have come down to us" (same source, 28). Both Testaments have theological reasons for portraying the past with concern for present meaning. In the NT the confession of the One who is risen and exalted and awareness of the activity of the Spirit have left their marks even on texts dealing with other topics. One thinks, for example, of the Synoptic accounts of Jesus' calling of His first disciples, which seems to assert that the mere command of a stranger compelled them to follow. Perhaps these narratives were molded by the church's awareness of the Spirit's evoking work in inner selves. Yet these Gospels, but primarily the Synoptics, are the main sources of information concerning the "Jesus of History"—Jesus as understood through historical-critical assessment of sources.

17. The opposite method, equally illegitimate, uses texts only as springboards for expressing current views.

18. Schleiermacher, *Hermeneutics*, 104.

as Schleiermacher attempted, may be too unrealistic to comprehend the "necessary movement in interpretation *from otherness, to possibility, to similarity in difference.*"[19]

As Richard Palmer has aptly stated, Schleiermacher's historical interpretation "'is the reverse of the act of composition, for it starts with the fixed and finished expression and [seeks to go] back to the mental life from which it arose.'"[20] Contrary to the common interpretation of Schleiermacher, he did not in romantic fashion seek to discern only the *feelings* of authors, but by historically studying authors' writings sought also to understand their *thinking*. Schleiermacher described texts as structured wholes that communicate subject matter using general patterns of language and individual styles.[21] He regarded the apprehension of writers' thinking as possible only by studying the unique ways authors utilized the language of their day.[22]

In the light of Schleiermacher's *Handwritten Manuscripts*, Gadamer seems incorrect in thinking that he was preoccupied with recreating the psychological experience of the author and indifferent to the content the author wished to communicate.[23] Schleiermacher, like Gadamer, Barth and many others, considered understanding to be about a topic.[24] Schleiermacher, unlike Gadamer, insisted that discerning an author's attitude and experience can shed light on his intention, and that knowledge of an author's probable intention contributes to our understanding of the texts he authored. This does not mean that we can comprehend a biblical texts' present meaning only when we have strong opinions concerning its original purpose.

Unlike Barth, some recent expositors seem to care only about the final or redacted form of Scripture and are largely indifferent to historical questions: Particular biblical scholars (such as Childs),[25] some theologians interested in literary/narrative approaches (Frei and others), a cultural/linguistic theologian (Lindbeck), a literary/pragmatic/churchly theologian (Kelsey),[26] and two hermeneutical philosophers (Gadamer usually and Ricoeur to an extent).[27] One hears the practical effects of such history-negating tendencies in an abundance of historically dishonest preaching.

Barth's general position was not historically indifferent: He did believe that the Risen Christ can and does speak through the redacted form of scriptural texts, especially when interpreted through preaching. But he also believed that an aspect of hermeneutical freedom and responsibility involves the historical-critical effort to understand texts according to their historical and literary contexts and meanings, with

---

19. Tracy, *Plurality/Ambiguity*, 20–21; my emphasis.
20. Quoted in Thiselton, *Two Horizons*, 224.
21. Jeanrond, *Theological Hermeneutics*, 72.
22. Schleiermacher, *Hermeneutics*, 97–98, 100.
23. Gadamer, *Truth/Method*, 259, 264.
24. Ibid., 158. See point 2 below.
25. See chap. 7, sec. 4.
26. Within the second point below is an evaluation of Lindbeck's and Kelsey's perspectives.
27. See the next paragraph and also chap. 16, sec. 4.

inquiry about the historical accuracy or inaccuracy of referents. He did not regard such historical and literary meanings as all-important or even as most important, but as penultimately useful for preparing to hear what God may be saying through Scripture today.

Gadamer is correct in thinking that what is fixed in writing has become to a considerable extent detached from the contingency of its origin and author and become free for new relationships.[28] In this respect Ricoeur learned from Gadamer: "An autonomous text calls for new appropriations without obliging these to conform to the possible intentions of the text's author, its original communicative context and its original addressees."[29] Certainly the meaning of passages is also somewhat indeterminate and open to more than one valid interpretation. Even so, interpretations are likely to be distorted if questions about authorial purposes are ignored.[30] The older historical-critical method should not be neglected for the sake of recognizing the dynamic role of the texts in the present.

A second facet of responsible hermeneutical activity is to reflect theologically concerning the Subject Matter to whom Scripture points.[31] "Barth called for a reasoned out, instrumental use of historical criticism in the service and interest of a theological interpretation that penetrates beyond historical analyses. . . . He demanded and practiced what Rudolf Smend has suggestively and happily termed a 'post-critical exposition of Scripture,' that is, an interpretation which does not stay with or mire down in historical-critical problems, but penetrates through them to the revelatory witness that shines from Scripture."[32]

Barth was unhappy that the historical scientific study of his day had tended to divorce scriptural expressions from the Transcendent Reference to whom they point. The difference between Barth's views of Paul and of other biblical authors, and the views of the critics was basic. The reigning biblical science regarded Paul as an object of interest in his own right; Barth saw him as a *witness* pointing Beyond.[33] Historians were studying Paul as though his faith focused upon his own piety and self-understanding,

---

28. Gadamer, *Truth/Method*, 357; see also 353.

29. Jeanrond, *Theological Hermeneutics*, 71, summarizing Ricoeur.

30. If the work of an author seems to have been altered by an editor we need to examine the theological differences between the two sources and in the case of conflicts choose between them. This was done in chap. 7, sec. 3 concerning possible differences between Paul and a Pauline editor of 1 Cor concerning women's leadership in the church. If a writing seems to be a composite, we need to perceive the various ingredients and theological purposes of the contributors and of the redactor, and inquire as to how the redactor may have enriched or distorted his sources. One thinks of the writers of Genesis through Joshua—the Yahwist (J), Elohist (E), Priestly (P), and Deuteronomist (D) sources—that were then reworked by a redactor, likely the writer of the J source.

31. Barth, *Romans*, "Preface," 2nd ed., 8; Barth, *CD*, 1/2:727. See chap. 3 above.

32. Stuhlmacher, *Historical/Theological Interpretation*, 49–50. One who is postcritical continues to learn from the Enlightenment, and should not to be confused with those who are precritical, who have not passed through the Enlightenment's cleansing fire.

33. McCormack, "Barth's Exegesis of NT," 327.

rather than upon the God whom he tells us was at the center of his faith and experience and reflection. Barth thought that if historical criticism did its proper scientific work, rather than expressing secular and psychological bias, it would attest that Paul's faith was in Jesus Christ, not in his own experience understood as autonomous.

Barth believed that real understanding arises only where the interpreter is confronted by the same Reality as the first witness. To *understand* Paul is not just to discover how what he said can somehow be repeated in a different language, "but how it can be *rethought*, and what it may perhaps *mean*."[34] Bultmann added that such exegesis "comes to what is meant only through what is said, and yet measures what is said by what is meant." "When I discover in my exegesis of Romans tensions and contradictions, heights and depths, . . . I am doing it from the point of view of showing where and how the subject matter is expressed, in order to grasp the subject matter, which is greater even than Paul. . . . No [person]—not even Paul—can always speak only from the subject matter itself."[35] As we stand before the God whom we come to know in Christ, we can feel obligated to extend particular lines of biblical thought or stand with one aspect of Scripture against another.

Since the primary theme of the Bible is God, if one is unwilling to reflect concerning Him, one's understanding of biblical texts will be limited. "Experience suggests that certain levels and dimensions of scripture are not explored except when [inquirers] are prepared . . . to think theologically, to ask the question how would it be if this were really true of God? Or, to take a simple illustration from philosophy, how much would the study of an ancient thinker like Plato have been impoverished if throughout the ages scholars had confined themselves to expounding the text and its internal semantic linkages and had rigorously excluded from their minds the question 'Is Plato right?'"[36]

H. Richard Niebuhr's referential hermeneutic (one that points beyond the text) was similar to Kierkegaard's and Barth's and likely influenced by them. It demonstrates the difference between reading biblical texts only descriptively versus descriptively and normatively, with the whole as subject to internal correction, reformulation and extension. "Dr. Richard Niebuhr well says of the prophets that 'One must look with them and not [merely] at them to verify their visions.'" For in looking with them we become contemporaneous with them in their seeing and in what they saw. "As far as it is given to us we are seeing now what they saw long ago."[37] Thus we are honoring their witness, rather than them.

We can more clearly understand referential reading by contrasting this with George Lindbeck's and David Kelsey's hermeneutics. Whereas Barth saw the Bible as pointing to the Living and Transcendent God, Lindbeck in effect regards the Bible as

---

34. Barth, *Romans*, "Foreword," 2nd ed., 91.
35. Bultmann, "Theological Exegesis/NT," 241, 120.
36. Barr, Biblical Study/Theology, 7–8.
37. Baillie, *Revelation/Recent Thought*, 107, who includes the quotation from *Meaning/Revelation*, 72.

pointing to itself. "The meaning of a text does not depend upon an outside referential verification, but scriptural meaning is understood only within a self-related whole."[38] Because the central feature of Lindbeck's biblical hermeneutic is its emphasis on "intratextuality" Childs is unconvinced that Lindbeck's view is the way the Bible actually functions or should function within the church. Though Childs also pays close attention to biblical interactions, he (like Barth) insists that the church should be listening for the voice of the Transcendent Lord, heard in part amid biblical interpretation, not autonomously seeking mere intratextual wisdom to solve her problems. Lindbeck either substitutes intratextual wisdom for the Holy Spirit or assumes that is itself God's voice. Lindbeck appeals to Barth's phrase "the strange new world within the Bible," suggesting that Barth also envisioned drawing the community of faith into the mere linguistic world of the Bible.[39] However, Lindbeck's hermeneutic does an injustice to Barth's understanding. For Barth the Bible above all bears witness to the Word of God who is Jesus Christ.[40] The real danger in much of Lindbeck's essay is that "'talk about text stands in the place of talk about God.'"[41]

Lindbeck's former colleague, David Kelsey, also takes a similarly literary approach to Scripture and in addition utilized the Bible within the confines of pragmatism.[42] Kelsey "places the emphasis on the functional role of the Bible to shape, order, and critique the continuing life of the Christian community. He argues that the authority of the Bible does not lie primarily in its content, but [in] how it is used 'to empower new human identities' (*The Bible and Christian Theology*, 395)." To the contrary, the Bible can legitimately function in the second sense only if it already decisively functions in the first. Childs's "reaction to this ecclesiastically functional view of theology is to question whether one can speak meaningfully about faithful forms of life within the Christian community before first establishing the identity and will of God who in Jesus Christ calls the church into being, and whose purpose encompasses the entire creation."[43]

In sum, Childs remains highly critical of any theological position in which intratextuality becomes the theological stopping point, rather than the springboard for listening for the Holy Spirit, or where pragmatic anthropological and ecclesiological

---

38. Childs, *Biblical Theology OT/NT*, 21.

39. Lindbeck's literary hermeneutic parallels that of Erich Auerbach—a literary and non-theological contemporary who taught at Yale University—not Barth. Auerbach also greatly influenced the narrative theology of Hans Frei.

40. Childs, *Biblical Theology OT/NT*, 21, 22.

41. Ibid., 22, quoting R Thiemann.

42. Pragmatic philosophies are controlled by concerns for the supposed practical benefits of ideas, beliefs or practices. See chap. 19, sec. 8.

43. Childs, *Biblical Theology OT/NT*, 23.

concerns take precedence over Christology.[44] Though I have plenty of disagreements with Childs,[45] I have learned much from him and entirely concur at these points.

A third aspect of hermeneutical activity, closely related to empathetically grasping Scripture's Theme, concerns seeking to apply it within one's life. Without this additional facet of interpretive activity the endeavor to understand Scripture in terms of its setting becomes a mere historical survey, and the reflective effort to think about its Subject Matter, idle speculation. Contrary to attempts to isolate understanding of the past from present meaning, *we who live in history have no hope of grasping what a biblical text meant in the past unless we not only struggle to perceive what it means today, but what it means morally.* God who speaks amid biblical texts wills to master our whole life.[46] We must, however, beware that concern for moral application inhibits us from seeking to understand the probable meanings of texts in their earlier contexts. Such indifference would ironically be morally self-defeating: "The appropriateness of the application of a transmitted text to a current substantive problem cannot be scrutinized without reflecting upon the historical difference between the present and the past situations, and on that which nevertheless links the two together. Indeed, just such historical reflection . . . may, under certain conditions, free one for the first time for the present's particular possibilities of action . . ."[47] Though we should respect the distance between past and present, God wills to use Scripture to renew our relationship with Him and to lift us morally (Rom 15:4–5). God intends to use Scripture not only for teaching, but *"for reproof, for correction, and for training in righteousness, that the [person] of God may be complete, equipped for every good work"* (1 Tim 3:16–17, my emphasis).

As mentioned with reference to Gadamer in chapter 16, section 4, seeking to apply a text is not subsequent to understanding, but is an essential part of the attempt to ascertain meaning. The thinking of pietists in general and John Wesley in particular is in agreement with Barth concerning the importance of inward appropriation and moral application for understanding the meaning of Scripture.[48] In German pietism interpreting meant reading texts in such ways that the reader's existence is given meaning. "In England in the early part of the seventeenth century application was already held [by the pietists] to be one facet of the procedure for preparing oneself to hear the word of God with understanding." Moral application in hermeneutics "is

---

44. Ibid., 23. Is not Kelsey guilty of secularizing Christian faith? Does not ecclesiastical pragmatism take the place of the Holy Spirit's independent and free activity? Even were God dead this biblical hermeneutic would still work.

45. See chap. 7, sec. 4.

46. Barth, *CD*, 1/2:736, 737.

47. Pannenberg, *Basic Questions*, 1:134. See chap. 16, sec. 4.

48. Augustine certainly interpreted Scripture with decisive concern for ethical application. He thought that Scripture's goal is to engender love of God and neighbor. Believing this he reverted to the only procedure he knew for blunting the force of passages that conflict with the double love commandment, figurative interpretation (Childs, *Biblical Theology OT/NT*, 38, citing Augustine, *Christian Doctrine*, 3, 9, 14).

not something one does after one has understood. It is inseparable from the process of understanding."[49]

To summarize this section to this point and to conclude it: True biblical interpretation entails seeking to establish probable original meaning and authorial intent, considering broader theological significance, and making moral applications. But more is involved. *Interpreters must fourthly listen for God's speaking through texts, judging and renewing us.*[50] All along—but especially concerning the previous two levels—God's Spirit is required to gain full insight. Both for us and for those to whom we bear witness, ultimately and finally "God is His own interpreter, And He will make it plain."[51]

3. A Culture Critical Warning

Lest the Gadamer discussion in chapter 16, section 4 encourage us to be one-sidedly affirmative concerning culture, it must be emphasized that we need to be critically discerning. Certainly those who preach or teach must seek to relate Christian Faith to the various contexts that have influenced the particular people with whom they communicate, for culturally that is where people begin. But no one should remain where they were. That would not help anyone to become Christian or to become more deeply so. Whether in Africa or elsewhere, people must not equate old or new cultural customs with God's commands. Furthermore, each person is influenced by variety of contexts, not just general cultural ones. Such conditioning backgrounds include the influences of parents, spouse and friends, as well as genetic factors, educational opportunities or lack thereof, and much more. But if we are seeking to be *Christ's* disciples we must allow God's revelation in Christ to challenge and redirect our prior understandings. Christ is to be our Master and we His servants.

Some of the natural theologies of the eighteenth century assumed that Christianity involves little more than a republishing of the laws of nature—including naturally perceptible morality. Thus Christian Faith was compromised in the name of whatever was culturally popular. I fear that some of the Christian theologies currently emanating from Africa and elsewhere may be doing something similar. Without explicitly reasserting supposed natural laws, tribal or national customs are nevertheless being uncritically reaffirmed by many Christians. With such conformity Christian Faith in effect becomes little more than a cheering section for what by nature is supposedly knowable—thus the parallelism with the eighteenth century natural theology that widely endorsed slavery. Yet, as in the eighteenth century, many of today's customs and ways of thinking do not agree with Christian Faith, and to a considerable extent

---

49. Michalson, "Hermeneutics/Holiness/Wesley," 129.

50. Barth, *CD*, 1/2:739.

51. From the hymn *God Moves in a Mysterious Way*. This fourth point is not really a "method," but an attitude of spiritual openness to the Living Word that God wills to speak amid the first three procedures.

ethnic groups disagree with other ethnic groups, and one nation's customs often conflict with those of other nations. May not Christian Faith as grounded in adaptation to various cultures fragment the Body of Christ, dishonor Christ's transcendent lordship, and negate Christians' pilgrim presence in the world? Eventually the only thing Christians around the world may have in common may be that (at least for the moment) they retain the name "Christian."

God once-and-for-all came into history in Christ and is known only as we come into fellowship with God through the Holy Spirit. Relationship with this God is not something everyone already has, not even "notoriously religious Africans" (Mbiti). Even such people do not by their natural religiousness know of nor honor the God disclosed in Christ. Nor can anyone's Traditional Religion legitimately be amalgamated with Christian Faith. When it is, Christian Faith becomes a way of trying to manipulate the divine into fulfilling our selfish desires for wealth and pleasure. Though western explicit paganism or Traditional Religion has long been eclipsed, an equivalent "prosperity gospel" paganizing has become popular in the West, in Africa and in many parts of the world.

To come to the God revealed in Christ involves overcoming an offense that guarantees the discontinuity of Christ with every culture. The offensiveness of faith in Christ was experienced in first century Jewish culture: The One whom Christians proclaimed as Messiah had died as a condemned criminal, but the OT had said that one who dies in this way is cursed by God (Deut 21:22–23; cf. Gal 3:13). Even if the curse theory is not convincing to people of non-Jewish cultures, dying a criminal's death on a cross is no naturally attractive way for God to reveal Himself. That the Messiah died in such circumstances means that to come to Christ people must surmount this barrier. The need to overcome this offense shows that Christian Faith is considerably different from religion in general and the prosperity gospel in particular. For the natural way to picture God is not as one who would humble Himself in this way, and similarly call His followers to take up their daily crosses and follow Him. The offense of Jesus's cross can be legitimately transcended only by those who by God's grace fall on their knees, confess their sin, and recognize their share in the world's rebellion against the true God that led to His rejection when incarnate. *Concerning faith in the Crucified Christ and much else, the point of contact is often the point of conflict*. If we minimize the conflict we will not help people to make decisive transition toward radical Christ-centering and costly discipleship, rather than some compromising alliance with worldly idolatries.

Let us consider an alternative model to one determined to adapt to culture. This comes from Karl Barth's personal example prior to World War 1 and 2. Barth pastored in neighboring Switzerland when Germany (under Kaiser Wilhelm) was engaging in the expansionist policies that led to World War 1. Though such imperialistic and militaristic tactics were terrible, the shattering event for Barth was related, but different. He became disillusioned when he learned that his revered theological lecturers in Germany had signed their endorsement of Kaiser Wilhelm's blatant aggression. Not only did the Kaiser want Germany to have more land and resolved to steal it, but the cultural theologians sprinkled holy water on the ghastly enterprise. Both the Kaiser and those theologians seemed to think that whatever was good for Germany could not be incompatible with Christian Faith. In the context of such compromises with culture Barth may have undergone the transition experience of his life. For him theology that blended seamlessly with culture collapsed, and a more direct relationship with the Living God was thereafter seen as essential for life and theology. For the remainder of his twelve years as a pastor, he, in his preaching and in the first and second editions of his commentary on Romans, struggled to develop a theology founded upon God's Word addressed to humankind, rather than on one emerging from easy alliance with the sinful ways of this world.[52]

Barth was later called to teach Christian dogmatics in Germany, where he had done much of his university study. He taught in three German universities for fourteen years, where his new theology that centered on Jesus Christ was eventually put to the test by Adolf Hitler: University teachers (as state employees) were required to sign oaths of allegiance to Hitler. Barth refused, since he thought the Nazis would understand such oaths as requiring complete endorsement of Hitler and whatever policies he chose to pursue. Barth insisted that he owed ultimate allegiance to God alone. He even had the audacity to explain his Christian reasoning to Hitler in a letter. Those actions could have gotten him killed, but (perhaps because he was Swiss) he was merely escorted by the gestapo to the German-Swiss border and told not to return. For the rest of his life he worked tirelessly to articulate a theology that was as free as possible from compromising entanglements with the assumptions of western or any other culture.

Barth's motivation for seeking to distance Christian Faith from culture was not primarily due to disillusionment with culture—western or otherwise—but had its source in gratitude for God's act of reconciliation in Jesus Christ. Is Barth not right? If God has spoken uniquely in Christ, which we must surely believe if we are Christians, must we not struggle to reorient our thought and life on "The Church's One Foundation"? Must not this be our focus, rather than preoccupation with our South African, Kenyan, Nigerian, American, British, Japanese or whatever other national background or tribal orientation?

We have all come from cultural contexts, and many aspects of our backgrounds are good or neutral—but many are not. However this may be, we come to Christ from where we are, and our backgrounds can help us to raise the questions that can begin hermeneutical dialogue. But to become and remain Christians we must become and remain people of the coming kingdom, which means that our backgrounds must be critically scrutinized in the light of our knowledge of Jesus Christ. Because we are

---

52. Jacques Ellul extended Kierkegaard's and Barth's critical approaches to culture by critiquing a variety of new commonplaces.

sinners none of us fully succeeds in making our thinking and behavior consistent with God's disclosure in Christ. But unless the various contextual ingredients of who we are become subjected to Christ's judgment and correction, we remain idolaters. Out of gratitude for what has been done for us and the world, ought we not to commit ourselves decisively to struggle to purify our natural thought and action in the light of the God manifest in Jesus Christ? Can we be satisfied with doing anything less?

Thematic Exposition Begins

Chapter 18

Relationship of Christian Faith to Historical Revelation[1]

WITH THIS CHAPTER AND the final one we remain within the more procedural discussions of *Volume 1* while moving into detailed consideration of theological beliefs.

The word "faith" is used in two interrelated ways in the Bible and by Christians today, and both are essential. This and the next chapter refer both to faith as the *relationship with Christ/activity of believing* in Him and to faith as the *content* of what one believes concerning Him.[2]

1. Essential Problem not Temporal Distance, but Gap Caused by Sin

The interpretive problem posed by the historical fact that Jesus lived long ago and far away is minor compared to the fact that the God revealed in Jesus Christ is holy and that we sinners have no natural right or capacity to live in relationship with this God. This greatest interpretive barrier to be surmounted was expressed by Peter when he recognized that because he was a sinful person he was not entitled to live in fellowship with God (Luke 5:8). The author of Isaiah 6:5 perceived the same hiatus: Upon seeing God high on a throne and hearing the words "holy, holy, holy" he confessed that he was a person of unclean lips who dwelt amid a people of unclean lips. Similarly, Malachi asked, "who may abide the day of his coming and who shall stand when he appears?" (3:2)

---

1. See chap. 2, sec. 5.

2. Throughout the remainder of this book we deal with both facets, though the emphasis will sometimes be on the subjective dimension (relationship with Christ and the activity of believing in Him) and at other times on the objective aspect (what is believed concerning Him). The traditional Latin distinction between *fides qua creditur* and *fides quae creditur*—the faith that believes and what faith believes—provides little help, since it considers faith entirely in terms of cognition. The formula does not attest that relationship with Christ and discipleship under Him are integral aspects of faith.

With the overcoming of the spiritual and moral problem of the relationship between Jesus Christ and us, the technical problem of the relationship between the then and there and the here and now also becomes solvable.[3] *Insofar as by the power of the Holy Spirit we accept God's judgment concerning our sinfulness and live from God's forgiveness in Christ and empowerment through Him we can perceive the relevance of God's saving deed in Him.* Such perception does not overcome all historical and interpretive problems, but challenges the idea that what happened long ago and far away has no significance for our lives today.

2. Need For Inward Appropriation of Biblical Tradition

Unless we live in relationship with the Savior and Lord our affirmation of biblical tradition concerning Him is mere traditionalism—mere intellectual assent to other people's convictions—mere faith in other people's faith. Under such circumstances we "creep into the existence of others."[4] For only something that inwardly transforms can constitute a *saving* fact for one who wishes to rise out of spiritual weakness.[5]

Christians' knowledge of biblical traditions concerning Jesus benefits from the precise understanding the historical study of the Bible makes possible. Yet purely historical investigation cannot reach Ultimate Reality, which can only be attained as our inner life is enriched by contact with the Living Christ. Such an encounter does not melt away historical problems, but inwardly kindles a spark that makes us certain of

---

3. Barth, Barth, *CD*, 4/1:290, 293.

4. Thielicke, *Modern Faith*, 115. This paragraph and the following, with accompanying notes summarize, critique and reinterpret insights of Wilhelm Herrmann.

5. Herrmann, *Communion/God*, 83.

what we experience.[6] Nothing can have revelatory meaning in our lives except what lifts us into communion with God.[7]

3. Resurrection-Enabled Experience of Justifying Faith Contemporizes Past Revelation in Christ[8]

That Jesus lived and then died on a cross are facts of world history *remembered* because of resurrection-enabled confidence in Jesus's ongoing significance for knowledge of God and for mediating forgiveness. What is special about faith in reconciliation in Christ is the togetherness of the "objective-historical element of revelation and the existential-subjective element."[9] And the paradoxical unity of Word and Spirit, of historical revelation and God's contemporary presence, of Christ for us and Christ in us, is the secret of the Reformation.[10]

In proclaiming Jesus's death and interpreting its meaning, Paul says that outside of us and apart from our personal involvement we have already died with Christ through the representative history that God in Christ effected on our behalf. Nevertheless,

---

6. Ibid., 384. My summary-reinterpretation smooths over two related problems in Herrmann's thinking. He spoke of a twofold action in which NT tradition becomes transparent *through the inherent power of Jesus's human life on the one side and through the inherent power of the believing Christian's experiencing intuition on the other* (Barth, *Theology/Church*, 265). In criticism of this statement, if Jesus's human life had such inherent power His human dimension would have been divinized, resulting in a rejection of the sharp biblical distinguishing between the human and the divine. Furthermore, how can Jesus's *human dimension* then and now be revelatory, since He was not widely recognized while on earth and since as a human He is no longer with us?

Against Herrmann's statement, Jesus's human nature must not be divinized. That "*God* was *in* Christ reconciling the world to himself" (2 Cor 5:19a, my emphases) means that God chose to be incarnate in Jesus and through unique relationship with Him to reconcile the world.

As for the problem on our side of the relationship, if we have the inherent capacity to bring ourselves into fellowship with God we are not the sinners that much of the NT (and of Herrmann's writing) insists we are.

Contrary to Herrmann's careless formulations, the Risen Christ as Spirit empowers our response to God's reconciling action in Jesus. And as the Spirit is active in our lives She connects us with the divine revelation in Jesus Christ, so that we can know the Father in the Son by the Spirit.

Presupposed in this triunitarian solution to Herrmann's conundrum is the recognition of the role of the Risen and Exalted Christ, which overcomes Herrmann's "singling out of the 'inner life' of Jesus as the unique bearer of revelation" (same source, 266). Also overcome is his elevating of Christians' experiencing intuition, which is greatly flawed.

With the above insistence on essential New Testament convictions Barth solved the two-sided problem that in Herrmann's thinking required a solution: How Jesus became God's unique revelation and how we can faithfully respond to God's disclosure in Him.

7. Herrmann, *Communion/God*, 74, 39. Barth learned well this pietistic emphasis from this his most revered teacher. "The fact is that a [person] *cannot* believe what is simply held *before* him. He can believe nothing that is not both *within* him and *before* him. He *cannot* believe what does not *reveal* itself to him, that has not the power to penetrate him" (Barth, *Word of God/Man*, 202).

8. See chap. 16, sec. 3 for ways in which this topic relates to the hermeneutical circle discussion.

9. Barth, *Word of God/Man*, 209.

10. Brunner, *Truth as Encounter*, 76.

Paul also insists that as we trust in Christ we can experience this reality, begin to die to self-centeredness and rise to life centered in Christ. Demonstrating this distinction, the words in regular print in the following passage refer to an immediate or direct personal experience made possible by the Holy Spirit, as well as personal faith in Christ; the emphasized words signify the action of God in Christ in the past. "I have been crucified with Christ; it is no longer I who live, but Christ who lives in me; and the life I now live in the flesh I live by faith in the Son of God, *who loved me and gave himself for me*" (Gal 2:20). Justification of sinners by God's grace in Christ received through faith implies distance and differentiation between God and humankind, with no mystical confusion here or hereafter. In true Christian understanding, the more we realize our relation with God the more clearly we become aware of what still separates us and the more our consciousness of sin intensifies.[11]

By being grounded both in present experience of the Holy Spirit and in historical revelation in Jesus Christ, Christian Faith avoids being a mere composite of subjective experiences or of positivistic historical assertions. That Christians begin with the Risen Christ as Holy Spirit, but seek to have their experience and its implicit knowledge deepened and corrected by historical revelation in Jesus Christ is a uniquely Christian exemplification of the process summarized by the words "hermeneutical circle."[12]

As we seek to interpret and proclaim the significance of the Christ event, we not only seek to understand Jesus's life and self-consciousness, but are to take seriously the NT's interpretations concerning Him. We must go one step further and interpret the meaning of Jesus by interpreting the NT interpretations. As we approach the matter in this way we are able to understand the present meaning of faith in Jesus Christ.

4. Hiddenness of Revelation in Jesus Christ[13]

Christian Faith by its very nature is odd in the extreme, for it claims that the Eternal, Transcendent and Wholly Other God penetrated time in a genuinely human life. Christianity proclaims this *paradox* and thus requires inward appropriation of what is an offense to Jews and folly to Greeks.[14]

Some have thought that faith in Jesus would have been easier had they lived in the days of His earthly life. This wishful thought naively forgets that until God raised Him from death no one *truly* understood who He was and what His coming meant. Because we have sinned away our capacity to know God, She must meet us through grace, thereby implying judgment concerning human perceptions and conceptions. You have hidden "these things from the wise and understanding and revealed them to babes" (Matt 11:25). But the recognition of divine hiddenness has nothing to do with

---

11. Aulen, *Faith/Church*, 21.
12. See chap. 16, sec. 3.
13. See chap. 9, sec. 4; chap. 7, sec. 8, for a brief reference.
14. Kierkegaard, *Unscientific Postscript*, 188, 191.

skepticism and agnosticism, since it is believers who confess that of themselves they have no capacity for knowledge of God.[15]

Because the gospel as God's disclosure is not a creation of mind or emotion or religious instinct it is not obvious (cf. 1 Cor 2:9). Paul certainly did not think that the gospel is absurd or obscure—he calls it wisdom (1 Cor 2:6)—but regarded it as a stumbling-block to those who fail to perceive that God humbled and still humbles Herself to demonstrate Her love. Paul affirmed God's self-emptying (*kenosis*, Phil 2:5–8; 2 Cor 8:9), and divine revelational condescension is elsewhere affirmed in the NT (John 1:9–14, 16–18; Heb 1:1–3a)

5. Eternal in Finite: Lack of Direct Knowability

God becoming an individual person is qualitatively different from being God in Herself, and therefore involves profound *incognito*.[16] Incognito means not being directly recognizable, as when a police person appears in plain clothes, or when the universe's Sovereign uniquely discloses Herself in a single human being.

That God was uniquely present in the Crucified is such an odd belief, overturning normal expectations concerning God's ways, that it will convince only as the Holy Spirit convicts hearers of their sinfulness and of their need for the Savior. The truthfulness of the Christ event *cannot be recognized by the mere receipt of direct knowledge*. Words can testify and clarify but cannot overcome the offensiveness of such an incarnational stooping. "Take away the possibility of offense . . . and Christianity is done away with, for it has become an easy thing, . . . that forgets the infinite qualitative difference between God and [humankind]."[17] Spirit is the denial of direct apprehension. If Christ be very God, He cannot be directly known, "'for to be known directly is the characteristic mark of an idol.'"[18]

Consistent with what has just been said, Barth understood the relationship of sacred history to biblical and general history as indirect, insisting on God's free speech with reference to both. To the contrary, Calvin equated sacred history with biblical history taken without critical appraisal. Against this, though God has revealed Himself in Christ, His Living Word is needed to understand past revelation aright and to hear God speaking amid biblical and general history. Seen in the light of Barth's perspective and Calvin's agreement that God's Living Word is required for knowledge of God, Calvin's equating of sacred history with biblical history is a "mythologizing biblicism."[19] "Biblical *history* in the Old and New Testaments is not really history at all, but seen from above is a series of free divine acts and seen from below [is often] a series

---

15. Cochrane, *Existentialists/God*, 128.
16. Kierkegaard, *Training*, 127.
17. Ibid., 139. See below, chap. 19, sec. 4.
18. Barth, *Romans,* 2nd ed., 38, quoting SK.
19. McCormack, *Barth's Dialectical Theology*, 305, citing Karl Barth, *Die Theologie Calvins/2*, 3.

of fruitless attempts to undertake something in itself impossible. From the viewpoint of ordered development in particular and in general it is quite incomprehensible."[20]

We also try to make Christ's authority directly comprehensible by smoothly integrating Him into our own systems of thought, rather than allowing Christ to challenge our thinking.[21] Contrary to this, God remains God precisely *in* His revelation. Therefore, gaining knowledge of God must not be equated with any worldly magnitude, whether that be our natural psychological experience, our ordinary moral self-consciousness, our speculative reconciliation constructions concerning general history, or even our historical-critical restatements concerning biblical events. Even after the divine reconciliation in Christ, faith is required to discern the meaning of this event.

6. Conflicts with Judaism, Islam, Rationalism, Mysticism, Kantian Moralism, Lessing about Normative Historical Revelation in Christ

Because Christian Faith centers upon God's act of historical revelation in Jesus Christ it differs from Judaism and Islam, which believe in historical revelation, but do not regard the disclosure in Christ as normative. Neither suppose that God uniquely embodied Herself in history to redeem us from sin. Guilt and divine forgiveness also play no essential role in Islam and a lesser role in Judaism than in Christianity.

Christian Faith also conflicts with rationalism, mysticism and Kantian moralism, which do not look to any form of historical revelation for knowledge of Ultimate Reality. Holding an optimistic understanding of human nature and drawing upon Plato and Stoicism, rationalism affirms that natural reason is the only basis for knowledge of all truth. Also, clinging to an optimistic conception of human nature, and well expressed by Plotinus and Eckhart in the West and Hindu and Buddhist traditions in the East, mysticism affirms that direct mystical experience is the sole foundation for "knowledge" of Final Reality.[22] With equal optimism, Kantian moralism regards humans as capable of producing a moral revolution. Kant regarded this as possible because he thought we have within ourselves what is unaffected by sin, an autonomous moral will by which we can provide ourselves with the moral law without needing to look to biblical disclosure. According to him the latter just happens to agree with the golden rule that influenced him.[23]

---

20. Barth, *Word of God/Man*, 72.

21. Thielicke, *Modern Faith*, 501. Schleiermacher thought Jesus had the highest level of (natural) God-consciousness; Ritschl, that He had the strongest amount of (natural) moral awareness; and Hegel and Strauss, that He was the supreme manifestation of their ideas concerning the reconciliation of humankind with God (Thielicke, *Modern Faith*, 501). With such "degree christologies" we regard Jesus as merely illustrating our prior conceptions, and consider Him as differing only in degree from us and thus as not truly God's Word from the other side. The same christological procedure is currently used in parts of Africa, for example, by speaking of Christ as the Great Ancestor.

22. Newbigin, *Gospel/Pluralistic Society*, 2.

23. Brunner, *Scandal/Christianity*, 19.

Relationship of Christian Faith to Historical Revelation

The reason guilt and forgiveness play no role in Muslim, rationalist, mystical or Kantian thinking is because humans do not want their pride infringed upon. Thus the "relation" to God is considered as established in a manner that shows no trace of sin's rupture. Only through the Spirit are we able to recognize that we are sinners redeemed through Christ, and realize that we could not have overcome our proud self-centering on our own.[24]

To elaborate further concerning mysticism: Mystics suppose that whatever affects us from without, even purported divine revelation in Jesus, is only a means toward producing in us a particular experience of calmness and unity. According to "Christian" mysticism, Christ may seem to lead people who become His disciples to the threshold of blessedness. But when at the highest points of their spiritual lives "Christian" mystics step across that threshold, they no longer have to do with Christ, but only with God. For according to mysticism when people find God, they are alone with Her,[25] or are they really alone with themselves?

Mysticism's total inner-outer split dissolves both history and historical revelation. In its logical structure mysticism is everywhere the same. Through contemplation or emotional experience mystics try to gain complete unification with the divine by disentangling the soul from all impressions from the outward world. We must empty our souls and thereby create the requisite conditions of receptivity. Since the initiative is primarily on our side, mysticism involves self-salvation through mystical procedure.[26]

A seeming exception to this rule is provided by the so-called grace mysticism of Hinduism's *Bhakti* doctrine. But by "grace" is only meant submersion in the divine and thereby the supplementing or expansion of the natural self. There is no deliverance from anything standing between God and humans (such as sin and guilt), no forgiveness of sin and no basis for knowledge of God's nature.[27]

In contrast to Ritschl, Herrmann, Brunner and Barth, Tillich thinks that at the last stage of ecstasy classical mysticism denies the possibility of self-salvation. He points out that in spite of all the preparations, when this point has been reached ecstatic reunion with the ultimate cannot be forced.[28] In contrast with this interpretation, not only is "ecstatic reunion" not the same as fellowship with God and others, but is largely seen as a human attainment. For we must climb to the point where God can take us by surprise. Also against Tillich's contention, much of the NT and of classical Christianity have insisted that even our initial impulse toward God is due to grace.

Christian encounter is dialogically personal, rather than merely introspective. Christian Faith not only radically differentiates between One who is holy and infinite

---

24. Ibid., 17, 22.
25. Herrmann, *Communion/God*, 30.
26. Brunner, *Scandal/Christianity*, 19–20.
27. Ibid., 20, 21.
28. Tillich, *ST*, 2:83.

and we who are sinful and finite, but regards God and people as personal agents who freely interact with each other. We learn of God not through mere rumination.

The Christian experience of the Holy Spirit not only differs from mystical religious experience, but from that of Jews and Muslims because the Holy Spirit continues the work of Jesus Christ. The Spirit does this by drawing people toward Him and helping them understand the meaning of God's disclosure in Him.

Agreeing with rationalism and mysticism that God is inactive in history, Lessing thought that whatever occurs in history is merely accidental and that "accidental truths of history" can never establish "universal truths of reason."[29] Lessing's rationalism wrongly assumed that there are universal truths of reason that can be recognized apart from the conditioning provided by historically influenced knowledge. Since Lessing's ahistorical assumption is incorrect, it is no weakness that Christian Faith's cognitions make no pretense of being so founded. The Christ event was no historical accident, but by God's initiative. And what God accomplished in Christ is of universal significance. Such insights are not irrational, but neither are they rationally compelling; were the latter so, Christian Faith would not require a decision of the whole self.

In *Philosophical Fragments* SK's summation concerning Socrates sheds light on the movements discussed above. Socrates, following the Orphic religion that believed in the preexistence of the soul, taught that people for that reason naturally possess ultimate truth. Thus philosophical midwives do not need to teach, but only to ask questions to recall people to what they inherently know. According to Socrates people are not in error concerning ultimate truth, but only in a humanly surmountable state of forgetfulness, that some questioning can overcome.

In contrast SK agreed with the NT that we are in ultimate error and are responsible for turning away from God; therefore we cannot find ultimate truth merely by looking within. Platonic idealism/rationalism, which continued Socrates's theory of knowing, is thus no gateway toward knowledge of the true God. Nor is neo-platonic inspired mysticism. SK disavowed the possibility of the mystical vision in which the individuality of people is swallowed up in the infinity of God.

7. General History Is not Revelation, but Revelation Occurs There: Evaluating Two Philosophies of History[30]

The Hegelian belief that general historical events equal "revelation" can as easily empty God's unique disclosure in Jesus Christ of meaning as can rationalism and mysticism. According to Hegel, God was not *uniquely present* in a person named *Jesus*, but *the Christ idea* exemplifies the increasing co-mingling of God with humankind in universal history. People will have one understanding if they regard history's whole development as God's revelation, as did Hegel, and will have another if they believe

29. Lessing, *Theological Writings*, 53.
30. See chap. 2, sec. 3; chap. 10, sec. 10; chap. 12, sec. 5.

that the normative revelation in Christ must ever again be grasped in its "original nature beyond its historical effects and forms, however important these may be."[31]

In criticism of Hegel's philosophy of history, Christian Faith believes that God has uniquely manifested Herself *only* in the Christ event, though that includes the OT history of promise leading toward Christ and the NT's Spirit-inspired interpretations of His meaning. General history is not regarded as inherently progressive and of itself cannot provide knowledge of God. God can speak within general history, and salvation history occurs there, but Spirit-guided discernment is required.

If we believe that God determines everything that happens in history, then God ordains the evil that She in Christ battled against. Under such circumstances, God wills contradictory things and is happy with whatever results. This is to equate God with fate, which is precisely what the NT does not do.

Certainly God permits the events that occur and affects something in everything that happens, but does not directly cause everything, else God has an immoral side that causes evil. To discover what God may will amid general occurrences we need first to look to the particular events where God's will has been decisively disclosed.[32] In this way we can find insights that help us to discern God's intentions and actions today.

Since Hegelianism regards the Absolute Spirit as immanent in humankind and as realizing itself in and through the human spirit "it virtually identifies the divine with the human. . . . Sin becomes only a necessary 'moment' or stage in the development of the finite spirit and is overcome when the finite spirit realizes its identity with the Absolute Spirit." By denying the transcendence of God and the awful gulf between God and humankind opened up by humankind's sin, Hegelianism, like Platonism in general, seems to make a real Incarnation unnecessary. "Thus, while Hegel and his disciples claimed to be defending Christianity, they were really seeking to 'go beyond' faith by dissolving Christian doctrines into mere symbols of the universal truths of Hegelian philosophy."[33]

Now to evaluate Oscar Cullmann's more recent philosophy of history that purports to reflect the NT perspective, but is in conflict with much of it. Paul understands God's actions in history as largely hidden, with history as a battleground between good and evil—ambiguous to the end. Paul's theology, which centers upon the reconciling work of God in Christ on the cross, requires the spiritual and moral discernment of Christ's will by those living within a sinful world. Rather than regarding God's manifestation as hidden within history, Cullmann's salvation history (Heilsgeschichte) understanding of the NT centers on a *recitation of self-evident, redemptive facts regarded as directly revelational*, with Christ as the mid-point of salvation history and of time.

---

31. Friedrich Gogarten agreeing with Barth's Second Edition Commentary on Romans, from Gogarten, "Holy Egoism," 84.

32. Hordern, *Speaking of God*, 166.

33. Thomas, *Religious Philosophies*, 294.

While conceding that Cullmann reflects a Lukan perspective, Käsemann does not agree that such a view summarizes the church's oldest or her theologically deepest perspective. Salvation history as Cullmann conceives it is an impersonal thing, with no idea of the ways in which sin so habitually challenges God's will. *It relegates faith to knowledge of saving facts, of which none are more important than others.* With both Cullmann and Luke, God's activity requires historically tangible rendition, beginning small with Abraham and resulting in Israel as humanity's representative. But because Israel did not prove to be faithful, the movement again began small, with Christ as the single Faithful One, and ended big, with the church. Käsemann contends that this understanding paralyzes Paul's doctrine of justification by subordinating it to a salvation history scheme, *as though if one gives intellectual assent to these facts one somehow has saving faith.*[34]

We move now from consideration of various theological attitudes concerning history's relationship to Christian Faith to discussing what Christian Faith should and should not expect historical-critical biblical scholarship to accomplish.

8. A Dialectical Perspective Concerning Historical-Critical Biblical Scholarship

Christian Faith does have an historical point of departure—God's unique revelation in Jesus Christ—but is not a direct function of historical-critical scholarship. It would be wonderful if all people were dedicated Christians and also understood historical-critical method. But many are greatly knowledgeable of such scholarship and are non-Christian; many others have no knowledge of biblical criticism and yet are genuinely Christian.

As we have seen in chapter 17, section 2, historical method only had flickering beginnings in the fifteenth and sixteenth centuries. Historical method developed in the eighteenth century and was refined in the nineteenth and following centuries. *Historical scholarship* as applied to the Bible is important for helping to understand the OT background to NT faith and for comprehending NT faith in its specificity. But it *can neither establish nor refute the Christian affirmations of meaning that the NT makes concerning God's manifestation in Christ.* Thus Christians should neither fear historical-critical biblical scholarship nor expect too much from it.

As for *not fearing*, if the promise of Christian Faith is true, that even hell cannot prevail against Christ and His church, neither can scientific historical honesty undermine faith in Christ. Thus Christians should stop suspending eternity on the spider web of historical evasions.[35] To the contrary, faith's certainty is menaced more by false assurances than by historical criticism. The stormy wind of historical criti-

---

34. Harrisville, *Bible/Modern Culture to Childs*, 256–57.
35. Thielicke, *Modern Faith*, 117. Thielicke rightly attributes such thoughts to Lessing, but Lessing's Christian commitment is far from clear.

cism's honesty can even bring "healing to those who dare to put themselves in[to] the storm."[36]

As for *not expecting too much* from historical scholarship but using it responsibly, Kierkegaard points the way toward a dialectical use of historical-critical method. Without rejecting that tool, he censures those who draw wrong implications from its usage, as for instance those who think that by such means one can "prove" essential New Testament beliefs. However, where important beliefs are linked to historically doubtful events, such as Jesus being born of a virgin, biblical criticism can show such "historical" connections to be less credible than other ways of affirming who Christ was and is. For example, instead of claiming that Jesus was born of a virgin, one can achieve the same christological result by appealing to the resurrection-inspired conviction that God was uniquely disclosed in Christ.

The important questions of Christian belief—such as whether God was uniquely present in Jesus Christ for the salvation of the world—cannot be answered by historical criticism. Such research can establish an astonishingly high probability that the early church believed this, since the NT evidence to that effect is overwhelming. The historical traditions about Jesus beneath the surface of the Synoptic Gospels point also to the strong likelihood that He understood His life and mission in some such terms, though not that He regarded Himself as God. I am convinced that the early Christian proclamation of the Crucified and Risen Christ is consistent with Jesus's proclamation of the kingdom that began to dawn with His person and work. Though it is highly probable that both Jesus and the early church believed that events in Jesus's life indicate God's saving activity, it does not prove that such convictions are true.

Christian Faith is interested in historical probabilities, but requires more. When Christ's Lordship and Saviorhood are regarded as probabilities, passionate commitment to Christ diminishes; decision tends to be indefinitely postponed and scholarly interest in the pursuit of objectivity replaces surrender of life. If faith were directly based on mere plausibilities, decision for Christ would need to be postponed until the eschaton, since only then will all the evidence be in.

SK believed that Christian Faith requires decision and commitment. He thought that the search for *objective* certainty concerning beliefs, for example trying to prove that Jesus was and is what the NT attests,[37] cannot succeed. But even if it could, it would not lead to the *certainty of faith*. The desire for such "proof" arises when Christians feel embarrassed or ashamed of their faith, and thus want outside reassurances. It is, SK suggested, "like a young woman for whom her love is no longer sufficient, but

---

36. Ibid., 118.

37. How could this be demonstrated? Before Jesus's resurrection even the disciples doubted and failed to have complete trust (Matt 14:31; see also 8:26 and 16:8) and according to one account even a supposed resurrection appearance did not overcome doubt (Matt 28:17).

who secretly feels ashamed of her lover and must therefore have it established that there is something remarkable about him."[38]

This brings us to the famous slogan used by Kierkegaard,[39] related to commitment to essential Christian beliefs, that *truth is subjectivity*. SK meant by this easily misunderstood phrase that *the truth of Christian Faith cannot be confirmed by anything other than biblical evidence substantiated by one's relationship with Christ*. Though Christian truth claims do not arise from subjectivity, but from NT testimony, the question of Christ's authority can be finally settled only as human subjects surrender to the Living Lord. Though God has disclosed a good deal about Herself through Scripture, and for this reason is an object of knowledge, Christian relationship with God must be between human subjects and God as Subject, not between human subjects and God as mere object.[40]

SK wrote that Christian Faith concerns "an objective uncertainty held fast in the appropriation process of the most passionate inwardness." Faith is objectively uncertain in that it is neither a logical truth of reason nor a mere historical probability. That God was uniquely in Christ will always seem unlikely to those who wish to remain uncommitted. Strictly speaking "the greatest attainable certainty with respect to anything historical is merely an approximation," but "an approximation when viewed as a basis for an eternal happiness, is wholly inadequate." "Without risk there is no faith. . . . *If I am capable of grasping God objectively, I do not believe, but precisely because I cannot do this I must believe.*"[41]

According to Revelation even coldness is better than lukewarm "commitment" (3:15–16). Faith in Christ requires such resolute dedication that one is willing to die for Him. But *only a fool is willing to die for a mere probability*. "Let him be offended, he is still human; let him despair of ever himself becoming a Christian, he is perhaps nearer than he believes"; but if concerning ultimate matters he is able to say that it is only true to a certain degree, "he is stupid."[42]

The important Christian claims involve transcendent, rather than immanent kinds of authority. Saying that Jesus Christ is the definitive revelation of God is not analogous to saying that "Napoleon was a great general." Being a great general involves widely recognized standards of military ability, in particular winning wars. To the contrary, God revealing Himself in a man who died as a condemned criminal entails a challenging of natural expectations.

---

38. Kierkegaard, *Unscientific Postscript*, 31; see also 28–30.

39. Coined by Lessing.

40. See chap. 2, sec. 3.

41. Kierkegaard, *Unscientific Postscript*, 182, 25, 182; my emphasis; see also 26. No one's ultimate commitments can be proven, and this is as true of the naturalist or rationalist as of the Christian (H. R. Niebuhr, *Christ/Culture*, 252).

42. Kierkegaard, *Unscientific Postscript*, 205.

That God was uniquely present in Jesus or that He offered Himself for the sin of the world are not "facts" in the empirical sense of the word. The most that the historians can affirm is that *various New Testament writers claim . . . and seem to mean . . . and the facts behind such testimonies are probable . . . and such writers' interpretations of such facts invite decision.*

9. Use of Historical Criticism in Biblical Analysis Theologically Motivated

Biblical criticism originated out of concern to understand biblical content discrepancies that perceptive biblical readers had discovered, as, for example, were evidenced in post-Reformation theological disputes. Consistencies as well as inconsistencies continued to be observed, which motivated theories to account for both. If we perceive differences between J (Yahwist) and P (Priestly) sources in the Pentateuch, it is primarily because we discern a common theological insight that runs through the J group of texts and a somewhat differing perspective in the P ones. Such analytical approaches reach authorship conclusions primarily by making judgments about theological differences and similarities and therefore must be alert concerning theological content.[43]

Historical-critical perceptions are thus *helpful* for understanding the Bible theologically.[44] "This is, indeed, the opposite of what has been thought by those who have argued that *for the sake of biblical theology* the role of historical criticism ought to be minimized. On the contrary, whatever the values of historical criticism from other points of view, for the enterprise of biblical theology it is particularly [useful]."[45]

The historical-critical study of the Bible likely helped Von Rad and Barth to perceive the interconnectedness of creation and redemption.[46] "'The historical-critical investigation of the biblical traditions of creation has made us aware how much these traditions look upon creation as the first of the series of God's redemptive deeds and how they describe it as analogous to it.'"[47] For another example of theological perceptions encouraged by biblical criticism, consider the recognition of the theological differences between Paul and Acts.[48] Here and elsewhere historical-critical method remarkably contributed to a recovery of the distinctive thinking of individual biblical authors.

---

43. Barr, *Concept/Biblical Theolog*, 80, 218–19, 81.

44. I cannot agree with Barr that they are "necessary" (ibid., 214), else no one could have understood the Bible until the ripening historical-critical method of the nineteenth century.

45. Ibid. Barr again says "necessary." For the sake of precise biblical theology historical criticism may be necessary, though imprecise biblical theology has also made contributions.

46. Ibid., 215.

47. Ibid., quoting Berkhof, *Christian Faith*, 66.

48. See chap. 6, n11 and sec. 7; chap. 7, nn49, 101 & sec. 8; chap. 10, sec. 6; chap. 13, n4.

Thematic Exposition Begins

10. Accuracy of Bible's Historical Details Requires Historical Evidence

In contrast to many of the theologians of the post-NT church and Middle Ages who regarded mere assent to saving facts as the heart of Christian Faith, Luther differentiated between trust in the God who meets us in Jesus and such acquiescence.[49] Though Luther's connected dichotomy eventually encouraged historical inquiry, much theology has tried to establish a secure basis for faith that ignores historical criticism's ongoing examination of historical details. In so doing, such theology separated faith from its revelational basis in history. One such approach *absorbed the object of faith into the act of faith* (one side of Schleiermacher), implying that the Christian experience of faith should disconnect from history. This aspect of Schleiermacher's thought encouraged a development in modern theology that does not regard the historical content of the biblical traditions as important, because talk about God and Her acts are seen *only* as utterances of faith and therefore expressions of one's understanding of existence. The other subjectively based perspective (another side of Schleiermacher, the theology of the Awakening, and the Erlangen theology) *supposed that faith can posit or create historical facts*.[50] Both views are historically dishonest. But what would constitute a fair regard for historical facticity, while remaining responsive to the supra-historical aspects attested by the historical record, as emphasized in section 8? To answer such questions we need to take account of the activities of historians in general, and see how biblical historians and we ourselves can learn from historical-critical work while remaining faithful to Jesus Christ.

11. Work of Historian

It is erroneous to regard history either as primarily "fact" (as with empiricism or positivism) or "meaning" (as with idealism and existentialism). "*What in any given case is called a 'fact' is always really one dimension of a*[51] *... scheme of meaningful interpreta-*

---

49. Pannenberg, *ST*, 3:144. "Even Satan, [Luther] wrote, can believe that Christ was born of the Virgin Mary" (Harrisville, *Hidden Grace*, 48).

50. Pannenberg, *ST*, 3:143, 149. Schleiermacher assumed that a sense of redemption can develop only in a fellowship that has found new life differing from sin. From that presupposition he speculated that *the very existence of the Redeemer* could be deduced from such communally derived "experience" of redemption. Behind such deductions was his assumption that the church's common life must have had a historical starting point. He, however, did not claim that communal faith-consciousness can establish the historicity of *details* from Jesus's life.

Later revivalist theology, reasoning from Schleiermacher's communally based predication of the Redeemer, went further and spoke more specifically, postulating that individual faith-consciousness can guarantee the historical reality of details concerning the biblical Christ (partially dependent on same source, 149).

51. Kaufman says "a contemporary scheme" (*ST/Historicist*, 270). Would not such terminology rule out Pannenberg's defense of aspects of NT apocalyptic interpretation or any other rehabilitation of ancient ways of thinking about history? For modern Christians to affirm a particular interpretation

tion, within which the fact is seen to be fact. [In terms of our knowledge of them][52] *facts thus have no existence apart from meanings.* However, the demand to 'get the facts' is not pointless. . . . The term 'fact' points to the empirical event that the 'meaning' renders comprehensible, if it is a genuinely historical meaning and not merely myth or poetry. Historical meaning is characterized precisely (and distinguished from fiction) by its being rooted in fact."[53]

Ernst Troeltsch sought to articulate *general guidelines for assessing historical probabilities.* He argued that historical inquiry rests upon three interrelated principles, all of which will require critique. *First, the principle of criticism* recognizes that judgments about the past are based on critical assessment of the evidence and historians can seldom classify these as simply true or false.[54] Not only do the historical disciplines yield only judgments of probability, but historians must investigate concerning degrees of probability,[55] and remain open to revision of formulations in the light of new evidence. Like a wise judge sifting evidence, the historian must critically "interpret the interpretations." If historians do not scrutinize their sources they are mere mediators of past beliefs and transmitters of traditions. The historian's evidence must credibly withstand critical dialogue among colleagues.

Because scientific historians weigh probabilities, they seldom completely agree or disagree but "agree and disagree with one another at various overlapping levels. They may agree, for example, that a certain policy was put into effect but disagree as to the motives of the policy-makers. They may agree that a certain event actually happened and concur on the details but differ as to the significance of the causal factors at work in it."[56]

Christian biblical interpreters should avoid understandings of the work of historians that oversimplify, as when a closed-minded person deduces from the premise that every historian has presuppositions, that this justifies one's own doctrinaire assumptions. Though like everyone else, historians have suppositions, the intangible quality that separates a sound historian from a tendentious and undiscriminating

---

requires that they find it meaningful—and in this sense it again becomes contemporary—but this does not require that it be widely accepted.

52. Kaufman says that "facts have no existence apart from meanings" (ibid.). To the contrary, we must concede that events happen apart from our knowledge of them. For example, scientific evidence indicates that organisms evolved for millions of years before humans were on hand to observe and draw evolutionary deductions. In terms of the traditional philosophical debate, we can conceive that many trees fall in forests even when no humans hear the sounds. Having later observed the effects, we can posit causes that existed prior to and independently of human observation.

53. Ibid.; emphasis mine. What we call myths or sagas (as in Genesis) can also be regarded as historical in that people once not only derived meaning from them, but took them literally. We may also derive meaning from these, but without taking them literally.

54. Harvey, *Historian/Believer*, 14.

55. Harrisville, *Bible/Modern Culture to Käsemann*, 155.

56. Harvey, *Historian/Believer*, 84.

one is that she weighs evidence fairly and carefully draws conclusions.[57] The historian "does not solicit mere assent but a quality of assent, not mere judgment but a properly qualified type of judgment ranging from tentativeness to practical assurance."[58]

In keeping with a love of truth, the sound and non-tendentious historian will not hold any proposition with greater assurance than the evidence it is built upon warrants. It is irresponsible to give heavy assent when only soft assent is deserved, or to convert one paragraph's highly debatable conclusion into the basis for an argument in the next. Such approaches undermine judgment, because they seem to require that assertions with low probabilities be converted into ones possessing high probabilities, and that logical possibilities be confused with likely probabilities.[59] With this approach the passion of faith becomes tied to beliefs, such as the virgin birth, that can be legitimately challenged by historical and natural science.

In contrast NT Christians' experience of Christ's risen presence, backed by NT attestation that God raised Him to eternal life, and our own confirming experience of Christ's presence more convincingly leads to the conviction that Jesus was God's unique historical disclosure.[60] Furthermore, the existence of the Christian Church following Jesus' crucifixion seems inexplicable apart from early Christian experience of and belief in Christ's risen presence. Even so, historians as mere historians can neither prove nor disprove such a conclusion, and they should not be asked to do so. Instead all people, including historians, are invited truly to share in the divine presence, forgiveness and moral empowerment that God through Christ wills to provide.

Nils Dahl agrees with Martin Kahler that the cardinal virtue of genuine historical research is the *modesty* of not overstating evidence, which Dahl insists means deriving rather than imposing interpretations on the material. Like all others, historians cannot work without presuppositions, but should allow their work to be enriched and

57. Ibid., 249, 121.
58. Ibid., 121.
59. Ibid., 123–24.
60. It's doubtful that Harvey believes even in the latter. He seems better at describing what he disagrees with than in affirming well-founded, historically related beliefs, and thus we see how easily Troeltsch's principle of criticism can be misused to encourage relativism. A healthy dose of Kierkegaard will, however, protect against relativism, while honoring the modest, but legitimate contributions of historians.

I, however, agree with Harvey that many evangelicals do not treat historical evidence fairly, and value conformity to group opinion and ideology over honest assessment of evidence. Such "orthodox believers often set aside the consensus in a given field for no other reason than that this is incompatible with a historical proposition they desire to believe. They are intellectually irresponsible, not so much because they want certainty, as because *they continually enter objections to our normal warrants for no principled reasons*. Consequently, their objections are themselves non-assessable [because not based on evidence] and lead to no advance in knowledge. Yet these same believers are most eager to welcome modern knowledge wherever it seems to support traditional Christian belief in any respect" (ibid., 118). Such people are apologists for prior dogmatic commitments. In terms of the morality of historical knowledge their procedures are dishonest. James Barr points out that fundamentalist Christians interpret the Bible literally or non-literally not on the basis of sensitivity to what texts intend to say, but alternate as needed to prop up their doctrine of inerrancy (*Fundamentalism*, 40–55).

corrected by the interpretations of events given by those who lived in close proximity to the events.[61]

A second principle for assessing historical probabilities is that of *correlation or interrelatedness*. This means that "the phenomena of historical life are so related and interdependent that no radical change can take place at any one point in the historical nexus without effecting a change in all that immediately surrounds it. Historical explanation, therefore, necessarily takes the form of understanding an event in terms of its antecedents and consequences, and no event can be isolated from its historically conditioned time and space."[62] Such a notion becomes objectionable to Christians only when overextended to imply that events are completely determined by prior conditioning factors, and thus understood as ruling out God's capacity to freely interact. When taken to that extreme the premise manifests complete historical determinism. In at least one place Troeltsch challenged such an interpretation of his own principle: He said that though new things *connect* to what precedes them, the new is not *established* by what precedes it, else nothing could ever be new, and change would be illusory.[63]

A third and final principle similarly becomes problematic when pushed too far. The principle *of analogy* means that when we attempt to reconstruct historical events we invariably assume a degree of commonality or homogeneity in the world over the centuries. If, for example, we now have good reason for recognizing the law of gravity, we have no choice but to assume that it also applied in ancient times, though the ancients lacked our scientific understanding and thus did not agree that such uniformity always held on earth. In this regard we must disallow the Acts of the Apostles claim that Phillip once flew through the air to get from one place to another (8:39–40).[64] Similarly problematic is the assertion that to offer Jesus two of the three temptations the devil transported Him miraculously both to the pinnacle of the Jerusalem temple and to a high mountain (Matt 4:5, 8a). Or to the Jerusalem temple and also into the heavens, so he could see all the kingdoms of the world (Luke 4:9a; 5). Though the OT says that the sun stood still that Israel could have more daylight to fight and thus win the battle against the Amorites (Josh 10:12b–13a), we can only understand the narrative as a way of giving God credit for the victory. The language supposes that the sun rotates around the earth.

However ancients may have regarded the natural world, the premise that earlier in the human era nature was not radically dissimilar from that of today is useful. *Such a postulate becomes problematic only when so overextended as to eliminate the possibility*

---

61. Dahl, *Jesus the Christ*, 45, 29.

62. Harvey, *Historian/Believer*, 15.

63. Troeltsch, *Christian Faith*, 151.

64. See chap. 13, n4 for a consideration of Jesus's ascension account (attested only in Acts), that presupposes ancient cosmology.

that unprecedented historical events can occur. Taken to the extreme the principle of analogy, means that "'anything that happens for the first time is to be discredited.'"[65]

Since Jesus' early resurrection encounter with Paul likely exhibits an unprecedented event, it challenges an exaggerated understanding of the principle of analogy. Also, Paul's conception of Jesus's resurrection as His enthronement with the Father reflects an absolutely unique event. One should give credence to Paul's historically early account of his divinely initiated, spiritual vision of the Risen Christ. For this was experienced and described by the only NT author who encountered the Risen Christ. His account is thus more credible than the Gospels' historically late (semi-physical, nature conflicting) accounts by non-eye witnesses.

12. Interim Reflection

The historical-critical method has had profound influence upon western interpretations of all traditions, challenging easy participation in these. *Historical exposure to the ambiguities of traditions has encouraged critical thinking.*[66] "Such reflection provides distance from all that simply 'is.' Historical critical methods show us how what 'is' came to be. All historical and social practices that seemed so natural are now understood for what they are: not expressions of nature but expressions of history."[67]

With whatever degree of certitude is possible, what happened in history should matter to us. "It is irresponsible for Christians not to care at all if Jesus ever lived and then go on to state their firm belief in Jesus of Nazareth as the Christ."[68] As historical work contributes its judgments concerning both historical probability and meaning, we must weigh evidence, but in the light of the understandings our historically well-considered events and carefully-scrutinized texts have helped to provoke. A usable past is a retrievable one.[69]

13. Could Christian Faith Be Historically Disproven?

The case against Christianity cannot be closed on historical grounds. We must remember that *strictly speaking* historians can neither "prove" nor "disprove" anything, but can only assess probabilities.[70] Convincing arguments for such a thing as Jesus's non-existence are difficult to imagine. If we try to conceive such conclusive argu-

---

65. Thiselton, *Two Horizons*, 79, quoting A. Boyce Gibson's comment concerning extreme empiricism.

66. Tracy, *Plurality/Ambiguity*, 39.

67. Ibid., 39.

68. Ibid., 36; a criticism applicable to Tillich.

69. Ibid., 39, citing Harnack.

70. As often seen in this work, natural science can and should rule out the Bible's linkage with ancient world views, and historians take natural science's evidence seriously.

ments about biblical history we need to remember that such interpretations would themselves be subject to scathing critiques. The only way that Christianity could lose its historical foundation would be if a vast array of facts were overturned by a massive amount of new evidence, such that the NT's entire history would require rethinking.

Is this a possibility? It is certainly not one we need to worry about. It is a possibility in the same respect that the non-existence of Martin Luther is a possibility, namely, that it is not a serious one. Could the *essential historical claims* on which Christian Faith rests be false? Too much of an inconceivable nature would have to happen to give this possibility any force, or cause one to doubt the historical truth that Christian Faith requires.[71]

But how wide-ranging are the historical claims on which Christian interpretation rests? Here the debate becomes intra-Christian. From this point *theological* discussion begins concerning how broad are the historical tenets to which Christianity is committed. Some theologians and other Christian thinkers "may define Christianity so that it includes a vast range of historical claims." Others "may not define the historical foundation of Christianity nearly as extensively"[72] and see much as coming from Spirit-guided NT interpretation. When "secular" historical critics challenge traditional assumptions, such Christians (some of whom are historical critics) can afford to enter into discussions and debates about how wide-ranging the evidence needs to be.

---

71. Whittaker, "Kierkegaard/Faith/History," 395–96.
72. Ibid., 396.

Chapter 19

Christian Knowing, Believing, Sharing in Faith

Part A. Jesus, Paul, and Johannine Tradition

1. Faith/Belief in Dawning of Kingdom in Jesus's Ministry, but

TOWARD THE BEGINNING OF Mark's Gospel Jesus is said to have summarized His message with these words: "The kingdom of God is near; repent and believe in the Gospel" (1:15). New Testament historians widely agree that the third aspect of Mark's introductory summary of Jesus's preaching—which is likely an allusion to belief in the Gospel of *God's coming in Him*—reflects the faith of the post-resurrection church, not Jesus's preaching. Such scholars have long suspected that Jesus proclaimed the coming kingdom, not belief in Himself.[1] Contrary to the Fourth Gospel and a few likely author-created synoptic additions to the historical tradition, Jesus probably called only for faith in God in response to God's action in His words, attitudes and deeds. Yet Christians must certainly agree that belief in Jesus Christ is essential to Christian Faith, for God instituted that belief and its linkage with Jesus's life and message by raising Jesus from death.

2. Faith/Belief According to Paul

Paul describes faith as a believing response to the proclamation of the message concerning the crucified and risen Lord (Rom 10:8–9). "Faith comes from what is heard and what is heard comes by the preaching of Christ" (Rom 10:17). "For since, in the wisdom of God, the world did not know God through wisdom, it pleased God through the folly of what we preach to save those who believe. For Jews demand signs and Greeks seek wisdom, but we preach Christ crucified, a stumbling-block to Jews and folly to Gentiles, but to those who are called, both Jews and Greeks, Christ the power

---

1. See Mark 9:42 & Matt 18:6a for highly unusual, explicit Synoptic references to belief in Jesus.

of God and the wisdom of God." For "God's foolishness is wiser than human wisdom, and God's weakness is stronger than human strength" (1 Cor 1:21–24 RSV, 25 NRSV).

Building from Gen 15:6 and in contrast to the traditional Jewish understanding of Abraham, Paul contrasts justification by faith with justification by works of the law. "To one who without works trusts him who justifies the ungodly, such faith is reckoned as righteousness" (Rom 4:5 NRSV). In Galatians 3:11 (NRSV) Paul appeals to Habakkuk 2:4b: "It is evident that no one is justified before God by the law, for 'The one who is righteous will live by faith.'"

In trying to comprehend why in soteriological contexts Paul contrasted faith so starkly with works, Bultmann followed a long tradition of Pauline scholarship. Bultmann perceived that Paul regarded the law as resulting in people calculating their relative merit and becoming boastful (Rom 4:2). Likely in reacting against such misuse of the law, Paul emphasized that our standing before God is based on God's act of grace in right-wising the unworthy, rather than even to a partial extent in rewarding the meritorious. In Paul's understanding, works issue from the grateful desire to be ever faithful and from participation in divine love (1 Cor 13).

According to Paul only those who continue to recognize their guilt and need for divine forgiveness can overcome the scandal of a crucified Messiah. They can continue to die to their own wills and rise to life centered in Christ—having surrendered their desire to live from their own resources and achievements. They can thus gain considerable freedom from conformity to the world by gaining considerable freedom from themselves.[2]

Truly to know Christ is so to trust in God's deed of love in Him that one is willing to suffer on His behalf. Thus Paul writes, "Whatever gain I had, I counted as loss for the sake of Christ. Indeed I count everything as loss because of the surpassing worth of knowing Christ Jesus my Lord. For his sake I have suffered the loss of all things, and count them as [rubbish], in order that I may gain Christ and be found in him, not having a righteousness of my own based on law, but that which is through faith in Christ, the righteousness from God that depends on faith" (Phil 3:7–9).

3. Faith/Belief According to Johannine Tradition

The author of the Fourth Gospel addresses the human longing for authentic life and attacks our false conception of this. The world that longs for such a life and thinks it has found it[3] is still in death. It supposes that it knows the "true God," but He remains unknown to it (5:37–38; 7:28), for He is known in the Son (17:3).

Christian Faith calls for the surrender of worldly security achieved without dependence on the Father known in the Son and asks that people accept the new life Christ gives and is (John 11:25), a life that from the world's perspective cannot be

---

2. Bultmann, *Primitive Christianity*, 202.
3. John 5:39 describes one such quest.

proven to exist. Faith involves no retreat from the world, but *desecularization* as the smashing of merely human standards and evaluations. In this sense believers are no longer "of the world" (15:19; 17:14, 16), since the world is no longer their determining origin. This is why the world does not recognize genuine believers, as it did not recognize Jesus (1 John 3:1). As Jesus's transcendent living led to suffering and death, so His disciples following of Him results in ill treatment by the world (John 16:1–4). Yet Christians must not retreat from the world, but gain freedom from evil (17:15). As God sent His Son into the world, so the Son sends forth His own (17:18).[4]

Having been drawn to Christ and thereby engaged in turning from sin, the Christian to a large extent has already passed through judgment and begun to participate in eternal life (3:18; 5:24). Faith as the act of believing constantly brings about this sharing in eternal life. Such true faith engenders faithfulness and constancy.

To understand the Johannine concept of faith we not only need to keep in mind its Christocentric focus and emphasis on eschatological distancing, but the integral relationship of faith to love. This relationship is shown by the discourse on the true vine (15:1–11). Verse 4 insists that abiding in Jesus is the prior condition for fruit bearing, but the vine analogy regards "fruit-bearing" as expressive of and required for "abiding" in Jesus. Such circular reasoning points to the unity of faith and love, which is a chief theme of First John: Believing in the Son cannot be separated from loving one another as He commanded (3:23b), doing what pleases Him (3:22c), and walking in the light (1:7a).[5]

"Walking in the light" gets a precise definition in First John 2:9–11 as loving one's brothers and sisters, and this commandment presumes the unity of indicative and imperative. Out of received love arises the *obligation to love*: "A new commandment I give to you, that you love one another; even as I have loved you, that you love one another" (John 13:34). Though we are sinners God has loved us as friends. "Beloved, if God so loves us, we also ought to love one another" (1 John 4:11). "We love, because he first loved us" (4:19).

The Johannine tradition sees a close relationship between believing in Jesus Christ as the One who has shown forth God's love and being disposed to please such a loving God through neighborly love. In line with this understanding is the notion of *faith as dispositional*. John Wesley wrote that faith is not "a cold, lifeless assent, a [mere] train of ideas in the head; but is a disposition of the heart."[6] Faith as a tendency does not mean that it is merely an attitude. Rather it signifies that one is disposed invariably and in the long run with new habits, a new love, and an acquired way of caring.[7] Wesley thus insisted that genuine faith and works cannot be separated, unless there is insufficient time to put faith into practice, as with the thief on the cross. Faith

---

4. Bultmann, *Theology/NT*, 2:75, 76.
5. Ibid., 78, 86, 80, 81.
6. Wesley, *Forty-Four*, 3.
7. Paul Homer, Lecture on Wesley's Theology, Yale Divinity School, 1966.

is not merely the inward reality while works are the outward expression. Rather, faith as a disposition is a springboard of behavior, and works are a way that faith shows forth its tendency. Nevertheless—and contrary to what Wesley sometimes wrote—the moral outworking of grace received through faith should not be regarded as one of the bases of salvation, as though in part we earn our deliverance.

Part B. Biblically Responsive Theological Reflection

4. Faith and Divine Transcendence

In his second commentary on the Epistle to the Romans Barth quoted Kierkegaard, who was a major influence at that stage of his life: "'Remove from the Christian Religion, as Christendom has done, its ability to shock, and Christianity, by becoming a direct communication, is altogether destroyed. It then becomes a tiny superficial thing, capable neither of inflicting deep wounds nor of healing them; . . . it forgets the qualitative distinction between man and God.'"[8]

In that Romans commentary Barth understood faith as first of all coming to terms with the transcendent, contradicting, and judging God, insisting that it is self-deceptive to think that from nature and history, from art, morality, science, or even religion direct roads lead to the impossible possibility of God.[9] To the contrary, "he who knows the world to be bounded by a truth that contradicts it, he who knows himself to be bounded by a will that contradicts him, . . . he who finally makes open confession of the contradiction and determines to base his life upon it—he it is who believes. The believer . . . puts his trust in God, in God Himself, and in God alone . . ." "Those who take on themselves the burden of the divine 'No' are carried by the greater divine 'Yes'. The wary and heavy-laden are refreshed. Those who do not avoid the contradiction are hidden in God."[10]

5. Christian Faith as Gift

As Luther insisted, the Christian believes and confesses that it is not by one's own reason or power that one believes in Jesus Christ as Lord or comes to Him.[11] Similarly Barth wrote that the revelation of God shines on and in a Christian, and "takes place in such a way that he hears, receives, understands, grasps and appropriates what is said to him, not with new and special organs, but with the same organs of apperception

---

8. Barth, *Romans*, 6th ed., 98–99. Barth claimed to be quoting SK here, but did not cite book titles. The passage is similar to one from Kierkegaard, *Training*, 139. For related SK material see chap. 18, secs. 4 and 5.

9. Ibid., 337.

10. Ibid., 39, 41.

11. Luther's Smaller Catechism, Article 1.

with which he knows other things, *yet not in virtue of his own capacity to use them, but in virtue of the missing capacity which he is now given by God's revelation.*"[12] Faith is activated as the Living Christ overwhelms us with the power of His *incontestable reality*—enabling us to share in God's forgiveness and beginning to free us from divisions within ourselves. As God in this way reveals Herself in us we experience both dependence and freedom, are humbled and exalted, and are awakened to senses of awe and trust concerning God.[13] The "Spirit itself . . . bears witness with our spirit, that we are children of God" (Rom 8:16).

But how can a person be free if their response to God arises from a conviction that comes from a Convictor who makes an overwhelming impression? Consider two analogies from the personal realm. Though a person should weigh the merits of those one dates, and should pray for God's guidance, falling in love is a won response and in this sense a gift. And yet who would doubt that such a response is free? Or, to choose another illustration, suppose you are sad and downhearted, but meet someone who flashes a friendly smile. You find yourself smiling back. Your smile is a gift given by the one who smiled. And yet who would deny that you had smiled freely. Our response to grace is similar.[14]

To have Christian Faith is to be so gripped by the Living Word—Jesus Christ—that one submits to Him.[15] Those so embraced receive an influx of spiritual and moral energy that redirects their powers to feel, think and act. This transformation is the presupposition of all that one is henceforth able to do. Faith is not the outcome of the use of human willpower, but the divinely enabled, indispensable condition for using one's powers in obedience to God.[16]

6. Faith as Evoking Affection for God Leading to Relationship with God and Trust in Her

Jonathan Edwards taught that in response to the gift of a new relationship with Christ "religious affections" are evoked, that thereby become the motivational force for living the Christian life. The grace-resulting religious affections involve love for and joy in

---

12. Barth, *CD*, 4/3.2:509; my emphasis.

13. Barth, *Theology/Church*, 247.

14. Hordern, *Speaking of God*, 169–70. The Fourth Gospel goes beyond believing that faith is a gift, and affirms that only those who believe were eternally destined to do so and only such people have prospect of salvation. "All that the Father gives to me will come to me" (6:37). "No one can come to me unless the Father who sent me draws him" (6:44; cf. 6:65). "Whoever is of God hears the words of God; the reason why you do not hear is that you are not of God" (8:47). "You do not believe, because you do not belong to my sheep" (10:26; cf. 17:6, 9–10, 24). Many of us may see theological disadvantages in pushing the gift nature of faith this far. Doing so also seems to conflict with the Johannine beliefs that God is love (1 John 4:8b, 16a) and loves all people (John 3:16).

15. Brunner, *Revelation/Reason*, 421.

16. Calhoun, *Lectures*, 42, 360, 359, 43.

God and are the source of both faith and morals. Though all people follow what they believe to be their apparent good, through experiential transformation Christians find their true good in knowing God and doing Her will.

Evoked trust in God through Christ is to be so wholehearted that one has confidence even when one's experiential awareness of God is weak. Yet such trust is possible only on the basis of a more direct relationship with God at other times. Like a relationship with a human friend, one at times directly converses with God and feels Her love, so that at less experiential moments one continues to trust in Her and Her love.

Faith looks away from its own self-sufficiency and clings to Christ. It takes confidence that since nothing can separate us from God's love in Christ (Rom 8:39), meaning in life is "higher than achievement and deeper than failure." Faith knows how to be abased and how to abound (Phil 4:12a). Faith as trust in God through Christ is that reliable assurance "that God is for us, and therefore we are secure come what may—failure, pain, disgrace, our own guilt, death."[17]

7. Christ-Centered Faith Implies Cognition

We cannot believe without knowing the One in whom we believe. For within the community that looks to Jesus Christ through Scripture, Christ has form and is an object of knowledge. We not only can have a true vision of the One in whom we believe, but can find some words to express such thoughts.[18]

According to the Apostles' Creed, trust is based on the Invisible Reality towards whom it is directed, namely, God the Father and His Risen Son present as Holy Spirit within the church. Trust is also related to what it hopes for from the reliability of the One on whom it depends, attested in the Creed as the forgiveness of sins, the resurrection of the dead, and eternal life.[19]

Calvin's triune understanding of faith as involving the Christ-centered recognition of God's benevolence, based on Spirit-generated trust in God through Christ, is faithful to the NT. Faith is both revealed to our minds and sealed upon our hearts through the Holy Spirit.[20] Being no mere cognition, such faith involves feelings and experiences, and leads to such assurance of God's goodness that one becomes confident and bold. "For the Word of God is not received by faith if it flits about in the top of the brain, but when it takes root in the depth of the heart . . ."[21]

According to Calvin, faith involves piety, that reverence for God joined with the love of God that the knowledge of Christ's benefits induces. Such piety equips disciples to serve God, not because they dread God's punishment if they do otherwise,

---

17. Clements, *Faith*, 39, 29.
18. Barth, *CD*, 4/1:764–66.
19. Loosely related to Pannenberg, *Apostles Creed*, 7.
20. Calvin, *Institutes*, 1:551.
21. Ibid., 583.

but because they have received God's love. Even if there were no hell, one would shudder at offending this God.[22] Although like Luther and most places in Paul's writings, Calvin uses the phrase "justification by faith alone," "he is careful to say that faith does not of itself effect justification, but embraces Christ by whose grace we are justified."[23]

A qualification needs to be introduced here that will be further elaborated in the next section: Though Christ-centered faith implies cognition, *the quality of faith is not directly proportionate to the extent nor precision of one's knowledge of God*. In a personal relationship between two friends, reflection and understanding are needed for the sake of the relationship itself.[24] Without those, friendship has little meaning and dialogue remains superficial. But the degree of friendship is not directly proportionate to the extent nor precision of friends' understandings of one another. The most perceptive student of another person's character is not necessarily that person's closest friend. Analogously, those who have the best researched and clearest theological understandings do not necessarily have the closest relationship with God—since knowledge concerning God is only one dimension of faith.

8. Christian Faith Involving Whole Personality as against Cognitive, Voluntaristic, Emotional Distortions

When a person responds to God's revelation in Christ his thoughts can become God-centered, along with his volition and feeling. Since faith is an activity of the whole personality, all three facets of the personality must be affected and consistently interrelated—intellect, will and feelings.

With the *cognitive distortion*, faith is understood as merely assenting to "knowledge" based on slight evidence, but supported by religious authority.[25] In contrast the early Reformers regarded faith as based on well-considered and heartfelt trust in God through Christ. Thus Melanchthon rejected a definition of faith as mere knowledge of the facts of salvation.[26]

Faith should not be regarded as simply making others' beliefs our own, even if those others are called apostles.[27] No one "'can be liberated by holding as true

---

22. Ibid., 41, 43.

23. McNeill, "Introduction," *Calvin/Institutes*, 1:lx. Calvin's position reflects the more precise wording found in Eph 2:8–9 (NRSV): "For *by* grace you have been saved *through* faith, and this is not your own doing, it is a gift of God—not the result of works, so that no one may boast" (my emphases). In Rom 3:22b–25a Paul himself writes in a similarly nuanced way: "For there is no distinction, since all have sinned and fall short of the glory of God, they are justified by his grace as a gift, through the redemption which is in Jesus Christ, whom God put forward as an expiation by his blood, to be received by faith."

24. Clements, *Faith*, 105.

25. Tillich, *Dynamics of Faith*, 33; Tillich, *Protestant Era*, x, xi.

26. Pannenberg, *ST*, 3:142.

27. Harvey, *Historian/Believe*, 129, describing Herrmann's criticism.

something that he does not inwardly understand to be true.'"[28] To know God as Judge is not only to believe there is a God who judges, but entails experiencing Her judgment (Jer 16:21). To know God as Savior is not just to believe that God is loving, but to be convinced of this because one has experienced God's forgiveness, which has capacitated one to trust in God's loving disclosure in Christ.

The voluntaristic distortion builds on the cognitive one and presupposes it. Aquinas regarded faith as involving little more than submission to what the church teaches, but believed that an act of will is required to make up for the unconvincing quality of the evidence.[29] To the contrary, faith involves an encounter with the Living God as disclosed in the Son by the Spirit, affects all aspect of a person, and entails costly discipleship.

Whereas Aquinas's voluntaristic distortion of faith minimizes individuals' adult responsibility for faith, one of the Protestant voluntaristic distortions (pragmatism) involves capricious willfulness. Faith's content becomes an arbitrary decision supported by insufficient evidence and by arguments that can just as easily lead in other directions.[30]

According to William James faith is only a working hypothesis, a persuasion that the odds in its favor are strong enough to cause one to act on the assumption of its truthfulness. Such a "faith" would have little power to make moral differences in peoples' lives, since such outward motivation has small capacity to move the affections and thereby the will. Furthermore believers do not regard their faith as a prudent gamble, but as involving knowledge of and love for God.[31] An additional problem is that "if it is rational to believe in the Christian God on the ground that this *may* be the only way of gaining the final truth, then it is equally rational to believe in any alternative religious system which *may* also be the sole pathway to Truth." In short, James conception of faith only recommends "wishful thinking." "Is he not saying that since the truth is unknown to us we may believe what we like and that while we are about it we had better believe what we most like?"[32]

As John Oman taught, faith is real only when the object of belief constrains us, and we have no need of constraining it. We have no right to believe anything unless it impresses us as true, since truth and its free recognition are required for right moral motivation.[33] Whether (with traditional Catholicism) we utilize willpower to consent to what the church requires or (with some forms of Protestantism) we force our

---

28. Ibid., 129, quoting Herrmann.

29. Tillich, *Dynamics of Faith*, 36. Since Aquinas regarded faith as little more than mental capitulation to truths concerning God, he considered faith as but the first step toward salvation, needing to be supplemented by hope and charity. With his understanding, all three combined—faith, hope, and charity—would not result in a saving relationship with God. Faith as mere assent to ideas, plus hope and love understood as humanly achieved virtues do not require personal relationship with God nor lead to it.

30. Ibid., 36.

31. Hick, *Faith/Knowledge*, 35, 42.

32. Ibid., 43, 44.

33. Clements, *Faith*, 44, quoting John Oman, *Grace and Personality*, 129.

wills to believe our own ill-founded preferences, such ways of "affirming" beliefs are inauthentic: With such approaches, people intellectually and volitionally acquiesce to what has not inwardly won their allegiance. "Our oscillating will cannot produce the certainty which belongs to faith."[34]

The emotional distortion identifies faith with vague feelings devoid of doctrinal content. Where Schleiermacher described Christian Faith as having to do with mere feelings of unconditional dependence—and as not implying specific beliefs concerning Christ—he stripped faith of the Christ-centered content the NT attributes to it.[35] "The word 'feeling' has induced many people to believe that faith is a matter of merely subjective emotions, without a content to be known and a demand to be obeyed."[36]

Though in very different ways from Schleiermacher, pietistic revivalism was and is often guilty of subjectivism. Also the temptation to self-salvation is present in much pietism and revivalism, since they can provoke the desire for emotions that are not genuine, but are artificially created.[37] It is as though people have to work themselves into emotional frenzies, and thereby achieve salvation by works.

Such criticisms of subjectivism are not meant to detract from the fact that faith as an act of the whole personality has strong emotional elements. Inward affection is an aspect of Christian Faith, but far from the whole. If Christian Faith involves mere feeling it is innocuous and no interaction with other fields of study is possible. Put safely into the corner of subjective feelings, Christian Faith poses no disruption of humankind's cultural activities.[38]

"Hegel was contemptuous of Schleiermacher's identification of religion with feeling. . . . Feeling is [a] form in which the consciousness of God is given, it is [a] place where God is in my being, and I am certain of him. But . . . to stop with feeling is to be able to make no discriminations concerning truth or value. Feeling as such is not distinctive of people but is shared with the animals—hence Hegel's remark that if religion were the feeling of absolute dependence, the dog would be the most religious being."[39]

Christian Faith does not entail mere intellectual assent, nor mere emotion, nor only acts of the will, but affects the whole person.[40] Faith involves the Divine Spirit of the Risen Lord working in our lives, and must be normed by God's disclosure in Christ.

---

34. Tillich, *Dynamics of Faith*, 39.

35. Ibid., 38. Fortunately Schleiermacher's *Christian Faith*, vol. 2 attests more content than his vol. 1 methodological statements seem to permit.

36. Tillich, *Dynamics of Faith*, 39. Inasmuch as Tillich advocated self-transcending naturalism and understood Christian Faith as mere ultimate concern, he did not escape the subjectivism he criticized. For these extreme problems in Tillich's thinking see, for example, *The Courage to Be*.

37. Tillich, *ST*, 2:85–86. Though this paragraph is influenced by Tillich, he was referring to religion in general.

38. Tillich, *Dynamics of Faith*, 39.

39. Welch, *Protestant Thought/Nineteenth Century*, 1:94.

40. Tillich, *Dynamics of Faith*, 51.

Conclusion

I HOPE THAT THE reader has seen that critical analyses from biblical, theological, and interdisciplinary scholarship can contribute to well-focused, constructive interpretations of Christ-centered biblical faith. It is also hoped that the reader has perceived the reverse, that continual concern to provide insight into the meaning of Christian Faith need not interfere with careful critical analyses. Furthermore, I hope that in its small way this volume may help to overcome the hiatus in the worldwide church between those who emphasize freedom and critical reflection and those who stress doctrinal content.

No synthesis is a final resting place and this as a first volume is even less so.[1] All syntheses should invite others to do better.

As for the themes to be discussed in the next volume: Early drafts of many topics and additional notes are largely in place, but the sequencing of these and others is still being fine-tuned. Likely to be considered at the beginning will be the Christian understanding of human nature and then the work of the Holy Spirit.

Here in proximate sequence are mentioned some other sectional headings with some of their sub-topics. In examining Christology, the plan is to deal with the Jesus of history-Christ of faith issues and with soteriological Christology. In considering a Christian conception of God will be discussed an understanding of divine triunity, God's freely expressed love and God's creative suffering. In pondering God as Creator and Governor will likely be included God's creational purpose for humans, the evolution of the species and emergent evolution, and humans as hereditarily influenced by other members of the animal kingdom.

Likely the final topic to be considered will be God's work of reconciliation, which will include: God's demonstration of Her love in reconciling humankind to Herself, justification and the righteousness of God, grace to appropriate atonement and to persevere in Christian Faith, the renewal of Christians, Christian witnessing as entailing suffering, religion and religions, the Church, Spirit baptism and water Baptism, and Christian hope concerning eternal life.

---

1. This work should help to clear the way for a well-focused discussion of particular Christian doctrines, where preliminary matters can be referred back to this volume, rather than being comprehensively considered at each point of doctrine.

Glossary with References[1]

Abstract Thought: Mental activity related to perceiving the connections between disparate ideas, texts or objects. This activity is utilized in scientific classifications and in systematic theology's drawing together of what it determines are the relevant biblical texts that shed light on the meaning of particular doctrines. Such thinking also facilitates the recognizing of conflicting texts and ideas (chap. 14, sec. 1).

Analogy of Being: Assumes that we have the same "isness" as God and therefore by nature relate to Him. This concept denies God's transcendence and our sinfulness and need for revelation for knowledge of God and relationship with Him (chap. 2, sec. 6). See Being Mysticism.

Apocalyptic Thinking: Contrasts this age with the coming eternal one and emphasizes the sinful and finite reality of this one (chap. 4, sec. 3).

Apologetics: Generally regarded as the defense of Christian Faith against attack, but see Eristics (chap. 9, sec. 6).

Apostle: One whose ministry of witness was authorized by extraordinary encounter with the Risen Christ (chap. 6, sec. 16 sub-sec. 4).

Aristotelianism: The philosophical belief that, by means of an analysis of sense experience, reason can perceive essential reality (chap. 9, sec. 4).

Atonement: Understanding of the way God brings about reconciliation or at-one-ment (chap. 4, sec. 5; see also chap. 7, sec. 7). Both Jesus's life and death and the New Testament's interpretation of His significance occurred in the past—but the Risen Christ as Holy Spirit can enable us to share in the atonement or reconciliation with God established in Christ. Thereby the effects of those past events penetrate into the present and affect our lives (chap. 18, sec. 3).

---

1. Citations only indicate the first usage of the definition, unless it is further expanded later. Some particular discussion listings are indicated in the Index, and more comprehensive listings can be located in the Expanded Table of Contents.

Being Mysticism: Supposes that by created nature we sinners and everything share in "Being Itself" (chap. 2, sec. 6). See Analogy of Being.

Biblical, Old Testament or New Testament Theology: Theology whose subject matter is limited to these sources (Preface).

Codex: Page book in contrast to scroll (chap. 5, sec. 5).

Canon: A circumscribing of some writings as of greater authority than others for determining the nature of Christian and possibly Jewish Faith (chap. 4, sec. 1). A relatively closed collection of books that is alone held to be scripturally normative (chap. 6, sec. 15).

Conflated: Combined (chap. 5, sec. 1).

Cullmann's Salvation History (Heilsgeschichte) Perspective: Rather than regarding revelation as hidden and requiring much discernment, this understanding of the NT centers on a recitation of demonstrable saving facts, regarding these as directly revelational. Salvation history as so conceived is impersonal, with no idea of the ways in which sin so habitually challenges God's will. It relegates faith to knowledge of saving facts—of which none are more important than others (chap. 18, sec. 7).

Demiurge: Gnostic term for an evil creator god (chap. 7, sec. 7).

Dialectics: The thinking and communicating process concerning the polarities (tensions) and paradoxes within complex ideas or between them (chap. 1, sec. 5). See Paradox.

Docetism: The belief that Jesus only *appeared* to be human and to suffer, as taught by the Gnostics (chap. 5, sec. 14). More generally, docetists also tend to minimize Scripture's humanity (chap. 7, sec. 8).

Dualistic Eschatology: Though we can share in eternity now, this world is thought to be under demonic influence; the place where the kingdom is to be fully realized is regarded as beyond this world (chap. 5, sec. 4).

Ebionites: Early Jewish Christians who, though placing their hope in Christ, practiced circumcision, observed the Mosaic law, and refused to converse or eat with Gentile Christians (chap. 7, sec. 7, sub-sec 5).

Eisegesis: Reading ideas into texts, rather than in historically and literarily precise ways seeking to derive meanings from texts (exegesis) and their considered applications (chap. 5, sec. 1). See Exegesis.

Epistemology: Theory concerning how we are able to know (chap. 2, sec. 4).

Glossary with References

Eristics: Polemical theology involving the intellectual critique of viewpoints and lifestyles contradicting Christian Faith (chap. 9, sec. 6). See Apologetics.

Eschatological Expectation: Salvation seen as transcending the historical plane; a biblical view that likely began with Isaiah (chap. 5, sec. 4).

Eudemonism: Where morally right actions are expected to bring earthly happiness and reward, and wrong actions, earthly misery and punishment (chap. 5, sec. 12).

Exegesis: Deriving meaning from texts and their expansions (chap. 5, sec. 1). See Eisegesis.

Existentialism: All forms regard the human situation as in many respects one of estrangement from the ideal. Equally common is the emphasis on the importance of personal experience and heartfelt knowing. Kierkegaard, for example, wanted to help people to experience the impact of truth in their own lives and to draw conclusions that affect feeling and action, not just knowing. Another characteristic widely shared by Existentialists is the recognition of the importance of suffering in coming to knowledge. All three emphases find a source in SK's Christian thinking (chap. 12, sec. 6).

Genres: Literary types (chap. 5, sec. 3).

Gestalt psychology: Regards perception as having to do with the intuitive interrelating of parts, thereby enabling the understanding of the whole (Preface and chap. 13, sec. 8).

Gnosis: The word used by Gnostics to refer to the speculative knowledge they regarded as essential for salvation (chap. 7, sec. 7).

Gnosticism: A docetic and speculative heresy that in the early centuries of Christianity infiltrated into much Christianity and competed with "normative" Christianity (chap. 7, sec. 7).

Hegelian Romantic Idealism/Rationalism: Did not believe that God was uniquely present in Jesus, but thought that the Christ *idea* exemplifies the increasing co-mingling of God with humankind in universal history. It so identified the divine with the human that sin was considered a necessary stage in the development of the finite spirit, overcome when it realizes its identity with the Absolute Spirit. Though Hegel and his disciples claimed to be defending Christianity, they were dissolving Christian doctrines into mere symbols of the supposed truths of their philosophy (chap. 18, sec. 7). See Hegel in Index.

Hermeneutics: The understanding of how we understand (Introduction).

Glossary with References

Historical Theology: The historical and theological discipline that studies post-biblical understandings of Christian Faith (chap. 9, sec. 9).

Historicism: Assumes that immanent explanations can be given to all historical events and that Scripture and all other historical texts can and should be read in purely historical ways. It naively believes in the impartial objectivity of purely historical methods that return us to the sources, as though historical methods transcend all influence from tradition (chap. 17, sec. 2).

Historicizing: Attributing particular teachings to earlier events, as, for example, ascribing later laws to God speaking to Moses (chap. 4, sec. 2).

Idealism: A philosophy confident that natural reason, independent of the senses and uninfluenced by history, can grasp ultimate reality (chap. 9, sec. 4). Mind-centered understanding of knowing, such as Platonic rationalism and Hegelianism (chap. 12, sec. 11).

Inerrancy, Verbal Inerrancy, Infallibility: The doctrinaire insistence that the Bible contains no errors or contradictions of any kind and is authoritative on all subjects to which it refers, including history, geography and natural science (for example, involving the universe's physical structure and history) (chap. 7, sec. 8).

Jesus of History: Jesus as understood through historical-critical assessment of the sources (chap. 17, sec. 2).

Kerygma: Christian preaching/message (chap. 5, sec. 2).

Liberal—Conservative: One who takes a caring and constructive attitude toward tradition, but evidences considerable freedom with reference to traditional understandings (chap. 5, sec. 12).

Liberal—Conservative Biblical Interpreter: One who takes a constructive attitude toward biblical tradition, but who does not exempt the Bible from critical reflection, and who thinks that only by making some distinction between essentials and non-essentials can the essentials be emphasized (chap. 5, sec. 12).

Literal or Plain Reading of Texts: Where normal linguistic procedures are seen to apply, but which include the recognition of metaphorical or symbolic meanings if those accord with one's perception of writings' intentions (chap. 5, sec. 1).

Marcion: A second century, somewhat gnostically influenced Christian who believed that the good Savior God disclosed in Jesus frees us from the evil creator god Marcion thought was depicted in the pre-OT. He was one of the first Christians to read pre-NT writings in more historical and literarily precise ways (chap. 5, sec. 14).

Masoretic Text: Hebrew OT text available for only 1,400 years and since its inception favored by most Jews (chap. 4, sec. 3).

Metaphysics: Philosophical speculation concerning the nature of reality (chap. 10, sec. 1).

Midrash: An interpretive method that enables non-historical and linguistically arbitrary meanings to be read into passages, as, for example, the way in which NT writers often found messianic predictions in OT passages (chap. 4, sec. 2; major discussion in chap. 5, secs. 6–7).

Monism: The belief that there is only one fundamental reality of which other beings are but attributes or modes (chap. 9, sec. 7). Compare with Pluralism and Relative Dualism.

Ontology: Philosophies based on an analysis of the concept of "being" (chap. 2, sec. 4).

Paradoxes: Ideas that when taken together seem to contradict each other, but upon closer examination can be seen to be compatible, though with polar tension or complexity. The paradox disclosed in Jesus Christ is not just that God became a human to the point of lowly suffering, but that God revealed Her eternal glory through such an act of condescension (chap. 9, sec. 4; also see chap. 1, sec. 5). Also see Dialectics.

Pelagianism/Arminianism: Understanding the decision of faith as within human creational capacities (chap. 9, sec. 6).

Pentateuch: The first five OT books (chap. 4, sec. 1).

Perspicuity: The Reformation idea that Scripture's central message is clear to Christian readers (chap. 7, sec. 1).

Pesher: Though the interpretive method called midrash sought the relevance of sacred texts by conjuring hidden meanings, pesher as a sub-genre may have been more allegory-like, imagining one-to-one correspondences between particular words and hidden references (chap. 5, sec. 6; major discussion in sec. 7).

Pietism: A movement (begun within German Lutheranism in the seventeenth century) that rebelled against Protestant orthodoxy's preoccupation with pure doctrine. It insisted that theological convictions need to be experientially internalized, lest affirmations make little difference (chap. 14, sec. 5).

Platonic Rationalism/Idealism: See Idealism.

Pluralism: The belief that reality consists of a genuine diversity of beings (chap. 9, sec. 7). See Monism and Relative Dualism.

Postmodern Philosophies: Emphasize that tradition is often a constructive factor in gaining knowledge, that interpretation is vital for learning, and that the understanding that reason's use of tradition and interpretation make possible can be and often is contested. Yet even when people differ in their interpretations, their views should not be regarded as purely subjective. Reasons and evidence can be given, discussion can occur—and for such reasons people can change their minds (chap. 16, sec. 4).

Pragmatic Philosophies: Ones controlled by concerns for the supposed practical benefits of ideas, beliefs or practices (chap. 17, sec. 2). With William James's pragmatic philosophy, faith's content became an arbitrary decision based on insufficient evidence and supported by arguments that could as easily have led in other directions. Because James regarded truth as unknowable, he recommended pursuing mere wishful thoughts (chap. 19, sec. 8).

Pseudonymous Writings: Ancient writers' use of well-known authors' names to entitle their own writings to help secure their acceptance, often implying that one's work was influenced by or in the spirit of the one named as the author (chap. 6, sec. 1).

Rabbinic Judaism: Phariseeism (chap. 4, sec. 2).

Rationalism: See Idealism.

Realism (philosophical): Object-centered knowing, such as Aristotelianism and Thomism (chap. 12, sec. 11).

Recension: Editor's version based on a critical examination of a text and its sources (chap. 6, sec. 15).

Redaction Criticism: Seeks to understand editors' perspectives (chap. 7, sec. 4).

Relative Dualism: The drawing of a sharp distinction between God and world, regarding the world as a battleground between good and evil, with God having supreme but not all-determining power (chap. 9, sec. 7). See Dualistic Eschatology, and compare Monism and Pluralism.

Septuagint (LXX): The earliest pre-OT, created for Greek language, non-Hebrew speaking Hellenistic Jews, parts of which were available approximately 2,200 years ago, likely from Hebrew fragments and partial versions (chap. 4, sec. 3).

Soteriology: The understanding of how salvation is attained (chap. 5, sec. 14; for more detail see chap. 7, sec. 7, sub-sec 3).

Teleological: Goal (telos) related (chap. 9, sec. 7).

Teleological Suspension of the Ethical: The telos or goal-related, case-specific divine suspension of what would otherwise be one's duty (chap. 9, sec. 7).

Testimony Books: Hypothesized selections and combinations of prophecies from those portions of the Septuagint then available, that made it easier to interpret pre-OT texts as predicting Christ and as pointing to eschatological meanings (chap. 4, sec. 4).

Traditional Religion/Animism: Regards nature as inhabited with and largely controlled by conflicting spirits (chap. 6, sec. 15).

Transposition: Concerning writings, changes of the relative position of letters within words, words within sentences, sentences within paragraphs, and changes through additions or omissions (chap. 6, sec. 5).

Truth as Subjectivity: Kierkegaard meant by this easily misunderstood phrase that the truth of Christian Faith cannot be confirmed by anything other than biblical evidence substantiated by one's relationship with Christ. SK thought that the question of Christ's authority can only be finally settled as human subjects surrender to the Living Lord (chap. 18, sec. 8).

Verbal Inspiration: That God inspired all of the words of Scripture (chap. 3, sec. 2; also see "Inerrancy, Verbal Inerrancy, Infallibility").

Bibliography

Ackroyd, Peter. "The Book of Isaiah." In *The Interpreter's One-Volume Commentary On the Bible*, edited by Charles M. Laymon, 329–71. Nashville: Abingdon, 1971.

Allen, Diogenes. *Christian Belief in a Postmodern World: The Full Wealth of Conviction*. Louisville: Westminster John Knox, 1989.

———. *Philosophy for Understanding Theology*. Atlanta: Knox, 1985.

Aulen, Gustaf. *The Faith of the Christian Church*. Philadelphia: Muhlenberg, 1960.

Baillie, John. *The Idea of Revelation in Recent Thought*. New York: Columbia University Press, 1956.

Barbour, Ian G. Barbour. *Religion in an Age of Science*. London: SCM, 1990.

———. "Science and Religion." In *Science and Religion*, edited by Ian G. Barbour, 3–29. New York: Harper & Row, 1968.

Barr, James. *The Bible in the Modern World*. London: SCM, 1973.

———. *Biblical Faith and Natural Theology*. Oxford: Clarendon, 1993.

———. "Biblical Theology." In *The Interpreter's Dictionary of the Bible: Supplementary Volume*, edited by Keith Crim, 104–11. Nashville: Abingdon, 1976.

———. *The Concept of Biblical Theology: An Old Testament Perspective*. Minneapolis: Fortress, 1999.

———. *Does Biblical Study Still Belong to Theology?* Oxford: Clarendon, 1978.

———. *Escaping From Fundamentalism*. London: SCM, 1984.

———. *Fundamentalism*. Philadelphia: Westminster, 1978.

———. *Holy Scripture: Canon, Authority, Criticism*. Philadelphia: Westminster, 1983.

———. *Old and New in Interpretation*. London: SCM, 1966.

———. "Revelation in History." In *The Interpreter's Dictionary of the Bible: Supplementary Volume*, edited by Keith Crim, 746–49. Nashville: Abingdon, 1976.

Barrett, C. K. *Paul: An Introduction to His Thought*. Louisville: Westminster John Knox, 1994.

Barth, Karl. *Against the Stream: Shorter Post-War Writings, 1946–1952*. New York: Philosophical Library, 1954.

———. *Church Dogmatics*. Vol. 1/1, *The Doctrine of the Word of God: Prolegomena to Church Dogmatics*. Edited by Geoffrey W. Bromiley and T. F. Torrance. Translated by G. T. Thompson. Edinburgh: T. & T. Clark, 1936.

———. *Church Dogmatics*. Vol. 1/2, *The Doctrine of the Word of God*. Translated by G. T. Thompson and Harold Knight. Edinburgh: T. & T. Clark, 1956.

———. *Church Dogmatics*. Vol. 2/1, *The Doctrine of God*. Translated by T. H. L. Parker et al. Edinburgh: T. & T. Clark, 1957.

———. *Church Dogmatics*. Vol. 3/4, *The Doctrine of Creation*. Translated by A. T. Mackay et al. Edinburgh: T. & T. Clark, 1961.

———. *Church Dogmatics*. Vol. 4/1, *The Doctrine of Reconciliation*. Translated by Geoffrey W. Bromiley. Edinburgh: T. & T. Clark, 1956.

———. *Church Dogmatics*. Vol. 4/3, *First Half, The Doctrine of Reconciliation*. Translated by Geoffrey W. Bromiley. Edinburgh: T. & T. Clark, 1961.

———. *Church Dogmatics*. Vol. 4/3, *Second Half, The Doctrine of Reconciliation*. Translated by Geoffrey W. Bromiley. Edinburgh: T. & T. Clark, 1962.

———. *Credo*. Translated by J. S. McNab. New York: Scribner's Sons, 1962.

———. *The Epistle to the Romans*. Translated by Edwyn C. Hopkyns from the 6th ed. New York: Oxford University Press, 1963.

———. *Evangelical Theology*. Translated by Grover Foley. New York: Holt, Rinehart, & Winston, 1963.

———. "Foreword to the Second Edition of *The Epistle to the Romans*." In *The Beginnings of Dialectical Theology*, introduced by James M. Robinson, and here translated by Keith R. Crim and Louis De Grazia, 88–99. Richmond: John Knox, 1968.

———. *God Here and Now*. Translated by Paul M. Van Buren. New York: Harper & Row, 1964.

———. *Göttingen Dogmatics*. Vol. 1. Edited by Hannelotte Reiffen. Translated by Geoffrey W. Bromiley. Grand Rapids: Eerdmans, 1991.

———. *Homiletics*. Translated by Geoffrey W. Bromiley and Donald E. Daniels. Louisville: Westminster John Knox, 1991.

———. *How I Changed My Mind*. Richmond: Knox, 1966.

———. *Karl Barth Letters 1961-1968*. Edited and translated by Geoffrey W. Bromiley. Grand Rapids: Eerdmans, 1981.

———. *Karl Barth's Table Talk*. Recorded and edited by John D. Godsey. Edinburgh & London: Oliver & Boyd, 1963.

———. *The Preaching of the Gospel*. Translated by B. E. Hooke. Philadelphia: Westminster, 1963.

———. "Prefaces" to the six editions of his Romans Commentary. In *The Epistle to the Romans*, prefaced and translated by Edwyn C. Hoskyns, 1–26. London: Oxford University Press, first edition, 1933, sixth impression, 1963.

———. *Protestant Theology in the Nineteenth Century*. Translated by Brian Cozens and John Bowden. London: SCM, 1972.

———. *Theology and Church*. Translated by Louise Pettibone Smith. London: SCM, 1962.

———. *The Way of Theology in Karl Barth: Essays and Comments*. Edited by H. Martin Rumscheidt. Allison Park, PA: Pickwick, 1986.

———. *The Word of God and the Word of Man*. Translated by Douglas Horton. New York: Harper & Row, 1928.

Barth, Karl, and Eduard Thurneysen. *Come Holy Spirit*. Translated by George W. Richards, Elmer G. Homrighausen, and Karl J. Ernst. London: Mobrays, 1978.

Barth, Karl, and Rudolf Bultmann. *Karl Barth-Rudolf Bultmann Letters 1922-1966*. Edited and translated by Geoffrey W. Bromiley. Grand Rapids: Eerdmans, 1981.

Barton, John. *Holy Writings, Sacred Text: The Canon in Early Christianity*. Louisville: Westminster John Knox, 1997.

———. "Marcion Revisited." In *The Canon Debate*, edited by Lee Martin McDonald and James A. Sanders, 341–54. Peabody, MA: Hendrickson, 2002.

Beare, Frank W. *The Earliest Records of Jesus*. New York: Abingdon, 1962.

Bibliography

Berkhof, Hendrikus. *Christian Faith: An Introduction to the Study of Faith*. Translated by Sierd Woudstra. Grand Rapids: Eerdmans, 1979; rev. ed., 1986. Quotations from first edition, unless otherwise indicated.

———. *Introduction to the Study of Dogmatics*. Translated by John Vriend. Grand Rapids: Eerdmans, 1985.

Biber, C. H. "Revelation, New Testament." In *Companion to the Bible*, edited by J. J. Von Allmen and translated by P. J. Allcock et al., 366–69. New York: Oxford University Press, 1958.

Bright, John. *The Authority of the Old Testament*. Nashville: Abingdon, 1967.

Brown, Raymond E., and Sandra M. Schneiders. "Hermeneutics." In *The New Jerome Biblical Commentary*, edited by Raymond E. Brown et al., 1146–65. Englewood Cliffs, NJ: Prentice Hall, 1990.

Brown, Robert McAffee. "Good News from Karl Barth." In *How Karl Barth Changed My Mind*, edited by Donald K. McKim, 94–101. Grand Rapids: Eerdmans, 1986.

Brunner, Emil. *The Christian Doctrine of Creation and Redemption*. Vol. 2 of *Dogmatics*. Translated by Olive Wyon. Philadelphia: Westminster, 1952.

———. *The Christian Doctrine of God*. Vol. 1 of *Dogmatics*. Translated by Olive Wyon. Philadelphia: Westminster, 1950.

———. *The Christian Doctrine of the Church, Faith, and the Consummation*. Vol. 3 of *Dogmatics*. Translated by David Cairns, in collaboration with T. H. L. Parker. Philadelphia: Westminster, 1962.

———. "Intellectual Autobiography." In *The Theology of Emil Brunner*, edited by Charles W. Kegley and Robert Bretall, 3–20. New York: Macmillan, 1962.

———. *Our Faith*. Translated by John W. Rilling. New York: Scribner's Sons, 1936.

———. *The Philosophy of Religion: From the Standpoint of Protestant Theology*. Edited by A. J. D. Farrer and Bertram Lee Woolf. London: Clarke, 1958.

———. *Revelation and Reason*. Translated by Olive Wyon. Philadelphia: Westminster, 1956.

———. *The Scandal of Christianity*. Translated by M. E. Bratcher. Richmond: John Knox, 1965.

———. *Theology of Crisis*. New York: Scribner's Sons, 1931.

———. *Truth As Encounter*. Translated by Amandus W. Loos, David Cairns, and T. H. L. Parker. Philadelphia: Westminster, 1964.

Brunner, Emil, and Karl Barth. *Nature and Grace*. Brunner, "Natural Theology"; Barth, "No!" Translated by B. Birch Hoyle. London: Geoffrey Bles, 1946.

Bultmann, Rudolf. *Essays Philosophical and Theological*. Translated by James C. G. Greig. New York: Macmillan, 1955.

———. *Existence and Faith*. Translated by Shubert M. Ogden. Cleveland: World, 1966.

———. *Primitive Christianity*. Translated by R. H. Fuller. Cleveland: World, 1956.

———. "The Problem of a Theological Exegesis of the New Testament." In *The Beginnings of Dialectical Theology*, edited by James M. Robinson and translated by Keith R. Crim and Louis De Grazia, 236–56. Richmond: Knox, 1968.

———. "Revelation in the New Testament." In *Twentieth Century Theology in the Making*, edited by Jaroslav Pelikan and translated by R. A. Wilson, 2:41–46. London: Collins, 1970.

———. *Theology of the New Testament*. Vol. 2. Translated by Kendrick Grobel. New York: Scribner's Sons, 1955.

Busch, Eberhard. *Karl Barth*. Translated by John Bowden. Philadelphia: Fortress, 1976.

Bibliography

Cairns, David. *The Image of God in Man*. New York: Philosophical Library, 1953.

Calhoun, Robert Lowry. *Lectures on the History of Christian Doctrine*. New Haven: Yale Divinity School, usage beginning in 1949. For private circulation only.

Calvin, John. *Calvin: Institutes of the Christian Religion*. 2 vols. Library of Christian Classics 20–21. Edited by John T. McNeill. Translated by Ford Lewis Battles. Philadelphia: Westminster, 1960.

Campenhausen, Hans von. *The Formation of the Christian Bible*. Translated by J. A. Baker. Minneapolis: Fortress, 1972.

Childs, Brevard S. *Biblical Theology of the Old and New Testaments*. Minneapolis: Fortress, 1993.

———. *Isaiah: A Commentary*. Louisville: Westminster John Knox, 2001.

———. *The New Testament as Canon: An Introduction*. Philadelphia: Fortress, 1984.

Clements, Keith W. *Faith*. London: SCM, 1981.

Cobb, John B., Jr. *A Christian Natural Theology*. Philadelphia: Westminster, 1965.

Cobb, John B., Jr., and David Ray Griffin. *Process Theology*. Philadelphia: Westminster, 1976.

Cochrane, Arthur C. *The Existentialists and God*. Philadelphia: Westminster, 1961.

Coulson, Charles A. "The Similarity of Science and Religion." In *Science and Religion*, edited by Ian G. Barbour, 57–77. New York: Harper & Row, 1968.

Croxall, T. H. *Kierkegaard Studies*. London: Lutterworth, 1948.

Dahl, Nils Alstrup. *The Crucified Messiah: and Other Essays*. Minneapolis: Augsburg, 1974.

———. *Jesus in the Memory of the Early Church*. Minneapolis: Augsburg, 1976.

———. *Jesus the Christ*. Edited by Donald H. Juel. Minneapolis: Fortress, 1991.

Dalferth, Ingolf U. "Karl Barth's Eschatological Realism." In *Karl Barth Centenary Essays*, edited by S. W. Sykes, 14–15. Cambridge: Cambridge University Press, 1989.

Davies, Paul. *God and the New Physics*. New York: Simon & Schuster, 1983.

Dunn, James D. G. *Jesus' Call to Discipleship*. Cambridge: Cambridge University Press, 1992.

———. *The Living Word*. Philadelphia: Fortress, 1987.

———. *Unity and Diversity in the New Testament: An Inquiry Into the Character of Earliest Christianity*. Philadelphia: Westminster, 1977.

Ebeling, Gerhard. *Theology and Proclamation: A Discussion With Rudolf Bultmann*. Translated by John Riches. London: Collins, 1966.

———. *Word and Faith*. Translated by James W. Leitch. Philadelphia: Fortress, 1963.

Ellul, Jacques. *The Humiliation of the Word*. Translated by Joyce Main Hanks. Grand Rapids: Eerdmans, 1985.

Erickson, Millard J. *Christian Theology*. Grand Rapids: Baker, 1985.

Fosdick, Harry Emerson. *A Guide to Understanding the Bible: The Development of Ideas within the Old and New Testaments*. New York: Harper & Row, 1967.

———. *The Modern Use of the Bible*. New York: Macmillan, 1961.

Funk, Robert W. "The Once and Future New Testament." In *The Canon Debate*, edited by Lee Martin McDonald and James A. Sanders, 541–58. Peabody, MA: Hendrickson, 2002.

Furnish, Victor Paul. "Prophets, Apostles, and Preachers: A Study of the Biblical Concept of Preaching." *Interpretation: A Journal of Bible and Theology* 17, no. 1 (1963) 48–60.

Gadamer, Hans-Georg. *Truth and Method*. Edited and translated by Garrett Barden and John Cumming. New York: Crossroad, 1985.

Gamble, Harry Y. *Books and Readers in the Early Church: A History of Early Christian Texts*. New Haven: Yale University Press, 1995.

———. *The New Testament Canon: Its Making and Meaning.* Eugene, OR: Wipf and Stock, 2002.

———. "The New Testament Canon: Recent Research and the *Status Quastionis.*" In *The Canon Debate*, edited by Lee Martin McDonald and James A. Sanders, 267–94. Peabody, MA: Hendrickson, 2002.

Gates, John A. *The Life and Thought of Kierkegaard for Everyman.* London: Hodder & Stoughton, 1961.

Gilkey, Langdon. *Maker of Heaven and Earth.* Garden City, NY: Doubleday, 1959.

Gogarten, Friedrich. "The Holy Egoism of the Christian: An Answer to Julicher's Essay: 'A Modern Interpretation of Paul.'" In *The Beginnings of Dialectical Theology*, edited by James M. Robinson and translated by Keith R. Crim and Louis De Grazia, 82–87. Richmond: Knox, 1968.

Goldingay, John. "Inspiration." In *A Dictionary of Biblical Interpretation*, edited by R. J. Coggins and J. L. Houlden, 314–6. London: SCM, 1990.

Gould, Stephen Jay. *Ever since Darwin: Reflections On Natural History.* New York: Norton, 1979.

Grene, Marjorie. "Introduction." In *Knowing and Being*, by Michael Polanyi, edited by Marjorie Grene, ix–xvii. Chicago: University of Chicago Press, 1969.

Gunneweg, A. H. J. *Understanding the Old Testament.* Translated by John Bowden. Philadelphia: Westminster, 1978.

Gunton, Colin E. *The Actuality of the Atonement: A Study of Metaphor, Rationality, and the Christian Tradition.* Edinburgh: T. & T. Clark, 1988.

Habgood, John. "Minds and Machines." In *Science and Religion*, edited by Ian G. Barbour, 300–308. New York: Harper & Row, 1968.

Haenchen, Ernst, *The Acts of the Apostles: A Commentary.* Translated by Bernard Noble & Gerald Shinn. Philadelphia: Westminster, 1971.

Hahn, Ferdinand. *Historical Investigation and New Testament Faith.* Edited by Edgar Krentz. Translated by Robert Maddox. Philadelphia: Fortress, 1983.

Hahneman, Geoffrey Mark. "The Muratorian Fragment and the Origins of the New Testament Canon." In *The Canon Debate*, edited by Lee Martin McDonald and James A. Sanders, 405–16. Peabody, MA: Hendrickson, 2002.

Harnack, Adolf von. *The Gospel of the Alien God*, which includes *Marcion's Antitheses*. Translated by John E. Steely and Lyle D. Bierma. Durham, NC: Labyrinth, 1990.

Harrington, Daniel J. "The Old Testament Apocrypha in the Early Church and Today." In *The Canon Debate*, edited by Lee Martin McDonald and James A. Sanders, 196–211. Peabody, MA: Hendrickson, 2002.

Harrisville, Roy A., and Walter Sundberg. *The Bible in Modern Culture: Baruch Spinoza to Brevard Childs.* Grand Rapids: Eerdmans, 2002.

Harrisville, Roy A., and Walter Sundberg. *The Bible in Modern Culture: Theology and Historical Method From Spinoza to Kasemann.* Grand Rapids: Eerdmans, 1995.

Harrisville, Roy A. *His Hidden Grace: An Essay On Biblical Criticism.* New York: Abingdon, 1965.

Harvey, Van A. *The Historian and the Believer: The Morality of Historical Knowledge and Christian Belief.* New York: Macmillan, 1966.

Hendry, George S. "On Barth, the Philosopher." In *Faith and the Philosophers*, 210–18. London: Macmillan, 1964.

Hendry, George S. *Theology of Nature.* Philadelphia: Westminster, 1980.

Herrmann, Wilhelm. *The Communion of the Christian with God*. Translated by J. Sandys Stayton, based on the 4th German ed. London: SCM, 1972.

Hick, John. *Faith and Knowledge*. 2nd ed. Glasgow: Collins Sons, 1974.

———. *Philosophy of Religion*. Englewood Cliff, NJ: Prentice-Hall, 1973.

Hordern, William. *Speaking of God*. New York: Macmillan, 1964.

Hultgren, Arland J. *The Rise of Normative Christianity*. Minneapolis: Fortress, 1994.

Jeanrond, Werner. *Theological Hermeneutics: Development and Significance*. London: SCM, 1994.

Jewitt, Paul King. "Emil Brunner's Doctrine of Scripture." In *Inspiration and Interpretation*, edited by John F. Walvoord, 210–38. Grand Rapids: Eerdmans, 1957.

Johnson, Robert Clyde. *Authority in Protestant Theology*. Philadelphia: Westminster, 1959.

Johnstone, William. "The 'Ten Commandments': Some Recent Interpretations." *Expository Times*, 100, no. 12 (1989) 453–61.

Jonas, Hans. "Gnosticism." In *A Handbook of Christian Theology*, edited by Marvin Halverson and Arthur A. Cohen, 148–51. London: Collins, 1962.

Kant, Immanuel. *The Philosophy of Kant: Immanuel Kant's Moral and Political Writings*. Edited and introduced by Carl J. Friedrich. New York: Random House, 1949.

Kasemann, Ernst. *Essays On New Testament Themes: Studies in Biblical Theology*. Translated by W. J. Montague. London: SCM, 1964.

———. *New Testament Questions of Today*. Translated by W. J. Montague. London: SCM, 1969.

Kaufman, Gordon D. *Systematic Theology: A Historicist Perspective*. New York: Scribner's Sons, 1968.

Kierkegaard, Soren. *The Concept of Dread*. Translated by Walter Lowrie. Princeton: Princeton University Press, 1957.

———. *Concluding Unscientific Postscript to the Philosophical Fragments*. Translated by David F. Swenson and Walter Lowrie. Princeton: Princeton University Press, 1963.

———. *Either/Or*. Vol. 2. Translated by Walter Lowrie with revisions by Howard A. Johnson. Garden City, NY: Doubleday, 1959.

———. *Philosophical Fragments or A Fragment of Philosophy*. Translated by David F. Swenson. Princeton: Princeton University Press, 1962.

———. *The Point of View for My Work as An Author: A Report to History*. Translated by Walter Lowrie and newly edited by Benjamin Nelson. New York: Harper & Row, 1962.

———. *Stages On Life's Way*. Edited and translated by Howard V. Hong and Edna H. Hong. Princeton: Princeton University Press, 1991.

———. *Training In Christianity*. Translated by Walter Lowrie. Princeton: Princeton University Press, 1960.

Kraft, Robert A. "The Codex and Canon Consciousness." In *The Canon Debate*, edited by Lee Martin McDonald and James A. Sanders, 229–34. Peabody, MA: Hendrickson, 2002.

Kummel, Werner Georg. *Introduction to the New Testament*. Comprising Kummel's complete reediting of the founding work of Paul Feine and Johannes Behm. Translated by A. J. Mattill Jr. Nashville: Abingdon, 1966.

———. *The New Testament: The History of the Investigation of Its Problems*. Translated by S. McLean Gilmour and Howard C. Kee. London: SCM, 1973.

Lessing, Gotthold. *Lessing's Theological Writings*. Selected and translated by Henry Chadwick. Stanford: Stanford University Press, 1957.

Bibliography

Leuba, J. L. "Teaching." In *Companion to the Bible*, edited by J.-J. von Allmen and translated by P. J. Allcock et al., 414–16. New York: Oxford University Press, 1958.

Lohse, Bernhard. *A Short History of Christian Doctrine*. Translated by F. Ernest Stoeffler. Philadelphia: Fortress, 1966.

MacIntyre, Alasdair. *After Virtue: A Study in Moral Theory*. 2nd ed. Notre Dame: University of Notre Dame Press, 1984.

McCormack, Bruce. "Historical Criticism and Dogmatic Interest in Karl Barth's Theological Exegesis of the New Testament." In *Biblical Hermeneutics in Historical Perspective*, edited by Mark S. Burrows and Paul Rorem, 322–38. Grand Rapids: Eerdmans, 1991.

———. *Karl Barth's Critically Realistic Dialectical Theology: Its Genesis and Development 1909–1936*. New York: Oxford University Press, 1997.

McDonald, Lee Martin. *The Formation of the Christian Biblical Canon*. Nashville: Abingdon, 1988.

McDonald, Lee Martin. "Identifying Scripture and Canon in the Early Church: The Criteria Question." In *The Canon Debate*, edited by Lee Martin McDonald and James A. Sanders, 416–39. Peabody, MA: Hendrickson, 2002.

McKelway, Alexander J. *The Systematic Theology of Paul Tillich*. Richmond: John Knox, 1964.

McLelland, Joseph C. "Philosophy and Theology—A Family Affair: Karl and Heinrich Barth." In *Footnotes to a Theology: The Karl Barth Colloquium of 1972*, edited by Martin Rumscheidt, 30–52. SR Supplements. Waterloo, ON: Academic Studies in Religion, 1974.

McNeill, John T. "Introduction." In *Calvin: Institutes of the Christian Religion*, edited by John T. McNeill and translated by Ford Lewis Battles, 1:xix–lxxi. Library of Christian Classics 20. Philadelphia: Westminster, 1960.

Meier, John P. *A Marginal Jew: Rethinking the Historical Jesus*. Vol. 1, *The Roots of the Problem and the Person*. New York: Doubleday, 1991.

Metzger, Bruce M. *The Canon of the New Testament*. Oxford: Oxford University Press, 1988.

Michalson, Carl. "The Hermeneutics of Holiness in Wesley." In *The Heritage of Christian Thought*, edited by Robert E. Cushman and Elgin Grislis, 127–41. New York: Harper & Row, 1965.

Migliore, Daniel L. *Faith Seeking Understanding*. Grand Rapids: Eerdmans, 1991.

———. "Karl Barth's First Lectures in Dogmatics: *Instruction in the Christian Religion*." In *The Gottingen Dogmatics: Vol. 1*, edited by Hannelotte Reiffen and translated by Geoffrey W. Bromiley, xv–lxii. Grand Rapids: Eerdmans, 1991.

Morse, Christopher. *Not Every Spirit: A Dogmatics of Christian Disbelief*. Valley Forge, PA: Trinity, 1994.

Newbigin, Lesslie. *Foolishness to the Greeks: The Gospel and Western Culture*. Grand Rapids: Eerdmans, 1986.

———. *The Gospel in a Pluralist Society*. Grand Rapids: Eerdmans, 1989.

Niebuhr, H. Richard. *Christ and Culture*. New York: Harper & Bros., 1951.

———. *The Meaning of Revelation*. New York: Macmillan, 1962.

Ott, Heinrich. *Theology and Preaching*. Translated by Harold Knight. Philadelphia: Westminster, 1965.

Outler, Albert C., ed. *John Wesley*. New York: Oxford University Press, 1964.

Pannenberg, Wolfhart. *The Apostles Creed*. Translated by Margaret Kohl. London: SCM, 1972.

———. *Basic Questions in Theology*. Vol. 1. Translated by George H. Kehm. London: SCM, 1970.

———. *Systematic Theology*. 3 vols. Translated by Geoffrey W. Bromiley. Grand Rapids: Eerdmans, 1991–1998.

Placher, William C. *Unapologetic Theology*. Louisville: Westminster John Knox, 1989.

Polanyi, Michael. *Knowing and Being*. Edited by Marjorie Grene. Chicago: University of Chicago Press, 1969.

———. *Personal Knowledge: Towards A Post-Critical Philosophy*. New York: Harper & Row, 1964.

———. *Science, Faith, and Society*. Chicago: University of Chicago Press, 1964.

———. *The Study of Man*. Chicago: University of Chicago Press, 1963.

———. *The Tacit Dimension*. New York: Anchor, 1967.

Rad, Gerhard von. *Biblical Interpretations in Preaching*. Translated by John E. Steely. Nashville: Abington, 1973.

Ramseyer, J. P. H. "Word." In *Companion to the Bible*, edited by J.-J. von Allmen and translated by P. J. Allcock et al., 460–63. New York: Oxford University Press, 1958.

Randolph, David James. *The Renewal of Preaching*. Philadelphia: Fortress, 1969.

Roberts, J. J. M. "A Christian Perspective on Prophetic Prediction." *Interpretation* 33, no. 3 (1979) 240–53.

Rood, Wayne R. *The Art of Teaching Christianity*. Nashville: Abingdon, 1968.

Schleiermacher, Friedrich. *The Christian Faith*. Vol. 2. Edited by H. R. Mackintosh and J. S. Stewart. New York: Harper & Row, 1963.

———. *Hermeneutics: The Handwritten Manuscripts*. Edited by Heinz Kimmerle and translated by James Duke and Jack Forstman. Missoula, MT: Scholars, 1977.

Schrader, George A. "Brunner's Conception of Philosophy." In *The Theology of Emil Brunner*, edited by Charles W. Kegley, 111–29. New York: Macmillan, 1962.

Smith, John E. "Existentialist Philosophy." In *A Handbook of Christian Theology*, edited by Marvin Halverson and Arthur A. Cohen, 124–31. London: Collins, 1962.

Stiver, Dan R. *Theology after Ricoeur: New Directions in Hermeneutical Theology*. Louisville: Westminster John Knox, 2001.

Stuhlmacher, Peter. *Historical Criticism and Theological Interpretation of Scripture*. Translated by Roy A. Harrisville. Philadelphia: Fortress, 1977.

Thielicke, Helmut. *Modern Faith and Thought*. Translated by Geoffrey W. Bromiley. Grand Rapids: Eerdmans, 1990.

Thiselton, Anthony C. *The Two Horizons*. Grand Rapids: Eerdmans, 1980.

Thomas, George F. *Religious Philosophies of the West*. New York: Scribner's Sons, 1965.

Tillich, Paul. *Biblical Religion and the Search For Ultimate Reality*. Chicago: University of Chicago Press, 1955.

———. *Dynamics of Faith*. New York: Harper & Bros., 1957.

———. *A History of Christian Thought*. Edited by Carl E. Braaten. London: SCM, 1968.

———. *The Protestant Era*. Chicago: University of Chicago Press, 1957

———. *Systematic Theology*. 3 vols. Chicago: University of Chicago Press, 1951–1963.

Torrance, Thomas F. *Karl Barth: An Introduction to His Early Theology, 1910–1931*. London: SCM, 1962.

Toulman, Stephen. *Foresight and Understanding*. New York: Harper & Row, 1961.

Tracy, David. *Plurality and Ambiguity: Hermeneutics, Religion and Hope*. San Francisco: Harper & Row, 1987.

Troeltsch, Ernst. *The Christian Faith*. Translated by Garrett E. Paul. Minneapolis: Fortress, 1991.

Vanderkam James C. "Questions of Canon Viewed Through the Dead Sea Scrolls." In *The Canon Debate*, edited by Lee Martin McDonald and James A. Sanders, 91–109. Peabody, MA: Hendrickson, 2002.

van Leeuwen, Arend Th. *Christianity in World History: The Meeting of the Faiths of East and West*. Translated by H. H. Hoskins. Edinburgh: Edinburgh House, 1964.

———. *Old Testament Theology*. Vol. 2. Translated by D. M. G. Stalker. New York: Harper & Row, 1965.

Vriezen, Th. C. *An Outline of Old Testament Theology*. Oxford: Blackwell, 1966.

Watson, Francis. "Philosophy." In *A Dictionary of Biblical Interpretation*, edited by R. J. Coggins and J. L. Houlden, 544–46. London: SCM, 1990.

———. *Text and Truth: Redefining Biblical Theology*. Grand Rapids: Eerdmans, 1997.

Weber, Otto. *Foundations of Dogmatics Vol. 1*. Translated and annotated by Darrell L. Guder. Grand Rapids: Eerdmans, 1981.

Welch, Claude. *Protestant Thought in the Nineteenth Century*. Vol. 1, *1799–1870*. New Haven: Yale University Press, 1972.

Wendel, Francois. *Calvin*. Translated by Philip Mairet. New York: Harper & Row, 1950.

Wesley, John. *Forty-Four Sermons*. London: Epworth, 1961.

Whitehead, Alfred North. *Adventure of Ideas*. London: Cambridge University Press, 1935.

———. *The Aims of Education*. New York: Macmillan, 1929.

———. *Dialogues of Alfred North Whitehead*. Recorded by Lucien Price. Boston: Little, Brown, 1954.

———. *The Interpretation of Science*. Edited by A. H. Johnson. Indianapolis: Bobbs-Merrill, 1961.

———. *Modes of Thought*. New York: Macmillan, 1958.

———. *Science and the Modern World*. New York: New American Library of World Literature, 1925.

Whittaker, J. H. "Kierkegaard On History and Faith." *Scottish Journal of Theology* 40 (1987) 379–97.

Wilson, R. McL. "Gnosticism." In *A New Dictionary of Christian Theology*, edited by Alan Richardson and John Bowden, 226–30. London, 1983.

Wood, Charles M. *The Formation of Christian Understanding: An Essay in Theological Hermeneutics*. Philadelphia: Westminster, 1981.

Ziesler, Paul. *Pauline Christianity*. Oxford: Oxford University Press, 1983.

——— *Paul's Letter to the Romans*. London: SCM, 1989.

Index

This index indicates page numbered subtopics under major themes and thinkers. (For ease of access some of the subtopics are listed in more than one place.) Smaller individual items are listed separately.

Analogy of being, being mysticism, 29–31.
Anselm's ontological argument, 210–11.
Anthropic principle, 215.
Apocrypha, Protestant & Catholic attitudes, 47–49.
Apologetics, 177–84.
Ascension, Acts's conception of, 232–3 (n4).

Atonement/reconciliation in Christ
  Anselm's satisfaction & representation theory, 74.
  Interrelatedness of historical & existential aspects, 305–6.
  Luther & Calvin's punitive conception, 74.

Barr
  Biblical theology, 187–8.
  Conflicting notions concerning revelation in history, 25–26.
  Historicalcritical perceptions helpful for understanding Bible theologically, 317
  Historical theology, 186–7
  Theological hermeneutic, 295

Barth (see Hermeneutics for his interpreting of Bible).
  Criticism of Existentialism's understanding of limit situations, 180–1.
  Critique of Orthodoxy, 191–2.
  Culture critical warning, 298–301.
  Faith & divine transcendence, 327.
  Hegel's influence upon Barth, 226.
  Interpretation of natural experience, 185–6.
  Opposed philosophical presumptuousness, 225.
  Theological balancing of Realism & Idealism, 227–9.
  Understanding relationship of sacred history to biblical & general history, 309–10.

Biblical personalism, 21.
Brunner, 20, 175, 176–7, 178–9, 185 n75, 195, 198, 200, 213, 218–9, 310–11, 311.
Buber, 221–2.
By grace through faith, 330.

Calvin
  By grace through faith, 329–330.
  Triune understanding of faith, 329.

Canon, canonizing, & precanonical writings
  Canonizing decisions, 112–6.
  Eight preNT writings not highly regarded in early years, 120.
  Precanonical & canonical writings' necessity, 118–9.
  Pseudonymous NT writings & the apostolicity standard, 122–4.
  Revelation's canonical inclusion questioned early, late, 106–7, 129, 130.
  Tatian's *Diatessaron*, 103–4, 115, (n85).

Child sacrifice, OT, 87.
Conservative—Liberal, 80–83.
Darwin, & Whitehead's critique, 214–5, 215.
Decalogue, ten commandments, 77–79.
Degree Christology, 310, n21.
Deputyship, 195–8.
Discussion & disputation, importance for Christian learning & teaching, 261–2, 263.
Dogmatics & catechesis, similarities, differences, 262.
Ecological crisis not due to Gen 1:28 deputyship teaching, 197, n17.
Edwards, Jonathan, affections as motivating force, 328–9.
Eschaton's delay, NT reinterpretations, 158–9.
Eudemonism, Jesus versus the OT, 82–3.
Evil, problem of, 313.

353

Existentialism, 222–3.

Faith & history
- Barth's literary & historical emphases, 290–1, 293–4.
- Biblicism, & critique of, 190–1.
- Conflicting notions concerning revelation in history, 25–26.
- Cullmann, salvation history, exposition & critique, 313–4.
- Dialectical use of historicalcritical method, 314–7.
- Efforts to separate faith from revelational base in history, 318.
- Evaluation of Hegel's philosophy of history, 222–3.
- Four Gospels, each relativized by relation to the others & by the gospel itself, 132.
- Hand copying of texts, inherent dangers of corrupting them, 116–7.
- Herrmann's biblical, theological insights, 169–71, 306–7, 311.
- Historicalcritical method challenges easy participation in traditions, 322.
- Historical-critical perceptions helpful for understanding Bible theologically, 317.
- Historical-critical scholarship cannot establish or refute NT affirmations of meaning, 322–3.
- Historical facts & their interpretations, 318–9.
- Historicism, 291–2.
- Objectivity, myth of presuppositionless understanding, 279–80.
- Principles for assessing historical probabilities, 319–22.
- Understanding relationship of sacred history to biblical & general history, 309–10.

Faith as involving whole personality, 330–32.
Gnosticism & Gnostic Christianity, 109, 119 (n107), 140–2, 143 (n61), 145, 145 (n65), 146–7, 147.
Hermeneutics, additional explicit, chap. 7, 129–57. See also "NT content analysis & critical appraisal" & "Faith & history".

Hermeneutics concerning interpreting of Bible
- Antiochan & Protestant plain reading biblical interpretation, 52.
- Barr, Theological Hermeneutic, 295.
- Barth, between remembrance & expectation, 36–37.
- Barth, Critique of Orthodoxy, 191–2.
- Barth, culturecritical warning, 298–301.
- Barth, honoring Christian theological tradition, 190–1.
- Barth, openness to God's critiquing & transforming of theological & moral perspectives, 297.
- Barth's literary & historical emphases, 290–1 293–4.
- Barth's moral application insights, 297.
- Barth's referential understanding, 294–5.
- Bultmann's interpretation of Rom. 7:14–24; 203 (n33).
- Bultmann's referential perspective, 295.
- Childs's canonical hermeneutic, exposition & evaluation, 134–6.
- Exegesis-exposition & meantmeans oversimplifications, 280–1.
- Four Gospels, each relativized by the others & by the gospel itself, 132.
- H. Richard Niebuhr's referential conception, 295.
- Jesus's hermeneutics and use of parables, 288–9.
- Kasemann's critical insights concerning NT interpretation, 135, 136–8, 150.
- Letter-spirit differentiation, 82, 137–8.
- Liberalconservative distinction, 80–83.
- Lindbeck's & Kelsey's intratextual approaches, 295–7.
- Pietism & Wesley's moral application interpretive understanding, 140, 297–8.
- Related to congregational preaching, 270–2.
- Scripture as inspired & inspiring, 32–33, 124–5.
- Spirit & interpreting, 37.

Hermeneutics general
- Ellul, 282–7.
- Gadamer, 278–82, 294.
- Gadamer, traditions' important in interpreting, 278–80.
- Hermeneutical circle, 277–8.
- Objectivity, myth of presuppositionless understanding, 279–80.
- Polanyi, 248–50.
- Schleiermacher, 292–3.
- Translating's similarities to interpreting, 280.
- Truth as manifestation, 281–2.
- Whitehead, 282–3.

Herrmann's biblical & theological insights, 169–71, 306–7, 311.
Hiddenness of revelation, 70, 75–77, 149, 309, 313.
Holy war (ban) & NT critique, 84–85.
Internal argumentative process for learning and teaching, 263.
Jesus as highly liberal, but not entirely so, 80–83.
Jesus's attitude toward His family, 83.

INDEX

Jesus's hermeneutic and use of parables, 288-9.
Jesus's interpretation of Old Covenant traditions, 54-55.
Jewish Christians & Ebionites, 147.

Kierkegaard
    Book of James, 142-3, n60.
    Christian apologetics, 178, 181-4.
    Christian Existentialist philosophy, 222-3.
    Contrast with Socrates, 312.
    Dialectical use of historicalcritical method, 315-6.
    Evaluation of Hegel's philosophy of history, 222-3.
    Hiddenness of revelation, 309.
    Individual as Responsible to God, 224.
    Truth as subjectivity, 316.

Law, relativizing of
    In Jesus's teaching, 80-83.
    In Paul's teaching, 83.

Letter-spirit differentiation, 82, 137-8.
Liberal—Conservative, 80-83.
Love disclosed in Jesus's person & work according to Paul, 85-86.
Marcion, 90-92, 107-8, 117, 143 (n61), 145, 146, 147.
Mysticism, 310, 311.

NT content analysis & critical appraisal
    Acts of the Apostles, 98 (n11), 100 (n16), 106, 120, 122, 123, 139, 139-40 (n49), 154-7, 159, 201, 232-3 (n4).
    First John's perfection teaching, 130.
    Fourth Gospel, nature of, differences from Synoptics, 107, 145, 153-4, 325-7, 328 (n4).
    Hebrews's problematic teaching, God as unforgiving to Christians guilty of willful sin, apostasy, 106, 130.
    James, book of, 130, 142-3 (especially n60).
    Pastoral epistles
        Discouraging of female leadership, 107 (n49), 133.
        Only pastor as having charismatic gifts, 107 (n49).
        Teaching concerning authority of available precanonical scriptures, 32-33.
        Women's salvation much to do with bearing children, 145 (n66).
    Revelation, canonical inclusion questioned early & late, 106-7, 129, 130.

Orthodoxy, 121-2, 137 (n42), 191-2; cf. 32-33.
Parables of Jesus, 54-55, 288-9.
Paradox & paradoxes, 12, 172-3.

Paul
    By grace through faith, 330 (& n23).
    His conception of his epistles, 98-99.
    His understanding of his apostolic authority, 99.
    Pauline school, theory of, 100-1.
    Paul's own writings occasionally distorted by editorial hands, 133.
    Pseudonymous Pauline letters, 96, 101, 124; cf. 96.
    Understanding of faith/belief, 324-5.

Philosophy
    Anselm, 210-1.
    Aristotelianism/empiricism, 208-9.
    Barth's theological balancing of realism & idealism, 227-9.
    Buber, 221-2.
    Coherence, consistency, comprehensiveness: logical tests, 263.
    Cosmological argument for God's existence, 211-13.
    Descartes, 208-9, 210-11, 247-8.
    Edwards, Jonathan, affections as motivating force, 328-9.
    Existence as relational, 221; (cf. 221-2).
    Existentialism, 222-3.
    Hegel
        Against identifying religion with feeling, 332.
        Critique of his philosophy of history, 312-3.
        SK's evaluation of Hegel's philosophy of history, 222-3.
    Idealism/rationalism, 208-14.
    Kant, 174-5, 178-9, 210-1, 216, 226, 310-11.
    Moral argument for God's existence, 216.
    Opposing philosophical presumptuousness, 247-8.
    Philosophies of methodological doubting, 247-8.
    Polanyi's Gestalt hermeneutic, 248-50.
    Scientific discovery, nature of, 243-8.
    Teleological Argument for God's Existence, 214-5

Pietism, 34 (n7), 263.

Polanyi
    Gestalt hermeneutic, 248-50.
    Nonscientific values required by science, 250-1.
    Scientific discovery, nature of, Polanyi, et. al., 243-8.

Proclamation, need to reflect transcendence, 260, 267-8.
Pseudonymous NT writings, 96, 101, 122-4.

Reason & experience in theology, 171
Schleiermacher, understanding of sense of absolute dependence, 216–7.
Scripture as inspired & inspiring, 32–33, 124–5.

Science/Theology Dialogue,
    Darwin, & Whitehead's critique, 214–5.
    Nature, science's current conception, 233.
    Nonscientific values required by science, 250–1.
    Objectivity, myth of presuppositionless understanding, 279–80.
    Realism's priority for knowledge of nature, 229–31.
    Science & theology revisable, 161–2.
    Scientific discovery, nature of, 243–8.

Slavery
    As reflected in Bible, 89.
    Response, 151–2.

Tatian's *Diatessaron*, 103–4, 115 (n85).

Teaching and Learning
    Discussion and disputation, 261–2, 263.
    Dogmatics and Catechesis, 262.
    Internal argumentative process, 263.
    Writing, importance for learning & teaching, 262–3.

Tradition, importance in interpreting, 190–1, 278–80.
Truth as subjectivity, 316.

Whitehead
    Basis of scientific quest, 244.
    Darwin, & Whitehead's critique, 214–5, 215.
    Hermeneutical insights, 282–3.
    Nature, science's current conception, 233.
    Realism's priority for knowledge of nature, 229–31.

Women's rights, the Bible, 87–89, 196.
Writing, important for learning, teaching, 262–3.

www.ingramcontent.com/pod-product-compliance
Lightning Source LLC
Chambersburg PA
CBHW080407300426
44113CB00015B/2425